Hot Thespian Action!

Ten Premiere Plays from Walterdale Playhouse

Hot Thespian Action!

Ten Premiere Plays from Walterdale Playhouse

Edited with a critical introduction
by Robin C. Whittaker

AU PRESS

CANADIAN PLAYS SERIES

Published by AU Press, Athabasca University
1200, 10011 – 109 Street
Edmonton, AB T5J 3S8

Library and Archives Canada Cataloguing in Publication

Hot thespian action! : ten premiere plays from Walterdale Playhouse / edited by Robin C. Whittaker.

(Canadian plays)
Includes bibliographical references.
Also available in electronic format.
ISBN 978-1-897425-26-8

1. Canadian drama (English)–21st century. I. Whittaker, Robin, 1976– II. Series: Canadian plays (Edmonton, Alta.)

PS8315.1.H68 2008 C812'.608 C2008-905017-7

This book is part of Canadian Plays series, edited by Anne Nothof of Athabasca University.

ISSN 1917-5086 Canadian plays series (Print)
ISSN 1917-5094 Canadian plays series (Online)

Printed and bound by AGMV Marquis
Cover and book design by Plumbheavy Design Inc.

To Walterdale's tireless volunteer artists, technicians, builders and administrators throughout the decades. May this anthology stand as a document of their original efforts and successes over the years;

and

to the unregimented artistic spirit of the playwright everywhere.

NOTES ON OBTAINING PROFESSIONAL AND AMATEUR PRODUCTION ROYALTIES

The Canadian Fact
© Wilfred Watson 1967
For production inquiries contact:
AU Press, Athabasca University, 1200, 10011 - 109 Street,
Edmonton, Alberta T5J 3S8
aupress@athabascau.ca

Chief Shaking Spear Rides Again or the Taming of the Sioux
© Warren Graves 1974
For professional production inquiries contact:
Playwrights Guild of Canada, 54 Wolseley St., 2nd Floor,
Toronto, Ontario, Canada M5T 1A5
orders@playwrightsguild.ca
For amateur or education performance rights contact:
www.playwrightsguild.ca
416-703-0201

Mutants
© Brad Fraser 1980, 2007
For production inquiries contact:
Ralph Zimmerman, Great North Artists Management, 350 Dupont Street,
Toronto, Ontario, Canada M5R 1V9
ralphzimmerman@gnaminc.com, bradfraser@bradfraser.net
416-925-2051

Swipe
© Gordon Pengilly 1981
For production inquiries contact:
Gordon Pengilly, 401 - 27 Avenue NW,
Calgary, Alberta, Canada T2M 2H7
gpengilly@nucleus.com

The Tenth Negative Pig
© Barbara Sapergia and Geoffrey Ursell 1983
For production inquiries contact:
Barbara Saperigia and Geoffrey Ursell, 48 Moxon Crescent,
Saskatoon, Saskatchewan, Canada S7H 3B9
ursell@sasktel.net
306-955-1912 (phone); 306-374-0993 (phone/fax)

CONTENTS

PREFACE AND ACKNOWLEDGEMENTS

This anthology recovers and collects well crafted, topical, and in some cases provocative Canadian plays that otherwise would have remained unavailable to wider readerships and audiences. Certainly today, Canadian plays too rarely receive a second production, particularly when premiered at an amateur theatre. At no point can this phenomenon be related to the quality of the plays because artistic directors and producers do not have the opportunity to read them (unless they take the initiative to contact the playwrights directly, or the playwrights contact them). This collection is a first step toward making ten plays available to a wider readership of producers, professional and amateur theatre artists, scholars, students, and an interested general public. That this collection is published at the moment that Walterdale Playhouse's production company, Walterdale Theatre Associates, commemorates half a century of play production gives cause for double celebration.

My own involvement with Walterdale has three "moments of origin." The first was as an audience member with my colleague James McKinnon in the fall of 1999 when we saw Kelly's *The Vampyre* directed by Cathy Lakin, who was president of Walterdale at the time. We had recently arrived in Edmonton to begin our studies in the master's degree program at the University of Alberta's Department of Drama, and we were keen to familiarize ourselves with Edmonton's highly touted theatrical landscape. James and I had moved to a city that boasted then, as it does now, more live theatre per capita than any other city in Canada (Old Strathcona Business Association), one in which over half of the population attends live theatre every year (Leger Marketing). I recall from my discussion with James then that the idea of seeing a play at a respected amateur theatre in our new home bestowed upon our theatre-going intentions an honest cachet, a healthy dose of cultural capital. We also had an eye toward producing theatre in Edmonton. After all, the opportunity to direct large-cast shows at a fifty-year-old theatre company with a variety of skilled actors, designers, and production team members is rare anywhere in this country. I would go on to see six more Walterdale productions in just over a year.

My second moment of origin at Walterdale came when I was appointed its twenty-fourth artistic director in February 2001. As a nonprofessionalized theatre company that produced a full season of seven productions a year, this was no slap-dash, "amateurish" operation. In fact, as I quickly learned—and was soon quick to inform others—an amateur theatre such as Walterdale requires its participants to wear their professionalism on their sleeves. Highly structured mechanisms are the glue that holds together all this unpaid talent and enthusiasm. For fifteen to forty hours a week, the artistic director position gave me invaluable experience in forming a well-balanced progressive season, dealing with people of all ages and experiences, handling administrative duties efficiently and effectively (this was before Walterdale hired a paid administrator for the first time in 2005), and doing theatre under the "disciplinary codes of timetables, collective training, exercises [and other forms of] total and detailed surveillance"—what philosopher Michel Foucault calls "systems of power" (218–21). These were useful—nay, *integral*—mechanisms, as I would discover throughout my two-and-a-half-year term there.

My third moment of origin at Walterdale came three years later, after I began research on nonprofessionalized theatre practices as a doctoral student at the University of Toronto's Graduate Centre for Study of Drama. All this disciplined theatre at Walterdale had, after all, led to critical and popular successes for half a century; it has a story to which other companies, amateur and professional alike, could relate. I returned to Edmonton in June 2006 to start researching in Walterdale's rich archives. A year later I returned again to include in my research the Provincial Archives of Alberta's Walterdale holdings. Clearly there was a traceable history to be found in executive and general meeting minutes, newsletters, correspondences, lease agreements, and season programs. I was glad to be back in my third capacity, as researcher, to begin uncovering these traces.

It is the opportunity to engage in this sort of tripartite role-playing experience—that of audience member, practitioner/administrator (for the two are never separate in any artistic director position), and researcher—that makes the art of theatre so unique. As a publicly created and produced art, it is highly disciplined (in all senses of the word) and well documented (due to the paper trails its creative moments leave behind). What is remarkable is that more collections of work produced by theatres have not been compiled.

This anthology of some of the best new plays produced at Walterdale during its fifty years is a critical collection. It is based on the belief that the historical and cultural underpinnings of plays are as important as their language, themes, and content. Plays emerge from artists, and artists emerge from their times and circumstances. It is from this point of view that I wish to begin.

Intended for a general readership, but of particular interest to theatre and culture specialists, this anthology is carefully researched and productively critical while providing a unique document for "fans" of Walterdale to cherish. As Walterdale celebrates its first five decades, a markedly rare accomplishment for any theatre company in this country, this anthology acknowledges the talent and commitment of thousands of Walterdale members who have thrived on the joys of bringing new creations to life. These new works, recovered and selected for publication, are products of the *amore* of amateur theatre artists and the powerful tradition upon which Walterdale and its membership have built a half-century of success. Amateur theatre practice often gains local community notice, but this collection takes an important first step in giving one influential amateur company national and international recognition. The title, borrowed from the name of Walterdale's 2004/05 season, foregrounds the passionate and focused work of Walterdale's volunteer members while alluding to its present firehall home.

Just as this anthology presents a variety of written voices, it has been made possible by a number of individuals and groups. This work, and my related research on contemporary amateur and professionalizing theatre practices, would have been inconceivable without the ongoing support of Walterdale Theatre Associates and its board of directors. In the first place, thank you so many times over to Walterdale's archive manager Lance Dittrich for his ceaseless accommodation in person and from across the country, which included scanning the pre-2002 production photographs from slides. Also, thank you to former president Judy Stelck and former artistic director Scott Sharplin for giving my on-site research the go-ahead in 2006. Kent Sutherland, Walterdale's administrator, proved an integral liaison. It is hardly possible to thank Mary and Frank Glenfield enough for offering me their lifetime of experiences at Walterdale. Theirs is the ongoing, lived memory of a theatre company, and of the city's theatre scene, for decades—a rare jewel indeed. Mary's master's degree thesis of 2001, duly cited herein, is an invaluable resource for all who intend to research the early years of Edmonton theatre. I also think of the numerous chats I had with Wendi Pope while I was artistic director and she was president. When we spoke of what it meant to be "amateur" and "professional" in the field of theatre, we were pushing away the sandy edges of a vital, insufficiently explored, discourse. David Owen—playwright, director, actor, educator, and former artistic director of Walterdale Theatre Associates (my predecessor in that position)—deserves acknowledgement for his original suggestion to me in 2001 in the lobby of Walterdale Playhouse that an anthology of Walterdale's new plays should be published. I regret that David's one-act play *Infidelity* (June 2002) did not make it into these pages, as it is an arresting and aesthetically challenging experiment in movement and dialogue.

I am indebted to Athabasca University's Press for having the foresight to publish new works produced by a nonprofessionalized theatre company. In particular I am grateful to Erna Dominey and Anne Nothof for guiding me through the publishing process. I heartily thank my two anonymous reviewers for their detailed insights and enthusiastic words. I am also indebted to Judith Johnson's careful copyediting of the manuscript. Susan Ivimey's timely transcription of *Mutants* was essential in preparing this collection. In the formative moments of the project, both Bequie Lake and the Playwrights Guild of Canada deserve thanks for helping me to contact certain playwrights. Diane Bessai's and Shirley Neuman's kind assistance in securing permission to print Wilfred Watson's play is most appreciated. At the University of Toronto, Bruce Barton's guidance has been integral to my work.

I also convey my gratitude to the kind and knowledgeable staff and volunteers at the Provincial Archives of Alberta for their assistance while I was working in Edmonton in 2007. Importantly, a University of Toronto School of Graduate Studies Travel Grant allowed me to return to Edmonton that year. My research also has benefitted from three Ontario Graduate Scholarships.

On a personal note, I wish to thank Ryland Alexander Lukiwski and Amy Zarzeczny for providing me with a place to call home while doing research in Edmonton in the summers of 2006 and 2007. And from my heart, thank you to Amy Franklin for her support, and to my father Brian and my late mother Marlene for, somehow, convincing me at a very young age that writing is vital.

Robin C. Whittaker, July 2008

Sketch of Walterdale Playhouse by Amy Franklin, June 2006.

GENERAL INTRODUCTION

Overview

This selected anthology of new plays produced by Edmonton's Walterdale Theatre Associates documents one influential aspect of that company's ongoing artistic contribution to Edmonton and to Canadian culture. It is the result of an undertaking to recover a number of important plays, written at various stages of their authors' lives, which in some cases might otherwise have been lost to desk drawers and storage boxes. It may signal the beginning of a sustained effort to trace the influence of contemporary amateur theatre companies and their impact on their communities and on theatre practices today.

It is common to view nonprofessionalized theatre practice as a phenomenon of the past. This view assumes that "amateur" is "preprofessional" and therefore outdated. It holds that Canada's "little theatres" evolved into professional theatres half a century ago (if they were any good), converted to producing decades-late off-Broadway hits, or simply folded. Certainly the former is true in specific cases in which an amateur theatre has professionalized: for example, the Winnipeg Little Theatre amalgamated with Theatre 77 to form Manitoba Theatre Centre in 1958, Calgary's Workshop 14 merged with the Musicians and Actors Club of Calgary to form MAC 14 in 1966 (becoming Theatre Calgary in 1968), and the London Little Theatre in Ontario professionalized to became the Grand Theatre in the 1970s. For these companies, professionalization was a sign of cultural progress in a Centennial-fevered national (and nationalizing) context.

However, many nonprofessionalized theatres remain and thrive in the professional era. This era had its direct origins in the 1950s with the release of the Royal Commission Report in 1951 (Canada), the opening of the Stratford Festival (1953–), and the opening of the Manitoba Theatre Centre (1958–), Canada's first state-sponsored "regional" theatre. A study of the changing practices of nonprofessionalized theatres during the professional era will help to clarify the function and relevance of theatre practice in contemporary society. Other amateur theatres not to be overlooked in this pursuit are Ottawa Little Theatre (1913–), Toronto's Alumnae Theatre Company (1919–), Regina Little Theatre (1926–), and the Victoria Theatre Guild at Langham Court Theatre (1929–). They are the country's longest continuously running theatre companies. They have also contributed in no small degree to new play production and, in some cases, new play development. That they have done so during the professional era is a testament to their often overlooked, and frequently renewed, artistic and administrative visions.[1] Within this latter set of amateur theatres, Walterdale Theatre Associates holds a significant place in terms of sustained new play production, having produced over sixty new plays in fifty years.

That Walterdale has done so consistently in one of Canada's most fertile new-play regions is remarkable. It is no secret that Edmonton has been an incubator of playwriting talent since the city's "coming of age in the performing arts" (Westgate) during the 1960s. Today, many professional theatre companies offer new play development and production opportunities. These include Workshop West Theatre's Kaboom Festival, Loud 'N Queer Cabaret, Springboards, Playwrights' Garage, and Playwrights Unit; Theatre Network's Nextfest; and Northern Light Theatre's Urban

Tales. As well, the University of Alberta's New Works Festival provides students with a production format for new one-act plays. And of course, in a less regimented lottery-selection style, the Edmonton International Fringe Theatre Festival—which, after the Edinburgh Fringe, is the second largest theatre festival on the planet—allows independent artists to produce shows of their own choosing, frequently new plays. Edmonton playwright David Belke notes that in the 2002/03 season alone, over one hundred new plays were premiered on mainstages, by co-op groups, and at festivals in Edmonton (Belke). An indication of Edmonton's new play prowess can be gleaned from a number of previous anthologies. *The Alberta Advantage* (edited by Nothof), the Nextfest Anthology series, *The West of All Possible Worlds* (edited by Day), *Staging Alternative Albertas* (edited by Demers and Kerr), and *New Canadian Drama* 3: *Albertan Dramatists* (edited by Salter) present a remarkable variety of Alberta talent. Alongside this frenzy of new play production, Walterdale Theatre Associates produced the formidable number of new works listed in Appendix I. Nationally and internationally recognized Alberta-raised playwrights Vern Thiessen, Brad Fraser, George Ryga, Frank Moher, Warren Graves, and Gordon Pengilly have all been associated with Walterdale as playwrights or directors.

As this anthology demonstrates by way of example and critical perspective, during the decades that mark the beginning of the professional era in Canadian theatre, Walterdale Theatre Associates created conditions that have allowed it to be a fruitful contributor to new play production and one of Edmonton's most recognized theatre companies.[2] The factors that led to these conditions are far more diverse than many people realize. By offering a selection of "lost" and recently premiered plays, this anthology considers key dynamics in amateur theatre practice. In so doing, it holds instructional value for committed professionals and amateurs as well as readers and audiences who are interested in the development and production of new plays today.

A Brief History of Walterdale Theatre Associates

Walterdale Theatre Associates, or Walterdale, is a not-for-profit amateur community theatre company and a registered society that produces a full season of six or seven plays at Walterdale Playhouse in Edmonton's Old Strathcona Theatre District. Today, Walterdale is run by a twelve-member board of directors, ten of whom are elected annually and two (the president and artistic director) biennially from among the company's constitutive paying membership of about three hundred. Its mandated objective is to "establish and promote vital, entertaining and self-sustaining amateur theatre in Edmonton" (Walterdale, Constitution). Under this markedly wide-open mandate, Walterdale has maintained a flexible niche among other Edmonton theatres by relying on programming variety and a creative mixture of commercial favourites and challenging, provocative plays. Participation in all aspects of play production remains on a volunteer, unpaid basis, which sets Walterdale apart from a number of other amateur or semi-amateur theatres in the country that sometimes pay directors, designers, technicians, actors, or front-of-house and building staff. Participant theatre artists at Walterdale are counted among the paying members and vary widely in age, experience, and training. While a few may become members who work on a specific show, most return for at least a few shows (Whittaker 1), and some stay on over the course of five or ten years to become part of a returning core of artists who may also practise theatre in other capacities around the city. Most specialize in one or two capacities, but some learn a variety of theatre skills. Still, most members (around two-thirds) are not involved in theatre production at all; their participation takes the form of audience support. Though membership numbers have ebbed and flowed, these dynamics have remained relatively consistent since the 1960s, when Walterdale began to attract Edmontonians at an enviable rate.

Walterdale Theatre Associates has produced plays in Edmonton since August 27, 1958. Originally called Edmonton Theatre Associates, it was founded by young actors who believed their demographic lacked opportunities to produce theatre in the city. As Mary Glenfield relates, Jack McCreath, the group's lead founder and first artistic director, "believed that there was an audience ready and waiting for good theatre, if one could tap into it" (46). The group officially registered under Alberta's Societies Act on May 13, 1960.[3] McCreath stated in the *Edmonton Journal* seven months later that the city was not ready for a professional theatre until "there exists an audience of regular theatergoers amounting to three per cent of our population" (quoted in Glenfield 53). He viewed Walterdale then as a possible "basis" for professionalizing theatre practice in Edmonton.

In response to the city's traditional fare of shows playing on large stages—particularly the Northern Jubilee Auditorium's mainstage—Theatre Associates gained public and critical recognition in the early years by staging a variety of well-rehearsed popular classics in smaller venues. Plays such as Hazelwood's *Lady Audley's Secret* and McCreath's reworking of Swan's *Out of the Frying Pan* (both in repertory August–September 1958, Jubilee Auditorium Social Room), Knott's *Dial M for Murder* (November 1960, Yardbird Suite), and Christie's *Ten Little Indians* (June 1961, Jubilee Auditorium Social Room) were directed by company founder Jack McCreath or members such as Frank Glenfield, Marjorie Knowler, and Bob Hedley.

Theatre Associates soon began offering edgier fare, including *Epitaph for George Dillon* (November 1961). Within three years the group was able to secure its own building by converting the John Walter School House at Walterdale Flats into a seventy-seat "thrust-style" theatre space (Rivet 6), with *Epitaph* as the opening show. It rented what had been "Edmonton's oldest one room school house" ("New" 1) from the city for $35 per month (Fritch 1). There, Theatre Associates could offer a full season of plays, the only company in Edmonton outside of the University of Alberta able to do so at the time. Weighty, relevant, and at times acclaimed productions of Lorca's *The House of Bernarda Alba* (March–April 1962), Pinter's *The Caretaker* (October 1963), Ibsen's *Hedda Gabler* (April 1964), Anouilh's *Waltz of the Toreadors* (March 1966), and Albee's *The Zoo Story* (May 1966) came to characterize the group as one that took theatre production seriously. It even produced its first original works during this time, Mary Baldridge's *Is This a Friendly Visit?* (December 1961) and Jack McCreath's Mexico-inspired play *Barranca* (November 1962). An article in the *Edmonton Journal* called the Theatre Associates "the only people consciously trying to fill the need [for theatre in Edmonton]" while fielding "some of Edmonton's best performers" ("Shavian"). Dozens were drawn to the local-minded group as working members, and performances routinely sold out,[4] but when the city decided to claim the schoolhouse-come-playhouse to build the Kinsmen Field House, Theatre Associates, after having staged over forty plays in eight years, was forced to move. It eventually found and renovated the Legion of Frontiersmen Hall; the ninety-eight-seat venue on Princess Elizabeth Avenue opened to a sold-out house with Gardner's *A Thousand Clowns* (November 1966).

The Theatre Associates' first location at the John Walter School House at Walterdale Flats (1961-66). Today, this is the location of the Kinsmen Field House.
Photo: Walterdale Theatre Associates.

The Theatre Associates' second location at The Legion of Frontiersman Hall (1966-74), today the site of Kingsway Garden Mall.
Photo: Walterdale Theatre Associates.

The move to Legion Hall came precisely twelve months after professional theatre descended upon Edmonton. With lawyer and local theatre enthusiast Joseph Shoctor's new regional theatre, The Citadel, addressing the demand for professional productions, members of Theatre Associates sought to clarify their niche in the city. Certainly, selections such as Kesselring's *Arsenic and Old Lace* (February 1967), Molière's *The Imaginary Invalid* (April 1967), Fry's *A Sleep of Prisoners* (October 1967), Albee's *A Delicate Balance* (January 1968), and Coward's *Hay Fever* (March 1972) were not unlike the fare now being offered at The Citadel. But edgier work continued to appear, such as Odets's *Awake and Sing* (November 1970) and Williams's *The Mutilated* (February 1973).

Theatre Associates was now frequently introducing new plays into its programming, premiering five between March 1967 and March 1968. By comparison, during the same Centennial months The Citadel produced no Canadian fare, new or otherwise, other than an "original revue" called *All the Crazy Things that Crazy People Do* (December 1966–January 1967). Works by writers such as George Ryga, Jimmy Richardson, Wilfred Watson, and Warren Graves were produced at the Legion Hall. During this time the theatre also began to make a name for itself with its "Walterdale Melodrama" as part of Edmonton's Klondike Days Festival.

By the time it held its annual general meeting in 1970, Edmonton Theatre Associates had officially changed its name to Walterdale Theatre Associates because, after all, the name "Walterdale" had stuck since the early years at Walterdale Flats. Its members, now paying their membership separately from ticket prices, grew to over one hundred. But the Legion Hall lease was set to expire in July 1972, and the city was making plans to give the land to a private developer for a shopping centre, what is now Kingsway Garden Mall. Following lengthy and at times heated negotiations with the city, Walterdale, facing homelessness once again, secured its current space at Old Strathcona's Firehall No. 6. When renovated, the new Walterdale Playhouse would seat 108 (today it seats 145 following a series of further renovations). This third building gave the company a home in a historic landmark in a central, and increasingly culturally vibrant, location. To date, the city's and the province's renewed support of the community-minded company has allowed it the freedom to produce relevant and challenging work. Coincidentally, the erstwhile firehall itself celebrates its one hundredth anniversary in the same season that Walterdale celebrates its fiftieth.

LEFT: Walterdale's third and present location at Old Strathcona's former Firehall No. 6. The firehall is 100 years old in 2009, following extensive renovations that have included the preservation of its façade. Photo: Walterdale Theatre Associates. RIGHT: Today's signage for theatres in the Old Strathcona Theatre District. Photo: David DeGagné.

When Orton's *What the Butler Saw* inaugurated the new building as a playhouse in December 1974, Walterdale boasted a membership of over 300. By 1980 membership topped 400, and it never fell lower than 250 for long. However, the larger building, leased from the city for $1.00 per year plus the costs of any city-mandated renovations (to be accomplished within historical code), would pose ongoing financial and administrative challenges to a group focused on producing plays and developing theatre practitioners and audiences.

The professionalization of Canadian theatre practice also created challenges for Walterdale in the years leading up to and following the establishment of the Canadian Actors' Equity Association in 1976.[5] In Edmonton, the growing number of new professional companies during the 1970s pressed Walterdale to further define its place. Theatre 3 (1970–81), Northern Light Theatre (1975–), Theatre Network (1975–), and Workshop West Theatre (1978–) provided professionalized opportunities for local theatre practice.[6] In the fall of 1977 Equity made it clear that its members could appear on Walterdale's stage only if they were paid as guest artists; in response, Walterdale made it clear that it would no longer avail itself of the services of Equity actors, thus asserting its commitment to amateur status (Sprenke 3; Rivet 22). Many in Edmonton's acting pool were now placed in a difficult position: eager to identify themselves as Equity professionals, they still counted on the exposure and experience that Walterdale provided. Following this hard split between professional and amateur practice, Walterdale was free to focus its energies on attracting the best non-Equity talent of all ages in Edmonton. Since the late 1970s it has contributed immensely to Edmonton's theatre scene while strengthening the city's artistic and social fabric by providing important theatre opportunities to non-Equity artists.

During the 1970s Walterdale further sought to clarify its niche by introducing children's programming and youth artist development with its Young Walterdale initiative and Christmas pantomimes, while furthering its reputation for producing the summer melodrama and original local work. To satisfy internal and public interest, it also turned, in part, to more commercial fare with plays such as Shaffer's *Sleuth* (November 1975), Stoppard's *Enter a Free Man* (October 1976), and Simon's *God's Favorite* (February 1977) and *Barefoot in the Park* (January 1978).

Challenging modern classics have also appeared at Walterdale, particularly since the late 1970s. These include Chekhov's *On the Harmfulness of Tobacco* (April 1979), *The Cherry Orchard* (May 1987), and *Ivanov* (April–May 1999); Shakespeare's *The Winter's Tale* (October 1983), *The Merry Wives of Windsor* (November 1986), *The Comedy of Errors* (October 1994), *The Taming of the Shrew* (March 2003), *King Lear* (February 2006), and *Antony and Cleopatra* (April 2007); Ibsen's *Ghosts* (April–May 1985) and *An Enemy of the People* (March 2001); Miller's *The Crucible* (April–May 1986, May 2002); Wycherley's *The Country Wife* (September–October 1987, January 2001); Behn's *The Rover* (April 1989); Williams's *A Streetcar Named Desire* (January–February 1995) and *The Night of the Iguana* (January–February 2003); Molière's *Tartuffe* (April–May 1996); and Marlowe's *Doctor Faustus* (January 2000).

Importantly, along with commercial and classical fare, during the past thirty-four years at the firehall Walterdale has expanded its reputation for introducing provocative works, many of them by Canadian playwrights, to Edmonton audiences. These include French's *Leaving Home* (January–February 1975), Ritter's *The Girl I Left Behind Me* (March 1977), Mitchell's *Davin the Politician* (November 1979), Tremblay's *Les Belles Soeurs* (May 1980 with Théâtre Français d'Edmonton, and February 2005), Walker's *Zastrozzi* (October 1980), Ryga's *The Ecstasy of Rita Joe* (March 1990), Brennen's *Tiger's Heart* (March 1998), Clark's *Jehanne of the Witches* (January 1999) and *Saint Frances of Hollywood* (April–May 2001), and Highway's *The Rez Sisters* (October 2005).[7]

For its efforts in the late 1980s and early 1990s, Walterdale garnered a string of Elizabeth Sterling Haynes Awards for Outstanding Amateur Production in each of the first six years the awards were handed out (1988–93).[8] In 1994, one year after winning the (not-amateur-specific) Sterling Award for Outstanding Costume Design for Jane Barclay's work on Anderson's *Elizabeth the Queen* (April–May 1993), Walterdale received an Outstanding Contribution to Theatre in Edmonton award, which at once rewarded the company for nearly four decades of work in Edmonton and rendered it ineligible for future recognition by the Sterling committee. Commitment to programming diversity is an important strength of Walterdale Theatre. And as this anthology shows, a significant element in this diversity is Walterdale's contribution to new playwriting.

A View of Amateur Theatre Practised in the Professional Era

> In the professional world the art sometimes gets lost in the business, which is sad, because no one gets into theatre in order to be more employable. No artist starts out with money as their [*sic*] first and foremost concern.
>
> ~ FORMER WALTERDALE ARTISTIC DIRECTOR SAM VARTENIUK

Acts of negotiating the borderlands between professional and amateur practices rank among the Western World's most difficult cultural challenges in the twenty-first century. For most of us, these challenges are unavoidable. In the case of a professionalizing art form, such negotiations frequently meet with impassioned responses. Today, few artists seek to be called "amateur," but few find consistent enough employment, payment, or recognition to be accurately called "professional." As a result, collections of dedicated artists have gathered to form union-styled associations in order to systematically define their art form's "profession" and therefore gain increased respect and security for their work. With a slew of emotional connotations following in the wake of professionalizing definitions, the result can be confusion in the way the art itself is viewed and practised.

In his influential study on public taste and cultural production, French sociologist Pierre Bourdieu observes that among the arts, theatre "divides its public and divides itself" both aesthetically and politically (19). In Canada, the effects of distinction in theatre practice are found, for example, in the divisions between regional professional theatres, mid-sized professional houses, co-op and collective productions, Fringe Festivals, and amateur theatres. More or less in this order, organizational bodies such as the Canada Council for the Arts, the Canadian Actors' Equity Association, the Playwrights Guild of Canada, and professional theatre training schools classify and order theatre companies, their practices, and their work, by degrees of "professional" and "amateur." These distinctions, it is important to note, barely predate the organizational bodies and constitutive artists and companies themselves. They are born in large part of the federal public policy document often referred to as the Massey Commission Report (Canada), named after the commission's chair (and future governor general of Canada), Vincent Massey. Today they reinforce the claim as articulated and questioned by theatre scholar Claire Cochrane that "'Professional' now carries with it connotations of ultra-competence. The amateur is non-professional and by implication incompetent" (234). This nominal segregation and superficial denunciation is largely responsible for delegitimizing the work of amateur practitioners (as well as that of a range of professionals). And because such negative views of amateur practice are endemic in and constitutive of the practice and study of theatre, they are rarely questioned.[9]

The sociopolitical location of amateur theatre practice is much ignored and highly misunderstood. This is true even for those theatre practitioners, critics, and scholars who, at one time or another, have worked in amateur contexts as artists, technicians, or administrators. I therefore want to take a moment to suggest a repositioning of amateur theatre practice in order to begin what I think is one of the most important, if rarely attended, projects on the contemporary theatrical landscape: the re-evaluation of the field of theatre as inclusive not only of those segments that identify as "professional," but also of those that identify as "amateur." Among the latter, a wide variety of amateur theatre practices continue to influence Western theatre culture. They operate, by their own choosing, in parallel with and in contrast to professionalizing practices. Many practitioners, such as the writers whose plays are included here, have worked in amateur theatre either as preprofessionals (anticipating future professional work) or as paraprofessionals (simultaneously pursuing professional work at other companies).[10] Still others devoutly remain nonprofessional, show little interest in professionalizing, and remain content with the designation "amateur" even as they produce compelling works for the stage. Importantly, the craft of playwriting, insomuch as it can be separated from the disciplinary economics of the practice, is comparatively demanding for writers identifying as paraprofessional, preprofessional, or amateur.

The professional asserts allegiance to a set of defined standards. The amateur practises, nominally, outside of the designated profession, drawing from professional standards when circumstances make it possible or appropriate. The borderlands of the post-industrial professions of medicine, law, teaching, nursing, and so forth are delineated by occupational regulations set out by unions or associations whose members deem anyone or any work operating outside of these regulations as "amateur." In other words, the modern day professions have simplified the definition of "amateur" during the past century in order to bolster the range and effects of their own collective powers for purposes that ostensibly include quality control and job security.

Undoubtedly, the word "amateur" is fraught with negative associations. For some it suggests "unfocused," "imitative," "dilettantish," or "inferior" work. Some have sought to disassociate these connotations from the term by arguing for a distinction between "amateur" and "amateurish," whereby the former conveys the pioneering spirit of a practice while the latter bears the pejorative meanings (Melvill 1; Perry 31). This seems to me to be a productive start. The *Oxford English Dictionary* makes a distinction between the two: the "amateur" is "One who loves or is fond of," "one who has a taste for anything," or "one who cultivates anything as a pastime" (the opposite of the "professional"); "amateur" is also used "disparagingly" as an adjective in opposition to "professional." Conversely, "amateurish" is used only to mean "having the faults or deficiencies of amateur work," thus allowing for space within amateur work that is not "amateurish." It is within this skill-based amateur space that nonprofessionalized companies such as Walterdale primarily operate.

Though the act of this sort of occupational designation may seem simple, the interplay of the terms' various functions is not. A number of factors traditionally separate, by measure, amateurs from professionals. A survey of amateur practices in the United Kingdom published in the early 1990s lists eight such factors: income, training, artistic aspirations, time allocated, experience, general approach, content and style (of the work), and importantly, status of the art form in society (Hutchison and Feist 10). At the amateur end of each factor's continuum there is a deficiency; at the professional end we might say there is not so much a surplus as a minimum point or borderland defined by the dominant union or association in the field. Professions tend to *exclude* those who do not meet their minimum qualifications, while amateur practices tend to *include* would-be practitioners, at least in principle, in the interests of both survival and variety. At any given time, practitioners or companies may situate their own positions at different points along each continuum, with the recognition that these positions may change.

As a volunteer-run amateur company, Walterdale produces within a populist context. This populist notion of artistic creation is one that views art not as the sole property of career specialists, but as part of a wider domain in which art is producible and transferable between and across lines of specific training, experience, income, and life focus. Traditions and genres are drawn upon according to the artist's autonomy within his or her own cultural position. While the playwrights represented in this collection may have been writing to (or for) particular constituent audiences ("on their own time," as it were), the theatre at which their plays appeared follows an "open-field" mandate, more or less unencumbered by limiting politicized aesthetic mandates.

It is important to note at this juncture that a critical discussion of amateur practice does not seek to vilify professional theatre work, nor does it seek to be an apologia for unpaid or underpaid theatre work. Quite the contrary: it seeks to reveal the mechanisms by which amateur practices contribute to and benefit from professionalized practices, and vice versa, and it seeks to free the discussion of the production of art, if only temporarily, from the strictures of prescribed regulatory and disciplinary systems.

New Play Production at Amateur Theatres

While the notion of placing contemporary amateur theatre practices within the context of theatre practice generally may be unfamiliar to many, the idea of an amateur theatre producing new plays may seem outright contradictory to the impressions that many hold of amateur theatre programming. The words "contemporary," "relevant," or "original" are not always attached to the programming expected of amateur companies. For some, an "amateur theatre season" brings to mind the production of decades-late off-Broadway productions, or the "feel-good" stock musicals you might find listed in the "Community Rentals" section of the Music Theatre International catalogue. While many amateur groups produce this type of fare with a good deal of popular response, the amateur theatre of which Walterdale is representative cannot be categorized among them.

Amateur companies such as Walterdale worked to find their niche during the state-sponsored influx of Canadian "regional" professional theatres between the late 1950s and the 1970s by producing hundreds of new works by Canadian playwrights. Regionals such as the Manitoba Theatre Centre (1958–), the Vancouver Playhouse (1963–), and Edmonton's Citadel Theatre (1965–) increasingly adopted the position that they could ill afford to take a chance on new play programming for fear that low attendance would trouble business-minded boards of directors and could result in the loss of state-granted public funds. Curiously, even in a mid-twentieth-century context in which efforts to nationalize Canadian theatre abounded, new Canadian play programming became synonymous with experimental theatre, which was viewed as a predictable "loss" on seasonal budget sheets and was therefore to be avoided (except as tokenism). Canada's established amateur theatres quickly learned, however, that freedom from government grants (in a democracy that values art but not necessarily *paying* for art) and operating budgets drawn primarily from box office sales and membership fees allowed for a marked freedom in programming. Some amateur theatres, particularly Alumnae in Toronto and Walterdale in Edmonton, ran with this freedom.[11]

An early catalyst for new play production by amateur theatres was the Dominion Drama Festival (DDF), the longest-running of Canada's state-initiated theatre events. The DDF was meant to build a national audience for theatre by providing contexts for play production and artistic improvement. For forty years (1932–71) it brought together approved nonprofessional theatre companies to compete at the regional and national levels. From its early years benefitting from private and (some) state patronage—which effectively ended when the Canada Council redirected its funding toward professional practice—to its later years scrounging for corporate funds, the DDF sought to encourage the practice of Canadian theatre in small towns and urban centres from coast to coast. Cultural organizers led by dignitaries such as DDF co-founder Vincent Massey and author Robertson Davies attempted to encourage the submission of new Canadian plays. Initially, companies were reluctant to take the chance on fare with which the festival's European adjudicators would not be familiar, yet new plays appeared occasionally and in 1967, in celebration of Canada's Centennial, all sixty-two plays presented at the DDF Finals were Canadian-written, and twenty-nine of these were premieres.

But Walterdale never participated in the DDF competitions. Its focus was not on contributing to a national network of theatre artists, but on building interest in theatre practice locally. Walterdale's founders were careful to familiarize themselves with their community and their potential audiences. By the early 1960s they were running the only continuously producing theatre in Edmonton (outside of the University of Alberta), a distinction that would last until The Citadel opened. During this time, Walterdale's members worked to ensure there could be no possibility that the development of theatre in the city would fail. Offering productions of the best quality was a must. A new play, for example, deserved not only a strong first production but also receptive audiences. New plays were included in a season only when they could be assured of an appropriate reception.

Amateur theatres such as Walterdale have proven to be well suited to producing new plays. This is due in part to a number of artistic freedoms inherent in amateur theatre practice. First, unburdened by union obligations that prioritize consistent employment opportunities for mid-career artists, amateur theatres are freer to open new play programming slots to all artists—in all stages of their careers—when the plays are strong enough for production. Second, taking a chance on an unknown playwright is less of a financial gamble, as normally no monetary compensation is involved. Third, amateur theatres can accommodate a wider variety of new plays because they are free from both the need to limit cast sizes (because participants are unpaid) and the need to follow ideological, topical, or political trends in style and theme in order to compete for government grants. Fourth, the overall emphasis on in-the-moment process as opposed to final product can be particularly conducive to staging untried, unsettled new work.

And fifth, by often having less of their operating costs tied to the changing winds of state funding, amateur theatres can, and occasionally do, produce unpredictable and controversial new plays that add cultural capital to the company and its membership. The various production conditions of the plays contained in this anthology illustrate, in combination, all of these freedoms.

Publishing Walterdale's New Plays: Selection and Content

Not since Vincent Massey's two-volume set, *Canadian Plays from Hart House Theatre* (1926–27), has a collection composed solely of plays premiered at an amateur theatre been published. In other words, this collection is the first of its kind in eighty years. Countless important new plays have disappeared from sight over the past half century simply because they were not first produced by a professional theatre. Granted, for many plays this may not be regrettable, but for many others it is undeniably so. On the whole, a Canadian play rarely receives a second production, and a play whose first production occurs at an amateur theatre may already have an unfair stigma attached to it. Regardless of the play's initial strength or success, it is relegated to the writer's drawer.

Like a number of important contemporary play anthologies—for example, *Staging the North* (edited by Grace et al.), *Testifyin'* I and II (edited by Sears), *Staging Coyote's Dream* (edited by Mojica), and *Lesbian Plays* (edited by Kerr)—this collection revisits traditional canonization practices in theatre, with Canadian plays as its focus. But, once again, it differs from other compilations in that each play had its premiere at an amateur theatre company.[12] By setting into print a selection of the many outstanding new plays introduced at one Canadian theatre, we move a step closer to charting the important and continued influence of amateur theatres on the country's cultural landscape. This collection may be the first in a series of studies of several largely ignored constitutive elements of contemporary nonprofessionalized theatre practice, elements that include play programming, production conditions, and audiences.

From the experimental 1960s to a bold resistance to professionalization during the 1970s, from the fruitful years of the early 1980s to the explosion of new one-act plays in the 1990s and the first decade of the new millennium, Walterdale has presented what its audiences and its members want while not shying away from challenging popular tastes. For Walterdale's audiences the two phenomena are hardly mutually exclusive, as the company has premiered more than sixty new plays during its first fifty years. The early 1980s were particularly productive years for new play production at Walterdale due to artistic leadership that focused to a great extent on new play programming and also to a one-time national playwriting competition held by Walterdale in 1980. And just as with any theatre company's production history, professional or amateur, there have been "hits" and there have been "misses."

Of Walterdale's "hits," only ten could fit in this anthology—a point that is quite simply cause for regret. Certain omissions may appear striking to the reader. *Is This a Friendly Visit?* (December 1961), written by Mary Baldridge, and *Barranca* (November 1962), written and directed by founding Walterdale member Jack McCreath, were the first new plays produced by Walterdale. The former won the Alberta Drama League's playwriting competition that year and the latter was lauded in the *Edmonton Journal* as "a smash hit" (Keeping), but both have been omitted because I could not track down a copy of either in time for selection. Seminal western Canadian playwright George Ryga's *Nothing But a Man* (March 1967), a stage adaptation of his teleplay *Man Alive* (1966), does not appear in this collection because it was published recently in *George Ryga: The Other Plays* (edited by Hoffman). Fans of Warren Graves's original melodramas will note that only one appears here, though three premiered at Walterdale. The reason why *Chief Shaking Spear Rides Again* has been chosen should be clear from its localized plot. Perhaps most difficult of all was the selection of new one-act plays from over forty produced at Walterdale between 1988 and 2008. Quite simply, a number of them were not available for examination. Among the plays that were available, I attempted to choose those that would reflect Walterdale's ongoing mandate to offer varied programming year by year. What I believe to be a comprehensive list of new plays produced by Walterdale thus far is included at the back of this anthology as Appendix I; the inquisitive reader should overlook none.

The ten plays herein have been selected in the first place for their quality, readability (on the page), and producibility (in performance). Most are published here for the first time, though three—*The Canadian Fact*, *Chief Shaking Spear Rides Again*, and *Swipe*—received previous, though limited, publication. Plays by relatively "known" writers Brad Fraser, Warren Graves, Gordon Pengilly, Wilfred Watson, and Barbara Sapergia and Geoffrey Ursell balance plays by emerging playwrights Trevor Schmidt, Jonathan Seinen, Scott Sharplin, and Mark Stubbings, and one-time playwright Mary Glenfield.

The selected plays cover most of the company's fifty years in order to illustrate its relevance to changing times. A variety of genres—including realism, historical drama, adaptation, comedy, melodrama, fantasy, and children's theatre—are represented because programming variety has always been characteristic of Walterdale. All favour ingenuity and integrity of craft over formulaic or "issue of the month" dramaturgy, and they are often provocative. No two plays are structured the same, nor do they stage duplicate agendas. Their diversity is attributable to the freedoms listed above and to Walterdale's approach to new play programming in which, normally, yearly open calls are sent out to the membership and the public for new scripts.

But while variety is a Walterdale hallmark, readers will no doubt pick out similar themes in a number of these plays. This is the result of reoccurring commonalities among national, rather than local, playwriting interests. Thus, we have come to recognize themes of identity in Canadian plays, including national coming-of-age mythologies, tensions with American and British cultural domination, the strengths and challenges related to multiculturalisms and authenticities, and the performative power of flags, anthems, and other symbols of nationhood. Many of these plays deal in some degree with Canadian identities, as reconsiderations of the past, comments on the present, or hopes or apprehensions for the future. Some characters celebrate their Canadian identity, while others are deeply troubled by it. (Curiously, almost half of the plays offered here include versions of "O Canada"[13] and two, produced a year apart, mention celebrities William Shatner and Céline Dion as iconic/ironic cultural symbols.) A number of characters express decidedly anti-American sentiments in order to address perceived "us/U.S." power binaries at play between Canada and the United States. It is ironic that in spite of this persistent tradition of producing plays on Canadian topics, the winner of Walterdale's 1980 national playwriting competition did not deal with Canadian-specific subject matter at all. Gordon Pengilly's *Swipe* is a utopian no-place/every-place swamp fantasy that evidences Walterdale's "open field" approach to the selection of new plays. Self-reflexive questions of identity are more generally played out by way of meta-theatrical situations found in the premises of both *Chief Shaking Spear Rides Again* and *The Trial of Salomé*, and to a lesser extent in theatrical conceits found in *The Beaver Effect* and *The Three Sillies*.

This anthology presents not only thematic variety, but also what we might call variety in points of professionalization. The playwrights whose work appears here were all at different stages of their careers when their plays were produced. Watson had already been writing poetry and plays in other contexts simultaneous to his career as an English professor. Graves, having worked as a civil servant, was embarking on what would become a new career, first as a playwright, actor, director, and administrator at Walterdale, then as a paraprofessional working at both amateur and professional theatres in the Edmonton theatre community, and finally as an identifying professional in the field. Fraser, benefitting from both his raw talent at an early age and from happenstance, effectively parlayed the success of *Mutants* into an international play- and screenwriting career. Pengilly, and Sapergia and Ursell, already prolific fiction writers, added the successful outcome of a national playwriting competition (first and second place, respectively) to their accomplishments. Glenfield once again came to the service of Walterdale, this time not with her acting skills but, for one time only, as a playwright. Schmidt—an emerging playwright, director, and actor at Edmonton's professional theatres—gained a production of his one-woman show before reworking it into part of a larger, award-winning venture. Stubbings and Seinen gained experience at the outset of their theatre careers with the plays included herein, and Sharplin, who had already transferred to Walterdale his leadership skills and aptitude with classical texts, gained a full production of his ambitious historical drama. The variety of career positions and interests here is astonishing. Not all were committed playwrights, not all proved to be long-time dedicated members of Walterdale, and none was forced by the theatre to conform to thematic or stylistic moulds in order to achieve selection or production. That Walterdale has served Edmonton artists in such a variety of ways has helped to define its niche and contribute to its longevity. The plays selected for inclusion here exemplify the great variety that nonprofessionalized practice can enable.

A final point I wish to make regarding selection is that these plays are not "representative." That is, no play stands in for the theme, content, style, or even production process of other plays produced at Walterdale over the decades. Together, however, they present compelling evidence that as an amateur theatre, Walterdale has a recorded history of staging a wide variety of outstanding new plays, many of which might influence the practice and study of theatre if disseminated more widely.

THE PLAYS

The Canadian Fact (1967)

by Wilfred Watson

> You can always be safe and predictable in the theatre, but it is best to take risks. If you are going to be a Canadian dramatist you can't win, so you might as well be experimental.
>
> ~ WILFRED WATSON QUOTED IN WESTGATE, "ANOTHER WORLD"

He has been called "The most fascinating playwright in the modern Canadian theatre and one of its most controversial" (Peacock, "Wilfred Watson" 9), "Western Canada's reigning absurdist" (Stuart 235), and "as Canadian as The Group of Seven or an inhabitant of Frye's *Bush Garden*" (Peacocke xii). Despite such accolades, the work of Wilfred Watson—playwright, poet, professor, essayist, University of Alberta Studio Theatre collaborator, and Marshall McLuhan co-author—remains, from a national perspective at least, an underground phenomenon. This paradox—representatively Canadian yet relatively unknown in Canadian popular culture—may exemplify Watson's writing career, but it also applies to Walterdale Playhouse, a company that has earned undeniable local recognition yet, as an amateur theatre, has flown under the national radar. Watson's ambitious theatrical events, which juggled with alarming linguistic rigour multimedia happening-style performances and theatre of the absurd sensibilities (what he called "radical absurdity"), were a natural fit with the experimental art of the 1960s.[14]

Watson was born in Rochester, England, in 1911 and spent his early years at a grammar school in Essex before immigrating with his family to Duncan, British Columbia, in 1926. He married writer Sheila Martin Doherty in 1941 before earning an honours BA in English literature at the University of British Columbia (1943). After serving in the Canadian navy, he enrolled at the University of Toronto, where he earned an MA (1946) and a PhD (1951). Watson met Marshall McLuhan in 1947 when they attended a play on the same night. Sheila, whose PhD supervisor at the University of Toronto was McLuhan, reintroduced her husband to the popular media theorist in 1959, initiating a decade of correspondence between them that culminated in their co-authorship of *From Cliché to Archetype* (1970), including the chapters "Theatre" and "The Theatre of the Absurd."[15] In 1949 Watson began his teaching career as a special lecturer at the University of British Columbia before becoming a professor of English at the University of Alberta, first at the Calgary campus in 1951 and then in Edmonton in 1953, where he remained until his retirement in 1977. In 1955 his first volume of poetry, *Friday's Child*, earned a Governor General's Award and accolades from T.S. Eliot (who had accepted it for publication) and Northrop Frye.

While living in Paris between 1955 and 1956 on a Canadian Government Overseas Fellowship, Watson was attracted to the new plays of the theatre of the absurd.[16] In the mid-1960s a number of his works written in the theatre of the absurd style were read and staged by founding Walterdale member Bud D'Amur at Edmonton's experimental performance venue, the Yardbird Suite.[17] When the Yardbird shut its doors to theatre performance in the fall of 1966, Watson, while continuing to produce at Studio Theatre, presented his less extravagant new plays at Walterdale's Legion of Frontiersmen Hall venue. But following the Studio Theatre premiere of *Let's murder Clytemnestra according to the principles of Marshall McLuhan* (November 1969), which received a notably scathing review from the *Edmonton Journal* (Westgate, "Wilfred Watson's"),[18] Watson opted to curtailed his more ambitious playwriting. In 1980 he and Sheila moved to Nanaimo, B.C. But when his unproduced trilogy *Gramsci x 3*, premiered at Studio Theatre in 1986, *Edmonton Journal* reviewer Liz Nicholls called it "a stunning theatrical experience," one "unlike any to be had in this burg. Not now. And not for a long time to come." The Watsons remained in Nanaimo until Sheila, and then Wilfred, passed away in 1998.[19]

During the 1960s, his most prolific decade as a dramatist, Watson's ties to university culture as a professor and playwright helped to shape his political and aesthetic convictions. He worked closely with students at Studio Theatre on his controversial extravaganzas *Cockrow and the Gulls* (March 1962), *O Holy Ghost, DIP YOUR FINGER IN THE BLOOD OF CANADA and write, I LOVE YOU* (December 1967), and *Let's murder Clytemnestra(...)*. His less ambitious, lyrical one-act plays *Wail for Two Pedestals* (December 1964); *Chez-vous, Comfortable Pew* (May 1965), which includes the "cultural Robin Hood" character "Bud Damur"; and *Tom Jones Meets Fanny Hill* (October 1965) premiered at the Yardbird. If his Studio Theatre plays were multimedia, large-cast performance events, his Yardbird plays were poetic performances played to inquisitive, bohemian audiences who would stay out until six in the morning.

Many of Watson's plays presented his dictum, as articulated in the prefatory essay "On Radical Absurdity," that "the central fact in modern civilization [is] its multiplicity of media" ("Poem" 43). Watson's multimedia events combined a contemporary theatre of the absurd sensibility with a McLuhan-inspired awareness of "multi-media man" ("Poem" 41). After all, was it not absurd that if anything is common among the people of the Western World it is that the majority of the experiences we hold are apprehended from a distance via new media—life as seen on TV? During the 1960s television aided in forming political opinions of far-off lands that resulted in countless demonstrations.

And grander still, the drawing together of so many people through television was ritual. "Theatre," said Watson, "repeats with increase of intensity—and its best expressions are ritual" ("Towards" 58).

But Watson's Walterdale plays were something else yet again. Closer to the Yardbird-styled plays in their minimalism, yet more focused in structure, *The Canadian Fact* (May 1967) and *Two Teardrops Frozen on a Rearview Mirror* (March 1968) are clearly inspired by theatre of the absurd.[20] Doubtless, *The Canadian Fact* is, in the main, a departure from his ritualistic sci-fi plays at the Studio Theatre or his more lyrical work at the Yardbird. These ventures were fantastical explorations, frequently infused with vocal acrobatics and new-media spectacles, whereas *The Canadian Fact*, while socially astute and rhythmically adroit in its prose, remains grounded in familiar, if persistently ridiculous, human discussion and is notably devoid of Watson's trademark mixed-media environment and fantastic ritualism. Indeed, *The Canadian Fact* might be seen as Watson's focused experiment in absurdist dialogue, leaving out the other elements of his dramaturgy in much the same way that Beckett's plays frequently dispense with certain dramaturgical elements in order to focus on one particular element: words without movement in *Krapp's Last Tape*, speech without body in *Not I*, and so forth.

Because the first wave of the theatre of the absurd in Europe was a forceful and personal inspiration in Watson's work, deconstructivist linguistic elements permeate his writings. "What theatre of the absurd is about," wrote Watson, "is the birth of a new kind of mind, through the labour pangs of the old simple-minded book mind" ("Towards" 58). In his essays Watson called for getting "rid of" what he termed "the freshman essay" type of playwriting in favour of a theatre in which "language is a mode of human behaviour" ("Towards" 55).

By the early 1970s Watson was urging Canadian theatre to take up those language-based intrigues common to Europe's theatre of the absurd in order to pursue—or was that problematize?—a national character. Thus, when he describes the scene for *The Canadian Fact* in the opening stage directions, he paints his view of the Canadian theatrical landscape, one that alienates and perplexes the very artists it contains:

> SCENE ... a Canadian theatre ... any Canadian theatre ... not so much a scene, as a milieu pervaded by a fascinating but devastating sense of the totally foreign, of the place furthest removed from home.

When Watson's university teaching career began at the University of British Columbia in 1949, it was the same year that the Massey Commission began its study of Canadian culture and the arts. The commission's focus on state-sponsored arts influenced Watson, as it did many of his contemporaries.[21] Watson viewed as obsolete the commonly held practice of framing Canadian theatre as the late-maturing offspring of "the mother country"—"England or France or both" ("Towards" 59). Instead, he preferred the view that Canadian theatre practises in antithesis to its American counterpart, particularly against the latter's "doomed" "attempt to avoid words" ("Towards" 58). Theatre, he said, is a national resource, "just like water, oil, coal, our fisheries, etc., etc. our workmen, our students—and our graduate students too"

("Towards" 58) and it needs state development if it is to thrive: "In further development of Canadian theatre we can make full use of the performed word as an essential element of theatre mimicry. The real problem is, how can we develop theatre as a national human resource?" ("Towards" 59). In answer, Watson singled out universities—not surprisingly, considering his lifelong affiliation with them—and state attention, in the form of "millions" of "tourist-dollars" that would convert "unemployment into leisure-employment [where] theatre will be a key activity" ("Towards" 59). In other words, in order for a sovereign Canada to find its theatrical voice, its theatre must become financially stable, and the best ways to accomplish this would be to generate popular interest internally at academic institutions and externally by generating income from British, French, and American tourists. As absurd as it may seem, Canadian theatre could mature by charging its "parents" and "neighbours" admission. Watson, like Robertson Davies, Vincent Massey, and other commentators of the day, sought to find a Canadian voice in the theatre by advocating for foreign styles of playwriting that would attract foreign audiences. Ultimately, this was an ironic strategy for a radically absurd national theatre.

In *The Canadian Fact*, a Canadian playwright (who no longer writes plays) and a Canadian director (who has never directed a Canadian play) conspire to produce a "Canadian" play about "the American bombardment of a lunatic asylum in Hanoi [Vietnam] while Peter Brook was directing a Canadian telephone directory there." The dialogue is as absurd as the struggle to find a Canadian theatre seemed to Watson, as it did (and still does) for many. The play is reminiscent of Robertson Davies's Lovewit and Trueman dialogue, and insomuch as it considers the place (figurative and literal) of a so-called maturing Canadian theatre and its constitutive writers and directors, it might be read as a response to it. The play deals with themes of nationalism and the theatre while commenting humorously on playwrights who are too literary and directors who ignore the text.

The Canadian Fact ran May 26–28, 1967, at Walterdale Playhouse (the Legion of Frontiersmen Hall) with the following cast and creative team:

THE DIRECTOR	Robbie Newton
THE WRITER	Jim Abrams
DIRECTOR	Peter Montgomery
PROPERTIES	Helen Martin
SOUND	Malcolm Leske
LIGHTS	A.E. Montgomery

The Canadian Fact was published previously in the Canadian literary journal *White Pelican* (2, no. 1, Winter 1972), of which Watson's wife Sheila was a founding editor. Watson himself edited another issue of the publication.

The Canadian Fact

by Wilfred Watson

Characters WRITER
DIRECTOR

Setting *... a Canadian theatre ... any Canadian theatre ... not so much a scene, as a milieu pervaded by a fascinating but devastating sense of the totally foreign, of the place furthest removed from home.*

WRITER But the first thing a Canadian writer feels when he goes into a Canadian theatre is a marked hostility. You shake your head in dismay, but it is so, I assure you. I am a writer, and that is what I feel. (*Director smiles disarmingly*) A Canadian writer is definitely *not*, N,O,T, *not* welcome in a Canadian theatre. (*Insisting*) He feels he's definitely not wanted.

DIRECTOR Oh my dear sir, that's not true.

WRITER But I tell you it is.

DIRECTOR No no no no no, definitely no! —I'm always on the lookout for a Canadian play.

WRITER That's your theme song. It's what Canadian directors sing all the time. (*Shakes head*)

DIRECTOR We're all of us looking for a good Canadian play. Mind you, it must be good.

WRITER (*Turning as if he'd got his companion trapped*) Well! I sent you one the other day!

DIRECTOR Yes you did, now I remember. Yes!

WRITER I don't know whether it was any good or not!

DIRECTOR Ah, yes, I remember, quite distinctly. Well...

WRITER It wasn't much good? No? (*Retreating*) You look dubious.

DIRECTOR Let me see. (*Thinks*) I remember it quite distinctly!

WRITER It didn't make much impact?

DIRECTOR I'm always pleased to get new scripts to read, always. (*Explains*) There are some purportedly new plays which aren't new. (*Pause*) But your play ... yes ... ah, yes! (*Pause*) I liked your play very much ... but...

WRITER You want some changes made?

DIRECTOR I'm just trying to remember...

WRITER I'm afraid I'm an awful bother?

DIRECTOR No bother at all. I remember. It did need some revision.

WRITER But you do think it will work? You think it will produce?

DIRECTOR I'm not making any promises. (*Pause*) But cheer up, man. Peter Brook, the great English director has shown us that a good director can produce anything.

WRITER Anything?

DIRECTOR Anything. (*Pause*) Just about anything.

WRITER Then you will produce it?

DIRECTOR I've seen some Canadian plays that ought not to have been produced. (*Pause*) We all have. (*Pause*) I've seen some Canadian plays which ought not to have been produced, yes. (*Pause*) Not even by Peter Brook. I think it should be produced. It ought to be produced. (*Pause*) Ought to. (*Pause*) Canadian theatre cannot afford to exclude Canadian writers.

WRITER Or the Canadian fact.

DIRECTOR Or the Canadian fact.

WRITER It's a question of relevance?

DIRECTOR You're right. (*Pause*) We ought to be holding the mirror up to life in Canada. (*Pause*) We ought to. (*Pause*) I won't say we always do. (*Pause*) But we ought to. (*Pause*) Don't you agree? (*Pause*) I hope you agree.

WRITER Dull as life in Canada may be...

DIRECTOR That's the trouble. Life in Canada is dull. And no audience will stand for it. They go to the theatre to get away from Canadian life. (*Pause*) They do.

WRITER But there are moments of rapture.

DIRECTOR Dull as it may be, we ought to hold the mirror up to it.

WRITER To show the age its form and pressure, what?

DIRECTOR I wish we could, and believe me, I do think your play ought to be produced.

WRITER We are a shattered people.

DIRECTOR We are.

WRITER A people of shattered identities.

DIRECTOR We are. (*Pause*) But don't despair.

WRITER You are going to produce it then?

DIRECTOR *Your* play? (*Pause*) Produce *your* play? (*Pause*) I'm just wondering whether our available ACTORS could manage some of the scenes.

WRITER You think some of the scenes are over difficult?

DIRECTOR Not for the right actors perhaps ... but that's the problem. We directors have to work with what we've got in the way of actors.

WRITER And that's not much?

DIRECTOR We've got no good actors. (*Pause*) Why? (*Answer*) Because they've all gone to the U.S. where they can get paid.

WRITER Which scenes do you think are going to be difficult? Not the scene where Mary...

DIRECTOR I haven't really got round to reading your script yet old man. I've been frightfully busy ... but, as I said, Peter Brook—

WRITER Can produce anything at all.

DIRECTOR Anything, anything at all. He can make anything work. So I don't suppose the Mary scene will get in the way—though I don't—without reading the play through, mind you—like the name Mary much—not much...

WRITER Not much.

DIRECTOR Not much.

WRITER It grates you, I can see by the look on your face.

DIRECTOR It doesn't send me.

WRITER Perhaps I'd better alter it.

DIRECTOR Don't alter anything. Just wait. I am having your script translated into French. (*Pause*) Just be patient. (*Pause*) It will take a little time, but I think it'll be worth it.

WRITER Into French?

DIRECTOR I'm having it translated into French.

WRITER You're going to attempt a bilingual production?

DIRECTOR My friend, I wish I could. But wherever could I find the actors? (*Pause*) Bilingual production? (*Pause*) Oh no. (*Pause*) You see, *when* it has been translated into French, I'm going to have it translated back into English. (*Pause*) This is my very own gimmick. (*Pause*) It takes time, ah yes!

WRITER But why translate it into French and back into English?

DIRECTOR It's too literary. By getting it translated I'll take down some of the values a notch or two.

WRITER It's too literary.

DIRECTOR Oh yes, much too literary.

WRITER But you haven't read it yet?

DIRECTOR No time, no time. Not a moment. I've been doing Mario Fratti's John Cage...

WRITER You mean, The Cage?

DIRECTOR John Cage is the Cage... After PB...

WRITER Peter Brook?

DIRECTOR John Cage is my chief inspiration he ought to be yours ... oh, those miraculous silences ... those miraculous modules of silence ... I find silence precious *per se* but Cage's silence is like Bach's St. Matthew Passion *sans* choir *sans* orchestra *sans* organ *sans* passion and *sans*...

WRITER St. Matthew?

DIRECTOR Yes, of course.

WRITER It's full of birds...

DIRECTOR Oh it's full of birds ... in fact, I do definitely try to turn the theatre into a cage full of birds ... and then I open the door ... (*Pause*) but it takes time ... I've been doing Ionesco's *The Bulky Soprano* and *Mother Courage* and *Hair*...

WRITER Not the New York *Hair*?

DIRECTOR Horrors no—the Birmingham *Hair* ... ah, yes, and *The Trojan Women* and *Marat/Sade*...

WRITER My play is set in a lunatic asylum.

DIRECTOR Your play is set in a lunatic asylum?—But I know ... without even reading it, your play is much too literary. (*Pause*) Too literary.

WRITER I see.

DIRECTOR You're a writer, aren't you?

WRITER That's what I thought.

DIRECTOR The theatre needs writers.

WRITER You think so?

DIRECTOR I'm sure of it. But writers are always so literary. That's why I think my scheme of a translation into and out of French will make it actable.

WRITER I actually wrote it in French, and translated it back into English.

DIRECTOR Wonderful. But you're still a writer and your translation would be a writer's translation, still too literary.

WRITER Peter Brook could do it.

DIRECTOR Not if it was literary.

WRITER But he does Shakespeare, and Shakespeare I suppose is literary?

DIRECTOR Shakespeare is very literary. (*Pause*) But he isn't literary in quite the same way. (*Pause*) But don't worry. I particularly want to do a play in a lunatic asylum.

WRITER Ah, good, then you will like my speech about all the world's a lunatic asylum.

DIRECTOR I want to do a lunatic asylum, but not a literary man's idea of a lunatic asylum.

WRITER You'll like my play.

DIRECTOR I'll probably have to change it a lot.

WRITER I've set it in a lunatic asylum in Hanoi.

DIRECTOR Peter Brook can make anything out of anything—I am not Peter Brook. —But he is my model, as a director. (*Pause*) Nothing daunts me.

WRITER Nothing daunts you.

DIRECTOR Not even your play.

WRITER Not even my play.

DIRECTOR Wonderful, wonderful Peter Brook. He can make anything out of anything.

WRITER That's just my theme. My play's about Peter Brook. He's gone to Hanoi, to see if...

DIRECTOR Not Hanoi? (*Pause*) The audience will never stand for that ... they've been bombarded too much with Hanoi.

WRITER But that's my theme. Instead of blowing them to bits, I'm going to stick them together.

DIRECTOR In a lunatic asylum in Hanoi?

WRITER Yes.

DIRECTOR I'd very much like to read your play, ever so much.

WRITER Well you've got it.

DIRECTOR That's right I've got it.

WRITER You've just said you'd sent it to be translated.

DIRECTOR I've sent it to be translated.

WRITER (*Dreamily*) It's a lovely play. —I think you will like it.—Especially since you want to do something with a lunatic asylum. (*Rapturously*) There's a brief moment ... a marvelous moment ... which I'm sure will enthrall you ... (*Pause*) It's a scene in which a strip tease dancer takes off all her clothes.

DIRECTOR Visual values.

WRITER She is in the lunatic asylum. (*Pause*) She has been entertaining the troops. But then she's captured by the Viet Cong, raped, and goes mad. (*Pause*) She's thrown into this wretched haven of a lunatic asylum in Hanoi. (*Pause*) And she's visited by a Roman Catholic missionary.

DIRECTOR But could this happen?

WRITER Anything could happen in Hanoi.

DIRECTOR Are you sure Hanoi is available to missionaries.

WRITER Anything could happen in Hanoi. That's why I chose Hanoi for my lunatic asylum.

DIRECTOR It's not a direct satire on American intervention? (*Pause*) I shouldn't want that. (*Pause*) The Canadian government doesn't give a sweet damn if we put on a Canadian play. (*Pause*) But Uncle Sam always is helpful when we put on an American play. (*Pause*) If it weren't for the U.S. we'd be out of business. Uncle Sam doesn't mind us putting on an occasional Canadian play, as long as it doesn't criticize American foreign policy. (*Pause*) This comes as a shock to you? (*Pause*) The ultimate aim of American imperialism is to display its image. (*Pause*) But don't worry. (*Pause*) As long as your play isn't a direct satire on American intervention.

WRITER I leave that to the Americans.

DIRECTOR You'd be wise to.

WRITER Well this lovely scene in which the strip tease dancer from Montana who has been captured by the Viet Cong, raped, tortured, and thrust into a lunatic asylum—is visited by a Roman Catholic father ... (*Emphasis*) She takes off all her clothes (*He starts to divest himself of his clothes*)

DIRECTOR She takes off all her clothes? (*Starts to disrobe too*)

WRITER The Roman Catholic father doesn't know how to behave.

DIRECTOR *C'est son metier.*

WRITER So he takes off all his clothes too. (*Disrobing further*)

DIRECTOR I must read this play.

WRITER There they are completely naked.

DIRECTOR Of course. (*Completes ritual disrobing*)

WRITER And they say nothing. (*Pause*) Nothing.

DIRECTOR Nothing?

WRITER I want to get away from words.

DIRECTOR I like that scene.

WRITER I knew you would. It's one of the best scenes I've ever done.

DIRECTOR I must read your script.

WRITER They take off their clothes together. They say nothing. (*Pause*) And they do nothing.

DIRECTOR I think I would have them say a prayer together.

WRITER I like it better without words.

DIRECTOR I don't think it would work. —Oh, if we had the right sort of actors. (*They put on the clothes they have discarded*)

WRITER Peter Brook could make it work.

DIRECTOR You're right. But I put myself in PB's place and when I do, I think, it needs an emphasis, a verbal emphasis.

WRITER Well the basic idea is a nice one.

DIRECTOR I'm not sure you're not too ambitious—I'm not convinced that you're not doing too much. A writer must be very careful not to upstage his producer. I like a play which leaves a good deal of scope to the director. (*Pause*) Most of the real work should be left to the director. (*Pause*) The ideal playwright is like a university president. (*Pause*) He goes out after the foundations. He gets the play discussed in the press. He makes appearances on TV. (*Pause*) But he leaves all the theatre details to the director. (*Pause*) He need write nothing more than the title. (*Pause*) The title should be a good one.

WRITER The title is the writer's province.

DIRECTOR It shouldn't of course encroach on the play itself. (*Pause*) That's what's wrong with *Six Characters in Search of an Author*. It competes with the play. It makes the play unnecessary.

WRITER The play comes as an anti-climax?

DIRECTOR The play itself should be left to the director. (*Pause*) And if the director is of the calibre of Peter Brook ... even a brilliant title...

WRITER Like *Mrs. Warren's Profession* or *The Importance of Being Earnest*?

DIRECTOR Won't unduly perturb him.

WRITER Well I leave a lot of scope to the director.

DIRECTOR I'm glad of that.

WRITER You see, I imagine Peter Brook in the lunatic asylum in Hanoi.

DIRECTOR I must read your play soon.

WRITER He has gone, let us suppose, to Viet Nam to get some research done for a documentary. And he's been captured by the Viet Cong.

DIRECTOR It doesn't sound very authentic?

WRITER The British government protests weakly—what else could it do under the circumstances.

DIRECTOR I would ask whether the British have any claim to world attention—except Peter Brook.

WRITER There's Shakespeare.

DIRECTOR He's of another time.

WRITER I thought he was of all time.

DIRECTOR Not any more.

WRITER Devouring Time, blunt thou the lion's paw, *etc.*, *etc* ... Pluck the keen teeth from the fierce tiger's jaw ... (*Sadly*) Alas poor Shakespeare! (*Recovery*) Well there is Peter Brook in the lunatic asylum in Hanoi and in his right senses too!

DIRECTOR Alas poor Peter Brook!

WRITER It was his finest moment! He rises to the occasion.

DIRECTOR Trust Peter.

WRITER One of the inmates accosts him, and says, I am a Canadian dramatist. (*Pause*) And Peter Brook said, very simply, I am Peter Brook, the British play director! (*Pause*) It's a nice recognition scene.

DIRECTOR What happens next?

WRITER I leave a lot of scope to the director. (*Pause*) Anything you like. (*Pause*) Within reason.

DIRECTOR But reason is posthumous.

WRITER So is life. We live it backwards. That's why we need the theatre. In the theatre we live life forwards into the future. This sort of reason is very mad. That's why I locate my play in a lunatic asylum in Hanoi.

DIRECTOR This is all very theoretical.

WRITER Well, to be practical, I suggest that they put on a play. (*Pause*) The bombs are falling all around them.

DIRECTOR They have to do something to distract themselves.

WRITER That's just it. Just simple madness is never distracting enough. (*Pause*) Peter Brook rises to the occasion sublimely.

DIRECTOR I knew he would.

WRITER He does. Let's ask, he decided, the medical superintendent for a budget.

DIRECTOR A sensible beginning.

WRITER That's what the Viet Cong psychiatrist thought.

DIRECTOR I can see the superintendent smiling.

WRITER But he was on the spot. He had been educated in the Harvard Medical School and he'd actually acted in a Brattle Street amateur production of Eugene O'Neill's *The Emperor Jones*. (*Pause*) Well, he stalls for time. (*Pause*) He asks them if they have a suitable play. (*Pause*) He's not opposed to the idea, mind you.

DIRECTOR Only to the budget.

WRITER He was on a budget himself.

DIRECTOR It's so difficult to find a suitable play.

WRITER Peter Brook told the superintendent of the insane asylum at Hanoi, No, I haven't a suitable play but I have got a Canadian playwright.

DIRECTOR This would be a challenge even for Peter Brook.

WRITER Oh it was a challenge to the Canadian playwright. (*Pause*) He had a captive audience. (*Pause*) And a captive director. (*Pause*) Peter Brook. (*Pause*) Unfortunately all his scripts were in a clothes closet in a room in a rooming house in Toronto. (*Pause*) You know the set up. There's a long hat-shelf. He'd piled all his MSS on this hat-shelf.

DIRECTOR Where'd he keep his hats?

WRITER He'd never had a hat—he kept his ear-muffs in his briefcase. In the summer-time he used them to polish his shoes. (*Pause*) But even if they long-distance telephoned for the scripts, there was still some back rent the Canadian playwright owed which would have to be paid before the script could be mailed to Hanoi.

DIRECTOR In the meantime, the bombardment was going on?

WRITER I've got a play about Sir Wilfrid Laurier, the Canadian playwright said. (*Pause*) Good, said Peter Brook. (*Pause*) I've got one about a forest fire in British Columbia. (*Pause*) Fine, said Peter Brook. (*Pause*) And I've got a play about Klondike Days. (*Pause*) Marvelous, said Peter Brook. (*Pause*) And a play about the Alberta Indians. (*Pause*) Great stuff, said Peter Brook. (*Pause*) And a play about the discovery of oil in Alberta. (*Pause*) Very interesting, said Peter Brook.

DIRECTOR Poor Peter Brook!

WRITER Which one shall I telephone for, asked the Canadian dramatist—the only book I have with me, he said is a telephone directory. I always carry an old telephone directory with me, he explained, in case I get stuck with names. (*Pause*) Peter Brook threw his hands in the air, in the wildest excitement. (*Pause*) You've got a Canadian telephone directory, he asked. (*Pause*) Yes, said the Canadian dramatist. (*Pause*) Well don't bother telephoning for any of your plays—I'll direct the telephone directory. It'll be a marvelous production. (*Pause*) Will you give me a part, asked the poor little strip tease dancer from Montana. (*Pause*) We'll all have parts said Peter Brook. Where's the directory. (*Pause*) It'll be difficult to cast, said the playwright handing it over. (*Pause*) There'll be some doubling, of course, said Peter Brook. (*Pause*) Here's our script, he told the superintendent, who, thinking Peter was madder than observation had indicated, authorized a budget.

DIRECTOR Well I get the situation.

WRITER It's a possible one?

DIRECTOR It just might work—Peter Brook directs a telephone directory in a lunatic asylum in Hanoi. (*Pause*) As soon as I get the translation back from the translators, I'll read it very carefully. (*Pause*) It seems to leave a lot to the director. It has an interesting if implausible situation—it doesn't exclude itself by being anti-American. It could even be taken as a satire on the Canadian playwright. (*Pause*) But what about an ending?

WRITER I think that should be left to the director.

DIRECTOR But supposing I do decide to produce your play, I'd like to know how you decided to end it.

WRITER I rather agree with you, that a writer's responsibility stops with the title. (*Pause*) I may even have committed an act of trespass there.

DIRECTOR Well, I'll see how you ended your script when it comes back from the translators.

WRITER I never gave you a script.

DIRECTOR But I'm waiting for your script to come back from the translators. (*Pause*) You said you'd sent me one...

WRITER I prevaricated.

DIRECTOR You lied to me. There's nothing I detest more than a liar. —You told me a bare-faced lie.

WRITER I prevaricated—it comes from my habit of fictionalizing.

DIRECTOR An occupational disease. —It doesn't excuse a downright lie. That is unforgivable.

WRITER Well, you lied to me.

DIRECTOR (*Relenting*) It's sometimes hard to face up to truth.

WRITER We've both prevaricated.

DIRECTOR Shake.

WRITER Gladly (*They shake hands*). An occupational disease.

DIRECTOR But really you must let me see your script.

WRITER Oh, I never write any more scripts.

DIRECTOR But you are a writer—how ridiculous to say you don't write any scripts.

WRITER Not any more ridiculous than what you do.

DIRECTOR How am I ridiculous?

WRITER Well you're a famous Canadian director and you never direct any Canadian plays.

DIRECTOR You mean, we're a prize pair?

WRITER I never write any plays...

DIRECTOR And I never direct any Canadian plays...

WRITER We're a pair all right.

DIRECTOR Well, I'm going to reform. You really must get this play down on paper.

WRITER But I'm a writer and I'd only get it all too literary. (*Pause*) Why don't we just go ahead and produce it. (*Pause*) Just think of me as the playscript. (*Pause*) An oral playscript.

DIRECTOR I think you have an idea. (*Pause*) You'll stand beside me and create the play at the same time as I direct it?

WRITER Yes.

DIRECTOR You did say the title was your total responsibility.

WRITER I was making an extravagant claim. But we could start with the *American Bombardment of a Lunatic Asylum in Hanoi while Peter Brook was Directing a Canadian Telephone Directory There.*

DIRECTOR I suddenly—for the first time in my career as play director—feel proud I'm a Canadian. (*Pause*) I think I may have discovered my identity. (*Pause*) Do you mind ... would it greatly disturb you ... if we sang "O Canada" together.

WRITER Let's. (*They remain silent*)

DIRECTOR Are you a tenor, baritone or bass?

WRITER My voice wanders between the lower registers of Caruso's tenor voice and the upper registers of Chaliapin's bass. (*They sing, a little shakily, but with great courage*)

DIRECTOR AND WRITER

O CANADA OUR HOME AND GRACIOUS LAND, *etc.*

DIRECTOR In discovering your play, I've discovered my identity. (*Pause*) I've discovered I am a Canadian. (*Pause*) I've always been something else. (*Pause*) I'd never thought that to discover one's true identity was such a touching experience. (*Pause*) Thank you, thank you. (*Pause*) Do you mind if I embrace you, French fashion.

WRITER Please do. (*They embrace*)

DIRECTOR Just once more. (*Pause*) I hope you don't mind. I hope you don't think I'm impossibly sentimental. (*They embrace*) But it's as if I took my own native land in my arms.

WRITER It's an awfully moving situation. (*Pause*) To be near when someone discovers his true identity. (*Pause*) I feel privileged.

DIRECTOR Thank you.

WRITER There is a constriction in my throat.

DIRECTOR But having discovered that I am a Canadian, I find myself beginning to question your script ... (*Pause*) which was the cause of my realizing a true sense of Canadian identity.

WRITER Oneness with the maple leaf, and all that? (*Pause*) Oneness with the French-Canadian separatist and oneness with the white Anglo Saxon protestant? (*Pause*) One foot in the Atlantic Ocean and one foot in the Pacific? (*Pause*) Oneness?

DIRECTOR Yes. (*Pause*) But is your sort of script really a Canadian play? (*Pause*) I'll put it on, mind you, even if it's the last play I ever direct. (*Pause*) But what has a script about Peter Brook in a lunatic asylum in Hanoi to do with myself and my fellow Canadians in Canada?

WRITER My script is still unwritten.

DIRECTOR That's not an answer. —You are your script, isn't that what you said. (*Pause*) It's an oral script? (*Pause*) There's no question of my not putting it on. But ... is it really a Canadian play?

WRITER Well, I am a Canadian. How could I write anything but a Canadian play? (*Pause*) The lunatic asylum is a metaphor for Canada. (*Pause*) Peter Brook is a metaphor for the Canadian theatre. (*Pause*) The Canadian telephone directory is a metaphor for the Canadian people.

DIRECTOR But what about the Canadian playwright, the mad Canadian playwright, who has written plays about Sir Wilfrid Laurier, forest fires in British Columbia, Klondike Days, the Alberta Indian, the discovery of oil in Leduc...

WRITER He is a metaphor for the writer who has never discovered Canada.

DIRECTOR You're right. (*Pause*) I'm feeling a little giddy. (*Pause*) It's like finding a sense of identity in a bottle of Scotch whisky. (*Pause*) Things are a trifle hazy. (*Pause*) The world very uncertain. (*Pause*) I'm not at all sure I haven't identified with something that doesn't exist.

WRITER Perhaps we should sing "O Canada" again?

DIRECTOR Singing "O Canada" wouldn't help at all.

WRITER No I suppose not ... I suppose not.

DIRECTOR It's what you said about life ... we live it posthumously. (*Pause*) Canada is so very much of the future, that we can only really be Canadians in the theatre, where we naturally live in the future. (*Pause*) I'm going to take a deep breath. Would you like to take one with me? (*They breathe a deep breath of air together*) (*Pause*) I feel better now. (*Pause*) I think I would like to sing "O Canada" again if you would join in with me. (*Pause*) You don't mind do you?

DIRECTOR AND WRITER
(*Singing*) O CANADA, *etc.*

Curtain.

Chief Shaking Spear Rides Again or The Taming of the Sioux (1974)

by Warren Graves

> Contrary to popular belief, I have finished writing the script for this year's melodrama and although it has all the ingredients of our classic form, it also has a whole heap of topical ingredients mixed in. [...] It is an "in" Melodrama. It is entitled *Chief Shaking Spear Rides Again or The Taming of the Sioux* and the whole mess will deteriorate rapidly from there. [...] This early in any project, all one can go on is the feeling at the pit of the stomach. It is either a warm glow or an ice cube. Happy to report warm glow which is feeding on response to the script and starting to move towards the extremities. Maybe I've written a melodrama after all.
>
> ~ WARREN GRAVES, WALTERDALE NEWSLETTER, MAY 1974

When Edmonton Theatre Associates produced its first two plays in August and September 1958 in the Social Room of the Jubilee Auditorium, one of them was Hazelwood's melodrama *Lady Audley's Secret.*[22] In March 1963 at the schoolhouse, Theatre Associates produced another melodrama, Johnson's *Dirty Work at the Crossroads*, as "a passing experiment received gleefully by the audience" (Fritch 2). The group was on to something. For thirty-five years (1965 to 1999), Walterdale was best known for producing one of Edmonton's most anticipated annual cultural events: the Walterdale Melodrama. From the time it was presented as part of the Klondike Days Festival in July 1965,[23] the summer melodrama frequently earned the company, particularly during the 1970s, enough money to fund a full season of shows. In 1978, for example, a particularly lucrative offering (Aulger's *Adrift in New York or Her First False Step*) netted the company nearly $20,000 (including sponsorship revenue), compared to the entire 1977/78 season of productions, which accounted for just over $9,000 in

Corporate sponsorship for Warren Graves's Chief Shaking Spear Rides Again *at The Citadel, July 1974. Sponsorship went a long way for Walterdale's Klondike Melodrama during its heyday. For many years, nearly a full season of productions was paid for by income drawn from the summer melodrama. Photo: Walterdale Theatre Associates.*

total income.[24] The 1980 Melodrama (Pratt's *Ten Nights in a Barroom*) netted Walterdale nearly $14,000, or 53 percent of the season's total show surplus that fiscal year. The Walterdale Melodrama was, as they say, a hot commodity.

The Walterdale Melodrama's first two Klondike Days appearances were, appropriately, at Edmonton's old music hall building, the Strand Theatre (formerly Pantages Theatre). In July 1967 it settled into The Citadel mainstage for a heyday that lasted well into the 1980s. It routinely played to sold-out houses as tourists came from across Canada and the United States to take in Klondike Days, which by 1971 was attracting an attendance of more than 600,000 over ten days. By the end of the 1970s many counted the Melodrama among the city's most anticipated performance events. Graves himself noted in 1974 that for the Melodrama, "There's a very high degree of acceptance in this city. [It] has become a very real contribution to the tourist industry. Now brochures sent out by the city and exhibition board include a piece on the melodrama" (quoted in Adams 73). But its fortunes declined in the late 1980s. Walterdale moved the Melodrama to the Playhouse (firehall) when The Citadel's rental prices soared (Nicholls). And because the Playhouse was rented to the Fringe Festival from late July to the end of the summer, Walterdale could no longer align the Melodrama's run with Klondike Days. Without the flood of tourists, attendance at the Melodrama suffered, interest waned, and the tradition ended in July 1999 with Kelly's *Dark Deeds at Swan's Place or Never Trust a Tattooed Sailor*.

These days, the melodrama form is often regarded as an outdated quirk of the theatrical past. As a genre and a performance style, it fell out of popular favour a century ago. Certainly it can be found in early film and in today's television soap operas and reality TV shows. When a stage melodrama is produced today it is inevitably played as an overdramatic parody of a genre that was, during the nineteenth century, considered to be "the most striking dramatic phenomenon of the period" (Booth 9). By distilling life into simplified idealizations of good and evil, the melodrama could provide its audiences with an escape from real life and the assurance of a virtuous and satisfactory ending. But as artists and their audiences adopted the skepticisms of the post-war Western world, melodramas came to be regarded as playing out over-sentimentalized naiveties. Stock characters,[25] prescriptive dramaturgical "rules," and the "re-assertion of a benevolent moral order" (Booth 10) became in the first instance existentially problematic, and in the next farcical. In the Western theatrical world melodramas were an aesthetic affront to modern realism and thus relegated to obscurity. Read in this context, how is it that Walterdale was able to capitalize on the form for the last thirty-five years of the twentieth century?

The many factors involved in the success of the Walterdale Melodrama are the shared result of two sets of circumstances: ideal local conditions on the one hand, and reaction to a professionalizing national theatre discipline on the other. Both circumstances are directly related to many of the freedoms of amateur theatre described in the general introduction. First, Walterdale tethered its melodramas to a nineteenth-century Klondike-themed entertainment festival; at their best the parallel settings and the hero-versus-hardship themes were a mutually definitive match, particularly in Edmonton, with its historical roots in the gold rush era as the so-called "Gateway to the North." Second, the recovery of a theatrical form that had long since fallen into obscure parody was ideal for a box-office-funded amateur company that did not need to justify the socio-aesthetic relevance of its repertoire to acquire state operating grants; instead, Walterdale sought to attract and maintain audiences and members with, for example, quality entertainment spectacles. Third, the large casts (frequently numbering in the dozens) that are integral to much stock-character melodrama can be prohibitive for many professional theatres, but not for high-profile amateur theatres; with the melodrama, Walterdale effectively created brand association. Fourth, the playing of melodrama called for an acting style eschewed by theatre professionals and their accredited training schools, but Walterdale's actors could participate in the form for entertainment's sake and personal fulfillment, actively in opposition to realism's familiar aesthetics and free from the restraints imposed by professionalized training on both practitioners and the norms of public reception. Fifth, the form gave local high-profile theatre personalities such as Jack McCreath, Wally McSween, Ron Wigmore, and John Rivet—who had gained a sort of celebrity status in Edmonton during Walterdale's early years—a vehicle in which to play stand-out characters (particularly villains) who could interact directly with their audiences. And sixth, the momentum of the Walterdale Melodrama was maintained in part when, in the 1970s, Warren Graves began to blend the old form with local political themes. His creations, part nostalgic melodrama and part contemporary satire, combined nineteenth-century circumstances with socio-political currency. The Walterdale Melodrama played an important role in Graves's development as a playwright and, conversely, at its peak it was an international phenomenon due in no small part to original "hits" written by Graves.

The University of Alberta's Gordon Peacock suggested that by 1971 Graves was something of a "playwright-in-residence" at Walterdale (62). Graves's plays *Yes, Dear* (March 1968) and *Love in a Greenhouse* (November 1968) had earned drama awards as well as favourable reviews and excellent houses at Walterdale under his direction. He also appeared in a string of Walterdale plays during the late 1960s and 1970s for which he garnered critical accolades.[26] A forthright administrator, he served as Walterdale's artistic director (1970–72), membership chairman (1973–76), and vice-president (1976–77), and from 1973 to 1975 he was the company's animated, and at times controversial, newsletter writer. During the early 1970s he led the committee that was instrumental in securing Walterdale's current location at the Old Strathcona firehall. A few weeks after the first production at the firehall, Graves wrote in the December 1974 *Walterdale Newsletter*, "It must be that I have become a Walterdale old timer, and the new grand upstart of a theatre is a vaguely terrifying stranger" (2). Graves resigned as Walterdale's vice-president in 1977 in order to pursue what would become an accomplished professional theatre career, leaving behind a company for which he had provided a public personality, an administrative fervour, and a host of celebrated new works.

Graves—playwright, actor, director, producer, and administrator—was born in London, England in 1933. He grew up watching London theatre where, he says, "I watched the beautiful people do beautiful things beautifully. As a Cockney urchin, I aspired to that" ("Interview"). In 1964, after working in an assortment of radio and television jobs and performing his required military service, Graves moved with his wife and two children to Calgary and then to Edmonton, where he took a job as an assistant clerk at the Alberta Legislature, leaving that position in 1974 to become a self-employed writer. When his one-act play *Yes, Dear* won the *Edmonton Journal* writing competition, Graves thought it should be tested on stage, so he sought out Frank Glenfield, who was then Walterdale's president (1965–68). Drawing from his earlier amateur theatre experience in the United Kingdom, Graves directed *Yes, Dear* to positive response.

While acting in a number of Walterdale productions in the late 1960s, Graves continued to write, eventually earning international recognition for his work. During the 1970s he wrote a number of plays for Walterdale, including his first melodrama, *The Mumberly Inheritance or His Substance Frittered* (1971; directed by Graves), which, along with *Love in a Greenhouse* and *The Hand the Cradles the Rock* (1974; written in 1969; directed by John Rivet), were reported by the *Edmonton Journal* in 1981 as having "produced a steady stream of residuals from the summer stock companies and schools that continue to perform them" (Ashwell, "Prolific"). *Chief Shaking Spear Rides Again* also earned much praise, as it drew on contemporary local politics for its satiric inspiration. By the early 1980s Graves's writing was being produced at professional theatres and television stations across the country and around the world.[27] The Lyric Players Theatre in Belfast picked up *Mors Draculae* after director and Walterdale member Kieran O'Malley invited his visiting parents to see the play—Mary O'Malley founded the Lyric Players Theatre in 1951. Graves's *Pamela Frankenstein or Adam and Eve Meet Apple II* (1984; directed by Graves) was his third and last new Walterdale Melodrama, though the company would return to his oeuvre frequently over the next two decades.[28] The Playwrights Guild of Canada, of which he was a member, has published fifteen of his plays. Graves passed away in Lethbridge in February 2008, nine days after celebrating his seventy-fifth birthday.

Graves wrote *Chief Shaking Spear Rides Again or The Taming of the Sioux* to celebrate the tenth anniversary of the Walterdale Melodrama.[29] It stands as the only play to date to be written about Walterdale Theatre Associates. The comic melodrama spoofs Walterdale in the early 1970s as it struggled to fund, acquire, renovate, and pay off loans for its firehall location (into which the group was moving). When the "ruthless land developer" Cramden Twinge informs the players of the Corn Exchange Theatre that they have a month to pay off their property mortgage to him (they own the building,

Twinge the land) or he will go ahead with plans to route the railroad through the very land on which the theatre lies, the group decides to stage a play to raise funds to buy the land outright. (Consider that it is the building, and not the heroine, that is threatened by the path of the train.) Even the lease's "cultural-identification preservation clause" cannot save them. It stipulates that if someone in the group was born in the area and has lived there his whole life, the lease will be voided and the company will own the land. But there is, of course, no "local talent" to be found! Or is there? Fortunately for all, the theatre burns down, the company collects the insurance money, and Twinge is spared the expense of tearing down the building. In fact, so pleased is Twinge with this turn of events that he arranges for the Corn Exchange Theatre to be relocated in the old firehall near the centre of town. Thus Graves's melodrama thwarts conventional expectations: in the end the villain is refashioned as a hero, and he attracts the affections of the woman after whom he had lusted. Says Rose Dale of Twinge, "There is no more attractive man to a woman than a rogue turned saint."

Chief Shaking Spear Rides Again is not merely a behind-the-scenes parody of amateur theatre practice, and theatre practice generally. The play speaks directly to Edmonton politics of the day and its controversies, and to Walterdale's position within them. By representing as caricature Edmonton's mayor (Twinge, the villain), its aboriginal population (Chief Shaking Spear), and the voice of Walterdale itself (Walter Dale, his daughters Millicent and Rose, and the exceedingly British Kenneth Haig-Fortescue), Graves provides a rare and timely staged send-up of 1970s Edmonton municipal affairs from the (somewhat) distanced perspective of a British expatriate. Historical allusions abound. For example, in 1974 Walterdale entered into a lease agreement with the City of Edmonton when it beat out the Strathcona Businessmen's Association for the firehall location. According to the agreement, the city owned the land and the firehall building; Walterdale would pay the city $1.00 a year for rent, but the company had to procure all necessary funds to keep the building up to safe (and historically accurate) code. Moreover, at the time the mayor of Edmonton was William Hawrelak, who had twice been ousted from office and convicted for questionable land sales. The lived material, still fresh on Graves's mind because he was Walterdale's primary venue negotiator with the city before the company was finally awarded the firehall, was ripe for his plucking. Moreover, that the music and lyrics to the melodrama's three original songs—"The Universe Is Going Wild," "Reputation," and "I Hate Edmonton"—were written by William Thorsell just a year before he assumed his first editorial position (with the *Edmonton Journal*) ("Today's Paper") signals an important creative moment in the life of an influential Canadian figure. Thorsell later became the editorial board chair and CEO of the *Globe and Mail*.

Predictably, critics did not miss an opportunity to play the genre infidelity card with *Chief Shaking Spear Rides Again*. Graves mused on this in the August 1974 *Walterdale Newsletter* a month after the play closed: "I was puzzled by critical reaction along the lines of 'but it's not the traditional melodrama.' How could it be? How many melodramas are there set in Western Canada celebrating the RCMP Centennial featuring an Indian Chief and telling the story of Walterdale Playhouse? If I could have found one I wouldn't have had to write it" (1). Of course, the critics (and Graves) were not entirely accurate. Numerous nineteenth-century melodramas were based on situations similar to those Graves describes. One popular theme was that of pioneer life, featuring North American "Indians" as villains attempting to thwart "heroic" settlers. Adhering to the genre, there was much violent spectacle and the hero-settlers were invariably victorious. The gold rush, a second popular theme, featured saloon and gambling scenes. *Chief Shaking Spear Rides Again* acknowledges some of the expectations raised by these types of melodrama, including treatments of racism, and draws upon an uneasy nostalgia to rework them to contemporary, potentially ironic effect.[30]

Chief Shaking Spear Rides Again or The Taming of the Sioux ran July 15–27, 1974, at The Citadel Theatre with the following cast and creative team:

NELLIE	Nancie Methuen
LULU	Troy Sprenke
DAFT WILLIAM	Bob McManus
MITZI	Edith Tusor
WALTER DALE	Don Biamonte
MILLICENT DALE	Patty B. MacDonald
ROSE DALE	Glenys Berry
CRAMDEN TWINGE	John Rivet
KENNETH HAIG-FORTESCUE	Patrick Spelliscy
EDDY NELSON	Len Crowther
CHIEF SHAKING SPEAR	Richard Davidson
RUNNING DEER	Donna Shandro
GIRLS	Sharon Jonzon, Barbara MacMillan, Joan Milroy, Carol Steinbring
BLADES	Sandy Shandro, Jim Watt, Joe Smith
CHAIRMAN	Victor Bristow
MUSICIANS	William A.W. Thorsell (pianoforte) Ken Jackson and Desmond Kucy (saxophones) Rusty Maher (banjo) Gerald O'Donnell (trumpet) Miro Mistric (drums) Elaine Christenson (vocalist)

DIRECTOR	Warren Graves
SONGS	William Thorsell
SET DESIGNER	Phil Switzer
COSTUME DESIGNER	Alice Switzer
CHOREOGRAPHER	Denise Kallal
STAGE MANAGER	Greta Pullishy

Walterdale produced the play again July 19–29, 1989, at Walterdale Playhouse (firehall), directed by Gilbert Allen.

Chief Shaking Spear Rides Again or The Taming of the Sioux

by Warren Graves

Characters
NELLIE HOGAN, *the Madame*
LULU, *one of the girls*
MITZI, *another of the girls*
DAFT WILLIAM, *stage manager of the Corn Exchange Theatre*
WALTER DALE, *manager of the Corn Exchange Theatre*
ROSE DALE, *his daughter, the Sarah Bernhardt of the Prairies*
MILLICENT DALE, *an ingénue*
KENNETH HAIG-FORTESCUE, *remittance man and thespian*
CRAMDEN TWINGE, *a ruthless land developer*
EDDY NELSON, *a Mountie*
CHIEF SHAKING SPEAR, *a playwright of the Plains*
RUNNING DEER, *his secretary*
and ASSORTED LADIES, GENTLEMEN AND MUSICIANS

Setting The play is set in Nellie Hogan's house of easy virtue at the turn of the century.

Act One, Scene One

Nellie's "house" is the subcultural centre of Edmonton in the early 1900s. Edmonton is becoming a city, the Mounties have been here a long time, there are aldermen, cowboys and pretensions to cultural activity.

At the centre of this area of endeavour are Walter, Rose and Milly Dale, who, aided by Kenneth Haig-Fortescue and Daft William, present a nightly entertainment at the Corn Exchange Theatre. Tonight they are celebrating a successful conclusion to their tenth season in the Corn Exchange with a big party at Nellie's place. Nellie has set up her place as near her idea of a Paris salon as possible and herself as near Mae West as possible.

As the curtain rises, her "string quartet" is concluding "I've Been Working on the Railroad." The room is full of blades and girls. Applause and whistles...

NELLIE That was fine, boys. Didn't I tell you? Finest string quartet west of the Lakehead.

GENT Never seen a string quartet with a trumpet and six people before.

NELLIE Who said that!?

Everybody points at everybody else.

Nobody, eh? Well, you can tell nobody from me that when Nellie Hogan hires herself a string quartet, she gets herself a string quartet. If that isn't a string quartet—they don't get paid. (*To the band*) Now don't be afraid to give it to me straight, boys. Are you or are you not a string quartet?

They hasten to assure her that they are.

NELLIE What did I tell you! Think musicians don't know what they are?

LULU It's coming up to eleven o'clock, Nellie.

NELLIE Thanks, Lulu. I've got a little surprise for everybody at eleven o'clock.

There is a panic for the doors.

Hold it, hold it! Where the hell's everybody going?

MAN We know your little surprises, Nellie. The Mounties have got another raid coming up at eleven o'clock, right?

NELLIE Heck, no. We were raided last week. We're not due for another six weeks now. No, this is a good surprise. Now you all know the people down at the old Corn Exchange Theatre, right? A great bunch of people. Well, tonight they're winding up their tenth season down at the old place and I've invited them all back here for a party.

MAN Will Miss Rose be coming?

NELLIE Sure she'll be coming. And Walter and Milly and Kenneth...

MAN Pretty high class people to be coming to your house, Nellie.

NELLIE Who said that?

Everybody points at everybody else.

Well let me tell you that they happen to be very good friends of mine, and I don't know whether you know it or not but I happen to be pretty high class myself. You don't think I could come up with genuine Parisian decor like this if I was a bum, do you? I was very big in Europe before I came here.

MAN Then why did you come here, Nellie?

NELLIE (*Vamping him*) How could I waste my life there when you are here?

MAN (*Ecstatic*) Oh Nellie. (*Slides to the floor*)

NELLIE What a way to go. Bury him while he's still happy.

MAN I thought you loved me, Nellie?

NELLIE I thought you swore you'd never tell?

MAN (*Ecstatic*) Oh Nellie. (*Slides to the floor*)

NELLIE (*To audience*) Either you've got it or you haven't.

Daft William enters.

WILLIAM Miss Nellie, Miss Nellie!

NELLIE William, my favourite sweetheart. What news do you bring from the thespians?

WILLIAM None. I've just come from the theatre.

NELLIE You've had a rough day, haven't you, William?

WILLIAM Not too bad, taking it all 'round, considering everything. I would have been all right if it hadn't been for me fly.

NELLIE Your fly? What was wrong with your fly?

WILLIAM It wouldn't go all the way up at the beginning of act two.

MITZI Ooo Willie! What had you been doing in act one?

NELLIE Pay no mind to them, William. They don't understand when we talk theatre talk. Tell me what happened to your fly.

WILLIAM Well, when I found it wouldn't go all the way up, I didn't know what to do at first.

NELLIE A tense moment for you, William.

WILLIAM It was. Then I thought, I know what I'll do. I'll tie it to me braces.

NELLIE You tied your fly to your braces?

WILLIAM Well, I had to do something. I didn't want anything unexpected happening in act two, did I?

NELLIE Like what?

WILLIAM Well, there's a lot of weight there you know. It could have all come crashing down on the stage.

MAN What, all of it?

WILLIAM Right in the middle of Miss Rose's death scene. Well, she's bad enough at the best of times, but there's no living with her when she's dying.

NELLIE I can imagine. But it all came out all right, did it?

WILLIAM No. It all stayed up all right.

NELLIE And the show was a great success...

WILLIAM Yes.

NELLIE And now it's finished...

WILLIAM Yes.

NELLIE And they are all on there way over here.

WILLIAM Yes.

NELLIE Good.

WILLIAM Oh yes, and Mr. Walter asked me to tell you that the show was a great success and now it's finished and they are all on their way over here.

NELLIE I wish I'd said that. Okay, everybody, places please. Mitzi and Jean—go get it. Lulu—go keep an eye on the door. (*To the band*) Are you guys ready? (*They nod*) Okay. Now let me hear you singing like you were going to bust out in something.

MAN Aw, Nellie. I can't sing.

NELLIE Well, that's up to you. Anybody I see not singing gets a punch in the throat to help them along. What'll it be?

MAN (*Sings*) Quanta bello archipulco...

NELLIE Okay, save it for the big moment.

Lulu returns.

LULU They're here.

NELLIE String quartet! Twang it!

The quartet strikes up with "Happy Birthday to You" and the ensemble joins in the singing. A couch and a small low table are brought downstage. Walter enters, assisting the pale Rose, Milly bubbles in with the poised Kenneth and they move to the couch, where Rose is seated. Mitzi and Jean bring in a cake with ten candles. All applaud at the end of the song; Walter is overcome.

WALTER So kind, so kind. I really don't know what to say.

NELLIE What's to say? Blow out your candles.

He does so.

MITZI (*Close to him*) You blew it again, Walter. (*Sashays off*)

Cries of "Speech, speech."

WALTER Well ... ladies and gentlemen...

MAN Aw come on, Walter, be serious...

Laughter.

WALTER No, I mean that. To me you are ladies and gentlemen. You are kind, you are generous, warm-hearted and so full of—

MAN (*Drunk*) ... alcohol...

NELLIE Who said that?

Everybody points at Kenneth.

KENNETH Oh. I say.

NELLIE Well, we know what some people are full of and it isn't alcohol. Say your piece, Walter.

WALTER I was just going to say, this is a momentous occasion. A full decade at the Corn Exchange Theatre, and don't forget we started out from humbler beginnings four years before that. Tonight, another full house ... another act of faith in our humble offerings. How wise we were to bring our arts from the warmth and comfort of the East and offer it here, in this cruel and barbarous place. And what a success we have been! Not one empty seat and not one good review in ten years! (*Applause*) It's a great comfort to know that you are making *everybody* happy. And tonight, again tonight. A theatre full of hardy citizens and Kenneth raised them to poetry, Millicent brought gaiety to their hearts, and Rose moved them to tears. What a performance. I cried myself when it came to the final curtain. (*Quoting Rose's curtain speech*) "The twinkling dew has gone from off the summer lawn ... the sun is rising in the sky ... and I, pale flower, shall wither in its firesome heat."

Rose coughs consumptively twice and "dies" on the couch—applause from the ensemble.

MILLICENT Oh you were beautiful, beautiful. I swear that when you lay down and died, I never thought to see you rise again.

ROSE It would have been difficult. You were standing on my dress.

MILLICENT Oh no.

KENNETH You were magnificent. Truly magnificent.

ROSE Thank you, Kenneth. I could not have done it without you.

KENNETH Oh no. I was a bumbling inadequate compared to your performance.

ROSE True.

NELLIE Another success, eh, Walter?

WALTER It was indeed.

MILLICENT How was the box office?

ROSE Millicent, how could you? We are talking about theatre.

MILLICENT Forgive my crude commercial streak, it is a source of great anguish to me.

WALTER There, there, my dear. Don't feel too badly. Everybody likes to eat.

NELLIE That goes for me too. Cut the cake, Walter, and, then the girls will see that everybody gets a piece.

Walter cuts the cake to applause, and Jean takes it to the kitchen.

Well done, Walter. And now I have another favour to ask.

WALTER Anything, my dear, anything.

NELLIE Sing us one of the old songs, one of the good old songs.

DRUNK Can you sing "Over the Hills and Far Away"?

WALTER Yes.

DRUNK Well, why don't you do that?

ALL Who said that?

The drunk points at himself grinning. A song from Walter, at the discretion of the director.

The villain enters.

TWINGE: Good evening.

LULU Heavens! It is Cramden Twinge, the ruthless land developer.

TWINGE Indeed it is. Forgive me for being late for the party, but, due to an oversight, you neglected to invite me. How could you do that to me, Nellie?

NELLIE You'd be surprised what I could do to you, Cramden. You're nothing but trouble and you make me nervous to have around.

TWINGE Nellie, Nellie. After all the trouble I had securing these luxurious accommodations for you.

NELLIE This place was a pigsty. The only trouble you went to was to make sure I couldn't find any place else. When are you going to sell me the land under this place?

TWINGE Sell you the land? My dear Nellie, Cramden Twinge never sells land—he only buys it. You don't have to stay on my land if you don't want to.

NELLIE How can I do that? The only land you don't own is the swamp across the river.

TWINGE And I am negotiating for that. You'll just have to face facts, Nellie. Land is money, and money is power, and it's power that makes the world go round.

MILLICENT Oh no. It's love that makes the world go 'round.

TWINGE Such a pretty thought, and such a pretty face. Don't you wish I would buy you a pretty dress?

ROSE We Dales do not need to be dressed by you, sir.

TWINGE Ah Miss Rose. It is not my intention to *dress* you—in fact, quite the reverse.

WALTER I must ask you to keep a civil tongue in your head, sir.

TWINGE And I would advise you to do the same. I am not here to participate in idle chit-chat and camaraderie, I am here on business ... and you, sir, will be most interested in what I have to say.

WALTER I doubt that.

TWINGE I thought everybody was interested—in the railway.

ALL The railway?

TWINGE Plans are proceeding apace. A thousand men and a Chinese cook are, at this very moment, defying the ravages of the prairies to bring steel to our very boundaries. Within the year we shall have a station, freight, silks and satins for the ladies, cigars and brandy for the men.

All cheer.

NELLIE You realize what this means?

ALL — It means that there's a whole lot of money heading right this way.

All cheer.

TWINGE — You are right, Nellie. The town is going to boom. We'll need bigger houses, hotels, general stores. Settlers will be coming in by the car-load looking for land, supplies, equipment—

LULU — Relaxation after a hard day's work.

WALTER — And what better way than an evening at the theatre?

NELLIE — (*To crowd*) Don't any of you ever tell him.

WALTER — Think how the rafters will ring with applause, faces flush at the antics of the comedians and tears fall at the bittersweet sadness of the tragedy.

TWINGE — Speaking of tragedies, I have something to show you.

WALTER — Me?

TWINGE — As owner of the Corn Exchange Theatre, I felt you should be the first to know. (*Produces papers from his pocket*) I have here the plan showing the proposed route of the railway through the city. You will find it of interest, I feel sure.

WALTER — Oh, yes indeed. How close will the station be to the theatre?

TWINGE — Oh, very close.

WALTER — But not so close that we would be disturbed by the noise?

TWINGE — From the station—no. But the line itself might present you with a few difficulties.

WALTER — Show me!

Twinge lays out the paper. Walter looks at it, clutches his heart and collapses. His daughters and Kenneth rush to him and he is taken to the sofa. Rose confronts Twinge.

ROSE — Show me that paper, sir.

TWINGE Now come, Miss Rose. There is no need for you to trouble your tranquil beauty with such mundane matters. My business is strictly with your father.

ROSE My father is indisposed as you can see. You now have business with me.

TWINGE I was saving that for later ... and in more suitable surroundings.

Rose snatches the paper from him and looks at it.

ROSE Kenneth! Come here and explain this to me.

TWINGE I would be pleased to undertake...

ROSE Thank you, sir, but no. I prefer to speak with someone who will tell me the truth.

She hands the map to Kenneth.

KENNETH Oh I say.

ROSE What is it?

KENNETH Rather bad news, actually.

ROSE Show me.

KENNETH Well you see, the railway comes in from the east here, runs south of jolly old Main Street, and then takes this deucedly necessary curve northwest in order to avoid falling in the jolly old river.

ROSE Well?

KENNETH Well, I'm afraid it cuts right across this jolly old corner ... on which stands the jolly old theatre ... our jolly old theatre ... actually.

ROSE You mean the railway runs straight through the theatre!

KENNETH As far as I can make out—in through the front door and out through the jolly old ladies whatnot, actually.

ROSE Then it must be changed.

TWINGE (*Laughs*) Changed? Changed? Do you think I have spent the last four years accumulating land along this line for it to be changed? Do you think that I will hear of it? Do you think that the railway will hear of it?

ROSE If you try to run it through our theatre, you will both hear of it!

TWINGE Then I suggest you move your theatre off my land.

MILLICENT Your land? But it belongs to us.

TWINGE I'm afraid that is not so.

ROSE Of course it is so. Father. Show Mr. Twinge the deed.

TWINGE I'm sure he wishes he could. But your father and I entered into a little business transaction some two years ago. A small matter of a mortgage. Let me show you... (*He produces another paper that Rose snatches from him*) a *copy* of the arrangement. If you examine it thoroughly, you will find that you own the theatre, but I own the land under it. And if you examine it minutely, you will find that I can throw you off it any time I wish to do so. I now wish to do so ... unless you would like to spend some time persuading me otherwise.

ROSE You cad.

MILLICENT You cur.

KENNETH You bounder.

TWINGE You better believe it. Let me leave you with your thoughts. You have one month! Either you fulfill the terms of this agreement, or I shall have your theatre removed from my land ... brick by brick if necessary. In the name of progress ... the railway must go through. (*He exits*)

ROSE Oh Father, what have you done?

MILLICENT He can't do this to us.

KENNETH I say. What a rough go.

NELLIE Looks like the party is over, everybody. Be grateful if you'd leave kinda peaceful while we get our heads together over this.

The crowd disperses; Rose settles to read the agreement, Kenneth sits by her, Nellie and Millicent go to Walter.

NELLIE What you been up to, Walter?

WALTER It seemed like such a good idea at the time.

NELLIE Yeah. They always do—at the time.

MILLICENT Tell me, Father. What was your arrangement with Mr. Twinge?

KENNETH Would you prefer me to leave, sir?

WALTER No, Kenneth, you might as well hear. I might as well tell all of you everything. It was the Chekhov that did it.

NELLIE The what?

WALTER The Chekhov. I've always wanted to do Chekhov's *The Seagull.* I thought the audience was ready for it. I mean you can't do Richard Brinsley Sheridan-type comedies forever can you? You have a duty to educate your audience, try more challenging theatre. So I did *The Seagull*, by Chekhov.

NELLIE And what happened?

KENNETH We got pooped on, actually.

MILLICENT Kenneth!

KENNETH Well, we did. I said we would if we did *The Seagull.*

WALTER I should have listened to you, Kenneth.

KENNETH Never mind, sir. Could have been worse.

WALTER How?

KENNETH We might have done *The Wild Duck.*

NELLIE I'd rather be pooped on by a seagull than a wild duck.

MILLICENT You mean the box office was bad?

WALTER Oh it can happen, my dear. And when it does, there's no food in the pantry, no heat in the stove and no money for the next show. What could I do? It was then that Mr. Twinge made me his offer.

ROSE This is hardly an offer, Father. This is legalized extortion.

WALTER Well, that's what the word mortgage means, my dear.

ROSE But this borders on usury!

KENNETH They usury do—haw haw!

MILLICENT Oh you stupid Englishmen. Why do you always laugh in the face of disaster?

KENNETH We have such excellent teeth.

WALTER Don't be hard on him, my dear. He is trying to put the best face on it that he can.

NELLIE He may not make it.

ROSE But Father, why did you agree to this? Could you not see that it would be impossible to pay off in the long term?

WALTER But it wasn't to be for a long term. I knew that once we put on another show in our own style the box office would pick up and I would pay off Mr. Twinge and his mortgage.

ROSE But after *The Seagull*, we did a riotous comedy and the house was full every night!

WALTER I know, I know.

ROSE Surely you could have paid off Mr. Twinge from that.

WALTER We could have—just.

MILLICENT Well, why didn't you?

WALTER Because—oh because he said why bother, things are going well, why lose all that capital just to pay off a mere loan.

ROSE A mere loan!

WALTER Don't scold me, my dear. Credit is so seductive and I have always been weak.

ROSE But what did you do with all that money?

WALTER For you, Rose—I gave you your own dressing-room with the star on the door. And Millicent, the dress you wore in *She Stoops to Conquer* was direct from Paris ... you were so pleased to have a dress from Paris, and you looked so pretty. Even Kenneth. Your silk top hat, Kenneth. Do you remember my giving you the silk top hat, Kenneth? And Daft William. His holiday to see his mother. All these things I was able to give through my possession of mere money. It made me feel so good, and all of you so happy ... and look where it has got us all. What foolishness.

MILLICENT Oh Father. You are such a good man.

ROSE Oh Father.

KENNETH Oh gosh, Mr. Dale, sir. I feel such a goose.

NELLIE Seagulls, wild ducks and now geese! What's the matter with you all? Do you think Nellie Hogan carved herself a place in this world by sitting around talking about birds all the time? Hell, no. If you are going to get anything out of life, you've got to attack it before it attacks you. Get right in there with the knees and the elbows, spit straight into the wind and duck fast so that it hits the guy coming up behind you. We are all going to have a belt and get some fighting spirit going here.

ROSE I don't drink.

NELLIE You'll do as I tell you because this is a fight you've got on your hands, and in your right mind, you don't look the fighting sort.

MILLICENT I think a belt will do us all good.

ROSE Millicent!

MILLICENT Well, I want to get my dander up, and I'm not even sure what it is.

WALTER You always were a spirited child, Milly. I wish I had some of it.

NELLIE Well, try some of this instead. (*Hands him a drink*)

KENNETH My dander could do with a little stimulation, under the circumstances.

NELLIE Help yourself. The bar is open to my friends.

WALTER You are very good to us, Nellie.

NELLIE Aw phoney-baloney. Us artists have got to help each other. Now let's start from the beginning. Is there anything in the contract that we can use to break it?

ROSE Not that I can see. Perhaps we should get a lawyer?

NELLIE Well, if you want to try pulling something crooked we could try that. But let's go the legal route first.

KENNETH Perhaps we could become a public nuisance.

NELLIE Is that a crack?

KENNETH Good Lord, no.

NELLIE I've been called a public nuisance in this town more often than I care to remember. So let's have no more public nuisance.

MILLICENT Why don't we just pay off the mortgage?

KENNETH I say! Why didn't I think of that?

WALTER There isn't time, my dear. You heard what Mr. Twinge said. We must fulfill the terms of the agreement by the end of the month. Oh why are we wasting our time like this? There is no way out. There's nothing we can do now—and it's all my fault.

MILLICENT Nonsense, Father. We have each other. We can do something. I could work for Nellie.

WALTER For Nellie!

MILLICENT Surely she must have washing and cooking and ironing for me to do, haven't you, Nellie?

NELLIE Well I have, but I'll tell you frankly—that's not where the money is.

WALTER Washing! Cooking! Ironing! My pretty little Millicent. I would rather die than allow that.

KENNETH Are you insured?

ROSE Kenneth!

WALTER He's right. Oh, woe is me! What a weak creature I have been. There is no help for any of us.

MILLICENT Nonsense, Father. Something will turn up. It always does. It's always darkest before the storm and every cloud has a silver lining. Hope springs eternal and who knows, maybe even now, something or someone is coming to help us. Probably from some entirely unexpected quarter, and probably through that very door.

WALTER Who could come through that door? And what could he possibly say or do that would help us?

Eddy Nelson the Mountie bounds in.

EDDY This is a raid! You're all under arrest.

NELLIE What's the meaning of this? We're not due to be raided for another six weeks. Who are you?

EDDY I'm a Mountie.

NELLIE I can see that. What happened to Frank Bell?

EDDY He's gone north to the Yukon. I'm his replacement.

NELLIE What's your name, son?

EDDY Nelson. Eddy Nelson.

NELLIE Hogan. Nellie Hogan. (*She shakes hands with him*) Let me introduce you to some local citizens. This is the Dale family from the Corn Exchange Theatre. This is Walter ... Miss Rose ... oh, and this is Kenneth. Never did know his other name.

KENNETH Haig-Fortescue. Eton, Harrow, and oblivion.

NELLIE And this is Miss Milly.

The lovelight explodes between them.

EDDY I do hope my sudden entrance didn't disturb you ladies, but I was on police business, you see. And, under those circumstances, we do not hesitate.

WALTER Are we really under arrest?

EDDY I was told that Miss Hogan ran a disorderly house ... (*Looks around*) It seems that my information is incorrect.

NELLIE It is like hell incorrect. I run the finest disorderly house west of the Lakehead and don't you forget it.

EDDY But there hardly seems reason to arrest anybody. It's so peaceful.

NELLIE If that gets out—my reputation is ruined. (*Yells*) MITZI!! LULU!! Get in here! (*To Kenneth*) Kenneth, can you do a drunk?

KENNETH (*Making his way unsteadily forward*) Well I shuppose if the necesstity-necessarity arose I could—hic—oblige.

NELLIE That'll do. I'll pay you fifty dollars and costs.

KENNETH (*Sober*) Costs?

NELLIE Yeah, you're going to get arrested.

KENNETH Oh I say.

NELLIE Better get some alcohol on your breath. (*She gets bottle and glass. Mitzi and Lulu enter*) Okay, girls, Walter and Kenneth—give'em the treatment.

Mitzi sits on Walter's lap and starts vamping him; Lulu goes to Kenneth but is stopped by Nellie.

Just a minute. He isn't ready yet. Here's your drink, Kenneth.

Kenneth walks forward to collect the drink: Nellie throws it over him.

That ought to do it.

Lulu zeroes in on Kenneth and vamps him.

(*To the pianist*) Play something disgusting.

Pianist strikes up and vamping proceeds.

Look at that. Isn't that terrible. Have you ever seen anything so licentious? There are decent people and small children in this town. Can this sort of thing go unchecked? (*To Eddy*) Well, don't just stand there for goodness sake—*do* something!

EDDY You are under arrest!

NELLIE (*Relieved*) He made it. Girls, plead guilty and here's fifteen dollars apiece for the fine. Kenneth, drunk and disorderly... (*Gives him a bundle of notes*) Keep the change.

The three of them move to the door.

EDDY (*To Walter*) I'm sorry, sir, I'll have to ask you to come along as well.

WALTER (*Shocked*) Me!

EDDY You were aiding and abetting.

WALTER Aiding and abetting!

NELLIE He wasn't exactly fighting her off. I've got an idea. Come here, Walter.

Walter stands and Nellie throws another glass of whisky over him. Walter starts to sing and stagger.

How about that?

EDDY Okay. Come along with me, you four.

ROSE Oh, Mr. Nelson. Couldn't you stay for a moment?

EDDY Stay? Well, I don't think...

MILLICENT Oh please stay. Please. I should feel so unprotected here alone with my menfolk taken from me.

NELLIE Sure you can stay. Mitzi and Lulu have done this a hundred times. (*Calls*) Turn yourselves in, girls, and tell them Eddy Nelson has been delayed.

Mitzi, Lulu, Walter and Kenneth exit.

EDDY I really don't think...

ROSE Oh please, Mr. Nelson. We do need your help.

EDDY My help?

MILLICENT As an officer of the law.

EDDY I see. (*Poses*) How can I be of service to you, ladies?

ROSE (*Producing agreement*) We would like you to read this document. It is a nefarious agreement between my father and that villain, Cramden Twinge.

MILLICENT He seeks to drive us from hearth and home, take the roof from over our heads and the floor from beneath our feet, the food from out of our mouths, the clothes from our very backs, the air we breathe...

ROSE That will do, Millicent.

MILLICENT I am just explaining to Mr. Nelson.

Rose looks at Millicent and Eddie gazing fixedly at each other.

ROSE I think you have done it very well. Now let us settle down with the agreement and see if Mr. Nelson can find some technical imperfection that might exonerate us from our obligations.

EDDY (*Coming to*) What?

NELLIE They need a loophole to get them off the hook. Sit down here and I'll make you some coffee. (*Exits*)

The three move to a table upstage, Eddy escorting Millicent most carefully.

MILLICENT This is most kind of you, Mr. Nelson. It is a comfort to a poor defenceless girl to know that your strength is available to us.

Seated at the table, Rose lays out the agreement, kicks Millicent, who still has Eddy hypnotized.

Oh! There is the object of our indignity, Mr. Nelson. Please help us.

EDDY Never fear, Miss Milly, Miss Rose. The law is here to protect the innocent and confound the wicked. If this document is contrived to place you at a disadvantage, I shall protect you against its iniquities. Are you prepared to place yourself in my hands?

Millicent is about to do so, but she is prevented by Rose.

ROSE You have our trust and faith, Mr. Nelson.

EDDY Thank you, Miss Rose. Well, then. Let's see what we have here. (*Reads document to himself*)

Act One, Scene Two

Street backdrop. Indian drumming begins. Chief Shaking Spear and Running Deer enter.

CHIEF Here we are, Running Deer. This is the land of the white man's tepees. Here we will find whisky, vice, greed, avarice, corruption and a whole heap of hymn singing. This is where I must come to bring my great writings because this is where they have the place. It is called the Corn Exchange Theatre and in my dream, the spirits told me that they would do my writings for all the world to see, for ten per cent of the gross. It is written. Mush!

He waves them on, drum strikes up and they move off to "This Land is My Land."

Act One, Scene Three

Travellers open to reveal Nellie's place with group still around the table. Eddy finishes reading the agreement.

ROSE Well? Is there any weakness in this arrangement that we might exploit?

EDDY It's tied up tighter than a calf at branding time.

MILLICENT Oh no.

EDDY Whoever wrote this is a specialist in fine print.

MILLICENT Oh curse that Cramden Twinge for the monster that he is.

EDDY There is just one clause that might help.

ROSE Which is that?

EDDY The cultural-identification preservation clause.

MILLICENT My goodness.

EDDY I think Mr. Twinge may have slipped up there. At one time, you see, it was a popular notion that land was for people to live on. This was before all the talk of the railway and real estate. Now, of course, it is just another trading commodity for making a lot of money. But the fact remains, it's still in this document.

ROSE But what do we do?

EDDY I'll read it to you. "Whereas the contractor, as aforesaid, may not, in the event of this section being applicable, and despite the provisions of sections 10, 11, and 13 aforementioned and sections 27, 28 and 29 hereinafter proscribed; initiate, commence or otherwise begin termination of this agreement if such termination may be described, construed or otherwise interpreted as being detrimental to the cultural identification preservation of one whose residence in the area commenced at birth and continues to be extant." That seems to be a possibility, doesn't it?

MILLICENT It does?

ROSE I'm afraid I don't see how.

EDDY Well, what you do is this...

Enter Cramden Twinge.

TWINGE Aha! A thorn between two roses. My name is Cramden Twinge—I don't think I have had the pleasure.

MILLICENT I'm quite sure you haven't.

EDDY Eddy Nelson. One of Western Canada's finest.

TWINGE To be sure, to be sure. These two ladies are not residents of this ... unusual hostelry. I hope you do not have them under arrest.

EDDY I am here to protect them.

TWINGE Not from me, surely.

EDDY Only in that they have come to me for legal advice.

TWINGE I see. You are going over the agreement, no doubt. A well-drafted document, is it not? Not a loose end to be seen from beginning to end, I am assured.

ROSE Mr. Nelson seems to feel that there may be one.

TWINGE Nonsense, my dear. It's tied up tighter than...

MILLICENT ...a calf at branding time...

TWINGE Precisely. And it will give me a great deal of pleasure to have both you charming ladies in the same predicament. I am not an unreasonable man. (*Moving in on Rose*) I'm sure that if you found it in your heart to show me special understanding and sympathy in my lonely life, this arrangement might be replaced by another of much more comforting aspects.

Rose begins to cough consumptively and "die."

MILLICENT My sister is not a well woman, Mr. Twinge. Surely you would not practice your villainy on her?

TWINGE You think I need practice?

EDDY I would remind you that I am here.

TWINGE Thank you very much, but I would rather practice on Miss Rose.

ROSE You cad. You unfeeling brute. Would you really close down the theatre and fling myself and my sweet young sister, to say nothing of my ailing father, unprotected into this western wilderness?

TWINGE What a way you have with words. I couldn't have put it better myself. There is, of course, the alternative.

ROSE The alternative?

MILLICENT You mean... ?

TWINGE Yes. Become my bride and, as Mrs. Cramden Twinge, this city will be laid at your feet.

ROSE No. No. I could not marry you if you were the last man on earth. Mr. Nelson. Please. Tell us what we must do.

TWINGE Yes, Mr. Nelson. Tell them what they must do.

EDDY All you have to do is to find somebody who lives here and include him in your theatre group and Cramden Twinge will not be able to foreclose on the agreement.

TWINGE WHAT?? What nonsense is this? They must be out of the theatre and off my land by the end of the month!!

EDDY Not necessarily.

MILLICENT Not if it may be described, construed or otherwise interpreted as being detrimental *etc., etc.,* ...

TWINGE You mean the old cultural-identity preservation clause?

EDDY Precisely.

TWINGE That fool lawyer. I told him to strike it out.

ROSE I am happy to say that he was negligent of your instruction and we now have you by the short ones, Cramden Twinge.

TWINGE I doubt that, Miss Rose. The clause reads, if I am not mistaken, "one whose residence in the area commenced at birth and continues to be extant." And to whom could that be applied? Not you, Miss Rose, nor you, Miss Millicent, nor your poor misguided father. Mr. Haig Fortescue is, by his own admission, a defrocked English nob, and Daft William is from Calgary. An alien group, if I may say so, and one that will do me the service of preparing to quit the Corn Exchange Theatre by the end of the month. (*Aside*) You'd have to get up very early in the morning to catch Cramden Twinge with his pants down. (*Exits*)

MILLICENT Oh dear. We are up the creek without a paddle once more. How are we to slough off Cramden Twinge's intolerable yoke?

EDDY Speaking of intolerable yokes, did you hear the one about brown bread?

ROSE Please, Mr. Nelson, this is no time for levity. We are confronted by ruination.

EDDY I'm sorry, Miss Rose.

Nellie enters with coffee.

NELLIE Well? How's it going?

MILLICENT It's no good, Nellie. We thought we had found a way out, but—alas.

ROSE Were you born here, Nellie?

NELLIE Me? Hell, no.

ROSE How about the girls? Were any of them born here?

NELLIE Wouldn't think so. Most of them are from the East, got one or two from the States, but none from these parts as far as I know.

ROSE There must be somebody somewhere that was born here and has artistic aspiration.

Walter hurries in. Drumming offstage.

WALTER Girls, girls. You'll never guess. We've just met the most amazing man. His name is Chief Shaking Spear, and he says he's written a play!

Shaking Spear and Running Deer enter, followed by Kenneth, Lulu and Mitzi. Street musicians play "This Land is My Land" for his entrance. Curtain falls.

End of Act One

Act Two, Scene One

At rise, Daft William, assisted by Kenneth, Lulu and Mitzi, is organizing the "scenery" for a rehearsal of the play. This consists of a tepee with a functional door flap, a couple of "trees," a totem pole and a "skyline." With the aid of ladders, they are stringing up the "skyline." William and Kenneth unroll the canvas.

LULU What is it?

WILLIAM It's the mountains. They're a bit creased—I've had them folded up all day.

MITZI Creased mountains?

WILLIAM They're not real, of course. It's what we call a backdrop.

LULU What do you do with it?

WILLIAM Well, you're supposed to hang it up.

MITZI Come on then, let's have some mountains. (*To Lulu*) Isn't it exciting? Our very own collapsible creased mountains.

KENNETH (*Pointing*) I think we could string them from there, catch them in the middle against that, and then carry them on to there. Are you going to nail them?

LULU Nellie'll kill you if you start driving nails into her French Provincial balustrade.

WILLIAM Her what?

LULU That balcony up there.

KENNETH It looks pretty solid, actually.

LULU Well, it isn't, "actually." It's fake—like everything else in this place.

MITZI Couldn't you tie it on?

WILLIAM I've put laces on it in case we had to. All we have to do now is get up there and do it. Pull the ladder over.

They pull the ladder over to one end of the balcony.

That's it. Now then, who's going up?

MITZI You are. You're the stage manager—manage it!

WILLIAM Oh I couldn't. I've got no head for ladders. I usually work from above.

LULU Well you're down here with the mortals now.

MITZI How about you, Kenneth?

KENNETH Me?

LULU Fancy tying one on Kenneth. (*Giggles*)

KENNETH Oh I say.

MITZI Oh come on, give it to me, I'll do it. You hold the ladder steady.

Kenneth and William hold the ladder while Mitzi climbs up and ties the end of the canvas. They are duly appreciative of Mitzi's legs as they go by.

(*From above*) How does it look to you?

KENNETH Fantastic!

LULU She's talking about the mountains.

KENNETH So am I.

LULU Come on down, Mitzi. You're making Daft William's knee tremble.

MITZI (*Descending*) That was fun. Can I do the next one?

LULU No. I get to do the next one. I think I've got the hang of it.

KENNETH (*Guffaws*) Oh I say, "got the hang of it," that's very good. Oh I say.

Lulu sashays up the ladder and subsides toward Daft William.

LULU Oh William. Help. I think I'm falling. Push me back on the ladder, William, quickly. (*She falls into his arms*) My hero...

While Lulu is fixing up the centre section, Walter enters with the Chief carrying bundles of scripts. They move to the director's chair and table down right.

WALTER That looks good, William. Have you finished the tepee?

WILLIAM I'll be bringing it in, Mr. Dale. I'm just a bit busy at the moment.

WALTER Yes. So I see. (*At table with Chief*) Well, Chief, I know this is the play you want us to do—but *The Taming of the Sioux*? Reminds me of another play.

You sure you thought of that title yourself?

CHIEF It came to me in a vision. When I was a youth, I went out onto the plains to talk to the animals and the spirits ... and after many days fasting, a spirit came to me and gave me my name and told me what I must do.

WALTER What did he say?

CHIEF As the sun touched the top of the mountains... (*With a sweep of his arm he finds himself pointing at Lulu on top of the ladder. She is bending over. To the audience*) Something like that could have screwed up my whole retreat, you know that?

WALTER But what did the spirit say?

CHIEF (*Still looking at Lulu*) Holy smoke! (*Recovers*) The spirit tell me that my name from that day will be Shaking Spear...

WALTER Shaking Spear?

CHIEF Those were his words. And he tell me that I shall write the stories that he will tell me and that these stories will tell of my people and their ways.

WALTER How many plays have you written?

CHIEF Many plays. First, there was *A Midsummer Night's Sweatlodge*—a comedy. After that, the words came quickly and I wrote *Two Gentlemen from Kelowna, The Factor of Venice, Henry Hudson, Parts One and Two, Troilus and Kalynchuk* ... then I got into the story of my people on the reserves applying for municipal status.

WALTER What did you call that?

CHIEF *Hamlet*. My next play will be more modern. I'm calling it *Who's Afraid of Crazy Wolf?*

WALTER What gave you the idea for *The Taming of the Sioux*?

CHIEF Two things. First there was the story of my people and Sitting Bull when he fled the longknives south of the Medicine Line...

WALTER Yes?

CHIEF Then there was this girl I met once in Winnipeg. She was a Sue when I met her, but a Gros Ventres when I left. (*Laughs*) That's what we call an Indian joke.

WALTER Oh, I see.

CHIEF Ethnic.

WALTER Yes, of course.

CHIEF Like "Hi there, Chief. What do you think of bilingualism?" Do you know what the Chief says?

WALTER I can't imagine.

CHIEF (*Folds his arms*) "White Man speak with forked tongue." (*Laughs*) Do you know the difference between a tepee and a wigwam?

WALTER No?

CHIEF Wholesale—about seventy-five dollars. (*Laughs*)

Rose enters in Indian costume, and joins them. Chief becomes solemn and raises his hand in greeting.

CHIEF When?

ROSE Don't you mean "How"?

CHIEF I know how. When? (*Laughs*)

ROSE Are you ready to start the rehearsal, Father?

WALTER I think we'd better. Kenneth, Mitzi, Lulu—go and get into your costumes. We shall be starting in a few minutes. William—get the rest of the scenery set, we'll try act three from the top. Excuse me, Chief. This is going to be a busy day.

CHIEF I'll just sit over here and read through my lines.

WALTER Yes, you do that. Now in this act, Rose, this is where the tribe that has adopted you brings in the white man and are going to put him to terrible torture... However, just as they are about to plunge the red hot pokers into his chest, you fling yourself across him and declare your love for him.

ROSE I seem to remember that story.

CHIEF It is loosely stolen from the legend of the hot pokers, or Pocahontas, as we say in Indian.

WALTER Yes, very well, but that isn't the first scene. Where's Millicent?

Millicent and Eddy enter.

MILLICENT Here we are, Father. I have been helping Eddy with his words.

WALTER Oh yes. It is kind of you to help us out with the production, Mr. Nelson.

EDDY My pleasure, Mr. Dale, but I'm not much of an actor, I'm afraid.

MILLICENT Isn't he wonderful—the way he *notices* things.

EDDY Part of my training, Miss Millicent.

WALTER (*Calling*) All right everybody. Places please for act three, scene one ... a sunny evening on Main Street, a friendly town in the West.

Activity as the cast gets arranged.

Okay, Chief, the narration starts ... now.

CHIEF Nose Creek was not a town to be sniffed at. A small settlement of sturdy pioneers, who couldn't make it in the old country, had settled here to chew up perfectly good buffalo pasture and grow cabbages. My people wondered at the many marvels they had in their lodges—steel knives, quick-shooting rifles, wool blankets and garbage bags. We did not know these things. To discover the secret of these wonders, a small band of warriors had captured a young white man and taken him back to the people. Meanwhile, back in town, his absence was beginning to be noticed.

WALTER Eddy and Millicent enter right, town activity begins...

Eddy and Millicent walk on and stop.

EDDY Mighty fine night, Miss Millicent.

MILLICENT It certainly is.

EDDY Sure is a mighty fine night to be accompanying you home from the second annual sodbusters' barbecue and masquerade ball like this. Did you have a good time?

MILLICENT Oh yes. I just love barbecued sodbusters.

A bank robber backs out onto the street, sees Eddy and is about to shoot, but Eddy shoots him first. His body is dragged away.

EDDY (*Without losing the speed*) Sure was surprised when you agreed to let me take you.

MILLICENT (*Coyly*) Oh come now, Eddy Nelson. You must know every girl in this town was just wondering who the big handsome Mountie would ask to be his partner at the ball.

The banker, bound and gagged, hops out onto the street. Eddy unties him as he speaks.

EDDY Don't have no eyes for any other girl in town except you, Miss Millicent.

MILLICENT Oh Mr. Nelson. I'll bet you're only saying that.

EDDY (*Thinks*) Reckon I was.

MILLICENT My guess is that the news will be all around the town in the morning that you took Milly Dale to the ball and walked her home after. Reckon that'll give rise to lots of talk and a whole heap of speculation.

The banker, now free, shakes Eddy's hand, picks up the bank's money and returns to bank. An old gent starts slowly across the stage.

EDDY Well let 'em talk, that's what I say. Talk didn't hurt no one.

MILLICENT Oh you just don't know. You should have been here before you came.

EDDY (*Puzzled*) Yeah?

MILLICENT This place was worse than Moose Jaw on a Saturday night.

EDDY Miss Millicent! How could a sweet young girl like you know what Moose Jaw was like on a Saturday night?

MILLICENT I've heard the stories. There was vice and sin and drunkenness and carryings-on and naughty ladies and men like animals. A girl just wasn't safe on the streets in the early hours of the morning.

EDDY If she was a lady, she wouldn't be on the streets in the early hours of the morning.

MILLICENT What! And miss all the vice and sin and drunkenness!

Two muggers leap out and start beating up the old man.

EDDY Excuse me, Miss Millicent. A man's gotta do what a man's gotta do.

Eddy strides forward to the muggers and thrusts his chest at them. They immediately turn tail and run. He puts a sling on the old man's broken arm.

MILLICENT My. You know all about broken bones and everything, don't you?

EDDY Pretty well. They teach us that at Mountie School.

MILLICENT Where was that?

EDDY Regina. That's why all the action was in Moose Jaw. There you go, oldtimer. Get a good night's rest and call me again in the morning.

Old man totters off. Young man enters right, girl enters left. They meet stage left.

MILLICENT You sure like people, don't you, Eddy?

EDDY Well, the way I see it, Miss Millicent, if you can't beat 'em, join 'em.

MILLICENT That's very erudite.

Eddy points a warning finger at the girl and she flounces off followed by the young man.

EDDY I get a lot of time to think, out there on the lonesome prairie, just me, my horse and the stars. Makes a man stop to consider. And do you know the conclusion I've come to, Miss Millicent?

MILLICENT What Mr. Nelson?

EDDY That prairie is pretty damned lonesome. I need to know that, somewhere, there's someone waiting for me to come back.

MILLICENT You mean like the Commissioner?

EDDY That wasn't quite what I had in mind, Miss Millicent.

MILLICENT Oh dear. My beloved brother has been captured by Indians.

EDDY I'm sorry to hear that, Miss Millicent.

WALTER Wait a minute, wait a minute! Millicent. Is that the right line?

MILLICENT Yes Father.

WALTER "Oh dear. My beloved brother has been captured by Indians"?

MILLICENT That's right, then he says he's sorry to hear it.

WALTER He's leading up to proposing to you and then you suddenly say your brother has been captured by Indians?

CHIEF In the trade, we call that a plot line. It tells the audience what has happened.

WALTER Yes, but when did it happen?

CHIEF While they were walking along the street there.

WALTER But how did she know it happened?

CHIEF She read the script.

WALTER That isn't good enough.

CHIEF So. My script isn't good enough? Running Deer!

Running Deer commences beat on drum, Chief chants.

WALTER Now what's he doing?

CHIEF I'm putting in a call to my agent.

WALTER All right, all right! We'll leave it in.

Drumming stops.

CHIEF (*To Running Deer*) Cancel that call.

Running Deer drums briefly: "Shave and a haircut," then the reply on a thunder sheet: "Two bits."

Okay.

WALTER Pick it up at "Oh dear," would you, Millicent?

MILLICENT Oh dear. My beloved brother has been captured by Indians.

EDDY I'm sorry to hear that, Miss Millicent.

MILLICENT He is in terrible danger and will be tortured cruelly if you personally do not gallop fearlessly into the teeth of danger and, by virtue of your sheer demonstration of raw courage, so impress the chiefs that they will set him free and you will bring him back safely thereby making me very susceptible to any suggestions you may have in mind.

CHIEF (*Smiling hugely*) Now that's a plot line!

EDDY I can see it is up to me. Through all travail, the code of honour of those fearless men in the red coats who bring peace and justice—shall prevail.

Eddy strides off leaving Millicent yearning after him.

WALTER Right, everybody. Indian encampment. William, get the tent in position. Where's Kenneth?

KENNETH Here, Mr. Dale.

WALTER Get yourself tied to the totem pole—help him, girls.

Rose enters in her Indian costume.

Rose, my dear, you look beautiful. Doesn't she look beautiful, Chief?

CHIEF Not bad for paleface woman. Indian woman more dark, more passion.

WALTER Yes, but she is the only survivor of a pioneer family and was adopted as a child by your tribe.

CHIEF Is that a plot line?

WALTER Yes.

CHIEF Pretty damn good plot line.

WALTER Now you go and get in your tent and await the arrival of the redcoat. Aren't you tied yet, Kenneth?

LULU He's fit to be, believe me.

WALTER Well please hurry.

Enter Cramden Twinge.

TWINGE Angels and ministers of grace defend us!

CHIEF (*Pokes his head out of the tent*) Who said that?

TWINGE I did.

CHIEF Do you mind if I use it?

TWINGE What is this nonsense, Dale? Are you really expecting to mount another presentation at the Corn Exchange Theatre?

WALTER I am indeed. This will be our finest show yet.

TWINGE That I doubt very much. And what is this? The delectable Miss Rose going native? That should attract a crowd.

ROSE This could be my greatest role.

TWINGE If you are looking for a role, Miss Rose, I would be pleased to arrange the daddy of them all.

ROSE How dare you, sir. You are not couth.

TWINGE For the last time, Miss Rose. Leave these nonentities to their plight. These fiddlings with cultural endeavour and caterings to human emotion, that is not the way of the future. Human achievement is to be measured in their ability to build great monuments. The railway, buildings, factories, banks, huge offices and stores—this is where the money is.

ROSE Why do you reduce everything to money, sir?

TWINGE Because life, when reduced to money, is reduced to its irreducible minimum.

ROSE And is that what you want, sir? A minimum life? I would rather raise it to its unlimited maximum through the beauty of the human spirit. Do you think that mere money should make us walk through life with our eyes downcast, searching for it in the gutter, when above it is—the sky?

CHIEF (*Head pops out of the tent*) Could you speak a little slower? I'm having trouble getting all this down.

TWINGE The gutter is where life is, Miss Rose, and achievement is the ability to climb out of it. Come with me and I will raise you to the heights. Stay here and you will grovel with the rest, begging for alms and help, at the mercy of those with *money*. I need your theatre for a railway. The town needs your theatre for a railway. The country needs your theatre for a railway. The whole world needs your theatre for a railway. And do you know why, Miss Rose? Because a railway means money, money, MONEY. How will you compete with that with your paltry offerings to the human spirit? Human spirit? Pah!! It can be bought and sold for MONEY!! (*Exits*)

WALTER Could we please get on with this rehearsal?

Nellie enters.

NELLIE Hi everybody. How's it going?

WALTER If we had a chance to get on, perhaps we could find out!

NELLIE Is that what they call artistic temperament or just plain bad temper?

WALTER I'm sorry, Nellie, but this isn't the easiest place in the world to rehearse.

NELLIE You want I should throw you out?

WALTER No, no. It's very kind of you to let us be here.

NELLIE Think you'll get back in the theatre for the play?

ROSE Of course we will. We have the clause in the lease and the Chief. Cramden Twinge cannot prevent us.

NELLIE Not in the lease, but maybe he'll come up with something else.

WALTER Come and sit with me, Nellie, and you can watch it and tell me what you think.

NELLIE I can tell you what I think. I think you've got about an hour before I shut you down for the day. I've got a business to run here, too, you know.

WALTER Yes, yes. All right everybody, places for act three, scene two. Lights. Okay, Chief. When you are ready.

Lights for this scene. Chief steps from the tent, a gale howls temporarily. Chief holds up his hand, and it stops.

CHIEF Now is the winter of my discontent. Can spring be far behind? All the world's a stage and men and women merely players. They have their exits and their entrances and one man, in his time, plays many parts. The warrior, by taking arms against a sea of troubles, can end them, or end up getting scalped himself. The unkindest cut of all. To be or not to be, that is the question. Whether 'tis nobler in the mind to suffer this outrageous fortune or take up slings and arrows and give the white man those thousand shocks that flesh is heir to. But could we win? A consummation devoutly to be wished. But then they trade us whisky, and then the mind is lost, determination flees and alcohol makes beggars of us all. White Horse, White Horse, my kingdom for White Horse!

Rose enters and throws herself at his feet.

ROSE Great chief, and my father. Do not speak from such a heavy heart. Look hopefully toward the new day and welcome tomorrow.

CHIEF Tomorrow and tomorrow and tomorrow creeps on this petty pace. I cannot wait until tomorrow. There is a tide in the affairs of men which taken at its flood, leads on to fortune. I must act! A gesture! A sign! How about my old red-hot poker routine with this paleface?

ROSE Father. You couldn't. You wouldn't.

CHIEF Wouldn't? 'Tis now the witching time of night when churchyards yawn and hell itself breathes out contagion to this world. Now I could drink hot blood and do such bitter business as the day would quake to look on. Find your tongue, white man, while still it roots itself in conscience. Speak the speech I pray you, trippingly on the tongue, before I cut it out.

ROSE Father!

KENNETH Help!

CHIEF Is this a dagger I see before me, the handle towards my hand. Come, let me clutch thee.

Rose flings herself across Kenneth, while the Chief stares glassy eyed at the dagger.

ROSE You cannot kill him. I love him.

KENNETH The quality of mercy is not strained. It droppeth as the gentle rain from Heaven.

CHIEF Fee, fie, fo, fum, I smell the blood...

ROSE Father, if you love me as I love you, spare this pasty, knock-kneed weakling from your wrath. To kill him you must first kill me.

Chief lunges and stabs Rose.

KENNETH Oh I say!

Rose staggers away in a prolonged death.

ROSE Father! How could you do this? How cruelly you betray me. (*Coughs*) There's no trust, no faith, no honesty in men. All perjured, all foresworn, all naught, all dissemblers. I should have listened to Mother. (*Coughs*)

CHIEF (*Lurching at Kenneth*) And you ... and you ... and you! What last words will you bequeath to mortal memory?

KENNETH (*Desperately*) Beware the Ides of March?

Eddy strides in.

EDDY STOP! (*Strikes pose, pointing at Rose*)

All turn to look at Rose, who has been waiting.

ROSE (*Coughs*) My last syllable of recorded time. Life is but a walking shadow. A poor player that struts and frets her hour upon the stage and then is heard no more. It is a tale, written by an idiot, signifying nothing.

(*Staggers dramatically*) Out ... out ... out ... out ... out. (*Falls to the ground, rises*) ... brief (*Falls, rises*) ... brief (*Falls, rises, coughs*) ... brief candle. (*Falls, pause, rises, Chief blows, she falls*)

Eddy strides across to Rose, listens to her heart. He raises her and she supports herself on one arm. When he gets up, she stays suspended.

EDDY Death lies on her like an untimely frost upon the sweetest flower of all the field. (*Rises*) I'm afraid I shall have to report this.

CHIEF I smell something...

WALTER That isn't the line.

CHIEF I don't mean the play. I can smell something else.

NELLIE I can only smell the play.

CHIEF Wait. Someone comes.

Daft William hurries in.

WILLIAM It's the theatre. The old Corn Exchange. There's a fire. The whole thing is going up in smoke.

Pandemonium as everybody rushes about and rushes offstage; Kenneth is left tied to the totem pole, shouting for help.

The travellers close. Street musicians enter; song connected with the fire, e.g., "Hot Time in the Old Town Tonight." Members of the cast cross behind with buckets and blackening faces. The curtain falls.

Act Two, Scene Two

The assembled group are in tatters, with blackened faces. Walter, sobbing, is comforted by his daughters.

ROSE There, there, Father. There was nothing that could be done.

MILLICENT Everything ... gone.

ROSE My dressing-room with the star on the door.

MILLICENT My dress from Paris.

KENNETH My silk top hat.

NELLIE My eyebrows.

WALTER We have nothing left ... after all these years. The laughter, the tears, the magic—all gone.

Cramden Twinge enters excitedly.

TWINGE I have excellent news!

ROSE That is impossible.

TWINGE Wait until you hear it, Miss Rose. Your theatre has burned to the ground!!

MILLICENT (*Wails*) How can you be so pleased?

EDDY Perhaps it was you that started the fire?

TWINGE I never thought of it! I mean the thought had never occurred to me. I mean ... what does it matter what I mean. All our problems are solved!

WALTER Solved?

TWINGE Don't you see. I am saved the expense of clearing the site—

WALTER Is that all you can think of at a time like this?

TWINGE —and you will collect the insurance money.

WALTER Insurance money?

TWINGE Part of our agreement was that I would advance the money if you would insure the theatre. You *did* insure the theatre?

WALTER (*With wonder*) Yes. I did. For fifteen thousand dollars!

ROSE Oh Father!

TWINGE And now the finest news of all. This conflagration has so impressed the mayor and the aldermen that they are sure the town needs more adequate protection. I have just arranged a lease with the fire chief on larger premises nearer the town centre.

MILLICENT So?

TWINGE Part of the transaction was that I was able to pick up the old fire hall for a song.

NELLIE Hum a few bars.

TWINGE It will be the site of the new Corn Exchange Theatre.

WALTER The new Corn Exchange Theatre. What are you saying?

Twinge falls on his knees before Rose.

TWINGE Miss Rose. If I cannot win you by foul methods, may I win you by fair. All these things I will give you and perhaps, in the giving, you may be persuaded to look upon me in a new light.

ROSE I may indeed. There is no more attractive man to a woman than a rogue turned saint.

Eddy pinches Millicent's bottom.

MILLICENT Oh! (*Smiles at him, interested*) The reverse may also be true.

TWINGE Say you will be mine, Miss Rose.

ROSE Will I have a dressing-room with a star on the door?

TWINGE You will.

ROSE And Millicent a dress from Paris?

TWINGE Indeed, yes.

ROSE And Kenneth a silk top hat?

TWINGE Even that.

ROSE Then I am yours. (*She bends him over and kisses him soundly*)

While all congratulate the happy couple, the travellers close and the Indian drumming starts. The Chief and Running Deer come to centre stage and, in a spot, the Chief makes the following speech.

CHIEF And I went out onto the plain and said to the Great Spirit, "In this play there will be a villain, and he will corrupt the minds of men and use them for his own design ... but there will come a great retribution and he will die the thousand deaths according to the White Man's Law. And the Great Spirit said to me, "Smarten up, dummy—they don't do things that way any more."

Travellers open and whole cast comes forward for closing song such as "Side By Side."

The End.

Mutants (1981)

by Brad Fraser

> It will be a long hard climb into professional theatre, but it will happen.
> ~BRAD FRASER QUOTED IN ASHWELL, JAN 1981

Few teen-angst plays are as compelling or as merciless as Brad Fraser's *Mutants*. Wrenched from his own high school experiences in the late 1970s and blasted through his infamously unforgiving and violently creative imagination, Fraser's first produced play introduced to Edmonton audiences his now internationally familiar scathing dialogue—what *Edmonton Journal* reviewer Keith Ashwell called at the time "a surgeon's appreciation of the jugular" ("Mutants"). Two decades later this same sensibility would endear Fraser to audiences and critics in the UK, particularly at Manchester's Royal Theatre Exchange, where two of his recent plays have opened, and in the United States, where *Poor Super Man* premiered. Given the controversial record of Fraser's subsequent writing, it should be no surprise that while Walterdale's board of directors nearly denied *Mutants* its first production, it was the company's highest-grossing show that season and a direct catalyst for Fraser's professional career.

Fraser was born in Edmonton in 1959. Following a difficult childhood, one that he has characterized as "nomadic" (quoted in Kirman) and "Dickensian" (Fraser, Interview), Fraser transferred from Edmonton's Eastglen High School to the Performing Arts program at Victoria Composite. There, theatre teachers Bill Brumbalow and Don Pimm influenced his artistic impulses while he gained something of a cult-of-personality following among his artistically inclined friends.

By the late 1970s Fraser's work was gaining notice. His play *Two Pariahs at a Bus Stop in a Large City Late at Night* won in the High School category of the Alberta Playwriting competition in 1977, and *With Love From Your Son* won in the full-length adult category the following year. Fraser also stage managed a Walterdale Christmas show, and in the fall of 1979 he designed for and appeared as Mr. Perry in Walterdale's production of Allen's *The Prime of Miss Jean Brodie*. In early January 1980 he appeared in the ambitious new Walterdale collective creation facilitated by Kevin Burns called *Shikata Ga Nai* (*It Can't Be Helped*), in which he played the journalist Sadeo "potently" (Ashwell, "Rewrite!"). That spring, shortly after Quebec's first referendum on separation, Fraser assisted director Stephen Heatley on Walterdale's production of Tremblay's francophone identity play *Les Belles Soeurs*. It was heralded as a "strong and frequently touching" Edmonton premiere (Ashwell, "Belles Soeurs"), with the English version staged at Walterdale and the French version staged at the University of Alberta's Faculté St. Jean by Théâtre Français of Edmonton. Fraser then appeared as the artist Verezzi in Walterdale's production of Walker's *Zastrozzi*, the first Walker play performed in Edmonton. By the time he began rehearsals for *Mutants* at the age of twenty-one, Fraser had already spent two summers in the Banff Playwrights Colony and had worked as a freelance writer for CBC Radio and ACCESS television, all while employed full-time at a graphic-arts supply company. With emerging Edmonton director Heatley as his "consultant" on *Mutants*, Fraser was prepared to navigate Walterdale's production conditions as director of his own play.

The formation of professional companies such as Theatre 3, Northern Light Theatre, Theatre Network, and Workshop West Theatre in Edmonton during the 1970s had created a vibrant Canadian play atmosphere in which Walterdale was, by the early 1980s, eager to participate. The 1980/81 season was remarkable in terms of Walterdale's Canadian play programming: Canadian writers penned half of the season's productions.[31] It was also remarkable for controversies related to Fraser, only part of which involved the premiere of *Mutants*.

The season-opening production of Walker's *Zastrozzi* that October had created a stir. The board, which became aware of the play's controversial material in the summer, voted to ban "total nudity" from the production despite the demands of the script's stage directions and strong objections from three board members. The issue stemmed from discussions regarding the opening of scene seven, in which Fraser's character, Verezzi, "is naked." Despite the board's ban on total nudity, Fraser elected to do a few performances without underwear. And he made sure, along with the actor playing Matilda, that the simulated sex that opened the scene was visually and vocally "offensive" (e-mail to author, 2007). For weeks the board fielded letters from disgruntled audience members who, in response to Fraser dropping trou, threatened to drop their season subscriptions. One such letter featured the flowery prose of a "long term supporter" who thought that in attending *Zastrozzi* she had sat "in the wrong pew."

It was in this charged environment that a revised version of Fraser's new play made its way into the hands of then board president Judy Tilley. The original draft of *Mutants*, Fraser estimated, would have run about seven hours: "It was everything I've ever wanted to say about everything" (quoted in Ashwell, "Mutants"). When some concerns were raised about the content of the now considerably shortened draft, Tilley sought advice from Walterdale's long-time membership. The ensuing commotion divided Walterdale mainstays: some felt the play's language and terrorist-style treatment of an adult youth worker were too much for the stage, while others "fought like hell" to keep it in the season (F. Glenfield, Interview), calling it a well-crafted piece by a promising writer.

The controversy found its way into the November board meeting, which Fraser attended. There was much discussion about the play's initial length, its "stylistic *vs.* realistic presentation, offensive language, and topical subject matter" (Walterdale, Executive, November 1980). In a preview interview in the *Edmonton Journal*, Fraser responded succinctly to the now-public accusations: "My position is it's colloquial. What people call offending words are not there for effect—I do nothing for effect, or I try not to" (quoted in Ashwell, "Mutants"). The board agreed to honour its commitment to produce *Mutants* in a vote from which eight members abstained (some admitting that they had not read the play in advance of the vote). The board agreed that a language warning would appear in all advertising. Auditions attracted a high turnout from local high school students. Years later, those board members who supported *Mutants* recall they did so with enthusiasm that evening, seeing in it the kernel of an already strong and undeniably promising artistic voice.

Mutants received "positive and enthusiastic" reaction, as reported at the first board meeting following the run, with solid 69 percent houses through to closing night. Fraser's work out-drew the other six Walterdale productions that season, including *Zastrozzi*, Ibsen's *The Lady from the Sea*, and Labiche's *The Italian Straw Hat*. But the production also sparked opinionated debate among audiences and reviewers. Its angry portrayal of ageism was immediately played out in the local media. Keith Ashwell opened his *Edmonton Journal* review as if shouting back at the play:

> Brad! What did I do? Why did you beat up on me like that?
>
> I came out of this show feeling I had to apologize. But to whom? For what?
>
> I've never, not wilfully at least, been the cause of adolescents going bad. I don't think I've even been guilty of denying their individuality, even by default, and yet Fraser never let up on me.
>
> I, representing adult society, was accused and condemned of an incredible catalogue of anti-social actions committed by the six delinquents in Mutants. And from them—hardly a word of remorse! ("Writer")

And in the University of Alberta's student newspaper, *The Gateway*, Emma Goldman wrote:

> But there is no way Fraser could subdue the play to make it less offensive to the middle-aged, middle-class family-type Walterdale patrons. They won't understand the play because they cling blindly to the system of values that Fraser attacks.
>
> For example, upon leaving the theatre Tuesday night I heard one of Edmonton's well-known theatre critics comment, "Now that he has gotten this out of his system, maybe he'll be able to write a play."

> Well, I'd say to that, "If the system doesn't get anything out of this play, maybe, if we are lucky, he will write another, just as powerful as this one."

Evidently it was not the twenty-somethings who were offended by the language and content they had been warned about in the show's publicity, but the "middle-aged, middle-class family-type[s]" who donned their moral armour. If various demographics found little to agree on, one thing seemed clear: Fraser was a playwright with opinions and something to offer both the art form and society.

Theatre heavyweights took particular notice of *Mutants*. Within days of the play's closing, Theatre Passe Muraille's Paul Thompson (in Edmonton at the time to direct David Fox in an adaptation of Kroetsch's novel *The Studhorse Man* at the University of Alberta) and Workshop West Theatre's Gerry Potter both approached Fraser with a keen interest in staging his next play at their respective theatres.[32] Fraser's *Wolfboy* played at Saskatoon's 25th Street Theatre the next year (November 1981) before he followed Thompson to Toronto, where they collaborated on what Fraser terms "a pseudo-collective" ("Biography") called *Rude Noises (For a Blank Generation)* at Passe Muraille (March 1982). Fraser's subsequent theatrical works include *Chainsaw Love* (1985, Edmonton Fringe), *Young Art* (1987, Theatre Passe Muraille), *Return of the Bride* (1988, Edmonton Fringe), *Unidentified Human Remains and the True Nature of Love* (1989, Alberta Theatre Projects), *Prom Night of the Living Dead* (1991, Citadel Teen Festival with Darrin Hagen), *The Ugly Man* (1992, Alberta Theatre Projects), *Poor Super Man* (1994, Ensemble Theatre of Cincinnati), *Martin Yesterday* (1997, Buddies in Bad Times), *Outrageous!* (2000, Canadian Stage Company), *Snake in Fridge* (2000, Royal Exchange Theatre), and *Cold Meat Party* (2003, Royal Exchange Theatre). He continues to work extensively in film, television, and print media.

Fraser's years at Walterdale were mutually beneficial. A few months after *Mutants* premiered he was elected member-at-large on Walterdale's board, but by the following November, having not had the opportunity to attend meetings, he withdrew. The next year the board considered commissioning him to write a new play, but this did not come to pass. Walterdale had given Fraser a very public start, and he had added to the company's production history of original, well-produced, and controversial fare.

Mutants captures six young "delinquents" in a condemned office building in the midst of kidnapping their group home counsellor, Mr. Goldwyn, in order to attract media attention to their mistreatment and to their general lot in life. But their plans backfire when they also kidnap Jett's straight-and-narrow friend Christine (daughter of the province's minister of culture), Judy reveals to Jim that she's pregnant with his baby ("Mutant children. How scary," observes Jett), and Jett is shot dead during an altercation with Plato. Fraser's skillful use of monologues and a Brechtian chorus give the play's us-versus-the-system theme a theatrical punch that was noted in reviews at the time. It offers strong, believable parts for young actors and deals convincingly with contemporary issues, including the treatment of prostitutes and young offenders as well as the use of terrorist tactics and fear to gain advantage and public notice. And yes, the play carries a language and content warning. That it is suitable not only to be seen but also to be performed by teen actors is clear. Importantly, subsequent productions of

Mutants will likely replay the same discussions in which Walterdale members and the Edmonton community engaged at the time of the play's premiere.

Mutants ran January 27–February 7, 1981, at Walterdale Playhouse (firehall) with the following cast and creative team:

JIM	Brian Rodomski
CAL	Greg Dovell
JETT	Les Bland
PLATO	Phil Zyp
JUDY	Darcia Parada
CHRISTINE	Collette Hebert
ABRA	Kat Mullaly
GOLDWYN	David Nattress
COP (OFF-STAGE VOICE)	Keven Smith
DIRECTOR	Brad Fraser
ASSISTANT DIRECTOR	Mark Plaudis Wilson
CONSULTANT/WORKSHOP DIRECTOR	Stephen Heatley
SET DESIGNER	Jeff Unger
LIGHTING DESIGNER	Tom Robertson
STAGE MANAGER	Deb Preston

Program cover designed by Brad Fraser for his first produced full-length play, Mutants, *for Walterdale Theatre Associates, Jan–Feb 1981.*

Mutants: A Play in Two Acts

by Brad Fraser

Characters JIM
CAL
JETT
PLATO
JUDY
CHRISTINE
ABRA
MR GOLDWYN
VOICE (OFFSTAGE)

Setting The top floor of a condemned office building. Lots of radiators, windows, ledges and things.

Notes Be imaginative.

This play is for Kat and Brian.

Act One

A lone spot on Jim.

JIM (*Whispers*) Are you here? (*Pause*) Hello. (*To Audience*) Hello. (*Pause*) I'm Jim. (*Pause*) Hot in here, isn't it? (*Pause*) I – I – uh – have some things to say. I have – you know – words. (*Pause*) It's just so hard to do. It's finding the right words. I know them, but I don't know them, if you understand any of that. No. I didn't think you did. It's like – sometimes you get fed up. The rules. You know. After a while you can't put up with it anymore. You've got to do something about it. You've got to say...

The others speak from the darkness.

ABRA We've had it!

PLATO We're through!

JUDY We're finished!

JETT We're done!

JIM And we're finally going to do something about it.

A lone spot on Cal.

CAL In my house it's very warm. In my house it's dim and all the shadows are very soft. My house is on a hill, beside some trees and in front of some clouds. In my house it's very soft. And I never hear anything but the sounds I like to hear. (*Pause*) Except sometimes, when I hear the far away, muffled sound of thunder in the distance. I don't like the thunder. But it's far away. In my house I'm always safe. And not even the thunder can get me.

JIM Cal?

CAL Not even the thunder.

JIM Cal?

CAL Not even the thunder.

Blackout. Lights up on set. The others enter. Cal follows Jim blankly. Jim holds a gun to Goldwyn's head.

JIM (*Pushing Goldwyn down*) Sit there.

PLATO And don't move!

JETT Christine?

ABRA Where is she?

JIM I don't think she's here.

JETT She's got to be. Christine.

PLATO I thought you said we could rely on this broad Jett.

JETT I did.

JUDY I don't think there's anyone here but us.

JETT Maybe she's in one of the other rooms. (*He wanders off to find her*) Christine. Christine?

ABRA We're fucked if she's not here!

JIM — We're not fucked yet. Don't go and get all excited until we know what's happening. (*Jim sits down*) Now you stay there.

JETT — (*Entering*) She's not here.

ABRA — Now I'll get excited. (*To Jett*) What the hell do you mean she's not here?!

JETT — I can't find her anywhere.

JIM — Jett, are you sure you told her to meet us here?

JETT — Yes Jim.

JIM — And she knew it was this building? She didn't get it confused with someplace else?

JETT — She knows the building.

JIM — Well maybe she's just late.

PLATO — And maybe she's on the phone with the cops right now.

JETT — Christine wouldn't do that!

PLATO — How do we know that?

JUDY — She gave Jett the gun didn't she?

PLATO — Lota good that was. It didn't even have bullets in it.

JETT — I told you, she couldn't find the bullets.

JIM — At least it got us out.

ABRA — That's right. And if it weren't for the gun we never woulda got Goldwyn to come with us.

PLATO — (*Pulling out a switchblade*) I could've got Goldwyn to come with us.

ABRA — Would you put that thing away.

JIM — And what would you have done if someone had seen us. Fought off six guards with a knife?

PLATO I might've.

JUDY I don't blame Jett's friend for not coming up here. This place gives me the creeps.

PLATO I think it's great.

ABRA You would. It's a dump.

PLATO Some people like dumps.

ABRA Yeah, and some people like vanilla.

PLATO You're a real riot.

ABRA And you're a royal pain in the ass!

JIM Alright! Let's not start fighting already. We've got a lot to do tonight.

JUDY We can't do much until Jett's friend gets here.

JETT Her dad probably wanted her to do something, so she couldn't get out when she was supposed to.

JUDY How well do you know this girl Jett?

JETT I've known her for years. She'll be here Jim. I wasn't lying.

JIM I know.

JETT Good. I wouldn't lie to you.

JIM I know that.

ABRA What if they found out she was the one who gave Jett the gun, and picked her up?

JETT She wouldn't talk.

ABRA Jesus, they could be surrounding this place right now.

JIM Alright Abra. That's enough.

ABRA This isn't a good place to hide out. It's right uptown.

PLATO And where would you suggest we go?

JIM We didn't exactly have time to get a car and get outa town.

ABRA But why this building? It's so obvious.

PLATO I told you, this is the best place. We used to come up here and party all the time. No one ever caught us.

JUDY I don't like this place either.

JIM If this thing's going to work we've got to stick together.

PLATO It's gonna be a piece of cake.

JIM If we're lucky.

ABRA All we gotta do is make one phone call, right?

PLATO Hell, I can make that phone call as easily as she could.

JIM I don't think that would be very smart.

PLATO Why not?

JIM Because they're going to be looking for us by now.

PLATO So I'll stick to the alleys. They won't see me. Which paper do you want me to call?

JIM Maybe later.

PLATO You think I'd go out there and just fuck it up.

JIM Don't be stupid.

PLATO Don't you trust me?

JIM Look, there are all kindsa people out on the streets right now. You might be able to get away with it, but what if you don't?

JETT Jim's right.

PLATO Jim's always right.

ABRA It must be thirty in here.

JETT At least.

CAL Rub a dub dub. Three men in a tub. And who do you think they be... (*He trails off*)

JIM (*Goes to Cal*) You okay? You need anything?

JUDY He's not going to answer you.

JETT (*Going to window*) It seems like years since I've seen downtown. All those lights...

JIM Get out of the window – someone might see you.

JETT Sorry.

ABRA I wonder if our parents have heard yet.

PLATO They're the first ones who those bastards'll get in touch with.

JETT My dad's going to be pretty upset.

ABRA Mine too.

PLATO I'd give anything to be able to see my old lady's face when they tell her I've escaped. She won't sleep for weeks. I hope she gets ulcers worrying about me. I hope she gets fucking bleeding peptic ulcers.

Cal rises and wonders around the set. Jim goes to him.

JIM You'd better sit down.

PLATO Night of the living dead or what?

JIM (*Sits Cal down*) Just stay here.

JETT (*To Jim*) Does he ever answer you?

JUDY (*Before Cal can answer*) No.

Goldwyn begins banging his feet against the floor. Plato walks up and slaps him, almost casually, across the head.

LEFT: Jett (Les Bland) commiserates with Jim (Brian Rodomski) while upstage Plato (Phil Zyp) lets their kidnapped group home counselor Mr. Goldwyn (David Nattress) have it in Brad Fraser's Mutants, *Jan–Feb 1981. RIGHT: Plato (Phil Zyp) gives it to Mr. Goldwyn (David Nattress). Photo: Phil McCallum for Walterdale Theatre Associates.*

PLATO Shut up ya old fart.

JIM Don't hit him Plato.

PLATO But I like to hit him.

JIM Well don't. (*Takes Goldwyn's gag off*) What is it?

GOLDWYN I can't breathe through that thing.

JIM You've done fine up to now.

GOLDWYN Look, Jim, you've got to let me go...

JIM (*Putting the gag back on Goldwyn*) Don't want to hear it.

JETT Christine should be here any minute now.

PLATO Y'know, this building's been condemned for years. (*To Judy*) You want to see the rest of it?

JUDY I don't know...

PLATO C'mon, it's not haunted.

JUDY Well, okay.

PLATO This way for the guided tour of Plato's House of Horrors.

JUDY Oh good, a tour.

PLATO (*As they exit*) Looking to your left we have the De Sade room.

ABRA (*Referring to Plato*) He pisses me off so much sometimes.

JIM You know what Plato's like.

ABRA He's always so fucking down on everything.

JETT I don't think he tries to be like that.

ABRA I don't think we should've brought him Jim. I don't trust him.

JIM I can handle Plato.

ABRA You sure of that?

JIM Yes.

JETT Maybe if I went out onto the roof I could see Christine from there.

JIM Just make sure no one sees you.

JETT It's just that ... I'd feel so horrible if she didn't show up after you guys trusted me and everything.

ABRA I think I'll go with him. It might be cooler.

Abra and Jett exit.

JIM (*To Goldwyn*) Guess you're pretty pissed at me huh? Can't blame you really. But we had to do this Mr. Goldwyn. We did. But don't worry. No one'll hurt you. We just need you – to make sure they listen to us. You'll be okay.

CAL (*Begins rocking*) Rub a dub dub. Three men in a tub. And who do you think they be? The butcher, the baker, and the candlestick maker...

JIM That all you've got? Nursery rhymes? (*Goes to him*) You're not fooling me Cal. I know you're still in there. Somewhere. And I'm going to get you back here. Somehow.

ABRA (*Entering*) No cooler. What're you doing?

JIM Nothing.

ABRA How are you?

JIM Huh? Oh, okay. You?

ABRA I'm scared.

JIM Don't start doubting Abra.

ABRA You know if anyone else tried to get me to do what we're doing now I would've told them to piss off. But I really think you can do it Jim.

JIM We've got to try.

JETT (*Enters*) No sign.

JIM We'll give her a little longer. If she's still not here we'll have to try something else.

ABRA What?

JIM One of us'll have to call the papers.

ABRA Not Plato!

JIM Of course not.

ABRA Who then?

JIM I'll go. But we'll have to wait until pretty late.

Abra finds a discarded newspaper.

ABRA Look at this.

JIM Anything in it?

ABRA No.

JETT I've always wanted to be in the paper.

ABRA As long as it's not the obituary section.

JETT (*To audience*) In the newspaper! Wow, would that be great! We could be heroes. Celebrities! People would know our names. I can see it already. My name in the newspaper. It would be just like in the movies. Or all those comic books I used to read. (*Pause*) They don't make comic books like that anymore. I – I don't usually tell people this, but I love comic books. Always have. I collect them. Or I used to. But I stopped when they changed. Comic books now, they aren't like they used to be. When I was a kid. They were really great then. I mean, the heroes were really heroes. Superman, Batman, the Creeper, the Shadow, Captain America. Now those guys were great. They never stopped to worry about whether or not what they were doing was right. They just went in there and slapped the shit out of those criminals. But they're not like that anymore. People don't want to read that kinda thing. They want their heroes to be just like they are. They want them to have problems and hang-ups and neuroses just like everyone else. Or they want them to be movie stars, or junkie rock and roll singers, or people who write about all the crappy things in life. They don't want heroes at all anymore. They want people just like themselves, with maybe a bit more talent. No one wants to be someone better than who they are anymore. Maybe that's why there are no heroes.

ABRA I can just see it on the four p.m. newsflash. Fat Girl and Friends Take Guidance Counselor Hostage. Details at six.

JETT Or, Courageous Youths Risk Lives to Blow Whistle on Provincial Institution.

ABRA That's not bad.

JETT We could be in *Maclean's*.

ABRA Or *Chatelaine*.

PLATO (*Entering with Judy*) Yeah, and maybe someone'll set fire to the bottom floor and we'll all burn up here.

ABRA And just where have you two been?

PLATO We were off – chatting. You know Jim this was the best place to come. There's only one entrance onto this floor of the building.

JIM Good.

PLATO (*To Jett*) Well, your friend show yet?

JETT No. Not yet.

JUDY That's really great! (*To Jim*) Have you figured out what we're going to do if she's chickened out?

JIM One of us'll have to make the call.

JUDY Which one?

JIM We'll decide that when we do it. We can't go out for a while anyway.

JUDY So we wait.

JIM Yes. We wait.

PLATO We wait.

Pause. They all wait.

ABRA I hate waiting.

PLATO Me too.

Pause.

JETT You know, when my father reads this in the paper tomorrow, he always reads the paper first thing, I hope he understands.

JUDY I'm sure he'll try.

PLATO I think your father's going to disown you the minute he hears about this.

JETT Plato...

PLATO Aw c'mon "buddy" you know I'm only funnin' ya because you're such a great kinda guy.

JETT (*Quietly*) No. I guess you're right. He won't understand.

JUDY Do they ever?

JETT Sometimes they try.

PLATO But do they ever succeed.

JIM How can we expect them to?

ABRA They don't know anything but where they're from. And Christ knows that's a different place.

Theatrical light change.

JUDY Different planet.

JETT Father?

ABRA Mother?

JIM Do you...?

JUDY Can you...?

PLATO Will you...?

ABRA Have you ever tried to understand me Mother? Have you ever really made the effort to look beyond the image of me you've always held in your eyes?

JETT I'm a person father. I laugh. I cry. I get in trouble. I win. I fail. I have things to say. I have opinions. I have ideas. I have feelings.

JUDY I'm desperate and I'm angry and I'm lonely and sometimes I want to punch you in the face and sometimes I just can't make myself care anymore.

JIM And sometimes I want you to stop existing.

ABRA And sometimes I want to hurt your feelings as much as you've hurt mine.

JUDY Tramp!

JETT Fairy!

ABRA Fat!

PLATO Loser!

JUDY Irresponsible!

JETT Immature!

ABRA Lazy!

PLATO Destructive!

JUDY Just like your father.

JETT Just like your mother.

ABRA Good for nothing.

PLATO More trouble than you're worth.

ABRA You should be ashamed!

ABRA Did you pray for me mother? Did you say make my daughter smart? Make my daughter beautiful? Maker her slim and svelte and attractive to men?

JETT Did you pray for me father? Did you say, make my son strong? Make him handsome and tall and good at all things. Make him a football player or a hockey player or a prize fighter?

JUDY Father.

PLATO Mother.

JIM My parents divorced when I was seven years old. My father was an asshole who didn't want anything out of life but a bottle and a lot of snatch to sleep with and when he left for the last time my mother had a type of breakdown and they took her away from my brother and me. My old man filed for a divorce and since neither of my parents would take responsibility for us we were put in an orphanage. I never saw my mother again after that. They tell me she killed herself. My father we never heard from again. We were in the orphanage for about three months before someone adopted my brother Tommy. He was four then. I felt bad about it, but a little bit relieved too. Because now that he was gone I didn't have to feel like I had to stay there to take care of him. I missed him sure, I missed him a lot. But I knew he was better off with his new family. And with him okay I could start making plans to get out of the fucking orphanage. So two days after he was gone I ran away. They caught me of course. But I never stopped trying to run after that. Every time one of the nuns turned her head I was gone. Usually they caught up with me within a couple of days.

Lights return to normal.

PLATO — No one's going to believe us. They've never believed us before, why the hell should they start now? Why don't we drop this whole thing and get the hell out of the province?

JIM — Because we have to do more than just get out of the home.

PLATO — So why can't we just ride write them a letter from Saskatchewan or something?

JIM — It's not just for us Plato. It's for the other kids there too.

PLATO — Fuck the other kids. They've never done anything for me.

JIM — We can't lose sight of things now that we're out.

PLATO — Why won't any of you ever listen to me?

Plato walks away from the others.

CAL — Rub a dub dub. Three men in a tub. And who do you think they be? The butcher, the baker, and the candle stick maker...

JUDY — Can't you stop him from doing that?

JIM — What do you want me to do? Gag him?

JUDY — It's starting to get on my nerves.

JIM — What did Plato say to you to make you so bitchy?

JUDY — Why do you always try to blame everything on him?

JIM — Forget it.

ABRA — I think I liked you two better when you were in love.

JIM — Stay outa this.

ABRA — Fine. (*Abra walks to Cal and sits beside him*) I'll spend my time with someone who appreciates the true sensitivity of my nature. (*To Cal*) Hiya chatterbox, read any good books lately?

JIM — (*To Judy*) Why are you so mad at me?

JUDY I'm not mad at you.

JIM Well there's something wrong.

JUDY Is there?

JIM What did you have to talk to Plato about?

JUDY Nothing important.

JIM Suit yourself.

Jim begins to move away.

JUDY Later. Okay?

JIM Okay.

ABRA (*To Cal*) So, what do you think of Kubrick?

JIM Leave him alone.

ABRA Sorry. You guys know how manic I am. Just ignore me. I'll – uh – sit in this corner and read the paper or something.

Abra sits in the corner and reads the paper.

JETT (*To Jim*) He really did a lot of acid huh?

JIM Yeah. We all did.

JETT How come you didn't turn out like him then?

JIM I'm not sure.

JUDY (*Joining Abra*) Anything interesting in the paper?

ABRA Not much.

PLATO Has that thing got a sports section?

ABRA (*Handing it to him*) There ya go.

PLATO Thanks.

ABRA You really used to hang around up here?

PLATO We used to skip school up here.

ABRA Why didn't you just hang around the Seven Eleven like everyone else?

PLATO Seven Elevens have no style.

JETT How long have you known him?

JUDY Since about grade six.

JETT Jeez, that's a long time to be friends.

JIM Yeah, I guess it is.

JETT Any of the friends I've had have never lasted more than a few months.

JIM Really? Why not?

JETT I don't know.

JIM Well how long have you known this Christine?

JETT Christine doesn't really count. She's more like my sister or something.

ABRA (*Who has returned to reading the paper*) Listen to this. "Mother puts Baby in Microwave Oven to Exorcise Demons."

JUDY Lovely.

JETT (*To Jim*) You ever done cocaine?

JIM Oh yeah.

ABRA Here's another one. "Nun Bludgeons Mother to Death With Crucifix." (*Laughs*) I love it!

JETT I've never really done anything but smoke drugs.

JIM Reefer is a real downer. I like something that's going to pick me up.

JETT Acid picks you up?

JIM Acid shoots you right into the fucking sky.

ABRA "Newborn Baby Thrown From Moving Car." Christ!

JUDY That's sick.

JETT You ever done heroin?

JIM Couple of times. It was just chipping though.

ABRA "Terrorist Group Bombs Cathedral."

PLATO Boring.

JETT Was Cal, like an addict?

JIM He was like an addict.

ABRA "Drinking Water Contaminated By Nuclear Wastes."

JETT What do you mean?

JIM I don't think he was physically addicted to drugs.

JETT There are other ways to be addicted?

JIM Sure.

ABRA "Acid Rains Exterminate Wildlife."

JETT Like how?

JIM Like when nothing's fun anymore unless you're stoned right out of your mind.

JETT Is it really that great?

JIM Yes.

ABRA "Junior High Suicide."

PLATO Sounds like a song.

JETT Can you describe it?

JIM No.

ABRA "Unidentified Remains Found by School Children."

JETT Try.

JIM I can't.

ABRA "Father Rapes Four Year Old Daughter."

JETT Why not?

JIM I don't know the words to use.

ABRA Oh good, another article about the energy crisis.

JUDY Which one?

JETT Is it anything like being drunk?

JIM No. It's nothing like that. It's like – like being in a good mood.

ABRA This newspaper is the most fucking depressing thing I've ever read.

JIM If everything was made outa chrome and lit with trails of moving neon that's what acid's like.

ABRA Even the weather report's depressing.

JETT I don't think I understand.

JIM Don't you ever want to get away?

JETT Sure. I like to escape.

JIM That's what it's all about. Escaping.

Lights change theatrically.

CAL Rub a dub dub. Three men in a tub. And who do you think they be?
The butcher, the baker, the candlestick maker...

ALL BUT JETT Acid. Acid. Acid. Acid. There are only three things to soothe my soul.
They're sex. They're drugs. They're rock and roll. I'll fuck 'til I drop.

I'll dance 'til I die. But without drugs I'll never really fly. Acid. Acid. Acidacidacid.

PLATO An ode to acid.

ABRA Ah little piece of paper. It is you that makes Friday nights fun again. It is you that gives life to all the old discos and sparkle to the conversation of mundane people. It is you that brings me up when I'm falling down and gives me the energy to go on and not care when I would be ready to stop. It is you that lets me soar above the heads of the boring and laugh at the frustrating.

JIM Ah little pill, little paper, little tablet, soothe me once more with the reality you alter and the brain cells you destroy.

JUDY Tingle my body and distort my vision. Make me witty, make me beautiful. Set the world afire and stop the bleeding in my soul.

PLATO Save me once more from the bondage of mediocrity. Lift me my little piece of paper.

ABRA My little bug of fun.

JIM My little lover of life.

ABRA My little friend.

JIM My little piece of paper.

BOYS But I'll pay your evil price if you'll take that away. I may forget my name but I'm alive today. Suck onto my body, bore into my head. If you live your life fast it doesn't matter if you're dead.

GIRLS It doesn't matter if I'm not loved. I don't care anymore. Once I've popped you into my mouth, I've evened the score. Rents can rise and atomic bombs can fall. The children unborn don't care at all.

ALL But give me for a moment the luxury of escape. Enter my system, don't make me wait. Take away the loneliness, take away pain, and when it rises once more, kill it again. I'm tired of caring and I'm sick of this shit. So I'll pay my five dollars and hide away from it. Acid. Acid. Acidacidacid.

Lights return to normal.

PLATO Where the hell is she?

JETT I don't know.

PLATO It's like a fucking oven in here.

ABRA So take some of your clothes off.

PLATO Very funny.

ABRA I will if you will.

PLATO Abra the last thing I want to see right now is your humongous sagging tits.

ABRA Slightly sagging tits.

Goldwyn begins to bang his feet against the floor.

JETT Now what?

Goldwyn continues to bang his feet.

PLATO (*To Goldwyn violently*) Shut the fuck up!

Goldwyn stops.

JIM (*To Goldwyn*) Don't be difficult, please. You've got nothing to worry about.

PLATO I wouldn't be too sure of that.

JIM And you leave him alone.

PLATO You gonna make me?

JIM If I have to.

PLATO I'd like to see that.

JIM Don't fuck with me Plato.

PLATO Sure boss.

JIM What the hell's wrong with you?

PLATO I'll bite, what's wrong with me boss?

JIM You never used to be like this.

PLATO I guess I've changed.

JIM Yeah Plato, you've changed.

PLATO I wouldn't worry about it too much.

Christine enters, unseen by the others. She stands at the back of the set and watches for a moment.

JIM Don't fuck this up.

PLATO You threatening me?

JIM I'm not going to let you ruin this.

PLATO How are you gonna stop me?

CHRISTINE Jett?

They all turn, very startled.

JETT Christine!

ABRA Well, it's about time.

JETT We were beginning to think you'd never show.

CHRISTINE The stuff you need's in that bag.

JIM Thanks.

JETT Boy Chris, you really had us worried for a while there. But I'm glad you're here anyway. And don't worry about being late. How are you?

CHRISTINE Fine.

JETT There's some buns and stuff in here if anyone's hungry.

ABRA (*Going for the bag*) Let me at it.

CHRISTINE There's a bottle in there too. I though you might like something to drink.

PLATO (*Pulling bottle out of bag*) Alright!

Plato begins to drink. He will continue to drink throughout the act.

JETT Where'd you get that?

CHRISTINE Dad's bar.

JETT Is there something wrong?

CHRISTINE No. No. I'm fine.

JETT You look sorta funny.

CHRISTINE Do I?

JETT Yes.

CHRISTINE Oh.

ABRA Well aren't you going to introduce us to your friend Jett?

JETT Of course. Christine, this...

ABRA (*Interrupting*) Hi there. My name's Abra. You must be Christine. I've heard so much about you. I have no morals.

CHRISTINE Uh – hello.

JETT Abra's such a card.

ABRA Yeah, funny fat girl. I've heard it all before.

JETT And this is Judy.

JUDY Hi.

JETT Plato.

Plato waves indifferently.

JETT And Jim.

JIM Hello Christine.

ABRA How do you like us so far?

CHRISTINE (*Indicating Goldwyn*) Why is that man tied up like that?

ABRA It's the only way we know how to tie people up.

CHRISTINE Jett, what's going on here?

JETT I told you. We escaped from the home.

CHRISTINE You never told me you were going to tie other people up.

JETT We had to take him.

CHRISTINE Why?

JIM We need something to make sure that if the cops find us they can't do anything. Taking someone from the home hostage was the best way to do that. We're not going to hurt anyone. We just need some insurance.

CHRISTINE I don't like any of this.

PLATO We're not doing it for you.

CHRISTINE Well I brought the stuff you needed. I think I'd better go now.

Christine begins to exit. Jim motions for Jett to stop her.

JETT Chris, wait.

CHRISTINE What?

JETT Why are you taking off so fast?

CHRISTINE I really should get home.

JETT But don't you want to stay and talk to me or anything?

CHRISTINE Look Jett, I'm sorry, but the only reason I came was because I promised I would. But I'm not going to stay. I could get into a lot of trouble.

JETT I know that Chris, but – I've missed you.

CHRISTINE Jett, do you know the police are looking for you?

JETT Yeah, well I figured they would be.

CHRISTINE You're going to be in a lot of trouble.

PLATO Too late.

JETT We're already in a lot of trouble.

CHRISTINE I don't think I want to be involved in this.

ABRA I thought you said we could trust this chick.

JETT We can trust her.

CHRISTINE Jett, if my dad found out I was helping you he'd have a fit. You know that.

JUDY I don't think I want her to help us.

JETT I know I've asked a lot of you Chris. But really, I wouldn't do it if it weren't very important.

CHRISTINE Jett, you're me best friend. But you know what dad's like.

ABRA What is this with her father? She makes him sound like Hitler.

JETT Chris's father is with the provincial government. He's very uh – aware of his public image.

JUDY With the government?

CHRISTINE He's the Minister of Culture.

PLATO Well La-de-fucking-da.

ABRA Great Jett, you didn't tell us she was one of them.

JETT One of whom?

ABRA One of them.

CHRISTINE I'm not one of them.

PLATO Who's them?

ABRA Shut up!

JETT Stick around for a while. Please.

CHRISTINE Well I suppose a few minutes won't hurt.

PLATO (*To Judy*) Drink?

JUDY Yeah, thanks.

PLATO When're you gonna tell him?

JUDY As soon as we know what's happening.

PLATO I was thinking that maybe, you know, if you didn't want Jim to know, we could like take off.

JUDY Take off?

PLATO Yeah, leave. Jim would never have to know.

JUDY You want me to leave with you?

PLATO Yeah.

JUDY Plato, I can't do that.

PLATO Why not?

JUDY It's Jim's baby.

PLATO He's not going to care. He's more interested in his faggot friend Cal.

JUDY That goddamn Cal.

PLATO I'll take care of you Judy. I'll get a job and be just like the kid's real father. You'll see.

JUDY I don't think so Plato.

PLATO Why not?

JUDY It just wouldn't work.

ABRA (*To Jim*) What're those two whispering about over there?

JIM Who knows?

PLATO (*To Judy*) Why do you all follow him around?

JUDY He means a lot to me.

PLATO And what about me?

JUDY You're a very good friend Plato. I like you. But I want to stay with Jim.

PLATO Jim's an asshole! Come with me?

JUDY I can't!

Judy walks away from Plato.

ABRA What are you two fighting about?

JUDY Nothing.

Abra goes to Plato.

JETT (*To Christine*) Have you seen Aaron lately?

CHRISTINE Not since you went into the home.

JETT He didn't come visit me or anything.

CHRISTINE You know what Aaron's like Jett.

JETT Yeah. (*Short pause*) It doesn't really matter anyway. I've got a whole new set of friends now.

CHRISTINE These people are really your friends?

JETT You've just got to look past what they show people. They're – nice.

PLATO (*To Abra*) If you don't quit breathing down my fucking neck I'm gonna cut your tits off!!

ABRA Yell at someone you can scare fuckface!

CHRISTINE Nice?

JETT Well Plato's sort of an off one.

CHRISTINE He looks like a lunatic to me.

JIM (*Approaching Jett and Christine*) Excuse me. I'd like to talk to you for a moment Christine, if I may. I think it's very – kind of you to help all of us out. Considering you don't even know us.

CHRISTINE Oh, it wasn't much trouble.

JIM No, I'm sure it was a lot of trouble.

CHRISTINE Okay, it was, kind of.

JIM It takes a very – concerned person to stick her neck out for a group of strangers like you have.

CHRISTINE I never thought of it that way.

JIM I can see why Jett's always spoken so highly of you.

CHRISTINE Jett, what have you told them?

JETT (*Not quite sure what's happening*) Oh, you know...

JIM Christine...

CHRISTINE Yes?

JIM I realize it's not very fair of me to ask anything else of you...

ABRA Here it comes.

CHRISTINE What is it?

JIM Well we have one more thing I need.

CHRISTINE One more thing?

JIM Yes.

CHRISTINE (*Her suspicion returning*) What is it?

JIM I don't know how much Jett told you about what happened in the home.

CHRISTINE Not that much.

JIM Well, you see, we didn't escape from that place just to get away. I mean, there were some very heavy things going down.

CHRISTINE What kind of things?

JIM The things aren't really important. What is important is that we've got to do something about it. And we've got to do it fast.

CHRISTINE What do you want me to do?

Cal rises.

CAL Thunder.

Pause.

JIM We have to call the newspapers.

CHRISTINE What?

JIM We have to call the newspapers and get some publicity happening. That's the only way we're going to be able to tell people what's going on.

CHRISTINE (*To Jett, indicating Cal*) What's wrong with that guy?

JETT Drugs.

CHRISTINE Figures.

JIM All it'll take is one quick phone call.

CHRISTINE What kind of drugs?

PLATO (*Violently*) Never mind that! Listen to what the hell he's trying to say to you!

CHRISTINE Don't you yell at me you bloody psychopath!

PLATO What did you call me?

JIM Plato, she didn't mean it.

PLATO She called me a psychopath!

JETT She didn't mean it.

CHRISTINE Yes I did.

PLATO Loud-mouthed little bitch!

JIM Slow down.

CHRISTINE Jett, I'm getting out of here right now.

JETT Wait a minute...

CHRISTINE These people are all crazy!

PLATO (*Very loud*) No!

Pause.

PLATO We can't let her go. She thinks we're all crazy. She'll probably be on the blower to the cops the minute she gets out of here.

JETT No.

PLATO Her father works for the provincial government – the bourgeois slut.

JUDY I think you're going a bit too far.

PLATO Am I? Do you want to take a chance?

ABRA Maybe he's right.

PLATO Do you want to see all your precious little plans turn to shit. All it'll take is one wrong word from her and bang.

JETT Stop it Plato.

PLATO Bang.

ABRA Jim, we can't take the chance.

CHRISTINE (*Turning to exit*) I don't believe this.

PLATO You'd better stop her.

JIM (*Going to stop Christine*) Goddamn you Plato!

CHRISTINE Let go of me!

JIM I'm sorry – we can't let you leave now.

CHRISTINE (*Slapping Jim*) Get your hands off me.

JIM (*To Christine, reasonably*) I can't let you go.

CHRISTINE You are all crazy!

JIM Just a few hours until we can get out to make that phone call ourselves.

CHRISTINE You can't do this. This is illegal. This is – this isn't right.

JIM I'm sorry.

Christly begins to scream, very loud. Jim slaps her.

JIM Please don't make this any harder.

CHRISTINE (*Trying to escape*) Let go of me you bastard! Let me go! Jett, make them let me go. (*Pause*) Jett? (*Very shocked*) Jett! You can't keep me here! I'll – I'll have you all arrested. I'll scream! I'll run away!

JIM Abra, give me the rest of that rope.

JETT Jim, do we have to?

JIM I'm afraid so.

CHRISTINE You wouldn't dare.

Judy and Abra hold Christine. Jim goes to the chair Cal is hiding under.

CHRISTINE Someone's going to pay for this.

ABRA — So call the cops angeltits.

CHRISTINE — Jett you little coward, how can you let them do this to me?

JETT — I'm sorry.

Jim ties Christine to the chair.

JIM — (*To Christine*) There. That's not too tight is it? If it's uncomfortable just say so and I'll loosen it.

Christine begins to scream again. Jim raises his hand. She stops quickly.

JIM — It doesn't make me feel good, hitting girls. But don't fuck with us.

JETT — Christine...?

CHRISTINE — You're supposed to be my friend.

JETT — I am your friend.

CHRISTINE — Friends don't tie each other up.

ABRA — My friends do.

JETT — We just can't take any chances.

CHRISTINE — But I wouldn't tell anyone anything.

JETT — It's only for a few hours. We'll let you go as soon as we call the reporters.

CHRISTINE — I hope you all get caught!

JETT — Don't say that!

CHRISTINE — I do! I hope you all get caught and they put you in prison for life!

JETT — If we do get caught we probably will go to prison. Most of us'll be eighteen next year.

CHRISTINE — Good.

JUDY — (*To Jim*) Things don't seem to be going according to plan.

JIM I know.

ABRA Don't go getting drunk.

PLATO Don't worry about me.

JETT (*To Christine*) You don't mean that do you? About us getting caught.

CHRISTINE No. I didn't mean it.

JETT I didn't think so.

CHRISTINE But I'm really mad at you.

ABRA (*To Plato*) Gimme a swig a that there bottle partner.

Plato hands her the bottle. Abra drinks and chokes.

ABRA You – uh – sure you're not drinking too much?

PLATO (*Warningly*) Abra...

Plato takes out his switchblade and begins to clean his nails with it.

ABRA I've always liked you Plato.

PLATO Yeah?

ABRA I used to like you more though.

Pause.

ABRA You're going to cut yourself with that thing.

PLATO (*Laughs*) I doubt it.

ABRA Can I see it?

PLATO No.

ABRA Why not?

PLATO No one touches my spike but me.

ABRA Hmmph, a phallic surrogate. I knew it all along.

PLATO I think it's more of a subliminal defense mechanism made tangible in slight phallic representation.

ABRA Is that the knife you got that teacher with?

PLATO Yeah.

ABRA Did he need stitches?

PLATO Sixteen I heard.

ABRA You're really scary sometimes.

PLATO (*Rising*) He never shoulda came at me like he did.

ABRA Where are you going?

PLATO Out onto the roof.

ABRA Why?

PLATO It's too hot in here

ABRA Someone might see you.

PLATO So what?

ABRA Why don't you care about this thing as much as the rest of us?

PLATO Because it's a stupid idea Abra. (*Forming his hand into a gun and pointing it at Abra*) Bang.

ABRA Stop being so stupid.

PLATO (*Aiming at Jim*) Bang.

ABRA Stop that.

PLATO (*Aiming at Goldwyn*) Bang.

ABRA Jeez!

CHRISTINE Jett, I have a Chemistry exam tomorrow.

ABRA So what?

Judy touches him.

JUDY You're so soft. I love the way that hair feels right there.

PLATO (*Who is observing all this from outside*) Fucking Jim. Why do they all look up to him so much?

ABRA Because he's handsome and has a big dick.

PLATO He's as fucked up as the rest of us.

CAL Rub a dub dub. Three men in a tub. And who do you think they be? The butcher, the baker, and the candlestick maker...

Cal begins to rock.

JIM Cal?

JUDY There's nothing you can do for him Jim.

JIM He looks so... (*He trails off*)

CAL (*The rocking increases*) Rub a dub dub. Rub a dub dub. Rub a dub dub. Rub a dub dub... (*The rocking becomes nearly violent*)

JIM (*Shaking Judy off*) Cal. (*And going to Cal*)

JUDY Jim?

JIM Cal? What's wrong Cal?

Cal rocks harder.

JIM Stop it.

The rocking grows.

JIM Stop it!!

Cal suddenly goes limp in Jim's arms.

JIM Jesus Fucking Christ!

CAL (*Remaining limp*) In my house, it's very warm.

Lights change theatrically.

JIM Cal? Shit Cal... When's it going to stop? How many times do I have to say I'm sorry? I'm so tired Cal? I want to talk to you again. I need you here. They're all watching me all the time. I didn't mean it. Really. It was just that – I was tired. It was all going too fast. We were losing touch with things. You always said we lived life like characters in a movie or a book. That we had an obligation to do all the things the hung up people wouldn't do. And we could do all the drugs and all the drinking and all the driving and all the fucking they were too scared to do. Hey, do you remember the time we picked those four chicks up at the club? What a riot! The looks people gave us when we walked out of there! And that time we booted that MDA and played on the swings in the park all night? But something happened. Somewhere we lost sight of things. We were doing things because that's what people expected us to do. We stopped being a couple of friends out for a good time and became what everyone wanted Jim and Cal to be. I got busted three times in a year. I got kicked out of school. You got kicked out of the house. I don't know what was happening – but things were changing. It was like we had to keep getting faster or things – I don't know what – things would catch up with us. I think – I think maybe we were trying to destroy ourselves. And I don't know why. Well except for our really fucked up families.

CAL In my house it's very warm.

JIM That's why I had to get away.

CAL In my house it's very nice.

JIM But I never thought you'd do – this.

CAL And no one can get in.

JIM I know you can hear me in there.

CAL Not even the thunder.

JIM Cal?

Lights return to normal.

CHRISTINE Jett, I've got to study for that exam.

ABRA Get off his back, would ya?

CHRISTINE I wasn't talking to you.

ABRA Ooh, the cheerleader's got a little fight in her after all.

CHRISTINE You don't scare me. And I'm not a cheerleader.

ABRA Don't be stupid. Of course you are.

JETT No Abra, she's not.

ABRA Well she should be.

A spot on Plato.

PLATO It's like an anger. It's like a loneliness. It's like some wired indefinable emotion welling up inside you. It's like you're the only person in the world and no one else can understand. (*Pause*) Mostly it's anger. (*Pause*) Mostly it's not knowing. (*Pause*) When I was in tenth grade they kicked me out of school for the first and last time. I'd always been a super student. I mean, I'm not talking nothing, but a ninety average since the first grade practically. And I didn't even have to try. No studying, nothing. I just knew things.

Anyway, when I hit high school I finally decided to hell with it. I mean, being brilliant and dependable had never gotten me anything but in fights with the other kids anyway. So I stopped going to classes. I still turned in my assignments. I still wrote the tests. I still got the highest marks in class. But within a week the principal was on the blower calling me down to his office. It started out pretty funny. I mean, the old fart was trying his hardest to be diplomatic and understanding about the whole thing. He hemmed and hawed for a while until finally I got fed up with the whole stupid thing and said Look man, why don't you cut the shit and get to the point. Well, that kinda shocked him. There was this sorta pause. And he said, Alright. I'm afraid if you don't start attending class we're going to have to ask you to withdraw from school. I said, why should I go back to class when I can maintain my marks without being there? He said if they were to make an exception for me they would have to make an exception for everyone in the school and they were running a school with some thirteen hundred students in it and they couldn't go about catering to individuals. I told him he could shove his school and his goddamn classes up his fat cocksucking asshole. He told me to get the hell out of his office. I said I'd love to and kicked the window out of one of his bookcases. He came at me across the desk. I don't like it when people rush at me. He called me a crazy little bastard and grabbed me. That was it. The old anger came up again. I tried to control it, but I couldn't. As soon as he grabbed me I pulled my spike outa my boot. I ended up cutting his arm open. Someone heard the noise and called the cops. I'm not sure what happened after that. Someone said I tried to knife the cops too. I don't know. (*Pause*) Sometimes you gotta fight back. Sometimes you gotta let them know that even if you can't win you're going to fight them.

Plato sits on the ledge and pretends to shoot people on the street. Goldwyn interrupts them by banging his feet against the floor.

JIM Jesus! (*Going to Goldwyn and removing his gag*) What is it now?

GOLDWYN Jim, this isn't going to work.

JIM We've got to do this.

GOLDWYN Why?

JIM Because – because we have to.

GOLDWYN Who are you doing this for?

JIM Us. We're doing it for us.

GOLDWYN But you broke the law. Probation didn't work. Foster homes didn't work. You had to go into the home.

JIM There are things you don't know about.

GOLDWYN What kind of things?

PLATO Don't tell him anything.

JUDY You wouldn't believe us anyway.

GOLDWYN Is this that Lucy Jordan thing again?

Lights change theatrically.

ABRA Lucy Jordan.

JETT Lucy Jordan.

JUDY Feet swinging.

JIM Lucy Jordan.

JUDY Neck angled.

PLATO Lucy Jordan.

JUDY Dried blood around her mouth.

ABRA Lucy Jordan,

JIM Lucy Jordan.

JUDY Lucy...

JIM Yes. It's got a lot to do with the Lucy Jordan thing.

Lights return to normal.

CHRISTINE (*To Jett*) Who was Lucy Jordan?

JETT Lucy was a friend of ours – theirs.

CHRISTINE What happened to her?

JUDY They say she killed herself!

GOLDWYN But she did kill herself!

JUDY She wouldn't kill herself.

GOLDWYN Judy, the coroner's report said that...

JUDY I know. I've heard it all before.

GOLDWYN How else could she have died?

JUDY There's no use talking to you!

GOLDWYN I don't understand what any of you are talking about?

JIM Leave it alone Mr. Goldwyn.

Jim moves to put the gag back on.

GOLDWYN No! I'll keep quiet. Please.

JIM (*Considers a moment*) Well okay, but you've got to keep your mouth shut.

CHRISTINE (*To Jett*) How long have you known these people?

JETT I told you, since I went into the home.

CHRISTINE I take it they all knew each other before that.

JETT Yeah, they've known each other for a long time.

CHRISTINE Why were they in there?

Lights change theatrically.

ABRA (*Stands*) Runaway. Truancy. Shoplifting.

PLATO (*Stands*) Breaking and entering. Auto theft. Assault with a deadly weapon.

JUDY Illegal possession. Runaway. Prostitution.

JIM Assaulting a police officer. Narcotics. Trespassing.

JETT (*Stands*) Shooting six dogs.

Lights return to normal.

ABRA What?

JETT Shooting six dogs.

ABRA Why the hell did you shoot six dogs?

JETT I hate dogs.

PLATO Don't worry Jett. I understand. Sometimes you just have to kill dogs.

GOLDWYN Jim?

JIM Yeah?

GOLDWYN You'd better watch Plato Jim. He's very – unstable.

JIM He's a little pissed right now, but he'll come around.

GOLDWYN He's angry because the others follow you, not him.

JIM No one's following anyone.

GOLDWYN They're all following you. They're all depending on you. And you know it.

JIM We're doing this thing together!

GOLDWYN Plato could ruin everything you're trying to do here.

JIM Isn't that what you want?

GOLDWYN I think I understand what you're doing.

JIM Don't patronize me.

GOLDWYN I know where you're coming from.

JIM Oh Christ!

GOLDWYN I understand your position. Jesus Jim, I come from practically the same background you do. I grew up in foster homes.

JIM Good for you.

GOLDWYN If this thing fails you won't go back to the home.

JIM I know.

GOLDWYN You'll go to prison.

JIM (*Indifferently*) I know.

GOLDWYN If you go to prison Cal won't go with you.

JIM What?

GOLDWYN If this thing falls apart you'll go to prison and they'll put Cal somewhere where they can take care of him.

JIM It won't fall through.

GOLDWYN They probably won't let you see him. They'll say you forced him to come here with you. That he's not responsible for his actions.

JIM There's nothing wrong with him!

GOLDWYN How can you say that? Look at him

JIM He's just fucking around.

GOLDWYN Jim he's retreated from reality completely!

JIM No. He's still there. He's just – hiding or resting or something for a while.

GOLDWYN Come on Jim. I grew up in the sixties. I saw what those kinds of drugs did to people. Speed. Mesc. Acid. It was a lot stronger and a lot cheaper then than it is now.

JIM He's not dead.

GOLDWYN Why do you feel so obligated to him Jim?

JIM He's my best friend.

GOLDWYN What happened? I really thought we were making progress in the home.

JIM You also thought Lucy Jordan committed suicide.

GOLDWYN Who would want to hurt her?

JIM There was so much going on there that you never knew about.

GOLDWYN What?

JIM The drugs, the sex, the fights. Couldn't you see any of that?

GOLDWYN We were – aware of some of the things the kids were doing.

JIM You stupid asshole! I'm not talking about the kids! I'm talking about the fucking guards!

Pause.

GOLDWYN The guards?

JIM (*Putting the gag back on Goldwyn*) So fucking blind. You don't deserve to hear anything else!

A spot on Judy.

JUDY I met Lucy Jordan the last time I ran away from home. It was just after my sister's funeral, and my dad and I were fighting again, and I finally decided "to hell with it." I was so goddamn tired of hearing about what a disappointment my sister was, and how I'd turn out just like her, that I figured I had to get out or lose my mind. So I packed my things and left. I'd met Lucy before, through some kids I knew, and since she was the only person I knew who didn't live at home, I went there. She was great. I mean she really cared about me. Well I moved in with her and we started hanging around with Jim and his gang. It was Lucy that first got me into working the streets. I was sort of nervous at first, but Lucy'd been at it since she was fourteen and she didn't seem to have any trouble handling it. It wasn't all that bad. You got some weird tricks sometimes, and the occasional dose, but nothing really awful happened. Jim and Cal were hustling then too, so it wasn't all that bad. And after the night was over we'd all get together and laugh about what we'd done. (*Pause*) In the home, Lucy was the bravest of us all. Braver than Jim even. I mean, she didn't take shit from anyone. When she didn't like something she said so. No one messed with her. She was a tough BITCH. I guess that's what finally did her in. (*Pause*) In a lot of ways Lucy was a lot like my older sister. They were both very brave. Now they're both dead. (*Pause*) I hate to think it, but maybe there's something to be said about being afraid. At least the rest of us are alive. (*Pause*) But I've got to admit, if I could start back in the home again I'd carry a knife with me, just like Plato does. And the first time one of those bastards came up to me I'd run it up his belly so fast he wouldn't have time to fall before his guts spilled all over his feet.

Lights return to normal.

ABRA This waiting is driving me out of my mind.

JIM I'll go out right away.

JETT Do you want me to come with you Jim?

JIM Thanks but no.

JUDY Are you sure? What if someone catches you?

JIM They catch me.

ABRA Maybe Judy or I should go. They're less likely to stop a girl than they are a guy.

JIM I think I stand a better chance of getting away.

JUDY But we need you here if something goes wrong.

PLATO (*Entering*) I could go. Maybe I should go, huh Jim?

JIM Maybe.

PLATO You mean you might let me go?

JIM I'll think about it.

PLATO I wouldn't screw anything up.

JIM Okay. Don't get all excited. We've got a little while yet.

PLATO I know what to do.

JIM Okay. I'll let you know.

ABRA (*Confidently, to Jim*) You're not serious?

JIM Of course not. But if it'll keep him quiet for a minute...

PLATO I'd just phone the paper and say, let me talk to the editors.

CHRISTINE (*To Jett*) Do you really think that's such a great idea?

JETT What?

CHRISTINE Calling the papers like that?

JETT Of course it's a good idea. Jim thought of it.

CHRISTINE Please, let's get out of here.

JETT I'm sorry. I can't. They'll let you go when Jim goes out to make that phone call though.

CHRISTINE But I want you to come with me.

JETT I can't do that Chris.

CHRISTINE I'll find someplace to hide you.

JETT I just can't.

ABRA (*Who has been listening*) Good stuff!

CHRISTINE You've been listening!

ABRA I had to listen to something.

CHRISTINE That's rude!

ABRA So my manners are bad. Sue me. Jett's not going to let you go.

CHRISTINE What have you done to him?

ABRA We made friends with him.

CHRISTINE Tried to make him just as sick as the rest of you.

ABRA He's comfortable with us.

CHRISTINE He doesn't know any better.

ABRA You talk just like a TV commercial.

CHRISTINE And the filthy way you talk is better I suppose?

ABRA I say what I've got to say. People understand me. That's the important thing.

CHRISTINE If people understood you, you wouldn't be where you are right now.

ABRA What would you know about it?

JETT Abra, please...

CHRISTINE I know your type.

ABRA It takes a type to know a type.

CHRISTINE You're a cliché!

ABRA And you're going to get a punch in the mouth in about three seconds!

CHRISTINE You're really tough when I'm tied up!

ABRA Tied up or not, I could rip your face off anytime!

CHRISTINE Fat girls don't scare me!

ABRA You bitch! (*To Jett*) Untie her, I'll show the stuck up scuz a thing or two!

JETT Stop it Abra.

ABRA I'll rip her arm off and beat her with the wet end!

CHRISTINE (*Loughs*) You're ridiculous!

ABRA Shut your mouth you fucking FAG HAG!

Long pause.

ABRA Sorry Jett.

JETT Don't worry about it.

ABRA I didn't mean to say that.

CHRISTINE I'm not a fag hag.

JIM Abra, leave them alone.

CHRISTINE (*To Jett*) Why did she have to call me that?

JETT She didn't mean it.

CHRISTINE I was your friend before I knew you were gay.

JETT I know.

CHRISTINE I'm not a fag hag.

JETT Of course you're not.

CHRISTINE I'm not afraid of men – or sex.

JETT Don't let it get to you Chris.

CHRISTINE Other people have said that too.

JETT What the hell do they know?

CHRISTINE They all know about you too?

JETT Sure.

CHRISTINE It didn't bother you to tell them?

JETT No.

CHRISTINE You've changed.

JETT Whatever I do is cool with them.

PLATO Judy, hey Judy. C'mere. Tell'im yet? Jim? You tell him the news? I will if you're scared to.

JUDY Don't you dare!

PLATO I will.

Abra joins them.

ABRA What's going on?

PLATO Mind your own business Pork.

CAL Rub a dub dub. Rub a dub dub...

Jim goes to Cal.

JUDY You think they've ever made it with each other?

ABRA I dunno.

JUDY Most guys do when they're close like that.

PLATO I slept with you Abra.

ABRA Please...

JUDY You ever sleep with Cal?

ABRA No. You?

JUDY Once.

ABRA How was he?

JUDY Not bad. Thick.

PLATO Remember when I slept with you Abra?

ABRA I don't like to Plato.

PLATO Why not?

ABRA We were both very drunk.

PLATO How was I?

ABRA You were a two.

PLATO A two?

ABRA On a scale of one hundred.

PLATO A two?

ABRA You're a real sloppy drunk.

PLATO Sometimes I cry too.

JETT (*To Christine*) Okay, so maybe they're not the most stable people in the world. But they make me feel like one of them.

CHRISTINE You're so different.

JETT A place like that changes you. (*Pause*) There were a lot of really rotten things happening there.

CHRISTINE What things? People keep talking about these things, but I still don't know what they are.

JETT Just things.

JUDY (*To Abra*) What're we going to do if we're caught?

ABRA Who knows? I know I won't go back to the home.

CHRISTINE: What kind of things?

JETT I don't know if you'd understand.

CHRISTINE I'll try.

JETT Well, there are these guards that work the night shift...

CHRISTINE Uh huh?

JETT They – uh – they do things to the kids in there...

CHRISTINE Things again.

ABRA Are you retarded? Do we have to spell it out for you?

Lights change theatrically.

JIM The home.

ALL The home.

ALL Grey walls. Dark corridors. Cement floors. Unbreakable windows. Wire fences. Small rooms. Communal cans. Cries in the night. Echoes in the dark. Blood on the tiles of the bathroom floor. School. Counseling. Recreation. Sleep. Smells of vomit in the halls. Graffiti scrawled on bedroom walls.

JETT Let me out.

JIM In black marker.

ABRA Fuck the world.

JUDY Scratched into the paint.

PLATO There are no heroes.

JETT I wrote that.

PLATO Slaughter the rich.

JUDY He wrote that.

ABRA Girls are virgins. Girls are sluts.

JIM I'm losing my mind. I'm going nuts.

ALL Watching your back. Watching your front. Fighting with the boys. Fighting with the girls. Knives made from razor blades. Scars across a wrist. Drugs smuggled in. Porn for trade. Secrets in the shower room. Someone planning an escape. The night staff...

JIM The night staff.

ABRA The night staff who take the place over when it's been shut down and all the kids have gone to bed.

JUDY Four men with the power and lack of intelligence to stop any rebellion that might form in the night.

JETT Four men in one of the lounges playing cards. Drinking beer. Waiting for the safety of midnight.

PLATO Then, when the lights are out.

JIM And they're sure most everyone is asleep.

ABRA They throw down their cards and hitch up their pants.

JUDY Step into the halls and tap on your doors.

JETT And you can hear them moving your way from the bed. And with every step they get closer to your door. And you hear their feet, and you hear the heaviness of their breathing. And they're getting closer and you shut your eyes and you pray, not me. Please not me. Not again tonight. Not me.

ABRA And their whispered voices carry the dirtiest words of all.

PLATO And those words are...

JETT Delinquents.

JIM Fuck ups.

PLATO Useless garbage.

JUDY Good for only a few things.

ALL And they tap on your door. And they tap on your head. And they enter your room. And they enter your bed. And they say, "Wake up little boys. Wake up little girls. Get out of your bed and get out of your underwear and get onto the floor and get onto your knees and get onto your back and get onto your belly" and they run your hands over their thighs and they run their fingers through your hair and they fill you up and make you hurt and make you choke and they pinch you. And they pant in your face and they let their sweat splash on your skin.

JUDY Leave me alone!

JIM And there's not a goddamn thing you can do to keep them from coming in.

ALL You hear the grunts and you hear the cries and you hear the moans and you hear the screams. And you want to yell out and you want to pound the floor and hit at the walls and claw at the windows and smash your head against the cement and yell "Make it stop. Make it stop!"

JUDY But you can't.

ALL Because how the hell do you fight the ones who are abusing you when everyone thinks they're helping you.

PLATO And even if you told them they wouldn't believe you anyway.

JIM And they'd make you very sorry.

JUDY Just like they made Lucy Jordan very sorry.

ABRA It's not the acts.

PLATO Because in another situation you might even enjoy the acts.

JUDY And it's not the pain.

JETT Because pain never lasts forever.

JIM It's knowing that they're using you. It's knowing that they're fucking you in every way possible because they honestly believe that that's all you're good for.

PLATO And the other kids may tolerate it. May even enjoy it.

ABRA But not us.

JIM Because we will not be used!

JUDY Lucy was the only one who ever stood up to them. She didn't care about their threats, or the fact that they slapped her around. She still fought them. Fought them with everything she had. She never gave in. They never got to her.

PLATO Never?

JUDY Until that last time. The time she told the guard to piss off and kicked him in the nuts. He slapped her, but went away. And we all laughed and celebrated and told her she'd finally shown them.

ABRA We should've known better.

JIM We should've protected her.

JUDY I found her the next morning.

Lights return to normal.

PLATO (*To Goldwyn*) Suicide! Fuck you suicide!

CHRISTINE Jett, why didn't you tell me?

JETT I didn't know how to.

CHRISTINE It would've made so much difference.

JIM I'm going to make that phone call now.

PLATO I thought you said I could go.

JIM You've had too much to drink!

PLATO You always treat me like a fucking kid!

JIM — I'll be back as soon as possible. If I'm more than an hour try to get the hell out of here.

PLATO — (*Pulling his switchblade*) No!

JIM — Put the knife away Plato.

PLATO — I'll cut you Jim. If you move I'll cut you bad!

JIM — I'm going now.

PLATO — Don't make me do it Jim.

JIM — I'm leaving.

Jim begins to exit. Plato steps in front of him, his knife to Jim's throat.

JETT — Leave him alone you crazy bastard!

JIM — If you're going to use that you'd better mean it.

Jim steps around Plato and continues to exit. Plato watches him, ready to pounce with the knife at any second. The others wait breathlessly. Finally Plato drops the knife. Jett picks it up quickly.

PLATO — Judy's pregnant.

Pause. Jim stops and turns.

JIM — What?

PLATO — You're fucked up good boy.

JIM — I don't believe you.

PLATO — Ask her.

JUDY — Plato...

JIM — Judy?

Judy nods.

JIM — We'll talk about this when I get back.

A flashing red light suddenly fills the stage. An amplified voice is heard offstage.

VOICE City Police. We're coming in.

Blackout.

Act Two

Lights up. All in same position as act one. Red lights still flashing. Pause.

VOICE Can you hear me?

Pause.

VOICE We know you're up there!

Pause.

VOICE We're coming in.

JIM (*Running to window*) No!

VOICE Who is that?

JIM My name's Jim!

VOICE I can hardly hear you.

JIM My name's Jim!

VOICE Jim?

JIM That's right.

VOICE Jim Stark?

JIM Yes.

VOICE Are the others up there too Jim?

JIM Yes.

VOICE All of them?

JIM Yes.

VOICE Mr. Goldwyn too?

JIM Yes.

VOICE Is he alright?

JIM He's fine.

VOICE Are you going to come down Jim? Or do we have to come after you?

Pause.

JUDY Let's give up.

JETT No!

JIM We're not coming down.

VOICE You're only making things difficult for yourselves.

JIM Jett, bring Goldwyn here.

Jett leads Goldwyn to Jim. Jim sets him out on the window ledge.

VOICE Don't do anything you'll regret.

JIM If anyone sets a foot in this building I'll push him.

VOICE Jim...?

JIM Do you hear me?

VOICE Yes, but...

JIM (*Cutting the voice off*) Listen to me! We have a gun. We'll kill him if we have to. Do you understand? We'll blow his brains out!

VOICE I hear you Jim.

JIM We don't want to hurt anyone. We don't want any trouble.

VOICE What do you want Jim?

JIM Reporters.

VOICE What?

JIM Reporters. Newspaper reporters. TV reporters. Any kind of reporters. I don't care. Just bring us as many of them as you can. Bring us reporters, or we'll kill him. Do you understand me?

VOICE Yes.

JIM Then do it. Now!

Jim pulls Goldwyn out of the window.

CHRISTINE (*To Jett*) He wouldn't really kill him, would he?

JETT (*To Jim*) What do you want us to do?

JIM Get over there by the ledge. Keep your eyes open. Let me know if anything funny is happening.

Jett goes to the ledge and stands look-out.

JIM Abra, Judy, go block the stairway. I don't care what you use, but make sure no one can get through without us hearing them.

ABRA Sure.

Judy and Abra exit. Pause.

PLATO And me?

JIM I don't care. Do whatever you want. Just don't fuck this up any more than it already is.

CAL Rub a dub dub. Three men in a tub. And who do you think they be?

JIM (*Low, but with force*) Stop it Cal. Now.

Cal stops.

JIM There's still a chance.

JETT Jim, you'd better come here.

JIM (*Going to him*) What is it?

JETT Look. Three cars just went into that alley. And there's men on top of that building over there.

JIM They don't fuck around, do they?

JETT They can see everything we do from up there.

JIM So let them see. (*Calling down*) Hey!

A spot hits Jim from the street below.

VOICE What is it Jim?

JIM Turn the fucking lights out!

The spot goes down.

JIM That's better.

VOICE What is it Jim?

JIM Why've you men on those buildings?

VOICE We just want to keep an eye on things Jim.

JIM I don't want anyone to get hurt.

VOICE That's good Jim.

JIM And if you cooperate with us, we'll cooperate with you.

VOICE That's all we want.

JIM As soon as we've talked to those reporters you can do whatever you want to do. But if you do anything to stop that from happening, we'll kill Goldwyn.

VOICE Can't you talk to me Jim?

JIM No! Just get the reporters! And tell those men to watch themselves!

PLATO (*Quietly to Goldwyn*) This is all your fault. Your fault. Your fault. Your fault.

JETT I'm not worried Jim.

JIM No.

JETT I know you'll make this thing work.

JIM Thanks Jett.

JETT You look kinda – kinda tired?

JIM Do I?

JETT Yeah. You're feeling okay, aren't you?

JIM Yeah. I'm fine.

Pause.

JETT You want me to stay here and keep watching?

JIM Sure.

PLATO I suppose you blame me for this whole thing.

JIM Drop it!

PLATO It's not my fault you know.

JIM I said drop it!

Pause.

PLATO You can't be sure it was me they saw. You don't know that for sure.

Pause.

PLATO And if they did, I didn't mean it. I just went out there to cool off. It was too hot in here. Too smoky. I was frying. I had to cool off. I had to... (*He trails off*)

Judy and Abra enter.

ABRA Well, we did the best we could.

JIM Great.

Pause.

ABRA What now?

JIM I guess we wait and hope they bring the reporters.

JUDY They're not going to bring the reporters.

ABRA Shut up Judy.

JUDY They're not going to come.

JIM So leave.

JETT They're up on some of the other roofs now.

ABRA They're on the roofs?

JETT Yep. All around us.

ABRA Shit! (*To Plato*) You ruin everything you stupid asshole!

PLATO You can't blame it all on me.

ABRA Why not? It's all your fault!

PLATO It's not my fault! (*Pointing at Goldwyn*) It's his fault!

ABRA That's right. Always someone else's fault!

PLATO If it hadn't been for him and his stupid home we wouldn't be here right now.

ABRA Yeah, and if you hadn't been so goddamn stupid that last time we got busted none of us would've ever been in the home at all!

Pause.

CHRISTINE (*To Jett*) What's she talking about?

JETT They all got busted together one night. They were on this fire escape and Plato...

PLATO (*Cutting him off*) Shut up Jett!

ABRA Why the hell should he? I'll tell you. We were all on this fire escape, drinking and talking on Friday night. Well there was this lounge across the street and all these disco queens and their boyfriends came out. We were sorta drunk and we all got up and started yelling at them. You know, just being rude. Nothing really heavy. The disco people weren't even worried about it. They were just laughing. Lucy yelled something like "Fuck the draft." And I yelled "piss on the world."

PLATO Stop it Abra!

ABRA Shut up. Anyway, I yelled "Piss on the world" (*Indicates Plato*) And this jerk off did it. I mean, literally. He whipped it out and pissed down four floors to the street below.

Christine giggles.

ABRA Sure, it sounds funny now. And it was funny at the time. But one of the disco ladies didn't think it was such a riot and called the cops.

PLATO I was drunk.

JIM Yeah Plato, you're always drunk when you do something stupid, or stoned.

JUDY I wouldn't talk if I were you.

ABRA The cops got us for illegal possession, trespassing, public indecency and about four other things I can't remember.

CHRISTINE None of those things sound so bad to me.

ABRA They weren't that bad. Except for like we were all on probation already, and Jim and Cal had just scored a hundred lot of acid that night. And the cops found it.

CHRISTINE Oh.

JIM Two weeks later we were all in court.

ABRA And shortly thereafter we were in the home. But none of it was Plato's fault. Oh no! Not his!

PLATO I hate you!

ABRA Yeah? So what're you gonna do. Knife me? Strangle me? Or just fuck me up like you have everyone else?

PLATO Go to hell!

JETT Look at them, just standing up there like that. It's kinda scary.

JUDY I bet there are fifty guns aimed at us right now.

JETT Jim's going to get us through. I know he is. And us, we'll be like little heroes, for helping him out. You know...

ABRA Heroettes?

JETT That's right.

CHRISTINE I hope so Jett.

JETT You mean that?

CHRISTINE I didn't realize – I mean, you never told me. It must have been awful.

JETT It was.

CHRISTINE No one deserves to be treated like that.

JETT I know.

ABRA Maybe you're right Jett. Maybe we will come out of this thing alright.

JETT Sure. Just like in *Rebel Without a Cause*. Jim'll be James Dean and I'll be Sal Mineo. Now those guys were real heroes.

Lights change theatrically.

PLATO Marilyn Monroe.

JUDY John F. Kennedy.

JETT Jimi Hendrix.

JIM Judy Garland.

ABRA Jack Kerouac.

ALL Lenny Bruce. Janis Joplin. Billie Holliday. F. Scott Fitzgerald. Jim Morrison. Freddy Prinz. Edgar Allan Poe. Keith Moon. Peter Sellers. Neal Cassady. Brian Jones. Vincent van Gogh. John Lennon. (*Repeat*) Be a hero. Be a rebel. Live in a leather jacket. Die in a sports car. Do it today. It may not be there tomorrow. Live life like a book. Live life like a movie. Squeeze it in. Cram it in. Fill it in. Colour it in. Ram it in. Stick it in. Jam it in. Stuff it in. Breathe it in. Suck it in. Make every second. Make every minute. Make every hour. Make every day of every week of every year of every lifetime count. Make it count. Never stop running. Never stop looking. Never stop searching. Never stop trying. Never stop laughing. Never stop crying. There's more. Somewhere there's more. There's more than money. There's more than sleeping. More than conflict. More than hurt. More than loneliness and more than death. And more than... more than... Look for it. It's there. It's got to be there. There is more than this. There must be more than this. There is more than this. There must be more than this.

ABRA There is.

PLATO There must be.

JUDY It's there.

JETT It has to be.

JIM There must be more than this.

They all chant, "There is more than this. There must be more than this" as Jim speaks.

JIM There is more. Somewhere there is more. More than getting up for a school you hate every morning. More than parents who don't understand and cops watching every move you make. More than nine to five jobs that pay shit for money and crush any creativity that there might be. More than getting drunk every weekend and scrambling to be one of the gang and trying constantly to prove yourself. More than getting married and buying a condominium and having two point three children and more than starting to die at thirty. There is more than that. I know there is because if there's not then there's no reason for us to exist. No reason at all.

ABRA Pray for me mother.

JETT Pray for me father.

ABRA John Lennon.

JETT Vincent van Gogh.

JUDY Brian Jones.

PLATO Neal Cassady.

JIM Elvis Presley.

All (*Very fast*) Peter Sellers. Keith Moon. Edgar Allan Poe. Freddy Prinz. Jim Morrison. Billie Holliday. Janis Joplin. Lenny Bruce. Jack Kerouac. Judy Garland. Jimi Hendrix. Marilyn Monroe. Montgomery Clift. James Dean.

James Dean. James Dean. James Dean. Rock and Roll casualties. Live fast. Die young. Stay pretty. Live fast. Live fast. Die young. Live fast. Die young. Live fast. Die young. Live fast. Die. Live. Die. Live. Die. Die. Die. Die. (*Pause*) Heroes!

Lights return to normal.

LEFT to RIGHT: Judy (Darcia Parada), Abra (Kat Mullaly), Jim (Brian Rodomski), Plato (Phil Zyp) and Jett (Les Bland) speak in a Brechtian chorus moment. Upstage their kidnapped group home counselor Mr. Goldwyn (David Nattress) sits tied up while their friend Cal (Greg Dovell) grows worse on a bad acid trip in Mutants, *Jan–Feb 1981. Photo: Phil McCallum for Walterdale Theatre Associates.*

CHRISTINE But don't you want to grow up and get married and have babies and things?

ABRA Things I might be able to handle, but babies repulse me.

JUDY (*To Jim*) I'm sorry.

JIM So am I.

JUDY I didn't mean to ... I – I guess I just forgot one of my pills.

JIM Yeah.

JUDY Everyone makes mistakes.

JIM What're we going to do?

JUDY I'll have an abortion.

JIM I guess there's no other choice.

JUDY No.

JIM Do you know what to do. Who to see and all that?

JUDY Yeah.

JIM Good.

JUDY Yeah.

VOICE Jim! Jim!

JIM (*Going to ledge*) What?

VOICE Could we see Mr. Goldwyn?

JIM What for?

VOICE We just want to talk to him.

ABRA They want to make sure we haven't disemboweled him or anything.

JIM Yeah, I guess so. (*To Goldwyn*) You heard him. Get up.

Jim leads Goldwyn to the ledge and removes his gag.

VOICE Samuel Goldwyn?

GOLDWYN Yes?

VOICE You're alright?

GOLDWYN Yes. I'm – fine.

VOICE You haven't been hurt?

GOLDWYN No.

VOICE We're going to get you out of this.

GOLDWYN Good.

VOICE Don't hurt him, Jim.

JIM Then get the fucking reporters.

Jim takes Goldwyn away from the ledge and makes to put the gag back on.

GOLDWYN No.

JUDY They're not going to call those reporters Jim.

JIM They have to.

JUDY They've got all the guns. We've only got one. They don't have to do anything.

JIM You don't have to stick around you know.

JUDY I know.

JIM If you're so sure we're going to fail why haven't you left already?

JUDY (*Pause*) Because.

JIM You can leave if you want to.

ABRA You don't mean that?

JIM Look, none of you have to stay up here. I'll finish this thing alone if I have to.

JUDY Maybe we should just take Cal and leave. All of us.

JIM Cal stays with me.

JUDY You've always got to be the rock.

JIM Any of you want to go?

JETT (*To Jim*) I'm staying with you.

ABRA Judy, they'll just take us back to the home.

JUDY (*To Plato*) Looks like you were right. He's not so special.

PLATO Yeah?

JUDY You coming with me?

Pause.

JUDY Plato?

PLATO I – uh – I... (*He trails off*)

JUDY Plato?!

PLATO Judy, I'm the one who fucked this whole thing up. I can't run out now. I – I have to stick here.

JUDY You're as bad as the rest of them.

PLATO I'm sorry.

JUDY (*Indicating Christine*) Well what about her? There's no reason to keep her here now. You can let her go.

JETT That's right.

JIM Yeah Judy, she can go with you.

They untie Christine.

CHRISTINE Thank you.

JETT I'm real sorry about all this.

CHRISTINE (*Pause*) Be careful.

JETT I will.

Jett and Christine embrace.

JUDY Let's go.

JIM Judy...?

JUDY What?

JIM You – you don't have to do this.

JUDY I thought you didn't care.

JIM Look, I'm not very good at saying what I feel. I didn't mean for it to sound like that. I just... (*He trails off*)

JUDY Just what?

JIM Just don't know what to say.

JUDY You always know what to say to Cal.

Pause.

CHRISTINE (*To Jim*) You take good care of Jett.

JIM I will.

JUDY Let's go.

Judy and Christine exit.

CHRISTINE (*Turning suddenly*) I can't do it!

ABRA What?

JETT Chris?

CHRISTINE I can't just leave. Now that I know why you're doing this, I feel like I'm part of it. I can't just leave you like this Jett.

JETT Christine...?

CHRISTINE I've never in my life had to do something – you know – fight for something. I'm probably crazy. But I can't just walk out.

JUDY You'll go to jail just like the rest of them.

JETT She's right Chris.

CHRISTINE Only if it fails. And I don't think it will. (*To Jim*) I want to stay with you Jett.

JUDY You're crazy.

CHRISTINE Jett's been my best friend for years. I want to stay with him.

JUDY Suit yourself.

Judy exits. Pause.

PLATO Jim?

JIM What?

PLATO I'm sorry.

JIM I know.

PLATO It's just that sometimes – you know?

JIM Sure.

PLATO I don't know why I do things like that. (*Pause*) I guess ... fuck! I don't know I'm just sorry.

JIM It's okay.

PLATO I want to be your friend again.

JIM Okay.

JETT (*At window*) My father's down there!

ABRA Where?

PLATO Right there. Beside the car.

ABRA And there's my parents. I don't believe it! (*Calling down*) Hi Ma, ya old wazoo!

JIM Cut it out Abra.

ABRA Sorry. (*Going to Jim*) I don't believe Judy really walked out on us like that.

JIM Neither do I.

ABRA Pregnant. Wow!

JIM Yeah. Wow.

ABRA I don't think she understands you very well.

JIM You're right.

ABRA It bothers her just about as much as it bothers you.

JIM It just gets in the way.

ABRA I guess it's not just something you can control.

JIM No, it's not.

ABRA I'm glad I've never loved anybody.

JIM Yeah. (*Going to ledge*) Hey! Hey down there!

VOICE What is it Jim?

JIM Where the hell are those reporters?

VOICE They're on their way.

JIM It's been too long.

VOICE We had to get most of them out of bed. They're coming.

JIM Well hurry it up.

GOLDWYN It's not working Jim.

PLATO Shut up, or we'll gag you again.

Judy enters.

JUDY I just couldn't.

PLATO Why'd you come back?

JUDY (*Quietly*) Because.

PLATO Because why?

JUDY Just because!

ABRA Great! I know what we'll do now that we're all back together.

JETT What?

ABRA When this whole thing is over, we'll all move to Saskatchewan and start our own commune. You guys can work out in the fields, growing brown rice and whole wheat and us girls can stay in the house and macramé cars and pigs and stuff. Then Judy can have her baby and name it something like Cranberry or Alfalfa or Rover and we'll all raise it. And we can put a sun porch just off the kitchen for Cal and Jim can go scrape moss offa his north side once a week.

CHRISTINE Sounds great to me.

ABRA I don't remember inviting you.

CHRISTINE Oh.

JIM I don't want to be a father.

JUDY You don't have to be. I already told you. I'm not having the fucking thing!

JIM There's nothing else we can do.

JUDY Guess not.

JIM What do you want me to do? Marry you? Get a job?

JUDY I'm not asking you to do anything.

Pause.

GOLDWYN You know Jim...

JIM What?

GOLDWYN You haven't hurt anyone yet. Except for escaping from the home you haven't really done anything wrong. If you let me go now, if you give yourselves up, I'll put in a good word for you all. I'll make sure you don't go anywhere but back to the home. And those guards, you won't have to worry about them anymore either. I'll make sure charges are brought against them. We'll work things out. You might have to spend a little more time in the home, but after that you'll be free to go.

JIM That's a great offer. But what are the conditions?

PLATO Conditions?

GOLDWYN Yes. I want you all to promise me that you won't say anything about the guards to the media.

ABRA Aha!

GOLDWYN We're a provincial institution. Funding is bad enough as it is. If people were to find out about that – well the bad publicity could ruin us.

JUDY Not to mention you'd probably lose your job huh?

GOLDWYN That's not important. If people find out about this thing they could well close us down. And if they did that there would be no place for people like you.

JIM And how would you make sure the guards were punished if you don't want to tell anyone about what they've done?

GOLDWYN We could take care of that privately. There's no use making a big stink about it anyway.

ABRA And what about Lucy Jordan?

PLATO That's right.

GOLDWYN What happened to Lucy was very unfortunate...

JUDY Very unfortunate?!

GOLDWYN But it's already been looked into. There's not much more that I can do.

JIM There it is. He can't do anything about Lucy, and he can't really do anything about the guards, but he can take us back to the home and make us healthy, productive members of society.

ABRA No doubt.

JIM In a year or so we can all get out of the home, and get jobs and get married, and never break the law again.

JETT No more guns.

PLATO No more fire escapes.

JIM No more drugs.

ABRA But a clean record and lots of security.

JUDY And we won't have to think about Lucy Jordan anymore.

PLATO Or getting fucked up the ass by a guard with whiskey on his breath.

JETT Or being beaten with the buckle of a belt.

JIM All we have to do is keep our mouths shut and watch out step. Now guys, what do you say to that?

Pause. They all turn their backs to Goldwyn.

JIM Thank you.

GOLDWYN You're all going to be sorry for this.

JIM Plato, gag him again.

Plato puts the gag back on.

PLATO (*To Judy*) I'm sorry I couldn't leave with you.

JUDY It doesn't matter.

CAL Rub a dub dub...

JIM (*To Cal*) Cal?

ABRA I wish he'd talk to us again.

PLATO You always say that.

JUDY What?

PLATO It doesn't matter.

JUDY Oh.

PLATO But things always do matter.

JUDY I guess I want them to stop mattering.

PLATO I know that feeling.

JUDY If there was just some way you could turn your feelings off. Like Cal did.

PLATO Do you think he did that?

JUDY Sure.

PLATO You're really going to have an abortion huh?

JUDY Guess so.

PLATO That doesn't bother you?

JUDY Should it?

PLATO It would bother some people.

JUDY Not Jim.

ABRA He has – trouble with girlfriends.

JUDY But how can he – not like me as much as I like him?

ABRA Some people are like that.

JETT Jim likes everyone equally I think.

JUDY Everyone but Cal.

JUDY But I tried to give him – so much.

PLATO Maybe you gave it too easily.

JUDY Huh?

ABRA I think I know what he means. Sometimes, nothing makes a person more uncomfortable than someone liking them too much.

JETT I don't like it when people like me as much as I like them, either. I get real suspicious when that happens.

PLATO I think I can sorta understand that.

JUDY Well I don't.

ABRA He loves you too Judy. He kinda loves all of us.

JETT There's nothing wrong with that.

ABRA You're one of his friends he slept with.

JETT I slept with him?

JUDY What?

CHRISTINE You did?

JETT Yeah. But there was no sex. One night, after the guards came to my room, I was pretty upset. Jim came and got me and took me to his room. And I slept with him. That's all. It made me feel – safe.

JUDY I just hoped...

ABRA That you were getting a little more from him than the rest of us?

JUDY Yes.

ABRA You're his friend. Is that so bad?

JUDY I've always wanted to be special to someone. Really special. My sister, Darlene, I was special to her. She looked out for me. And after she died, Lucy looked out for me. I wanted Jim to be like that. I need someone to look out for me.

JETT Jim looks out for all of us.

PLATO How did your sister die?

JUDY Overdose.

JETT Smack?

ABRA Heroin's pretty heavy shit.

JUDY But I lost her, and I lost Lucy, and the way it's going, I could lose Jim too.

ABRA Don't you worry. Jim's going to get us out of this.

CAL Rub a dub dub. Three men in a tub. And who do you think they be?
The butcher, the baker and the candlestick maker and they all... they all...

JIM Not looking too good buddy. I think they're fucking with us Cal.

JUDY Jim?

JIM Yeah?

JUDY You've done the best you can.

JIM Don't start talking like it's all over yet.

JUDY I didn't mean...

JIM It's okay.

JUDY We can't say anything without one of us taking it the wrong way.

JIM I guess not.

Pause.

ABRA Young love, ain't it wonderful.

JETT She wants to marry him, doesn't she?

PLATO Sure.

ABRA The girl's crazy.

CHRISTINE Don't you ever want to get married?

ABRA Me? No way.

CHRISTINE Why not?

ABRA Too boring. I'm a real slut.

JETT Oh Abra, you are not.

ABRA I am so. Deep down.

PLATO Me too.

JETT (*To Plato*) How about you? You ever want to get married?

PLATO Naw.

ABRA (*Referring to Judy*) I think she made the right decision about not wanting to have this baby.

CHRISTINE Why?

ABRA After all the drugs Jim's done, who knows what she'd give birth to.

PLATO It could be anything.

ABRA Like an eight pound four ounce foot.

JETT Mutant children. How scary.

CHRISTINE Does that really happen?

ABRA I don't think so.

PLATO I know a lot of people who've done a lot of drugs. Real heavy shit. And their kids all turned out fine. Big. Healthy.

ABRA Able to lift things with their minds.

JETT Those reporters are taking an awful long time.

JIM They've got an ambulance down there now.

ABRA An ambulance? What for?

PLATO There's a fire truck too.

JETT They always call in ambulances and fire trucks. Don't you guys ever watch TV?

JIM Maybe we should pack it in.

CHRISTINE You can't just give up now.

JIM If the reporters were going to be here they would've arrived by now.

ABRA Maybe the reporters don't care.

JIM I guess we aren't as smart as we thought we were.

CHRISTINE I have – oh forget it.

JIM What?

CHRISTINE I had an idea. But it's dumb.

JETT What is it?

CHRISTINE It'd never work.

JIM Let's hear it.

ABRA Yeah. At this point I don't think we can get too fussy.

CHRISTINE Well I don't think it's very good. But this is it. What if I were to go down there and tell the cops that you guys made me come up here. You know, like your prisoner or something. Then maybe they'd take me home. I'd pretend to be real upset so they had to take me home, and I'd call the reporters for you.

JETT That's a great idea.

CHRISTINE You really think so?

JIM Sure.

JETT You'd do that for us Christine?

CHRISTINE Yes. I mean – I'm sort of part of this thing aren't I?

JIM Let's do it then.

CHRISTINE Okay.

JUDY Good luck.

CHRISTINE Thanks.

JETT Be careful Chris.

CHRISTINE I will.

Christine exits.

ABRA Now there goes one hell of a woman.

JIM We're gonna make it Cal.

JUDY Jim, have you ever stopped to consider that maybe Cal really is burnt out and's going to stay that way permanently?

JIM No Judy. I've never considered that.

JUDY It's a possibility.

JIM No. It isn't.

ABRA Judy might be right Jim.

JIM No. She's not. I know Cal. I know what he's doing. He can't keep it up forever.

JETT What do you mean?

JIM You wouldn't understand.

ABRA We knew Cal too Jim.

JIM Not like I did. There are things none of you knew.

JUDY Like the fight on the fire escape?

JETT (*At ledge*) I hope Chris is alright.

JIM What about the fight on the fire escape?

JUDY Wasn't it just after that that Cal did all that acid?

JIM How did you know about that?

JUDY You told me. Remember?

JIM No.

JUDY Don't you remember the night you came to my place. Drunk out of your mind? You cried on my shoulder all night long.

JIM And I told you about that?

JUDY Yes.

Pause.

ABRA What fight?

JIM It doesn't matter.

JUDY You can't feel guilty for the rest of your life Jim.

JIM I didn't mean to ...

PLATO To what? I thought Cal just went out and did lots of drugs one night.

JUDY No. There was a reason.

ABRA What reason? Jim, you never told me about any of this.

JETT Jim doesn't have to tell us if he doesn't want to.

JIM I was so tired.

JUDY No one blames you for that.

JIM It wasn't fun anymore.

JUDY We'll understand.

ABRA Understand what?

JIM You can't run forever. It all catches up with you, eventually.

ABRA What did you do?

JIM I told him to get the fuck out of my life.

Pause.

JIM After that last time we got busted, when we were waiting to go to court, I told him to meet me on the fire escape one night. Then I told him I couldn't do it anymore.

ABRA You said that – to Cal?

JIM He didn't understand at first. He thought I was joking or something. I said, I'm sorry Cal, but it's stupid. Then he got mad, called me a pussy. Said I was selling out. He told me I was a chickenshit. That I didn't have the guts to enjoy myself, to really live. I told him he was a...

CAL Thunder?

JIM Fuck up. I called him a fuck up and took off!

Pause.

JIM Two days later his mother called me. Said Cal was in the hospital. Some kind of overdose. The doctors said he'd recovered fine, physically. But something had happened. To his head.

Pause.

JIM Even his mother said it was my fault.

PLATO You did what you thought you had to do.

JIM I should've known what he would do.

JUDY No one knows anyone that well.

JIM Cal and I did.

CAL Thunder.

JIM (*Going to him*) Cal?

Jim and Cal are singled out. The others all disappear into the darkness.

JIM Cal? I'm running out of time. Why the fuck do I always let people down? I don't know. I've got to talk to you Cal. Cal? Cal? (*Jim pulls Cal to a standing position and slaps him across the face*) Prick! (*Jim slaps him again*) You're dead meat! (*Slapping him again*) You stupid son of a bitch! You fucking asshole! You goddamn fucking stupid...

Jim pushes Cal away angrily.

JIM I'm too tired. I-need-you-Cal.

Pause. Slowly Cal begins to rise. Cal changes slowly to the person he once was. He walks to Jim, who doesn't see him at first.

CAL Jim.

JIM Cal?

CAL Yes.

JIM I don't believe it.

CAL It's true.

JIM But Cal...

CAL You said you needed me.

JIM I need to talk to you.

CAL So talk.

JIM I'm not sure what to say.

Pause.

JIM I've – I've missed you.

CAL Yeah?

JIM Yes. (*Pause*) Have – have you missed me?

CAL I don't miss anything Jim.

JIM What?

CAL I don't miss anything anymore.

JIM That's not like you.

CAL I'm not like I used to be.

JIM I don't understand.

CAL I don't expect you to. What did you want to talk to me about Jim?

JIM Everything. All the thing's you've missed. All the things that've been happening.

CAL I know what's been happening.

JIM You do?

CAL Yes.

JIM But how...?

CAL I'm still aware of what's happening. I just don't let it matter to me anymore.

JIM Nothing matters to you anymore?

CAL No.

JIM I don't believe that.

CAL I don't expect you to.

JIM Judy's pregnant.

CAL Yes.

JIM I don't know what to do.

CAL Neither do I.

JIM I'm not ready.

CAL Is anyone ever ready?

JIM And the cops are down there. I don't think they're going to bring the reporters.

CAL Of course they're not.

JIM You believe that too?

CAL They always win.

JIM No. No they don't.

CAL Oh yes, they do.

JIM They can't.

CAL They will.

JIM Don't say that.

Pause.

JIM I wasn't selling out. I was just – tired.

CAL Tired?

JIM Sick.

CAL Fed up?

JIM Yes.

CAL Scared?

JIM No.

CAL Scared!

JIM Alright then. Scared. I just wanted to stop it for a while. Slow it down.

CAL Slow it down?

JIM We were burning ourselves out.

CAL We were living!

JIM We were dying!

Pause.

CAL Dying isn't so bad, if you live right.

JIM I want to live.

CAL Live or exist?

JIM Live. But there's got to be a medium somewhere. An in between ground.

CAL Sure. Mediocrity.

JIM And are you any better? You're dead. Or as good as dead.

CAL I'm safe.

JIM Safe? You're a fucking vegetable!

CAL I don't hurt like you do. Not anymore.

JIM You can't live if you don't hurt.

CAL I'm tired of being hurt.

JIM It wasn't the drugs at all. Was it?

CAL They helped.

JIM You just – stopped.

CAL Yes.

JIM How can you do that?

CAL It wasn't so hard.

JIM And you tell me I don't know how to live?

CAL I know what I've done. I'm weak. I admit it. I'm just as weak as you are.

JIM We were strong when we were together.

CAL Yes.

JIM We can be strong again Cal. Together. We can get all of us out of this thing.

CAL No.

JIM Why not?

CAL I don't know anymore.

JIM You're still mad at me.

CAL I don't feel anything anymore.

JIM That's worse than being dead!

CAL Only in your mind.

JIM Why didn't you just take a razor and slice your wrists? Why didn't you run your car off a bridge? Why didn't you die? Do the job right? Any of those things would've been easier for both of us. Why didn't you just die?

CAL I used to think you were different. That you knew.

JIM Knew what?

CAL The things I knew.

JIM But I did know.

CAL I thought you knew about living. About turning on the night and going underground and taking everything that was offered. Because experience is the only lasting thing in this fucked up world today. I thought you knew about being friends and remaining safe from everyone else. I really thought you knew.

JIM Come back. I'll make it this time. I'll know. I'll live. Just come back to me.

CAL I can't.

JIM Why not?

CAL Because – because, I won't be hurt again. By anyone. Not ever again.

JIM I won't hurt you!

CAL You have to.

JIM Why?

CAL Because you're my friend!

Pause.

JIM Please.

CAL No. (*Pause*) You're going to fail.

JIM You've got as much to lose as any of us.

CAL You forget. They've decided I'm no longer responsible for my own actions.

JIM You bastard!

CAL I'll survive.

JIM I hate you.

CAL You can come with me Jim.

JIM Never.

CAL It's not such a bad place.

JIM You're insane!

CAL And it's not hard to get there.

JIM Not in a million years.

CAL And you won't be hurt. Ever again.

JIM Fuck you!

CAL It's very warm, and it's very nice. And no one gets in unless you want them to. (*Cal returns to his childlike state*) It's soft and warm and nice. Nice Jim. It's very very nice.

JIM Cal? Cal?

Sudden pandemonium from outside. Horns going off. Many voices yelling. Lights return to normal. The others return.

VOICE Come back! Come back here! Someone stop her!

ABRA What is it?

PLATO What's going on?

JIM I don't know. They're sure excited down there.

Sound of someone running up the stairs. Christine bursts in, very out of breath.

JETT Chris.

JIM What happened?

CHRISTINE Those bastards!

ABRA What happened?

CHRISTINE They wouldn't even take me home. They thought I was involved in this somehow. They were going to make me sit in that car until they got you guys.

ABRA Got us guys?

CHRISTINE Look at the roof of that building over there!

JIM Holy Jesus.

JETT What is it?

CHRISTINE It looks like a whole goddamn SWAT team.

ABRA Oboy!

CHRISTINE They've got them up on every roof that faces this place.

JUDY Goldwyn was right. They're never going to let us out of here.

Pause.

VOICE We're losing patience, Jim.

PLATO Those assholes.

ABRA What'll we do now Jim?

JETT Jim?

JIM I don't fucking know!

PLATO Look at them up there. Looking down on us.

JETT (*Taking gun out*) Maybe we should load this now.

PLATO It's so goddamn hot in here.

ABRA One gun? What the hell will we do with one stupid gun?

JIM We're so close.

JETT Jim, should we load it?

JIM Let me think a minute.

PLATO They're going to kill us. They're going to shoot our fucking brains out.

JUDY Plato?

JIM I don't know what to do.

PLATO Assholes! Assholes!

JUDY Plato, are you okay?

Plato sudden rushes at Jett and takes the gun away from him.

PLATO Assholes!

JETT Plato!

Plato rushes to the window, brandishing the gun wildly.

PLATO Bastards! Goddamn fucking bastards! You can't win. We're right! We're the ones who are supposed to win! You can't get us! We've tried too hard!

JUDY Plato!

JETT Get down from there!

PLATO I should blow your fucking brains out! I should kill every one of you!

JUDY Plato, put the gun down. They'll...

Pandemonium. Plato continues to rant at the cops. The others try to talk him down. The Voice calls out "Hold your fire. Don't shoot." Jett rushes Plato to get the gun away. Plato and Jett fight for possession of the gun on the ledge. Judy and Abra scream. Jett gets the gun. A shot rings out. Plato and Jett waiver on the ledge. Jett falls dead. Christine screams.

CHRISTINE Jett?!

JIM Jett?

CHRISTINE Jett, get up.

JIM C'mon buddy. Get up.

Abra goes to Christine and holds her.

CHRISTINE No! No!

Jim goes to Jett and cradles his head in his arms.

JIM Why him? Why did it have to be him?

CHRISTINE (*To Jim*) This is your fault! It's all your fault! He respected you! You were his hero!

JIM Please, don't say that.

CHRISTINE All he wanted to do was be your friend. He – he said he loved you.

JIM Don't say that.

ABRA (*Gently, to Christine*) Leave him.

JIM Please...

PLATO We're finished.

JIM Not quite.

Jim begins to load the gun.

JUDY Jim?

JIM Not quite.

JUDY What are you doing?

JIM Don't touch me.

Jim stands and aims the gun and Goldwyn.

JIM Someone stand him up.

Goldwyn rises on his own.

ABRA Jim don't...

JIM Jett's dead.

JUDY Killing Goldwyn won't accomplish anything.

JIM We're all dead anyway.

JUDY It's murder. You'll lose everything Jim.

PLATO Don't do it Jim.

JIM (*Aiming the gun at Goldwyn's head*) For Jett.

CHRISTINE It's not for Jett, and you know it!

JIM And Lucy Jordan.

JUDY No!

JIM And for Cal.

PLATO No!

Jim pulls the trigger. There is a loud gunshot. The lights go red. Goldwyn falls, dead. The others scream and twist in pain.

JIM (*Dropping the gun*) Now we're even.

The others rise. Lights return to normal.

ABRA Jim.

PLATO Jim.

JUDY Jim.

CHRISTINE Jim.

JIM Keep away.

The lights change, they get dim and ghostlike. They will stay like this until the end of the play.

VOICE Jim...

ABRA Jim?

JIM Don't any of you come near me.

VOICE Can you hear me in there?

JUDY Jim?

JIM Just-leave-me-alone.

VOICE Was that a shot?

JUDY What's wrong with you?

JIM Cal?

CAL (*Rising*) I hear you.

VOICE Jim, anyone – talk to me.

JIM I'm caught Cal.

JUDY Jim?

CAL It's not so hard.

JUDY You look so...

CAL Jim?

JUDY Strange.

CAL It's warm.

JUDY Like...

CAL It's nice.

JUDY Like Cal.

CAL And no one can hurt you.

JUDY You look just like Cal!

CAL Come.

JUDY Jim, no.

CAL Come into my house.

The others begin to move about the stage. They do bits and pieces of their monologues and dialogue. Judy and Cal stand on either side of Jim.

JUDY Don't escape Jim. You can still make it.

CAL It's not hard Jim. It's not hard at all.

JUDY I'm having your baby.

PLATO Jim?

CAL Just let go.

JIM Judy?

JUDY Jim?

JIM Cal?

CAL Jim.

ABRA Don't go.

The others stop moving around. They stand in place and continue to do their monologues without making a sound.

JIM I – I don't know.

CAL It's warm.

JUDY You can't escape everything.

CAL No responsibilities.

JUDY You have to face life.

CAL No feelings.

CHRISTINE Stay.

JIM I'm so sorry Jett.

JUDY I need you.

CAL Come Jim.

JUDY I love you.

CAL Join me.

JUDY You don't have to be alone.

CAL It's not hard Jim.

JUDY Jim.

CAL Just let go.

JUDY Jim?

CAL Just let go.

JIM I...

Jim walks to Cal.

JUDY Jim. Please.

JIM What – what do I do?

CAL Sit. Here. Beside me.

JIM Sit.

They sit.

CAL Now rock.

JIM Rock.

They rock.

CAL In my house.

JIM In my house.

CAL It's very warm.

JIM It's very warm.

CAL Very nice.

JIM Very very very nice.

The light on Jim and Cal fades very slowly as they continue to rock. The sound of the sirens and the flashing of the red light fade with the main lights until all is black.

LEFT: Jim's (Brian Rodomski) magnetism draws in Judy (Darcia Parada) as their kidnapped group home counselor Mr. Goldwyn (David Nattress) looks on helplessly. Photo: Phil McCallum for Walterdale Theatre Associates.

BELOW: Cast and crew for Mutants. *BACK ROW (Left to Right): Greg Dovell (Cal), Brian Rodomski (Jim), David Nattress (Goldwyn), Tony Dawkins (lights). SECOND ROW (Left to Right): Tim Preston (hairstylist), Phil Zyp (Plato), Kat Mullaly (Abra), Keven Smith (Off-stage voice of Cop), Les Bland (Jett), Deb Preston (Stage Manager). FRONT ROW (Left to Right): Collette Hebert (Christine), Brad Fraser (playwright, director), Darcia Parada (Judy).Photo: Phil McCallum for Walterdale Theatre Associates.*

Swipe (1981)
by Gordon Pengilly

> Gordon is one of those Canadian playwriting treasures insufficiently recognized in this country.
>
> ~ PLAYWRIGHT SHARON POLLOCK QUOTED IN HUNT

It is difficult to disagree with theatre historian E. Ross Stuart's assessment of Gordon Pengilly's critically acclaimed *Swipe*, a play that explores blind faith and its value to humanity. In Canadian theatre, Stuart notes, a fantasy play, particularly one set on a run-down Mississippi riverboat, is an "oddity" (Stuart 235). Indeed, Ron Wigmore—longtime Walterdale member and member of the selection committee that awarded Pengilly's play top spot in the company's 1980/81 national playwriting competition—anticipated Stuart's assessment by offering context from among the sixty-three other plays submitted to the competition: "We had Women's Lib themes, peace-in-our-time plays, parents trying to cope with disabled children, two or three very competent little comedies.[...] In terms of language, subject matter, structure [*Swipe*] was a sheer delight to read" (quoted in Ashwell, "Winner"). It was also a delight to watch. The *Edmonton Journal* called it a "marvelously lusty flight of fancy [...]. The play is escapist, absurdist... and absolutely entertaining. [T]he superbly mysterious and evocative set by Phil Switzer and the electric direction by Larry Farley could not be more professional" (Ashwell, "Flight"). The success of Pengilly's "tragicomic fantasy" at the Walterdale competition provides food for thought in the context of a Canadian theatre atmosphere that teems with politically topical new plays. That it succeeded within the structure of a national writing competition is indicative of the way theatre has been nurtured in Canada.

The maturation myth that has come to define the "growth" of theatre in Canada from birth to adolescence to maturity—akin to what scholar Alan Filewod has called the "anthropomorphism" of Canadian nationalism (62)—has been nursed, in no small part, by competitions and awards variously arranged at the regional, provincial, and national levels. From the Musical and Dramatic Competition (1907–11) initiated by competitive rugby fan and ninth governor general of Canada Earl Grey, to the forty-year landmark Dominion Drama Festival (1932–71), to contemporary regional theatre awards such as the Elizabeth Sterling Haynes Awards in Edmonton, the Betty Mitchell Awards in Calgary, and the Dora Mavor Moore Awards in Toronto, Canadian theatre practices, both amateur and professional, have been built from above by rewarding notable plays that satisfy diverse criteria with any combination of trophies, money, or first or further production. Competitions serve three important public purposes: they celebrate the "best" among eligible entries, they celebrate all constitutive entries by proclaiming (implicitly or explicitly) the strength of the field, and they celebrate the population and the geography from which the entries originate. Yet ironically, by awarding *Swipe* a top national prize, Walterdale's committee eschewed political topicality for more fantastical themes.

Walterdale's playwriting contest was local in funding, provincial in name, and national in range. In the spring of 1980 Walterdale applied for and received $8,500 from the City of Edmonton to organize, adjudicate, and award a prize for the best full-length play in a national playwriting competition to be held in honour of Alberta's 75th anniversary.[33] Over the course of ten months between April 1980 and February 1981 a selection committee of notable Walterdale members Ron Wigmore, Troy Sprenke, Frank Glenfield, and artistic director Vivien Bosley was organized, contest criteria set, and a national press release dispersed. The winning entry would receive $1,500 and a full production as the last show of Walterdale's 1980/81 season, with Wigmore slated to direct it.[34] During the fall of 1980, while Walterdale's board was dealing with controversies related to its season productions of *Zastrozzi* and *Mutants*, the subcommittee was preparing to choose the winner of the new play competition. Diverse scripts from across Canada had poured in, and by November sixty-four entries were ready to be distributed for blind adjudication. *Swipe*, then titled *The Apprentice of Swipe*, eventually emerged as the selection committee's unanimous favourite.

Along with Brad Fraser's play and the second Walterdale production of Warren Graves's *The Mumberly Inheritance*, *Swipe* was one of three plays written by Albertans to be staged at Walterdale during that provincial commemorative season, and it already had an extensive history. The play was conceived as a 1978 Alberta Theatre Projects commission titled *Rooster and the Captain*, which "fell through for 'political' reasons" (Ashwell, "Winner"). Pengilly rewrote it at the Banff Playwrights Colony in 1979 as *The Apprentice of Swipe*. It then underwent a three-day Workshop West workshop in 1980 (while he was playwright-in-residence and a board member there) before winning the Walterdale competition. At the time it represented a turning point in Pengilly's writing. As he entered his late twenties with *Swipe*, he moved from darker writing to what he called "a new whimsy" (quoted in Ashwell, "Winner"). It was yet another success in Pengilly's impressive oeuvre.

Award-winning playwright and theatre advocate Gordon Pengilly was born in Lethbridge in 1953 and raised on a farm south of there. Throughout the 1970s he lived in Edmonton, finishing a BA in drama at the University of Alberta in 1975, followed by an MFA in playwriting in 1978, the first person to receive that degree at the U. of A.

He has written over fifty works for the stage, radio, television, and film and has won a dozen provincial, national, and international playwriting competitions, including a 2007 BBC International Radio Playwriting award for *Seeing in the Dark* (out of 1,200 entries) and a number of screenwriting awards, including the Writers Guild of Canada Jim Burt Prize for screenwriting for *Drumheller or Dangerous Times* (2003).[35] He has been playwright-in-residence and associate playwright at a number of theatre companies across Canada, including Workshop West Theatre, Northern Light Theatre, Theatre Network, Theatre Calgary, Theatre New Brunswick, and the Banff Centre for the Arts, as well as theatres in Red Deer and Toronto. His contribution to Alberta writing at the time of and following Walterdale's production of *Swipe* is remarkable: instructor for a number of playwriting workshops across Alberta (sponsored by Alberta Playwrights' Network, Workshop West Theatre, Theatre Calgary, and Alberta Culture), reading staff at The Citadel Theatre and the CBC, editor of *Dandelion Magazine*, and dramaturge for Alberta Playwrights' Network. His plays have been produced internationally in New York, Los Angeles, Philadelphia, Holland, Germany, Japan, and Australia.[36] Today he lives in Calgary.

Though it appeared in the same remarkable season as plays by Fraser and George F. Walker, *Swipe* shares none of their edgy controversies. Years later, Pengilly described his play as "highly poetic. It's nearly written in a kind of meter form. And it's set in a kind of ether zone, which means that it's not in any recognizable place, it's sort of a place in someone's head, if you like.[...] It has spoken songs in it, several of them, and otherwise it's very consciously rhythmic" (Pengilly).[37] The philosophical fantasy play is set in a lagoon where the paddlewheel steamer *Empress* lies wrecked. Chief thief Peck Woodstick rules over the other tramps and his young apprentice Rooster. When Peck reports that their mystical old friend Clancy will finally return from the stars to bring them all "transcendence," expectations mount until Peck is exposed for the liar that he is. After the tramps deal with Peck in revenge for his deception, Rooster rekindles Clancy's legend and keeps the myth alive.

Swipe opened as *The Apprentice of Swipe* May 19–30, 1981, at Walterdale Playhouse (firehall) with the following cast and creative team:

GUPPY	Pierre Lafontain
DUKE	Bob Brophy
WORM	Troy Sprenke
PECK WOODSTICK	Frank Glenfield
ROOSTER	Jim Farley
BECKY	Bethany Ellis
TINKER	*not in Walterdale premiere*
DIRECTOR	Larry Farley
SET DESIGNER	Phil Switzer
LIGHTING DESIGNER	Luciano Iogna

COSTUME DESIGNER	Jackie Bland and Phil Switzer
PROPERTIES	Larry Lawson
SOUND	J.E. Lyszkiewicz and Carla Nolan
STAGE MANAGER	Larry Savage
PRODUCER	Ron Wigmore

Swipe then ran December 5, 1981, to January 5, 1982, at Toronto Free Theatre, produced by the NDWT Company, with the following cast and creative team:

DUKE	Patrick Sinclair
WORM	Kay Hawtrey
GUPPY, TINKER	Jerry Franken
PECK WOODSTICK	David Fox
BECKY	Denise Naples
ROOSTER	James Crammond

DIRECTOR	Keith Turnbull
MUSIC	Patrick Godfrey
SET DESIGNER	Sue LePage
COSTUME DESIGNER	Ingrid Hamster
LIGHTING	Robert Thomson
STAGE MANAGER	Susan Monis

Swipe was also produced at the University of Lethbridge February 9–17, 1990, with the following cast and creative team:

DUKE	Jim Wright
WORM	Michelle Fuller
GUPPY	Roger Hamm
PECK WOODSTICK	Tom Gillespie
BECKY	Tammy Kovacs
ROOSTER	Brad Erickson
TINKER	Ron Christensen

DIRECTOR	Ches Skinner
MUSIC COMPOSER	Lael Johnston
SET, COSTUME, AND LIGHTING DESIGN	Terry A. Bennett
SOUND DESIGN	Neil Sheets and Lael Johnston
STAGE MANAGER	Tracy Cook

Swipe was previously published in Denis Salter, ed., *New Canadian Drama 3: Albertan Dramatists* (Ottawa: Borealis, 1984). The author has since reworked the play into the present version.

Swipe
by Gordon Pengilly

Characters
GUPPY, DUKE, WORM — *The aging lagoon tramps*
PECK WOODSTICK, *An old tramp with a captain's hat, a bum leg, and a wooden stick*
ROOSTER, *A young tramp with fiery-red hair, Peck's apprentice of swipe*
BECKY, *A young runaway*
TINKER, *An old, blind tinkerman*

Setting Evening in the thick of a blue-dark lagoon.

Note An act break can be inserted after Becky's cry for police.

"Hope never leaves a wretched man that seeks her."
~ BEAUMONT AND FLETCHER, *THE CAPTAIN*

Rooster (Jim Farley) petitions Peck Woodstick (Frank Glenfield) as Becky (Bethany Ellis) looks on in Gordon Pengilly's Swipe *(produced at Walterdale as* The Apprentice of Swipe*), May 1981. Photo: C.W. Hill Photography for Walterdale Theatre Associates.*

An old paddle wheel steamer, christened "Empress," sits wrecked in a blue-dark lagoon surrounded by bramble. It is heeled and sunk in mud and weed such that the lower deck is nearly at ground level. A ribbed plank bridges the deck to the ground. A rickety ladder leads up to the hurricane deck and steering station. The paddle wheel rests forlornly in the lagoon. The Empress is a portrait of heartbreak – so weathered, worn and rotting.

It is evening. A ribbon of red sky will gradually give way to nightfall and storm clouds.

Three old river Tramps, two men and a woman, are standing together in the mud beside the boat gazing into the sky.

DUKE We are the tramps of this lagoon.

WORM Our time is sworn to come.

GUPPY If fiddles were pickles...

DUKE And pillage were ham...

WORM This legend would fit inna bun.

DUKE Once upon a timeless moon
the moon picked a partner.
A golden bolt of moonlightning
poked its hot finger
into the green eye of Clancy Dougal
and evaporated him into thin air.
Such wuz the fate of Clancy Dougal
Fer nobuddy's seen him since.

GUPPY Oh, there was magic in that tramp.

WORM He come and took over the wheel.

DUKE He danced and he fiddled...

GUPPY That put lumps in your guff...

DUKE And he stole like a breeze picked dandelion fluff.

WORM Then one day Clancy hadda vision.
Said his time had come
to shake this old lagoon.

So the cap'n of thiefs he went to the moon.
He got there by the jam of his blazin' fiddle
and said someday he'd return
with revelation and inspired blueprints
to gather his brotherly crew.

GUPPY He promised to raise the old Empress outa the mud...

DUKE And spin a course for the starry blue!

TOGETHER (*Rapturously*) AAAHHHH!

Pause. Duke looks askance at Guppy.

DUKE Psst. Hey, Guppy, speak up. It's yer turn, ain't it?

GUPPY Aw, go on without me, Duke. I gotta bone in my guffer.

DUKE Like hell you do! You forgot the words again!

GUPPY Well, just between you and me and the slapped-ass of the settin' sun, I'll remember again when I see Clancy fiddle back down with a sackful of universal secrets. In person! I'm get tired of those plain old words. Fifteen years of hanging on tender hooks and I ain't the man I used to be.

WORM Have hope, old boy. Can't be long now.

GUPPY Hope schmoke! Look at me! My hands are both thumbs, my fast tail is frozen-like, and my bum's gettin' so baggy I can barely crawl outa bed and go to work in the morning. I ain't pilched a pocket in three weeks. Have you?

DUKE I've had the flu.

WORM I sprained my ankle.

GUPPY Damn! See what I mean? We're all gettin' crotchety waitin' fer Clancy. Countin' Peck Woodstick and young Rooster we're the last tramps in the whole lagoon. The rest've all died off. Charlie, Tinker, Palimino, Turdface—they all took those crummy words to their muddy graves.

DUKE May they rest in peace.

WORM Ditto.

GUPPY And tomorry it might be me! Why just yesterday I strolled straight inta Ernie's Snake Pit. Now I ain't never done that before. I been pickin' coily creatures outa my wardrobe ever since. I can't hang on forever, Duke. I gotta case of creepin' senility and it scares the hell outa me.

WORM Don't let the bandit be burned outa yer heart, Guppy. Clancy promised transcendence and we're gonna get transcendence.

GUPPY Worm, stuff it! We gotta crisis to consider! I'll say it straight out—There's sumpin' smelly like dead fish when it comes to Peck's prophecy about Clancy's homecomin'.

DUKE Yer rockin' the streamboat, Guppy.

GUPPY It needs rockin', you old fool! It's needed rockin' fer a decade!

WORM But Peck saw Clancy fiddle up and he wuz his best buddy in the whole lagoon.

GUPPY So sez Peck. He wuz the on'y one who saw, tidy.

WORM Rooster believes! The red-haired bandit is got lotsa hope. Why don't you go fishin' together and get refueled?

GUPPY Aw, he's Peck apprentice. He'd do anything that moldy ol' crowbait told him to, ring in the nose-like. I don't trust neither one of'em any more.

DUKE Guppy—

GUPPY And I'm sick in the gills fer layin' my good plunder 'n booty in the mud of the Empress, prophecy or no prophecy. I mean, when wuz the last time you saw Peck swipe for hisself? Huh?

DUKE Well ... now that yuh mention it I ... I ... Iyiyi.

GUPPY Duke, listen to me, buddy. I know it hurts to think, but damnit we're nearly dead and we got nuthin' but promises to show fer it. Right?

Pause.

DUKE Clancy wuzza finger man. The best in the business. Taught me everything I know about the art of river robbery. On the other hand I ain't made a clean swipe in ages. On'y from the slow and very stupid.

WORM I'm gettin' scared! If we don't transcend soon we're gonna be all washed up fer sackin' the universe!

DUKE Don't crack up, Worm. Okay, Guppy. What're yuh sayin'? Spit it out.

GUPPY I say now's the time we put the screws of our discontent to Peck Woodstick. And if he don't communicate our crisis to Clancy in the sky I'm gonna take his phony prophesy and stick it where the moon don't shine. Then we'll see about whose bony hands is fer grippin' what wheel.

DUKE Nobuddy's on the make here, Guppy. This is gotta be a team effort or not at all.

GUPPY I on'y want some answers to one damn question: What the hell is up? Plain and simple. No make.

DUKE No mutiny.

GUPPY We'll see.

WORM I think we should all go home and ferget about it.

GUPPY You would.

WORM Oh be quiet.

DUKE Both be quiet. Here comes Peck.

WORM Oh no.

DUKE Let me do the talkin', Guppy. You always make him mad.

GUPPY Okay, but don't fag out on me, some guts.

Peck Woodstick comes out of the steering station on the hurricane deck above. He is eating from a can of sardines with his fingers and whistling a little tune. He looks down at the tramps out of the corner of his eye, then emits a huge yawn. Guppy gives Duke a nudge.

DUKE Hi, Peck!

PECK OH! Yuh scared me. I wuz havin' a little nap. Ain't half awake yet.

DUKE Sorry, Peck. We wuz tryin' to whisper.

PECK Naw, that's okay. Y'coulda snuck up on me with a tractor. Where's the moon?

DUKE High as a kite!

WORM Bright as a honeyed apple!

PECK Look! There goes Clancy Dougal dancin' two-step through a crate!

TRAMPS WHERE?

PECK ...Yuh missed'im. (*Laughs*)

Dontcha just love little customs. (*He comes down to the deck*)

Hey! I got an idea! If it don't rain tonight whaddya say we go on a little picnic? Eh, Worm? Fry up a chicken, get summa Guppy's cocktail, go uppity Chuck's Point and watch the barges go by. Whaddya say, gang?

WORM Sounds good to me, Peck. I'll fry up the chicken.

PECK Like on'y you can do it, girl. Whaddya say, Duke? We could roll out the old checkerboard and play best outa seven fer matchsticks. Eh? Eh? (*Laughs*) Whatta shark!

Guppy gives Duke another shove.

DUKE Uuuh, Peck...?

PECK Uuuh, what? Duke, what? What? Whenever you open your move with "Uuuh" I know it's a biggy. What?

DUKE Well ... we wuz just wonderin' ... the three of us here ... like sooo what's up with the prophecy these days? That is I mean, if we ain't doin' sumpin' to bring it to the boiling point we'd just as soon be doin' it as not be doin' it. (*Laughs weakly*) If yuh get what I mean?

PECK Vague.

GUPPY Then maybe I could sharpen it up some, mind?

PECK Guppy! Good idea. You be the one. I'd like that. Truly.

GUPPY My pleasure.

So Guppy walks up to the Empress and yanks a rotting board off the portside. Then he raises it above his head and brings it down hard on Peck's foot up on the point of the prow. Peck doesn't even flinch. He scratches his head.

GUPPY Sharp enough?

PECK Medium.

GUPPY No pain, right?

PECK Look, Guppy, ev'ry dog knows I'm half-dead from the knee down on this leg. So what's yer point?

GUPPY The point is that you ain't the on'y one anymore who's draggin' chunksa body around like they wuz spare parts or sumpin'. And the bigger the chunks the slower yuh get. It's a simple law of nature, Peck. Hell, I could wrap this board around Duke's head and probably get the same reaction.

DUKE Yer the one with snakes in yer closet not me.

Worm laughs.

GUPPY And Worm's a giggly birdbrain. It all fits what I'm sayin'.

PECK Well somewhere's I already fell outa the boat. I mean, what's all this petty pitter patter got to do with Clancy's prophecy which is time-honored, respected, most noble, classified, bigger than a bread basket, kinda creepy, and otherwise beyond the normal human grip?

GUPPY It's the "grip" part. And biggy is this—When is Clancy comin' home to gather his brotherly crew? It's been fifteen years, seven hundred and ninety-odd full moons, and who knows how many words of hope ... When?

PECK Duke?

DUKE Yeah, Peck, I hate to admit but I've been countin' the days more than usual too.

PECK Worm?

WORM I just wanna hear Clancy's sweet fiddle again, that's all.

PECK Well, gang ... the answer is this ... I dunno! Why ask me? I'm just a tramp like youse.

DUKE But you got mental telepitty with Clancy in the cosmos. Right?

WORM You always sez so.

PECK A direct line of communication I sez, sure, but it takes awful heavy contemplation fer a man with a bad ticker.

DUKE Well if you ain't up to it nobuddy is.

PECK True. But, gee whiz, it takes a full moon to copy the blueprints under.

GUPPY It's a full moon tonight, ain't it?

PECK (*Looks up*)
Pretty close, I s'poze. But, hey, what about the lagoon marchin' band? We gotta conjure up a musical highway fer Clancy to fiddle down on, and like yuh said - more'n half the orchestra is dead. Charlie, Palimino...

GUPPY I thought you wuz nappin'.

PECK Eh?

DUKE We can do it! We'll just hafta toot twice as hard, that's all.

WORM I'll toot! Just gimme the chance!

GUPPY Atta go, Worm.

DUKE C'mon, Peck! Let's make prophesy come to pass!

TRAMPS YEAH!

Pause.

PECK Gee, brothers. I dunno. Man-oh-man.

He walks away from them, muttering and shaking his head. He looks up at the moon and scratches his beard with both hands vigorously. Then a light comes to his eyes. He raises his brows and smiles a little. He turns back around to them.

PECK ...Alrighty. I'll do it.

The Tramps cheer and adlib encouragements.

PECK Hold on! Hold on!

They quiet down.

I'm gonna need plen'y of time fer meditation and a whole lotta plunder'n booty. Fer Clancy. So go to your various homes and wait for my word. I'll go to the cave-in-rock and put my bad ticker to work. If I connect with Clancy on the air waves I'll letchya know. Now go! Disperse!

The Tramps cheer. Peck moves away from them and stands gazing at the moon.

WORM Holy crow! I feel like jumpin'!

DUKE I'm goin' fer a snooze. I wanna be clear-headed and fluless fer the marchin' band. Gotta get shipshape fer transcendence!

GUPPY If and when.

WORM Me, too! I gotta go home and feed my skinny chickens!

GUPPY Them scrawny birds is stayin' back, Worm. Chickens don't transcend.

WORM Will if I want!

GUPPY Oh yeah?

WORM Yeah!

DUKE Stop fightin', you two! Let's go home and leave Peck with a little peace. And who knows what midnight will release. C'mon!

Duke heads off into the bramble. Worm follows excitedly. Guppy lags behind. He stops. Turns.

GUPPY Hey, Peck?

PECK Hey, what?

GUPPY There's no such thing as a free lunch. (*Starts to go.*)

PECK Hey, Guppy?

GUPPY What?

PECK If yuh open up a can of worms, the on'y way to get'em all back in is to use a bigger can.

Guppy grins slyly. Peck grins back. Then Guppy disappears into the bramble. Peck turns to the audience.

PECK Oh me shattered soul. It looks like a storm is gonna fall down boom on my lagoon. Now there's a fright full of thought. Them tramps is gettin' the drift of their predicament. Ah me, now what? Gotta think fast-like, Peck Woodstick. Gotta set me royal beans to work again. I ain't called Cap'n fer nuthin'!

He squeezes a look at the moon.

Damn you, Clancy Dougal! How long y'gonna haunt me bloodstream, yuh fiddlin' jerk? How many more legends I gotta spin to keep them old tramps offa me bony neck? Holy, holy, so long ago I almost ferget ... I wore the pants in this lagoon. I had me castle in the mud. Me legs always got me from the cops. I took no bunk and I ate no crud from nobuddy. Then Clancy came to town. Wearin' that garter on his sleeve. He laughed at me leg and swiped me crew but nobuddy's seen'im since! ...Yer thinkin' I'm dupery, dontcha? Well, horsepucky! Bumps on the log of life that's what you are! I'M THE CAP'N!—And I intend to pretend to stay that way... Oh, I've got me faithful followin' in the likes of me apprentice of swipe. He's got red hair like a shootin' star, flyin' feet like the wind, sticky fingers like atomic glue, and a boss in the likes of me. He's good in the crunch. Get the point?

Starts moving around and rubbing his hands together.

I ain't no slouch tramp. They'll spinnin' legends around me before I'm dead. Oh I got business and items of mischief tonight. I gotta plan up me hairy-arm sleeve. I got plunder and thunder bangin' in me skull. Gonna make masquerade into prophesy! You just wait and see. Ha ha. Ho ho. Hee hee.

Peck hobbles off into the bramble. A moment. Suddenly a sack of something is thrown over the bramble on the opposite side of the stage and then Rooster comes barrel-assing into view like a Hollywood stuntman. He peeks back through the bramble and laughs.

ROOSTER Stupid tourists.

Then, satisfied with his safety, he jumps onto the deck of the Empress. He drops his sack down and looks around.

ROOSTER Peck? Hey, Peck, are you here?

He grins to himself, then he climbs up the ladder to the hurricane deck. He disappears into the steering station and reappears with an old striped deck chair, which he unfolds and sits in. He sighs with gratification and begins to whistle Peck's tune from before. Now we hear a rustling in the bramble in the direction of Peck's exit. Rooster gasps and begins to refold the chair, catching his finger in it, just as Becky makes her appearance. She is wearing a dress and has a traveling bag over her shoulder. She tiptoes gingerly through the mud. She sees the Empress and stops in her tracks. Rooster hides.

BECKY Wow!

She takes a diary from her bag and begins to write in it.

"Dear Mr. Twain: Today I came upon an old river boat of ... indeterminate age and dimensions. It was dirty ... smelly ... lopsided ... and absolutely defied any purposes whatsoever. Some kind of swamp animal had defecated on the deck. There were cobwebs strewn all over the hogging. It was a sore sight for pretty eyes and indeed a minor curiousity but I decided to board it anyway."

She moves closer. Stops.

"I hesitated. There were spiders in the cobwebs and the swamp animal stuff looked fresh. I concluded it was a dumb idea."

She puts her diary back into her bag and begins to walk away. Rooster comes quietly out of hiding and leaps toward her.

ROOSTER Look out!

She screams and trips over into the mud. Rooster laughs hard.

ROOSTER What's the matter, girl? Did I scare yuh?

BECKY No! Who are you?

She gets to her feet.

ROOSTER Nobuddy. Who're you?

BECKY None of your business. Oh! Look at my dress!

ROOSTER Pretty colour. Except for the mud.

Laughs.

BECKY Ha ha.

ROOSTER What's that smell on you?

BECKY Perfume!

ROOSTER Are you lost?

BECKY Definitely not!

ROOSTER Don't worry, it on'y shows a little. Ev'rybuddy gets lost around here. I've been lost for months. What's in the bag?

BECKY Just some—none of your business!

ROOSTER Havin' a picnic? Out for a stroll in the summer air maybe?

BECKY I don't stroll. I'm ... passing by.

ROOSTER Must be nice. I'm goin' around in circles myself. What's that around your neck?

BECKY What does it look like?

ROOSTER A chain with a rock on it.

He reaches out to touch it. She gasps and covers it with her hand.

BECKY Do you mind?

ROOSTER Mind what?

BECKY I want to be alone.

ROOSTER I was here first.

BECKY Shoo!

ROOSTER I'll flip you for it.

BECKY No!

ROOSTER Just as well, I don't have a nickel. Hey! Got any spare change for the likes of me? I'm a traveller and a tired soul who din't have no supper for three days back.

BECKY I'm a traveller myself and I don't have much money to begin with.

ROOSTER Maybe just a crust of raisin bread left over from your picnic.

BECKY I only had one sandwich and I already ate it.

ROOSTER How about a toothpick to keep my mouth busy?

BECKY Good idea.

Now we hear the low, mellow sound of a distant river boat.

ROOSTER That's the *W.B. Dance* goin' to the sea.

BECKY If you run you can still make it.

ROOSTER So! You're a traveller, huh? Havin' a little holiday away from the humdrum. Well, the swump is a fine choice. You got style. Maybe you'd like to reach into my sack. What you pull is what you get. Twenny-five bucks. Take a chance. Why not? Souvenir! Like I said, twenny bucks.

He gestures to his sack on the deck.

BECKY Don't you have any scruples?

ROOSTER Maybe. Reach in and find out. What you pull is yours. But do it quick or you might get bit. There's a serpent inside. Yeah, really! He got hold of my leg back there in the bramble and wouldn't let go so I clobbers him over the head and there he lays. I'll sell'im to yuh for fifteen bucks.

BECKY You're full of bunkum.

ROOSTER I like your shoes.

BECKY Oh, thanks.

ROOSTER Ten bucks and he's yours. Take'im home before he comes to. Stick'im under an old wash tub and sit on it.

BECKY Are you crazy?

ROOSTER Never been saner. And when he starts screamin' to get out yuh whupple on toppy the tub with a wooden spoon or a soup bone until he starts to bawl. Then yuh takes a handful of pepper and yuh throws it quicklylike under the tub. He'll start wheezin and sneezin' and you'll hafta get your ugly fat cousin to sit on it with yuh. After he's gone and sneezed all the snort outa hisself yuh lifts up the tub and yuh poke his eyes out with a sharp fork. All that good 'n done he'll make the best housepet for a classy girl you've ever seen. Five bucks.

BECKY We already have a dog.

ROOSTER Three bucks.

BECKY You are crazy.

ROOSTER Oh yeah? Watch this, pretty miss.

He steps on the sack. A loud screech emits. Becky jumps back.

He's still a little groggy I reckon. I whuppled'im real good. Take that!

He steps again—Another screech.

BECKY My goodness.

ROOSTER Two bucks? It's a bargain.

BECKY You're trying to trick me.

ROOSTER Have a peek inside if yuh don't believe me. Grab'im by the scruff of the neck and pull him out. Kick'im once in the ribs and he'll sit up like a cocker spaniel. Go ahead.

BECKY No.

ROOSTER Chicken.

BECKY I am not.

ROOSTER Prove it.

Pause. She considers the sack. Then bends over it cautiously. Rooster delicately removes her necklace and slips it into his pocket like honey. The river boat calls again. Becky draws back from the sack.

BECKY I'm not going to fall for it.

ROOSTER It's your loss.

BECKY I think I'll catch that river boat.

ROOSTER Ten minute call. Y'better run.

She nudges the sack with her tiny foot.

BECKY Hogwash.

Then runs off into the bramble the way she came.

ROOSTER (*Waving*) So long!—sucker. (*He laughs and playfully kicks the sack*)

Take that, yuh mean little bugger. (*Laughs again, then takes the necklace out of his pocket, examines it, smells it, bites on it, and drops it in his sack.*)

PECK'S VOICE (*In the distance*) Rooosterrr! Rooosterrr!

Rooster remembers the deck chair unfolded above.

ROOSTER Ho-jeez! (*He scampers across the deck and up the ladder.*)

PECK'S VOICE (*Getting closer*) Rooosterrr!

Rooster quickly folds up the chair, slamming his finger in it...

ROOSTER Ow!

... and puts it back in the steering station just as Peck hobbles excitedly into view. Rooster clamours down the ladder, sits on the bottom rung, and begins whistling nonchalantly.

PECK Rooster!

ROOSTER Over here. Peck.

PECK Oh Rooster! (*Boards the Empress.*)

ROOSTER What's the matter? You look awful.

PECK I just had awful news land on me skull!

ROOSTER What news?

PECK Where's the moon?

ROOSTER High as kite.

PECK Bright as a honeyed apple! Look! There goes Clancy Dougal dancin' two-step through a crater!

ROOSTER Where?!

PECK Yuh missed'im.

ROOSTER Damn!

PECK Oh-oh-oh, Rooster! I've just come from heavy contemplation at the cave-in-rock.

ROOSTER What for?

PECK Guess.

ROOSTER Tell me.

PECK Hold onta yer underwear, me grand loyal swipe— (*Takes a deep breath and lets it out*) —I gained telepitty with the Starry Bandit.

ROOSTER You're lyin'.

PECK Like drinkin' moonlight through a straw.

ROOSTER No!

PECK He poked his hot finger inta me beans and twirled them around. I got the shakes in ev'ry bone in me body. Ev'ry bitta marrow wuz grindin' and cracklin' from me head to me toes. Tonight's the night!

ROOSTER (*Struck*) ... Yuh mean...?

PECK CLANCY'S COMIN' HOME!

Rooster freezes, his mouth agape. Peck looks at him, then boots him in the bum. Rooster blinks.

ROOSTER Ho-jeez.

PECK Rightly so. This is it.

ROOSTER I think I'm gonna crack up.

PECK Don't crack up. Whatever yuh do don't crack up. Y'gotta be in one hopeful piece fer the homecomin' party.

ROOSTER Ho-jeez.

PECK Whatsa matter?

ROOSTER I can't think straight.

PECK Yes yuh can.

ROOSTER No I can't. It's all mixed up.

PECK No it ain't.

He boots Rooster again—off the deck and into the mud.

ROOSTER Whaddya do that for?

PECK Fer strength and hope, yuh stupid nitwit.

ROOSTER What if Clancy don't choose me for his crew? What if I ain't good enuff for the blast-off?

PECK Horsepucky!

He beans Rooster with his stick.

ROOSTER Ow.

PECK I taught yuh ev'rything yuh need to know about the art of river robbery. Din't I? Don't lose yer grip, me loyal swipe, or Clancy might get mad.

ROOSTER Ho-jeez.

PECK Rightly so.

ROOSTER Tell me again.

PECK Tell yuh what?

ROOSTER All about hope.

PECK Yuh don't deserve it.

ROOSTER Yes I do!

PECK Horsepucky.

ROOSTER TELL ME!

PECK (*Quickly by rote*) "Hope is feelin' and feelin' is believin' and believin's gonna bring Clancy outa the cosmos with moonbeams on the brim of his hat and all the secrets of the universe in his sack."

ROOSTER Wow.

PECK So sez I.

ROOSTER Tell me how Clancy fiddled to the moon.

PECK Nope.

ROOSTER How come?

PECK It's too beautiful fer words.

ROOSTER Aw, c'mon, you crud! I gotta have that sparkle in my beans for the homecomin' party! ... Please?

PECK Who am I?

ROOSTER You're the cap'n of thieves, Peck.

PECK Who're you?

ROOSTER Your apprentice of swipe through 'n through.

PECK Yer the best little bandit this river has ever seen.

ROOSTER Right.

PECK Since me.

ROOSTER Right.

PECK Alright.

ROOSTER Whew!

Peck sits on the railing.

PECK — But don't breathe a word to no strangers.
Just between you and me.
That wuzza night of wonder.
A night of glory-be.

Peck taps the deck at his feet. Rooster sits there joyfully.

PECK — Well...

Clancy Dougal wuzza tramp-a-travellin',
he come to this here swump.

He fiddled and danced and told such stories,
in yer guff he put a lump.

ROOSTER — Get to the good part.

PECK — Hold yer horses! ... Where wuz I?

ROOSTER — Lump.

PECK — Lump?

ROOSTER — Lump!

PECK — Right...

No sooner had Clancy parked his bum
on the throne of his lagoon,
then all of a suddy morn he woke,
said, "I'm goin' to the moon!"

ROOSTER — Wow.

PECK — "I got ants in my pants
and cobwebs in my hair,
I'm gonna pick up me fiddle
and march outa here!
I'm gonna bathe in the moonlight
and dunk my head in the Milky Way.
I'm gonna trail on the tail
of a star," said he.

ROOSTER — He can do all that???

PECK Rightly so and a whole lot more.
He said, "When I come home
some full-moon night,
I'm gonna gather my brotherly crew.
I'm gonna lift this boat outa the mud
and spin a course for the starry blue!"

ROOSTER Aaahhh!

PECK Stars in the paddle wheel.

ROOSTER Just think.

PECK The ring of Venus blowin' through yer beard.

ROOSTER I can't stand it!

PECK Stealin' quasars and stuffin' cosmos in yer sack.

ROOSTER Whuppee! I'm goin' to and I ain't comin' back!

PECK So Clancy and me went straight into town
to find a launchin' pad.

ROOSTER On'y you!

PECK Nobuddy else.

ROOSTER Cuz you wuz the buddy he never had!

PECK Hit it!

Rooster begins pounding a drum beat on the deck.

PECK So at the stroke of midnight, Clancy Dougal clumb to the top of the tallest buildin' we could find. Yup! Straight up the side of'er! He chewed out hunks of brick 'n boulder to make foot-holds fer his feet as he went. He carried his fiddle in his teeth and his bow under one ear. He clumb to the tip of the flagpole and stuck his chest at the moon. Then he started to play. His fiddle blazed in the moonlight and the clouds assembled. They crawled outa their bunks in the sky and started to march. Clancy fiddled. He had no fingers now. Just one eye and a bright red garter. The wind she started to blow. Then all of a suddy a golden bolt of moonlight come blisterin' outa the sky and struck ol' Clancy on the square of his head!

Rooster stops the beat.

... And he wuz gone.

ROOSTER Gone.

PECK Evaporated into thin air.

ROOSTER Clancy Dougal wuzza stargazer.

PECK The noblest wretch you could ever meet.

ROOSTER Who wuz last seen chewin' on the corner of the moon—

TOGETHER With both crooked teeth.

Silence. Rooster gazes upwards with his mouth open, then...

ROOSTER Look! There goes Clancy dancin' two-step through a crater!

Peck looks up. Then looks at Rooster.

PECK Right. Now. Lemme see whatcha brung in yer sack.

ROOSTER What?

PECK Yer sack!

ROOSTER Oh! Sure, boss, yeah!

Rooster scurries to get his sack. Peck climbs up the ladder and disappears into the steering station. Rooster climbs the ladder. Peck reappears with his deck chair, unfolds it on the hurricane deck, and sits. Then he stands. Looks down at the chair suspiciously. Re-sits. Rooster quickly opens his sack.

ROOSTER Have a look.

PECK Bring it out.

Rooster takes out a small globe and a Magic Cube and juggles them a few times.

ROOSTER Pretty good, huh?

PECK Dazzlin'. What else y'got?

He pulls out a pair of lady's nylons and holds them up proudly.

PECK How the hell didya manage that?

ROOSTER Oh I've got the quickest two hands you've ever seen.

PECK How old are you, Rooster?

ROOSTER Fifteen I think. Why?

PECK One of these we're gonna hafta have a long talk.

ROOSTER About what?

PECK About the guiles and willies of women. What else y'got?

He pulls out Becky's necklace and shrugs.

ROOSTER A little do-dad. Ain't much.

PECK Lemme look closer. Hmm. Now that's a rarity. Give to me, boy. It's a keeper.

ROOSTER No, it's mine. I made the swipe.

PECK Who's the boss you or me?

ROOSTER You are but—

Peck boots him in the bum. The necklace springs loose. Peck catches it.

PECK Thanks. What else?

ROOSTER Nuthin'.

PECK What's in the bottom there?

ROOSTER It's mine.

PECK Lemme see!

Rooster frowns and pulls out an old concertina. He produces the "serpent" noise and grins.

PECK What sort of item is that?

ROOSTER It's a squeaky-link accordian that's what.

PECK Maybe Worm'll give us a sack of chickens fer it.

ROOSTER No! It's a keeper! For me! I mean, we gotta resemble the old lagoon marchin' band, don't we? We gotta conjure up a musical highway for Clancy to fiddle down on. Remember?

PECK 'Course I remember, yuh nitwit!

ROOSTER Well, Clancy's got his blazin' fiddle, you got your rusty-dusty bugle, and I ain't got nuthin'.

PECK The band wuz long before yer time, Rooster.

ROOSTER So what? All I need is practice. Please?

PECK Yer serious, eh?

Rooster screws up his face seriously.

Alright. You may keep it.

ROOSTER Whuppee!

PECK —on one condition if.

ROOSTER If what?

PECK Y'promise me sumpin'.

ROOSTER What?

PECK That you won't turn yer back on me no matter what. I mean, don't trust nobuddy else, boy. Tonight is wrought fer treason.

ROOSTER Aw, Peck, don't worry. You're the cap'n!

PECK Swear it!

ROOSTER Shit.

PECK Alright.

There is a low rumbling of thunder in the sky.

It looks like a storm is gonna fall down boom on my lagoon. Better I be driftin' out in the night-wash to deliver the invitations to Clancy's homecomin' party. Tuck this stuff in the boiler.

ROOSTER Can I come with yuh?

PECK No. I'll be movin' too fast. You'll never keep up.

Peck climbs down the ladder. Rooster follows him with his sack and accordion.

ROOSTER Hey, Peck?

PECK Hey what now?

ROOSTER What's it gonna be like?

PECK What's it what gonna be like?

ROOSTER When the Empress rises outa the mud and Clancy makes a course for the starry blue. How're we gonna breathe? How're we gonna find food outer in space? What kinds of things we gonna see?

PECK Use yer imagination.

ROOSTER Gimme some fer example.

PECK Lookee, boy, stop worryin' about details. Clancy's got it all figured out in his own way. He's got revelation and inspired blueprints. Right? So with Clancy in the cabin and yers truthfully at the wheel, we'll navigate the course of things most people just dream about. We'll up and away to the bedazzlin' blue hole of the heavens!

ROOSTER Wow.

They gaze at the moon together.

PECK Clancyyy? Is that yooou?

ROOSTER Think he can hear yuh?

PECK Telepitty maybe. Who knows?

Rooster is transfixed by the moon. Peck hobbles to the edge of the bramble. There is another low rumble in the sky.

PECK Look out, storm. Peck Woodstick is comin'. I'm off in the wrinkly-dinkly night with a plan up me hairy-arm sleeve. I'm crippled as sin, but I'm the cap'n of thieves!

He disappears through the bramble.

ROOSTER ... Hey, Peck, what if—?

He looks around for Peck. Then he smiles and quickly runs and stuffs his sack of booty in the boiler under the hurricane deck. He takes the concertina in his hands and sits on the prow. He begins to practice, badly, but with growing enthusiasm.

Now, through the bramble, comes Guppy, crawling on his belly toward the Empress. In his hand he holds a whiskey bottle full of bronze liquid with a twisted rag dangling out of the neck. He crawls to the portside and stuffs the bottle into the gap where earlier he tore off the board. The bottle rests inside the shell of the boat with an inch of rag poking out. Guppy then begins crawling back toward the bramble. There is a low rumble in the sky. Rooster stops playing and looks up.

Is that yooou?

Guppy freezes face down in the mud.

ROOSTER Lookee here. Pearl keys. No more crawlin' through cracks, leapin' outa trees or duckin' under mud for me. Just see me swingin' through the stars tootin' this little baby.

Another rumble above.

Clancyyy?

Rooster (Jim Farley) plays the concertina in Gordon Pengilly's Swipe *(produced at Walterdale as* The Apprentice of Swipe), *May 1981. Photo: C.W. Hill Photography for Walterdale Theatre Associates.*

ROOSTER Lookout!

Rooster begins playing again. And Guppy crawls into the bramble and disappears. Now, through the bramble in another place, comes Becky again, looking quite disheveled and perturbed. She sees Rooster playing and decides with a vengeance to sneak up on him. But Rooster catches a whiff of her perfume and smiles to himself. As she comes up behind him—

ROOSTER Did I scare yuh?

Becky screams and falls over in the mud. Rooster turns around laughing.

BECKY No!

ROOSTER I thought you wuz catchin' the *W.B. Dance*.

BECKY So did I.

ROOSTER What happened?

BECKY Help me up.

She holds out her hand. Rooster smiles, takes her arm, pulls her up and steals her bracelet all in one motion.

BECKY Thank you.

ROOSTER My pleasure.

BECKY I was halfway to the dock when I realized I'd lost my necklace. I came back to look for it.

ROOSTER Really, eh?

BECKY Don't just stand there! Help me!

ROOSTER Sure.

They both look around in the mud.

BECKY My luck is lousy today.

ROOSTER So is mine. My serpent got loose. Sack sprung a leak. Must be around here somewheres. If yuh happen to turn the bugger up lemme know. It's easy to spot. Looks like a big snake with leathery wings. It's a variety both in the water and out. Has deadly green powder on the tip of its tail and makes a whole other sound not unlikely to this—

Rooster lets out a loud, weird yelp. Becky jumps back.

ROOSTER Pretty good, huh?

BECKY It's absolutely obnoxious!

ROOSTER I've been practicin'. Cuz I plan to bait'im. And if I had one square meal under my belt I'd have just enuff strength to strangle the bounder and be done with it. But as you see I'm skinny as a rake from the weary road. Hey! Got any spare change—ten dollars or so that I could feed myself on and maybe buy a knife?

BECKY No!

Becky starts to cry. Rooster pulls back and stares.

ROOSTER What's the matter?

BECKY I'm crying!

ROOSTER How come?

BECKY Because!

ROOSTER You ain't even hurt.

BECKY You don't have to bleed to cry, you maniac.

ROOSTER Well if yuh ain't hurt yuh must be sumpin'.

BECKY I'm FRUSTRATED!

ROOSTER What's that?

BECKY I'm fifteen going on sixteen and I can't get past the lagoon!

ROOSTER Follow the river.

BECKY You don't understand me!

ROOSTER Well, you ain't helpin' a whole lot, girl.

BECKY My name's Becky!

ROOSTER Are the cops after you?

BECKY What makes you say that?

ROOSTER You gotta way of lookin' over your shoulder without turnin' your head.

BECKY Do I?

ROOSTER Are you on the run?

BECKY (*Sighs—nods*) I ran away from my stepfather this morning.

ROOSTER How come?

BECKY Because he's an old, fat, retired magistrate with grey hairs poking out of his ears.

ROOSTER Does he kick yuh around the yard?

BECKY No, but sometimes he locks me up in the library and makes me read.

ROOSTER You're kidding.

BECKY Every morning he crawls out of bed and calls for his stupid warm milk and eggs. "Come here, Rebecca, and help me find my blasted socks!" Ooo!

ROOSTER Dirty old bugger.

BECKY Oh he'll be going barefoot for the rest of his days.

ROOSTER If you get your way.

BECKY (*Stamps her foot*) I will!

ROOSTER (*Laughs.*)

BECKY Are you making fun of me?

ROOSTER Well, it don't sound that bad.

BECKY Plato's *Republic* behind a locked door is a fate worse than death. I hate books! I want to be a writer!

ROOSTER I can't even read.

BECKY Not at all?

ROOSTER Not a word.

BECKY Didn't you learn in school?

ROOSTER Never.

BECKY Never???

ROOSTER Nope.

BECKY Are you a vagabond?

ROOSTER Probably not. I'm skin and bones and weak with hunger but I'm as happy as a snake in the grass.

BECKY Amazing.

ROOSTER Yup, that's me.

Becky whips open her bag and takes out her diary.

BECKY What's your name?

ROOSTER What's that book for?

BECKY It's a journal of my adventures. I'm dedicating the whole summer to Mark Twain.

ROOSTER Who's he?

BECKY He's the freewheeler who lies inside of Plato when my stepfather isn't looking.

She giggles; Rooster cocks his head at her.

BECKY Never mind. Tell me your name.

ROOSTER It's Rooster.

BECKY Very good. Why? (*Begins writing.*)

ROOSTER Cuz of my red hair so sez Peck.

BECKY Who's he?

ROOSTER Peck Woodstick that's who. He found me in a basket in the mud after a river boat sunk. Ev'rybuddy else wuz killed I wuz just a baby who floated into shore. Peck scooped me up, stuck a bone in my mouth, and made me his apprentice of swipe.

BECKY (*Writing furiously*) What's that?

ROOSTER That's what I do. Write it down.

BECKY I need more detail.

ROOSTER Slink. Snatch. Pilch.

BECKY Steal???

ROOSTER Yup! He taught me ev'rything I know about the art of river robbery. I'm topnotch for my age. Ask anybuddy. Sackin' paddle wheelers is my special.

BECKY I don't believe you.

ROOSTER I've got the quickest two hands you've ever seen!

BECKY That's disgusting!

She turns her back haughtily. Rooster snatches the ribbon from her hair.

... How do you do it?

ROOSTER Lots of ways! Sometimes I sneak aboard at night and cheat the gamblers at poker.

BECKY Really?

ROOSTER Really sure! Other times I pretend to be a traveller marooned on the riverbank. Some stupid tourist always pulls me aboard and feeds me. Then I wander around and pick pockets. (*Laughs.*)

BECKY No scruples.

ROOSTER Not that I know of.

She bends over her diary. Rooster swipes her earring.

BECKY What else?

ROOSTER On good days I pick the calking from the seams of the boat so's it sinks downriver where Peck is waitin'—he can't steal for hisself no more, gotta bum leg—and stuff just floats into shore. Peck picks it up and hobbles into the bramble whuls ev'rybuddy is screamin' for their lives. Nice timin', eh?

BECKY But what happens to you?

ROOSTER Oh, I gotta swim like hell from the alligators!

BECKY Now you're exaggerating!

ROOSTER I got bit once. Wanna see?

BECKY Okay!—no. I'm a lady ... Is it a big bite?

Rooster smiles and lifts up his tattered shirt revealing a scar. A long look from her.

BECKY Can I touch it?

ROOSTER If yuh want to.

She moves her fingertip along the length of his scar delicately. Her diary falls from her lap. They look at each other. There's a low rumble in the sky. They turn away from each other rather perplexed. Rooster quickly tucks his shirt in.

ROOSTER There's a storm comin'.

BECKY (*Dreamily*) Ah! Yes. There's a mist on the lagoon, chum. It's rolling in like folds of lavender waves. (*She quickly writes that down.*)

ROOSTER Yuh better be lookin' for shelter, girl. You'll get blowed hither-de-pither all over the bramble. I mean, yuh just can't take the chance of gettin' caught without a coop around here.

BECKY "Chance is the providence of adventurers." Napoleon said that.

ROOSTER He probably had a roof over his head.

BECKY And so do I.

ROOSTER Where at?

BECKY Here.

ROOSTER Oh. —WHAT?

BECKY I'll wait out the tempest in the bosom of this majestic Queen of the swamp. Wow! (*She writes that down.*)

ROOSTER No! You can't!

BECKY Why not?

ROOSTER Cuz—you ain't been invited!

BECKY Nonsense.

ROOSTER It's a private party tonight!

BECKY What're you babbling about? It's a free lagoon.

ROOSTER No it ain't!

We hear the sound of someone coming through the bramble who clatters and tinkles as he walks.

BECKY Hush! What's that sound? ... Someone's coming!

ROOSTER If it's Peck and the tramps yuh better duck your butt, girl,
cuz tonight is rotten with treason!

BECKY Good! The more the merrier! Open the flood gates!

ROOSTER Ho-jeez.

Enter, through the bramble, an old blind tinkerman, singing. Over his back and around his shoulders are ropes bearing cups and pans, kettles and spoons, socks and shoes, and an assortment of other things that hang okay but probably don't work worth a damn. He wears dark sunglasses and an old raincoat. Becky takes one look at him and dives behind a barrel. Rooster has already hidden behind the boiler.

TINKER My body's a bag,
My head is a bone,
I'm blind as a bat
and I've got no home.
But mamma,
Ooooh, mamma,
I got some pretty things to sell.

He boards the Empress tapping his cane. And stops,

There's somebody here. I smell dirty feet. I smell perfume.

Y'wanna sweep your floor? I sell you a broom.

Speak up. I won't bite. I don't have any teeth.

He laughs. Rooster and Becky peer out from their hiding places. They look at each other. Rooster puts his finger to his lips. She glares back at him. Then stands—

BECKY Who are you?

TINKER Who're you, little miss?

BECKY I asked first. What's your name?

TINKER It's Tinker in the north and Kettles in the south.

BECKY Where do you come from?

TINKER I come and I go. Been following this river for ninety-five years. I've got no sight but I do have bearing.

BECKY Are you really blind?

TINKER Are you a brunette?

BECKY (*Lying*) No I'm blond.

TINKER Then I must be blind.

BECKY Oh.

Rooster stifles a laugh. She glares at him.

TINKER What's your line of business?

BECKY I'm a writer.

TINKER How romantic.

BECKY It's very rewarding. Today I'm exploring the ups and downs of the paddle wheel steamer.

TINKER It's a dying breed. Take my word for it. Every last one is gonna crumple-dust-'n splinter to the mud. And, baby, there ain't no heaven for steamboats.

ROOSTER Oh yes there is!

TINKER Hi, smelly feet.

Becky laughs; Rooster glares.

ROOSTER The Empress, she's special, and if you don't drag your hide out of here I'm gonna throw you in the river!

BECKY Rooster!

TINKER (*Laughs.*)

BECKY Don't mind him, sir. He's delinquent.

TINKER People are this, people are that,
nothing less and nothing more.
I'm a tinker with eyes like lead,
but I got a pie plate you'd adore.

BECKY No thank you. I don't cook. We have a nanny.

TINKER I see.

BECKY No, you don't—you're blind.

Tinker and Becky laugh.

TINKER Clever girl.

BECKY I think so. (*She sticks her tongue out at Rooster.*)

ROOSTER Ho-jeez.

TINKER Come have a closer look, blondie. My rope is loaded with adventure for a girl like you. And the prices are negotiable.

BECKY No offense, sir, but this is only junk.

TINKER Pretend it's not.

BECKY Pretending's for children.

TINKER And writers.

BECKY Oh.

During this exchange Peck pokes his head through the bramble and listens with growing intrigue to the tinkerman. He becomes loaded with "ideas" as the scene progresses.

ROOSTER Ha!

BECKY Be quiet. Okay, sir, I'll look a little. But I really don't think I need anything.

TINKER Browse around. Take it slow.
And I'll tell you a story as you go

Becky begins looking through the tinkerman's wares.

BECKY I'm listening.

ROOSTER I'm not.

TINKER Imagine a riverboat captain, and a gambler,
and a certain kind of lady,
all who worked this river many years ago.
The captain loved the lady,
or as much as he could love,
and the gambler worked the tables down below.
He had a reputation for marked cards.
He had an ace up his sleeve for a certain kind of lady.
Well, one night there was a storm
which kept the captain at the wheel
while the lady painted her toenails at the bar.
The gambler threw his hand beside the discards on the table
and his eye across the room fell on a garter.
Her heels clicked when she went into her chamber.
She left the door ajar.
The storm was over in an hour
and the captain came below
to put a slug of whiskey to his needs.
He watched the gambler dealing Black Jack
from the bottom of the deck
with a certain kind of garter on his sleeve.
The captain walked over.
There was a look in his eye like thunder.
But the gambler saw him coming,
drew a pistol from his pocket,
turned and shot the captain in the leg.
But the captain kept a-comin' with a certain kind of madness
and stuck a dagger nicely in his lung.
It was a single-shot Derringer.
It was a six inch Remington blade.

The rest is history I guess
and the boatswain told the rest
about the morning after storming he went in.
The chamber was in shambles
and a certain kind of lady
was lying on her bed in a bloody mess.
The captain disappeared.
So did the lady's garter.
And the terrible name of that riverboat—
was the Empress!
A vessel of treachery.
A darling of murder.

Silence. Now Tinker pops off the top of a dangling teakettle and smiles at Becky. She reaches inside and brings out a frilly red garter. And gasps. Rooster rolls his eyes.

TINKER Something special. Don't be shy.
It's fine and pretty. For your thigh.

BECKY Where did you get it?

TINKER I pulled it off a dead man's arm who I found floating in the river many years ago.

BECKY How much do you want for it?

TINKER It's priceless.

BECKY I'll give you anything.

TINKER Then it's yours. All you have to give me is the truth in return.

BECKY The truth?

TINKER That's what I'm asking. For that's what a blind man banks on.
Tell one single thing that you know to be true, big or small,
it doesn't matter at all, and the garter is yours for the taking.

BECKY Well...

TINKER Going once...

BECKY I can't think straight!

TINKER Going twice...

BECKY Give me a moment, please!

TINKER Going...

BECKY Rooster!

TINKER ... going...

BECKY Help me!

TINKER G—

ROOSTER It's Clancy's Homecomin' tonight!

Pause.

TINKER False. (*He snaps the top of the teakettle open.*)

BECKY It isn't fair! You didn't give me enough time to think!

TINKER The truth come quickest when simply told.

BECKY But... (*She sighs and drops the garter back into the teakettle.*)

TINKER Sorry, blondie.

BECKY I'm brunette.

TINKER Then you can't be trusted. As for me it's time I made my way through the darkness.

BECKY Don't step in any holes.

TINKER Nor you, sweet thing.

BECKY I don't plan to.

TINKER But I've seen more than one fair youth fall into the hole of a full-moon night without the slightest intention at all. So fair thee well ... and beware.

He taps his way off the Empress and moves slowly into the bramble. Peck, still watching, hides deeper.

My body's a bag,
My head is a bone,
I'm blind as a bat
and I've got no home.
But mamma,
Oooh, mamma,
I got some pretty things to sell.

He disappears. Peck, holding his stick like a club, disappears after him.

ROOSTER That's the biggest load of crap I ever heard of.

Suddenly Becky kicks him in the shin.

Ow! Whaddya do that for?!

BECKY You—you—you—OH! (*She begins crying.*)

ROOSTER Ho-jeez. Here we go again.

BECKY And again and again and again! You idiot! You're ruining my life!

ROOSTER It was on'y a dumb ol' garter.

BECKY No it wasn't! It was—a CLUE to my EXISTENCE! (*She cries harder.*)

ROOSTER Y'wanna see my alligator bite again?

She shrieks and kicks him in the other shin.

Ow!

BECKY Clancy's Homecoming! What the HECK is that???

She sits down hard on the railing with her head in her lap and sobs. Rooster looks at her. Looks at the moon. And then decides.

ROOSTER It's the truth, Becky. It truly is. And it's the best damn story you ever heard of, too!

BECKY (*Muffled in her lap*) Hogwash.

Rooster picks her diary off the deck and bops her on the head with it. Becky jerks up.

Don't touch me!

ROOSTER Here.

She snatches it from his outheld hand.

ROOSTER Now open it to a clean page.

BECKY What for?

ROOSTER Well yuh asked who Clancy wuz so I'm gonna tell yuh. And if it don't blow your socks off I'll be a monkey's uncle.

BECKY You're already a monkey's uncle.

ROOSTER Open your damn book. ... Please?

BECKY Okay, okay, don't rush me. This better be good, Rooster, because you're looking at a woman with a broken heart. (*She opens her diary*)
Go on. Get with it.

ROOSTER ... Tonight is Clancy Dougal's prophesy come true. He's gonna drop back down and gather his brotherly crew.

BECKY Where's he been?

ROOSTER The moon.

Becky closes her diary and gives him a big dubious look.

BECKY Is Clancy an astronaut?

ROOSTER Better'n that. He got there by the jam of his blazin' fiddle. And when he transcends down tonight he's gonna scoop the old Empress outa the mud and hang'er in the stars! Write it down.

BECKY (*Re-opens her diary and writes*) Sounds like cheese to me.

ROOSTER Cheese! Clancy's got revelation 'n inspired blueprints! We're gonna pillage and plunder from one corner of the universe to the other! Come midnight I'll be sippin' moonlight through a straw on a course for the Milky Way!

BECKY Have you ever seen this Clancy Dougal?

ROOSTER He wuz before my time.

BECKY They always are.

ROOSTER But I've got hope.

BECKY What's so big about hope?

ROOSTER "Hope is feelin' and feelin' is believin' and believin's gonna bring Clancy outa the cosmos with moonbeams on the brim of his hat and all the secrets of the universe in his sack." So sez Peck.

BECKY (*Slams her diary shut*)

Awww hogwash! Double hogwash! Don't give me that line of cosmic turnips. If it's not between your pinkies then it's not worth squeezing. Rooster, your appenticeship is clearly a trap and if you don't get out of it you'll be picking up Peck's blasted socks and chasing his warm milk and eggs for the rest of your days. And, furthermore, I wouldn't spend the night with you on this rotting riverboat if it was the last place of sanctuary in the whole lagoon. I'd sooner sleep in a cave! Goodbye!

She offers her hand stiffly. Rooster takes it. They shake. He steals the ring from her finger. She stuffs her diary back into her bag, hoists it, and then notices her naked finger.

BECKY Did you steal the ring from my finger?

ROOSTER Did I what?

BECKY You did! I trapped you redhanded, you hoodlum! Open up! That one—the right!

He opens his hand, sees the ring, and is genuinely surprised.

ROOSTER Ho-jeez. I did. I made a swipe without thinkin' about it. Now don't that take the cake.

BECKY You—you—OH! (*Snatches her ring back*) I'm only fifteen but nobody NOBODY makes a fool out of me!

She kicks him in the other shin then wheels off the deck and moves toward the bramble. Rooster leaps off the deck and tackles her from behind into the mud. She screams.

BECKY What're you doing?!

ROOSTER I'm fifteen, too, and I'm stealing you!

BECKY WHAT?

ROOSTER (*Laughs and picks her up*) I'm swipin' your whole self, yuh big mouth! Can't seem to stop myself! You're a keeper! For me! I'm gonna take you on board the flyin' Empress and sell yuh to a Martian! Whaddya think of that?

BECKY HELP! POLICE!

He carries her struggling back onto the deck. Just then Peck comes hobbling through the bramble with a sack full of goods.

PECK HEY! Who's that trezpassin' on me private property?! Rooster!

ROOSTER I made me a swipe, Peck—ouch!

PECK What kind of plunder'n booty is that?

ROOSTER It's a keeper—ouch!—for me.

BECKY Let go of me, you—you—!

Rooster covers her mouth.

ROOSTER Pretty good, huh?

PECK No it ain't pretty good! Since when didya get permission to pilch whole people?

ROOSTER I din't know I needed permission.

PECK Don't gimme no guff, boy! Yer throwin' this one back!

Becky bites Rooster's thumb.

ROOSTER OW!

BECKY —Monsterrr!

Peck boots him in the bum; Becky springs loose from his arms and falls to the deck.

BECKY Ooo! (*Hops back up.*)

PECK Use yer head, Rooster!

ROOSTER Aw, Peck—

Peck raises his boot again; Rooster steps back and tumbles over the railing into the mud.

PECK Aw nuthin'! Holy-moly! What would the tramps think with that panty-waist here onna night like tonight?!

BECKY Hey! Just a minute! This is a free lagoon!

PECK Beat it!

BECKY Ouch! Yoooou—!

She shoves Peck over the railing and into the mud beside Rooster. Then she stands above them with her hands on her hips defiantly.

BECKY I've been dying to do that for a long time! I'm nobody's piece of merchandise! My whole life I've been passed around, pushed around, groomed, schooled, styled, and otherwise locked up in stuffy places! I've had it up to HERE with other people's petty restrictions on my free time! This panty-waist will be here if she WANTS to be here and to HELL with what the tramps think!

Silence. Becky is momentarily stunned by her own speech and then a smile comes to her face. She looks around the boat as if re-designing it in her head. Rooster is mesmerized by her. Peck has a sly look on his face.

PECK Rooster?

ROOSTER ... Huh?

PECK Rooster!

ROOSTER What, boss?

PECK Help me up, me lovely.

ROOSTER Right. (*Helps him up*) Are you okay, boss?

PECK I never felt better, me laddie. Cuz me old milky eyes have been opened up to your own fine prowess.

ROOSTER My what?

PECK Yer smarts.

ROOSTER Me?

PECK You.

ROOSTER Thanks, boss.

PECK Stop with the "boss," yuh nitwit. You've graduated into near-partnership. That you had the sheer parcel of mind to make such a good clean swipe of it—this yummy thing standin' deck-wise above us. You got instinctive know-how, boy, but more even than you frankly put together whuls absorbed in natural swipe. And Clancy's gonna be impressed.

ROOSTER Ho-jeez.

PECK Rightly so.

BECKY What're you getting at, you old geezer?

PECK I'm gettin' at this, jammy-pie—that yer standin' onna awful slippery hunka boat there ... cuz guessy-pooh-pooh what I seen tonight?

ROOSTER AND BECKY
What?

PECK I seen a cop in plain-ol'-clothes snoopin' around the docks askin' questions fer the anywhereabouts of one, bonified, runaway, rich kid.

BECKY Hogwash.

PECK Horsepucky.

BECKY My name's Belinda.

PECK Becky.

BECKY No.

PECK With a big reward stamped on her little bum.

Becky gasps, whirls, and looks desperately for some means of escape.

PECK Rooster—GRAB'ER!

Rooster hesitates.

PECK GO-O-O-!

Becky screams and darts. Rooster cuts her off and grabs her around the middle. She kicks like crazy.

PECK Now take that item and stuff it in the boiler!

BECKY No!

PECK And close the hatch!

BECKY NO!

PECK And lean on it!

Becky screams.

ROOSTER (*Struggling with her*) But, Peck, hey, why don't I just rope'er down to the hogging somewheres and—

PECK DO WHAT I SEZ!

ROOSTER Okay!

BECKY Rooster, no!

PECK And hurry up! We don't have much time left!

Rooster drags Becky to the boiler while Peck rummages through her travelling bag, mumbling anxiously to himself. He finds her diary and reads —laughs!—then stuffs it in his shirt. Rooster is trying to stuff Becky in the boiler but she keeps wriggling out—all arms and legs—like worms in a can.

"I'm swipin' your whole self, yuh big mouth!" Rooster (Jim Farley) grabs Becky (Bethany Ellis). Thanks to a provincial playwriting competition grant in honour of Alberta's 75th Anniversary, Walterdale's production budget could accommodate a remarkable set, including a new cyclorama upstage and mud covering the stage. Photo: C.W. Hill Photography for Walterdale Theatre Associates.

BECKY Please, Rooster, save me! I don't want to be a writer anymore!

ROOSTER Don't worry, I won't let anybuddy hurt you.

BECKY But he's crazy!

ROOSTER Just think of the ring of Venus blowin' through your hair and you'll be fine.

BECKY If you loved me you'd let me go!

ROOSTER I ain't never gonna let you go, Becky.

BECKY Then I hate you, you thief!

ROOSTER We got lots to figure out, girl. In the boiler!

He shoves her hard; she tumbles into the boiler with a shriek.

PECK Rooster!

ROOSTER Comin'! ... See ya soon.

BECKY Roo—!

Rooster slams the hatch and locks it. Then he scampers to Peck who is taking some candles from his sack and placing them strategically around the deck.

PECK Go take a watch fer them tramps whuls I make arrangements fer the party.

ROOSTER Right. Hey, Peck?

PECK Hey what?

ROOSTER Everything's smooth for Clancy's landing, right?

PECK Right. Like silk. Get goin'.

ROOSTER How come you're breathin' so hard?

PECK Fer the joy pure joy of the occasion.

ROOSTER Right.

PECK Go!

Rooster leaps from the deck and disappears into the bramble. Peck lights the candles. Becky is reaching through the boiler vent trying to unlock the latch. Peck sees and hobbles to her.

Hey! Hey! Hey! (*He slaps her hands away.*)

BECKY Let! Me! OUT!

PECK SHUT! (*He slams his stick on the boiler, echoing.*) Me and you is gonna make a little deal.

BECKY I don't make deals with strange old men

PECK Wanna bet? (*He takes the red garter from his pocket and waves it in front of the vent. Becky gasps inside*)

BECKY Mine!

PECK Yours.

BECKY Yes!

PECK —on one condition if.

BECKY If what?

PECK Glad yuh asked. Y'see, jammy-pie, them three tramps of mine is trudgin' through the bramble with their hapless hope. There gonna be here inna minny.

BECKY What the heck do I care?

PECK You vouch.

BECKY Vouch what?

PECK That you been delivered from the cosmos to be Clancy Dougal's sacrifice, magically-like, on the night of his homecomin' .

BECKY I will not be party to a swindle.

PECK What swindle where? All I'm sayin' is let's give this whole thing some class and circumstance. That yer from Venus precisely to throw yerself at the starry bandit's feet. And yer such a sweet thing of purity it could make a grown man fall on his face fer just thinkin' about it.

BECKY That's disgusting! I won't lower myself just so you can—

Peck puts the garter between his teeth and begins eating it.

BECKY Okay! ... I'll do it.

PECK Like I knew yuh would.

BECKY Poor me.

Peck opens the boiler hatch.

PECK Stick yer leg out.

Becky's bare leg comes out. Peck gazes at it in rapture. Now, off in the distance, we hear singing—the Tramps singing "Old Man River" and getting closer. Peck snaps back to reality.

PECK The tramps! They've come. I can hear'em wheezin' through the bramble.

He slides the garter up her leg to her thighs and in the process puts his whiskered cheek on her knee. She gasps and jerks her leg inside.

BECKY You wretch! (*She slams the hatch shut.*)

PECK And you— (*He locks the hatch.*)—no fuss, stay hid, and notta word edgewise til I sez. Then sweetly. Like an angel of certain proportions. Y'got that,lambykins? Cuz if yuh don't that cop at the dock is gonna find one lonely leg with a garter attached floatin' in the river.

BECKY Alright, buster—if you want a certain kind of lady, you're going to get a certain kind of lady.

PECK I can hardly keep from cryin'.

Rooster comes running out of the bramble and leaps onto the deck. The Tramps' song is very near.

ROOSTER They're almost here, Peck! What do we do now?

PECK Follow me uppity the hurricane deck. The time is come fer prophecy to come ta pass.

Peck reaches into his sack and pulls out a music box. Then he climbs the ladder to the steering station. Rooster runs to the boiler and looks through the vent just as Becky looks out. They bump noses.

TOGETHER Ow!

ROOSTER Are you okay?

BECKY Thrilled.

ROOSTER Great! Hang on! Pretty soon we'll be up-and-away through the bedazzlin' blue hole of the heavens and never come back to this muddy ol' swump again!

BECKY Rooster, you're dangerously naive.

ROOSTER What's that?

BECKY You'll see.

PECK (*From above*) Rooster!

ROOSTER Comin'!

He tears himself away from the boiler and scurries up the ladder to Peck who is winding the music box. Carnival music bubbles out. He stuffs it in Rooster's hands.

PECK Here. Play.

ROOSTER I got my squeaky-link, Peck. It's just down there.

PECK This is better.

ROOSTER But I've been practicin'.

PECK Play!

Rooster sighs heavily and holds the music box in both hands. Peck slaps his shoulder and goes into the steering station. Rooster follows.

PECK Now ... We'll give'em just a few seconds to ripen their imagination and then we'll start the party.

Peck ducks down below the viewing frame and pulls Rooster with him.

BECKY'S VOICE (*Echoing in the boiler*) Shoot-t-t! Warm milk-k-k and eggs again-n-n.

Footfalls and rustling through the bramble—Duke and Worm appear. They have sacks over their shoulders with gifts inside for their hero. They also have black mud smudged on their faces for camoflage. They finish their rendition of "Old Man River" and stand gawking at the candle-flooded Empress.

WORM Holy crow!

DUKE Tonight's the night, girl.

WORM I feel fifteen years younger already.

DUKE Lookee the moon, wouldya? It's right outa the book.

WORM High as a kite!

DUKE Bright as a honeyed apple!

WORM Painted right off the blueprints sure as shootin'!

DUKE I wonder where Guppy is? I ain't seen'im since sundown.

WORM Think maybe he din't get an invitation fer rockin' the steamboat?

DUKE My heart would bust if he got left behind by himself.

WORM Yeah, mine, too.

DUKE I ain't never seen such a beautiful sight in my whole miserable life.

WORM There's even music.

DUKE Heroic.

WORM Yeah.

DUKE Do you see Peck and Rooster? It's nearly midnight.

Now there is more rustling in the bramble and Guppy appears. He also has a full sack but his face has not been blackened. There is a slim-necked bottle dangling from his arm. He is supremely drunk.

GUPPY Old Man Riverrr! That Old Man Riverrr!—hic!

WORM It's Guppy!

DUKE Alright! We're a trio!

GUPPY Hiya, kids! (*Laughs*)

WORM Oh, no. Cocktails.

GUPPY So whutz shakin' down in the ol' lagoon tonight?

DUKE Are you drunk again, boy?

GUPPY So am I! —hic. (*Laughs*)

WORM Didya get yer invitation to Clancy's Homecomin'?

GUPPY That I diddy-do-do, Worm, but it din't say nuthin' about a circus. Where's the elephants and tigers? Is there a flyin' trapeze? I could put my eyes on some jugglers with no problem. (*Laughs*)

DUKE I'll juggle for yuh! I'll juggle yer neckbone, yuh big goof! I mean, dotcha have no respect?

GUPPY Beep beep!

WORM Clancy's comin' home!

GUPPY Toot toot!

DUKE What's the matter with you? We got prophecy on the boil and yer a plain hopeless mess.

GUPPY Well just between me 'n you and the risin' moon I'm gonna keep my suspicions on simmer til I sees Clancy come fiddlin' down. —hic!

DUKE Team. Effort. Remember? No. Make.

GUPPY Yeah yeah. Paddy-cake. So where's the bumleg and his dope? Let's get the show on the road.

Suddenly there is a bugle blast and Peck and Rooster pop up in the steering station. Peck has a bright ribbon pinned to his chest and a big smile pinned to his face. Rooster, holding the music box, looks very nervous.

WORM There they are! Up there!

DUKE We made it, Peck! We're here for the homecomin'!

PECK And glad yuh are, Duke! Welcome to the mighty Empress! It won't be long now! Clancy Dougal is just around the corner! He's inna holdin' pattern in the upper stratosphere just a-waitin' fer his musical highwaaay! (*He blasts his bugle again*)

WORM Whuppee!

DUKE Can we approach the deck, Peck?

WORM We camouflaged our faces just like yuh said fer sackin' the universe!

Then Worm reaches down, grabs a handful of mud, and slaps it on Guppy's face.

PECK Rightly so, yuh did! And there's gonna be wonderful times fer sackin' when the time fer sackin' comes! (*He clangs the station bell*) Aaall aboooard!

The Tramps board the Empress and arrange themselves in a line as Peck and Rooster come down the ladder to the deck. Guppy takes a big drink. Duke grabs the bottle from his hand and tosses it overboard.

PECK (*Looks at them—Sighs deeply*)

Man-oh-man! What a loverly crew fer the blast-off. Clancy's gonna be proud.

GUPPY (*Stepping out of line*) Hey, Woodstick...

PECK What is it, sweet Guppy?

Duke and Worm look at each other.

GUPPY How's Clancy gonna come? Did he tell yuh? Will he transcend down inna blaze of fire? Will he paddle outa the cosmos in a solar canoe? Will he rise outa the swump like a dead haunt? I mean, I figure we gotta right to know—just so's we can cover all the angles—right?

DUKE He's gotta point there, I s'poze.

PECK Rightly so! I'm glad yuh asked. Today in extreme contemplation Clancy told yers truthfully that his landin' wuz gonna be... a surprise!

GUPPY A surprise.

PECK (*Shrugs*) That's what he said. Who knows? He could take any shape you might think of—and some yuh might not think of. Why he might materialize right inside of yer sack, Guppy, so's yuh better not doze off.

Peck, then Duke and Worm, laugh it up.

GUPPY Not fer a second, Woodstick.

Duke and Worm exchange anxious looks.

PECK Hey! And speakin' of sacks—didya bring along yer plunder 'n booty to lay at the champion's feet?

DUKE Yup we did!

WORM Ev'ry last drop!

PECK Now that's what I call hope. Ain't that right, Rooster, me grand loyal swipe?

ROOSTER ... I thought hope wuz feelin'
and feelin' wuz believin' and
believin's gonna bring Clancy
outa the cosmos with moonbeams
on the brim of his hat and all
the secrets of the universe in
his sack.

PECK (*follows each of Rooster's lines above:*)

True.
Uh huh.
Just that.
Right.
Sure.
Shut!

DUKE Atta boy, Rooster!

PECK Exactly what I meant.

WORM Like a summer breeze liftin' dandelion fluff into the sky!

PECK Ooo! Well put, Worm. I can see the solar ladder in yer eyes tonight. And a little booty sure ain't gonna hurt in the form of loyalty now, is it?

DUKE AND WORM
Alright!

Duke and Worm dump their sacks of gifts on the deck: gloves and shoes, a handkerchief, a baseball, the odd wallet, a candy bar, a checker board, and various other trinkets and trifles that lay there nicely. Guppy, however, just watches.

PECK Guppy? Yer lookin' a little short, eh? No offense.

GUPPY I ain't layin' down no plunder fer no champion til I have proof of.

PECK Yer a cautious ol' bugger, ain't yuh? (*Laughs*)
But that's what I like about you. Clancy thought so, too.
... Yuh want proof? I got proof.

GUPPY Whip it out.

PECK I wuz savin' fer a surprise.

GUPPY So wuz I.

PECK You first.

GUPPY (*Darkly*) Peck.

PECK But if you insist ... It's this!

He pulls Becky's necklace from his pocket. It glimmers in the candlelight. Rooster gawks.

WORM Holy crow!

DUKE It's beautiful.

PECK It's a magical moonstone.

WORM What does it do?

DUKE Where'd yuh get it?

PECK It dropped outa the heavens flat on me very own skull. It had extraterrestial postage and wuz hotter than a burnin' bun. So I cooled it off in the lagoon and wiped it clean under me hairy-ol' armpit, like so ... and BINGO! —She appeared.

DUKE AND WORM
Who???

PECK Oh it wuzza mighty revelation that fell on me head and proof that Clancy wuz comin'. This here moonstone makes it official-like. What comed from me hairy-ol' armpit put tears in me milky eyes. A beautiful sacrifice, gonna lay down her body fer the champion. So sweet! So pure! Like an angel of certain proportions. ... Rooster! Fly open the boiler!

ROOSTER (*Worried*) Peck...?

PECK I sez fly open the boiler!

ROOSTER ... But — (*Doesn't move*)

PECK (*Laughs*) The boy's as stiff as a cream can. All the excitement. So I'll do it meself.

Peck glares at Rooster and hobbles to the boiler. He opens the hatch and then blows on his bugle. A moment. Now we see smoke curling out of the boiler. Then Becky comes out, having used the contents of the plunder inside to transfigure herself into "a lady of certain proportions": her hair piled on her head, bright red lipstick, a ribbon at her throat, an earring in her nose, her dress over one shoulder and split up one thigh, sleezy nylons and the garter, a cigarette with holder in one hand and the stolen globe in the other. A stunned moment. The Tramps are speechless, including Guppy, who rubs his eyes. Rooster stares.

DUKE Look! It's Clancy's garter on her leg!

Finally Peck, a big smile, turns and looks.
His jaw drops.

BECKY My name is Hope. Kiss the mud.

Worm cries and drops to her knees. Duke follows. Then Guppy. Rooster hasn't budged an inch. Becky gives a big, bad wink to Peck and drapes herself against a pillar. Peck, looking around at the effect, suddenly brightens up again.

PECK (*Then with profundity*) It's midnight, me lovelies. It's time fer the marchin' band. Bring out yer instruments. We're gonna conjure the musical highway. We're gonna bring Clancy down to play.

The Tramps plunge into their sacks and bring out an assortment of musical instruments of original and makeshift design. Rooster, looking confused, finds his concertina. Becky poses.

PECK Alright, you wretched thieves. Ready?

WORM Just a sec, Peck. I got kidney pains. If I don't take a leak
pretty damn quick I ain't gonna be able to toot a single note.

PECK I am sorry, girl. But yer just gonna hafta hold it. Dontcha understand the calibre of this occasion. We can't wait any longer! Let's make music! Play the Blue Lagoon! Send a musical highway from here to the moon! ... BEGIN!

They all play. The music is grotesque but passionate. Becky shifts her hips to it as best she can. Peck brings his stick down on the deck. Music stops.

PECK Clancy Dougal played fiddle like no man alive.
He could fiddle the dimes from yer pockets ten atta time.

TRAMPS CLANCY!

Silence. All gaze upwards. Nothing.

PECK ... Again.

More grotesque music, louder and more passionately. Becky begins dancing. Peck brings his stick down for silence.

PECK Clancy Dougal ate nickels, boulders and spoons.
But when he farted the sky filled up with the ballons.

TRAMPS CLANCY!!

Silence. Upward gazes. Nothing.

PECK ... Again.

Music. Passion. Becky, swirling, is completely caught up. Peck slams his stick.

PECK Clancy Dougal wuz sharper than the tooth of a cat!
He milked up the public and drank it straight back!

TRAMPS CLANCYYY!!!

Long silence. Long gazes. Nothing.

GUPPY It ain't workin', Peck.

DUKE Where's the Starry Bandit?

WORM (*Whimpers*) I don't see nuthin'.

PECK I—I don't understand. Clancy gave me his word of honour on the launchin' pad. ... Just a rainy! Hold yer horses! Didya hear that?

DUKE Hear what?

WORM Where?

GUPPY I din't hear nuthin'.

PECK There it goes again! Oh me shattered soul! I'm gettin' the shakes in me legs! I feel me bones scratchin' at me skin!

Me beans are swimmin' around like crazy! I'm gonna crack up! I'M GONNA CRACK UP!

Peck freezes in a strange pose with a glazed look in his eyes.

DUKE Hey, Peck? What's the matter with you? What's the matter with him?

GUPPY He's frozen stiff.

WORM It's Clancy's surprise landing I betcha! ...Oh! I think I just wet my pants.

Peck starts to move and talk strangely.

"PECK" Rise O people of the swump! This is yer captain speakin'. Yer spokesman and hero has returned. This is Clancy Dougal comin' to yuh LIVE from Peck Woodstick's very own body. That's right, folks. It is I. Yer champion. Thanks kindly fer the musical highway—though it wuzza little bumpy in spots. But it's good to be back in the ol' lagoon seein' all yer hopeful faces.

DUKE Is it really you, Clancy?

"PECK" Is that you, Duke?

DUKE It's me, Clancy.

"PECK" It's me, Duke. Long time no see. Where's ev'rybuddy else?

DUKE The rest all died off. This is it.

"PECK" Too bad. I woulda come sooner but I wuz busy sackin' the universe.

WORM When're we gonna transcend, Clancy?

"PECK" Is that you, Worm?

WORM It's me, Clancy! I'm just a little bit fatter that's all. But I'm as ready as I ever was! Are yuh gonna choose yer brotherly crew now? We're all packed!

"PECK" Well, gang—I've got some good news and I got some bad news. First the bad news. It looks like we're gonna hafta postpone transcendence fer a while.

WORM Oh, no!

DUKE But, Clancy, how d'ya figure that? I mean, how much longer are yuh keep yer brothers earthbounded?

"PECK" Ain't much longer, Duke. Ten years at the most.

DUKE Ten years!

WORM T— ... no.

GUPPY (*Screams*) I MIGHT BE DEAD BY THEN!

"PECK" I know how yuh feel, gang, but transcendence calls fer special development. I barely made it topside meself. I din't have one drop of hope left to spare and there ain't no fillin' stations on the way. Fact is—there's on'y one of yuh who meets the mark even close.

Tramps WHO?

"Peck" takes an envelope from his coat and opens it. Sparkle dust falls out.

"PECK" Ooo!

Silence as "Peck" opens the piece of paper inside.

"PECK" (*Reading*) ... And the winner is ... Peck Woodstick!

Everybody slumps heavily except for Guppy who bristles and looks at Becky who is looking at Rooster who is stymied.

And now fer the good news! Peck Woodstick is stayin' earthbounded, too! He's stayin' back down by my command to teach you tramps the true meaning of transcendence. He's more inspired than all yer muddy souls put together. He's got prophesy and revelation in his heart and he's gonna put all yer plunder 'n booty fer the next ten years or so to good use. Let's hear it fer Peck Woodstick!

"Peck" claps his hands—but nobody else does. Guppy steps forward.

GUPPY (*Low and black*) Hey, Clancy...

"PECK" Is that you, Guppy?

GUPPY One and the same, Clancy.

"PECK" How nice. How are yuh, boy?

GUPPY Not bad. But I'd be whole lot better if yuh took a crack at yer sacrifice now.

"PECK" My—sacrifice?

GUPPY The pretty little moonstone baby.

"PECK" Oh! That! ... well ... (*Laughs uncomfortably*)
I wuz thinkin' I'd just take'er up in one piece and save it
fer a rainy day.

GUPPY I wuz thinkin' we'd split it up right here. I mean, a little
vessel virgin blood is what we need, no? Just to make it all
official-like. So sez Peck.

Becky, wide-eyed, begins shifting toward the edge of the deck. Rooster puts down his concertina.

"PECK" (*Laughs*) Gee-whiz—I dunno, brother. Sounds awful nice, but I'm not sure if I got the right taste in my mouth after the long trip down. I mean—

Suddenly Guppy lunges and grabs Becky by the ankle. She shrieks.

GUPPY Since when do sacrifices cry out, Clancy?

"PECK" (*Laughs—shrugs*) Venus brand.

Guppy moves his hand up her leg to her thigh and feels the garter.

GUPPY It's Clancy's garter alrighty. The one he wore on his arm those many years ago. Faded, frayed, but found. Where'd yuh get it from, baby? Tell old Guppy the truth.

Becky looks at Rooster who swallows hard; then at "Peck" who snarls his lip and narrows his eyes.

BECKY I ... I found it cast on a solar wind and plucked it with my toes.

"Peck" smiles. Rooster shakes his head to himself. Duke and Worm clutch each other's hands.

GUPPY Then yuh wouldn't be opposed throwin' yerself at the champion's starry feet now, wouldya?

Then Guppy grabs her arm and throws her down on her knees toward "Peck's" feet.

GUPPY Throw yerself!

DUKE Fall flat, girly!

GUPPY Throw yerself down!

WORM Kiss'em! Kiss'em!

Becky, shaking, lies down on the deck and tries to force herself to kiss his feet. It is a humiliating experience for her. She begins crying.

ROOSTER NO! Don't, Becky, don't! Guppy! She ain't no sacrifice! She's just a swipe I made and the garter came from an old blind tinkerman who pulled it off a dead man in the river! I don't know how it got on her leg but it ain't solarized and that's the truth!

Silence. Everybody looks at "Peck" who breaks out in a cold sweat. Now Becky raises up and points her finger at him.

BECKY Rooster's right. He put me up to this whole thing against my free will. It's all a big hoax and you've all got mud on your faces for nothing.

Pause.

PECK Lookee the moon! IT'S ME!

They all look up. And Peck runs. The Tramps chase him. Becky runs to Rooster; they hug. Peck is finally cornered. He swings his stick a few times, then leaps off the boat. Guppy jumps after him and knocks him to the mud. The Tramps gather around him. Heavy breathing...

GUPPY Yuh might as well fess up, Woodstick. You been lyin' through yer broken teeth all these years concernin' Clancy Dougal. You made up the whole legend just to keep yer boney hands on the wheel and yer slimey thumbs in our sacks.

DUKE Is that true, Peck?

WORM Is that true?

PECK No! No!

GUPPY And it's my personal thinkin' that yuh killed Clancy outa jealousy and that's why the champion disappeared all of a suddy fifteen years ago and never came back.

DUKE Is that true, Peck?!

WORM (*Crying*) Is that tru-u-ue?

PECK No! I swear it!

DUKE Where's yer evidence, Peck? Yer back's up against the steamboat now! Are you pissin' in the wind or did Clancy Dougal fiddle to the stars?

Peck looks desperately into their faces above him but can't find the words to speak. Now Rooster goes to him and kneels in the mud face to face.

ROOSTER ... Peck?

PECK Aw, Rooster. Listen to me, boy. You were me legs after mine bummed out. You were me hands after mine lost their glue. You were me eyes after mine turned to milk. Now look at us. Look at us! How we gonna steer the boat from this position? Y'gotta stick up fer me, laddie. Hope ain't nuthin' but feelin' anyhow. You can still do it if yuh try. Put it inta words. Draw it inna picture in the mud. Do sumpin' damnit before the whole thing drips away! I NEED YOU!

ROOSTER Didya kill Clancy?

Pause.

PECK I thought I did. I mean, the first time. When we wuz both young and wild and the river wuz fast. But then he came back when the river changed. We laughed at each other's scars and became best buddies in the whole lagoon. ... I thought.

ROOSTER What happened, Peck?

PECK (*More to himself now*) So long ago I almost ferget. It wuz one wee-night on the river again. When we wuz playin' onna log. We wuz drunk and Clancy fell in and got caught inna unddy current. I, uh, sorta, panicked. I watched him go down.

ROOSTER Yuh coulda helped'im but yuh din't???

PECK THE BASTARD SWIPED MY CREW!

Pause.

GUPPY That's good enuff fer me. I say we drown the murderer. Duke?

DUKE ... Alright.

LEFT: Rooster (Jim Farley) and Peck Woodstick (Frank Glenfield), May 1981. RIGHT: Peck Woodstick (Frank Glenfield), May 1981. For Glenfield, among Walterdale's stalwart long-time directors and actors, the commanding role ranks among his fondest acting memories. Photo: C.W. Hill Photography for Walterdale Theatre Associates.

They grab Peck and drag him kicking and screaming to the paddle wheel resting in the lagoon.

PECK No! No! Yuh can't do this, yuh traitors! I'm the captain! This is mutinyyy!

They drape him over the wheel and bind him there with long reeds.

PECK Rooster! Help me! Rooster!

Rooster covers his ears. Becky tries to comfort him.

PECK I'm doomered! I'm DOOOOMERED!

The Tramps turn the wheel over by hand. Peck disappears headfirst into the lagoon. We hear choking in water. His legs kick wildly in the air. A moment. His kicking subsides. They turn him back up in the moonlight. He has Becky's diary clutched in his hand.

DUKE Peck wuzza tramp of this lagoon.

WORM His time wuz sworn to come.

GUPPY If murder were pickles...

DUKE And cheatin' were ham...

WORM His legend would fit inna bun.

Pause.

DUKE Now what?

GUPPY It's my vote we duck our tails into the bramble and never come back.

Duke and Worm cast long looks at the Empress.

C'mon, droppit clean! Let's get outa here. Go play some poker, get cocktailed to the gills, and divvy the booty up three ways. Whaddya say?

WORM I think I'll go home and feed my skinny chickens.

DUKE I think I'll go home fer a nice ... long ... snooze.

GUPPY Suit yerselfs, yuh cruds. But don't come cryin' to me when the chips get down cuz I'll be gone.

Worm looks up at the moon fluttering with clouds racing by. Then she looks at Duke who shakes his head saddly. Her face sags and she walks toward the bramble, putting her hand gently on Rooster's head, then disappears. Duke walks up to Rooster, starts to say something—can't—and disappears into the bramble, too. Guppy, meanwhile, is stuffing all the booty in one big sack. He hoists it over his back with difficulty and walks by the portside in the opposite direction. He stops beside the twisted rag poking out of the shell. He takes a lighted candle from the railing. Gazes up at the steering station—then back across to Rooster who is gazing at the moon. He squeezes a look at the moon himself—sighs—and blows out the candle. Then he retrieves the bottle. Drinks. And disappears. The wind gathers more strongly now.

Becky begins dressing down from her masquerade; last to come off is the garter. She holds it to her cheek.

ROOSTER There ain't nuthin' left.

BECKY Don't say that.

ROOSTER Nuthin' but nuthin'.

BECKY What a terrible, terrible thought

Thunder booms above. Becky dares to go to the paddle wheel. She tries to take her diary out of Peck's dangling hand. But it won't budge free. She leaves it. Finds her travelling bag. Puts the garter inside. And then goes to Rooster in the mud.

BECKY Do you want to come with me, Rooster? We could have such wonderful times on the river together.

Pause.

ROOSTER Peck always talked about inspired blueprints like they wuz really sumpin'. And y'know what, Becky? I still think he wuz right. Ev'rything down here has its very own blueprint hangin' somewheres up there. I mean there's nuthin' you can think or do that ain't already out there in the solar system. If yuh whip down your pants and fart at a butterfly I betcha a dollar there's some starry shape that stands for it.

We hear the low, mellow sound of a river boat calling.

BECKY The *W.B. Dance* going to the sea.

She bends and kisses Rooster. Then she picks up a candle and walks to the edge of the bramble. Stops. Turns around.

BECKY Don't worry, Rooster. There is life in space. And it's us.

She takes a deep, resolved breath and disappears. The candle flickers and fades. Now Rooster stands and walks slowly to the paddle wheel. He turns Peck into the lagoon to be buried. Thunder booms and lightning flashes. Rooster picks up his concertina and sits on the point of the prow. Begins playing softly.

ROOSTER He wore the pants in this lagoon.
He had his castle in the mud.
His legs always got him from the cops.
And he took no bunk and ate no crud from nobuddy.
Now he's driftin' through space.
Sittin' on the brim of his old slouch hat.
Strange way to travel but it suits the bounder.
Goin' out for a gulp of golden moonlight.
Oh he's got business and items of mischief tonight.
He's gotta plan up his hairy-arm sleeve.
He's gonna lick the honey off the face of the moon.
You just wait and see.

He plays. It rains gently. Dim to Black.

END.

Becky (Bethany Ellis) comforts Rooster (Jim Farley), May 1981. Photo: C.W. Hill Photography for Walterdale Theatre Associates.

The Tenth Negative Pig (1983)

by Barbara Sapergia and Geoffrey Ursell

On June 22 1981, Walterdale's outgoing artistic director Vivien Bosley received recognition from the board for her "dynamic and adventuresome work [which] achieved a lot in the promotion of new authors, new plays, and young people" between 1979 and 1981. In gratitude, the membership elected her board president, a position she held from 1982 to 1984. Her impact on Walterdale was tremendous. Between 1980 and 1984, under Bosley's direction, Walterdale organized a national playwriting competition and produced five original season plays (Kevin Burns's *Shikata Ga Nai*, Brad Fraser's *Mutants*, Gordon Pengilly's *The Apprentice of Swipe*, Barbara Sapergia and Geoffrey Ursell's *The Tenth Negative Pig*, and Warren Graves's *Pamela Frankenstein*) and four new one-acts (Mary Glenfield's *The Three Sillies*, Raymond Storey's *The Immortelle*, Warren Graves's *Would You Like a Cup of Tea?* and Gerald St. Maur's *Sister Virtue*). Bosley had, in fact, aligned Walterdale with the recent new play production explosion at many Edmonton theatres. She kept Walterdale's material provocative and relevant in a city whose theatre audiences were growing to demand new plays.

Walterdale's national playwriting competition had introduced the company to a number of workable new scripts. Three in particular the board felt deserved further attention. A few weeks after the first of these, Pengilly's *Swipe*, closed in May 1981, the board decided to include in its 1981/82 activities two workshops that would for the first time involve the company in new play *development*. The first workshop was of a play by local playwright Tom McGovern called *Charlie Is My Darling*, led by long-time member John Rivet with *Edmonton Journal* reviewer Keith Ashwell.[38] The second was of a play set in a tuberculosis sanatorium in Saskatchewan at the end of World War II, led by Frank Glenfield. Interest in the play, titled *The Tenth Negative Pig*, had grown over the summer of 1981, and the board decided in September that the play's co-authors, Barbara Sapergia and Geoffrey Ursell, would be flown in from Regina to see a two-day workshop of their creation the following March. For their expenses, $500 came from funds remaining in the national playwriting competition grant. University of Alberta English professor Diane Bessai was dramaturgical "critic" for the workshop and reading.

Frank Glenfield, also a member of the selection committee, had taken particular notice of Sapergia and Ursell's play during the adjudication process for the competition. He recalls, "The [selection] group, the four of them, picked *The Apprentice of Swipe*. I didn't. Turned out that I had never seen it. Somebody had seen a little mark on the script and thought I'd had it. I'd never seen it. So I had picked the second play which we later did: *The Tenth Negative Pig*" (Interview). When Glenfield did read *The Apprentice of Swipe* he agreed that it was more appropriate for immediate production and the unanimous decision was made, but he saw strong workshop potential in *The Tenth Negative Pig*. Following the March 1982 workshop, interest in mounting a full production of the play was high, and the board decided to stage it the following season with Glenfield as director.

Playwrights, poets, and novelists Barbara Sapergia and Geoffrey Ursell were both born in Moose Jaw, Saskatchewan, in 1943. Sapergia received her BA in English literature from the University of Saskatoon in 1964 and her MA from the University of Manitoba in 1966, while Ursell received his BA and MA from the University of Manitoba and his PhD from the University of London (England). Eight of Sapergia's plays have been produced, including *Lokkinen* (1982), *Matty and Rose* (1985), *Roundup* (1990), and *Winning the Prairie Gamble* (2005), the latter written with Ursell. Ursell's plays include *The Running of the Deer*, which won the Clifford E. Lee National Playwriting Award in 1977; *Saskatoon Pie!*, which won the Persephone Theatre National Playwriting Award in 1981; and *Gold On Ice* (2003). With Bob Currie and Gary Hyland, Sapergia and Ursell co-founded Coteau Books in 1975, and in 1982 they were founding members of the Saskatchewan Playwrights Centre.

Described in an *Edmonton Journal* review as a "well-cast and at times spellbinding play" (Coady), *The Tenth Negative Pig* was another early-1980s "hit" for Walterdale. While visiting the Saskatchewan Summer School for the Arts (1967–91) in the Qu'Appelle Valley, Sapergia and Ursell learned of the site's history as a tuberculosis sanatorium (1917 to the mid-1960s) before the provincial government had refashioned it as an arts retreat in 1967. Their play provides a moving fictional account of "Fort San" set at Christmas and New Year's in 1944, just as trials of the antibiotic streptomycin are being introduced to treat and cure the disease. The play follows four patients—Johnny, Lorene, Nan, and Michael—through personal interactions and fevered hallucinations. We learn that Nan is doing well and may soon be released if she passes the usual tests: fluid from her lungs is injected into a guinea pig; if there is a negative reaction—that is, no infection—for ten successive tests, she could be free to go. Her hopeful news comes as she is falling in love with an air force pilot, Michael, who faces a long stay in the sanatorium. As well, small-town girl Lorene is smitten with Johnny, a "pig-sticker" from a meatpacking plant. A fifth patient, Mariana, conveys the devastating impact of TB on First Nations people.

Discussions about our place in a world filled with violence and disease are interwoven with flowing original folk music composed by the playwrights (see Appendix II). Though tuberculosis was widely viewed as a preventable disease in the developed world when *The Tenth Negative Pig* appeared on Walterdale's stage in 1983, the emergence of drug-resistant strains since the early 1990s heightens the play's socio-scientific relevance for contemporary audiences. The play uses a subtle lyricism to focus on an important part of Canadian history.

The Tenth Negative Pig ran March 17–26, 1983, at Walterdale Playhouse (firehall) with the following cast and creative team:

JOHNNY DOMBROWSKY	Claudio Mascuili
NAN WILKIN	Karen Redford
LORENE EVANS	Suzi Max
MARIANA	Karen Anthony
CHARGE NURSE (Laura)	Linda Pollard
ELVA STEWART	Gaye LePage
MICHAEL	Rainer Kraps
DOCTOR DEVON	Alan Tovey
DIRECTOR	Frank Glenfield
SET DESIGNER	Alli Ross
STAGE MANAGER	Andrew Thompson
PRODUCTION MANAGER	Tim Marriott
MUSIC PERFORMER	Rob Jerrak

The Tenth Negative Pig

by Barbara Sapergia and Geoffrey Ursell

Characters DOCTOR DEVON, *in his 40s.*

JOHNNY DOMBROWSKY, *from a Ukrainian farm background. Worked in a Moose Jaw meatpacking plant on the pig-killing floor. Was a volunteer in the Spanish Civil War. 35 years old.*

NAN WILKIN, *was a teacher. 25 years old. Tries to idealize things. A "model patient."*

LORENE EVANS, *from a poor family. Used to be a waitress in Swift Current. Sarcastic, trying to be tough. In love with Johnny.*

MARIANA, *Cree. From a northern reserve. Pregnant, about to give birth. In her early 20s.*

CHARGE NURSE (LAURA), *in her late 30s. Efficient, brisk. Likes to be in control of herself and her surroundings.*

ELVA STEWART, *a Nurse. Around 45–50. A very limited experience of life. Religious. Spinsterish.*

MICHAEL, *from a well off background, a ranch in Alberta. Served briefly in the RCAF in Ceylon. Tries to romanticize his war experience and illness. In his early 20s.*

Act One

A tuberculosis sanatorium. At the very front of the stage are two sleeping porches, open to the air but screened in, where the patients sleep at night. Johnny's bed is pushed out onto the porch that is connected to the Men's Ward, behind it and Stage Right. The beds of Nan and Lorene are pushed out onto the sleeping porch connected to the Women's Ward, behind it and Stage Left. There is an empty bed in the Men's Ward, and there are two bedside tables, with tissue boxes, thermometers, and sputum cups on them. There are two bedside tables in the Women's Ward. There is a shelf of books and magazines in Johnny's room, near where the bed will be.

At Stage Centre is the Maternity Ward, where Mariana is sleeping. At the back of Stage Left is an Examination and Operating Room, with a fluoroscope, pneumothorax equipment, and a table that doubles as an examining and operating table. At the back of Stage Right is a place for the musician(s).

It is 6 a.m. The stage is in complete darkness. It is Sunday, December 24, 1944. The musical intro for "In the Sanatorium" begins softly. Doctor Devon, standing near the musician(s), begins to sing. As he sings, a spot comes up slowly on him, and then the lighting on the porches and wards comes up slightly, as in winter just before dawn, so that the beds are visible. Lorene stirs in her sleep and groans.

DOCTOR (*sings*)

Oh the days go on forever
And the nights are just as long
When you're lying in your bed
And you're lying all alone
And you know that somewhere out there
Folks are living normal lives
But you're waiting for the angels to arrive
Yes, you're waiting for the angels to arrive
In the Sanatorium
In the Sanatorium
Waiting for the angels to arrive

Oh, the summer's so long coming
Then it goes by so fast
And the days are like a dream
You know can never last
And was it only yesterday they took the harvest in
And you were waiting for the winter to begin
Oh, so afraid of winter moving in
On the Sanatorium
Yes, the Sanatorium
Waiting for the icy touch of wind

Pause. Then Charge Nurse and Elva come on briskly and go into the wards, Elva into the Women's and Charge Nurse into the Men's. They flip the lights on in the Wards. The lights are bright. Elva pushes first Nan's bed and then Lorene's from the porch to the Ward. Charge Nurse moves Johnny's from his porch to his Ward. Conversations take place on both sides of the stage, although they do not overlap. They have put jugs of warm water on the bedside tables.

ELVA Rise and shine, you two.

NAN (*Waking up*) Is it morning already?

Elva puts a thermometer in Nan's mouth, then goes for Lorene's bed.

JOHNNY (*Waking up*) What? What time is it?

NURSE (*Looks at watch*) It's six-oh-four. We're four minutes behind.

JOHNNY Behind what?

Elva pushes in Lorene's bed.

LORENE Jeez! First they freeze you, then they blind you. (*Rubs her eyes, shivering.*)

ELVA Open up. That's it.

Elva slaps a thermometer in her mouth. Elva fusses about, straightening the beds, lining up the sputum cups and checking the supply of "cellu wipes."

JOHNNY We need a goddam union around here to regulate the hours. Patients of the world unite!

NURSE I don't see that you have anything to complain about.

JOHNNY You never ask! Now, if we had a patients' committee—

NURSE I don't think you'll find much support for an idea like that, I really don't. Now here (*Puts a thermometer in his mouth*) ... be quiet. I need your temperature.

Elva takes out Nan's thermometer and marks down the temp on her chart. Charge nurse fusses around, straightening up.

NAN How is it?

ELVA Fine. It's just fine.

Elva takes out Lorene's thermometer, and Lorene immediately grabs a tissue and coughs into it. Elva reads her temp and makes a clucking noise with her tongue. She enters it on the chart.

LORENE What's wrong, have I got a temperature?

ELVA You got your usual two degrees.

LORENE You'd think with this fever I'd at least be warm out on the porch at night. Christ!

ELVA I've asked you before not to take Our Lord's name in vain.

NAN Lorene...

ELVA And on the day before Christmas.

LORENE Ok, I'm sorry. But it must have been twenty-five below out there.

ELVA (*Gloating a little*) Thirty below, actually.

LORENE Oh my God, I'll never get out of here!

NAN LORENE!

Elva walks out of the Ward, offended. She goes into Mariana's room, carrying one of the jugs of water. She puts the water on the table, gently shakes Mariana away and gives her a thermometer.

NAN Couldn't you watch your language in front of Elva?

LORENE I SAID I was sorry. It's just this goddamn cold, I don't know what I'm saying.

NAN Are you sure you're not exaggerating? I don't find it so bad.

LORENE (*Incensed*). Are you kidding? Some things I don't fool around with. Keeping warm is one of them.

NAN Ok, Ok. Why don't we wash up?

LORENE I hope the goddamn water's hot.

Nan sighs and they both begin to wash up. Nan and Lorene take out combs, mirrors and make-up and work on hairdos and make-up. Nan does her hair in a tight bun. In Johnny's room, the Nurse reads his temp and records it. In Mariana's room, Elva washes Mariana's face. Johnny has picked up a book and is reading it.

NURSE What's that you're reading—some union book?

JOHNNY Nope. Hemingway ... about the war in Spain.

NURSE There's a war on right now, in case you hadn't noticed.

JOHNNY I read the newspaper.

NURSE General Patton's stopped the Germans.

JOHNNY If we'd had a little more help in Spain, he wouldn't have had to bother.

NURSE You'd better watch yourself—

JOHNNY Is that right?

NURSE —we're not having any of that Communist nonsense around here.

JOHNNY Whatever you say. (*Mock salute*)

NURSE Don't do that.

JOHNNY (*Moves into clenched fist salute.*)

NURSE (*Angry*) There's hot water. You better wash up.

JOHNNY Sure thing.

Charge Nurse leaves. Johnny puts the book down and washes. He shaves, looking sadly at his reflection in his shaving mirror. Charge Nurse stops at Mariana's room.

NURSE (*Emphatic*) Stewart!

ELVA (*Comes out of Mariana's room*) Yes, nurse?

NURSE Help me with the breakfast trays.

ELVA I'll be finished here in a moment.

NURSE Right now, Stewart.

ELVA Of course.

She puts cloth in basin of water and brings them out. They go off to get trays. Elva comes out first, with Johnny's. She takes it to him.

ELVA Time for breakfast, Mr. Dombrowsky.

JOHNNY (*Still shaving*) Just set it down on the bed.

ELVA (*Sets it down*) Did you have a good night?

JOHNNY Not so great.

ELVA You're going to get better. I know.

JOHNNY Oh sure.

ELVA I can always tell. (*Looks at empty bed*) I knew he wasn't going to make it.

JOHNNY Maybe you better not mention that to anybody else. About knowing who's going to live and who's going to die.

ELVA Oh, I don't.

Elva goes out of room, and goes to get tray for Mariana. Charge Nurse passes her in the hall, carrying trays for Nan and Lorene. When Elva takes the tray in to Mariana she stays there, trying to feed her. Mariana does not eat much.

NURSE (*Sets trays on beds*) Here's breakfast.

Nan tucks in. Lorene just stares at the food.

LORENE I just don't think I can manage it.

NURSE I expect you to eat it.

LORENE It's just too much ... how could anybody? (*She watches Nan eat*) I mean, three eggs, and all that sausage and bacon, and FAT ... and mixed milk and cream to DRINK—ugh. I grew up on skim milk, pig food, Mom called it, but skim milk is all we ever drank.

NURSE Well, do your best, will you?

LORENE Sometimes I think that's where this fever comes from—having to burn up all this food. I'm like a furnace working overtime ... every time I turn around, somebody's shovellin' in the coal.

NAN Try it, Lorene ... it's good.

LORENE I'm just not hungry. I'm tired. (*Picks up glass. Takes a sip, and grimaces.*)

NAN (*Changing subject to protect Lorene*) After we take our pneumo today, I think I'll go for a little walk.

NURSE You better ask the Doctor first.

LORENE (*Picking at food*) Jeez, wish I could go for a walk.

NURSE You have to rest until that temperature starts to come down.

LORENE I don't see what difference it makes.

NURSE It makes all the difference in the world. You have to give the body a rest so it can fight.

LORENE Is that why we have to freeze at night? It slows our bodies down?

NURSE The fresh air's good for you.

LORENE I've have enough fresh air to last me a lifetime. Two lifetimes!'

NAN Fresh air and bed rest and good food have helped a lot of people.

LORENE Yeah, well they haven't done much for me.

NAN Come on, Lorene, give us a break, will you?

LORENE It's all right for you. Everybody knows you're getting better.

NURSE And so would you, if you'd just stop fighting it. (*Picks up wash basins to take away.*)

LORENE I'm not. (*But she's lost interest in the subject*) Say, Nurse, do you ever give the men patients a bath?

NURSE Certainly not. We've got orderlies to do that sort of thing. I am a nurse.

LORENE Yeah, I know that. But wouldn't you like to?

NURSE Your mind's in the gutter. (*Going out*) Eat your breakfast.

Charge Nurse goes to Mariana's room.

NURSE Stewart.

ELVA Yes?

NURSE Collect the trays when they've done with them.

ELVA Yes, nurse.

NURSE And get Mr. Dombrowsky reading for his pneumo. (*Turns away*)

Charge Nurse goes to op room and begins to prepare it. Elva stops trying to force Mariana to eat.

ELVA I wish you'd eat something, Mariana.

Elva takes this tray off.

Lorene is picking at her food. Nan is well into hers. Johnny has a spell of coughing, which is taken up by Lorene, both of them coughing loudly together. Nan watches as Lorene tries to control it.

NAN (*Softly*) Remember, your cough can be controlled.

LORENE (*Between coughs*) Sure thing, Nan. You sound like Doc Devon. (*Mimics "Nobody needs to cough." Coughs into tissue*) Jeez.

NAN Well, it's true.

Watching Lorene, Nan has to relax and breathe deeply to keep from coughing herself. Lorene slowly gets it under control, then Johnny's coughing stops abruptly. He buries his face in his pillow, and may be crying.

LORENE Jeez, I hope Johnny sneaks down here today.

NAN You're getting lonely.

LORENE I haven't seen him for a couple of days. I need him to hold me.

NAN He must be pretty upset.

LORENE I guess we all are. We try and forget about the bone wagon, and then pouf! Some careless bugger goes and—

NAN Lorene. Really.

LORENE We have to face it.

Reprise of music of "In the Sanatorium." Lights dim, then rise as Elva comes back to get their trays.

ELVA (*Takes trays*) Time to get ready for your pneumo.

NAN Sure, Elva.

Elva goes with trays. Nan and Lorene get dressing gowns on and move towards op room. Elva returns for Johnny's tray. She thinks he is sleeping.

ELVA Mr. Dombrowsky? Johnny?

JOHNNY (*Turning from pillow*) Yeah?

ELVA It's time for your pneumo.

JOHNNY Yeah, O.K. I'll be there in a minute.

ELVA All right.

Elva takes Johnny's tray off, then goes into Mariana's room. She gets to her knees and prays silently. Doctor enters and walks towards op room, passing Nan and Lorene.

DOCTOR Morning, Nan. Morning, Lorene.

NAN AND LORENE
Good morning, Doctor.

He goes in the op room. Nurse hands him charts. He looks at them. Nurse comes to door of op room.

NURSE Miss Wilkin.

Nan goes into op/exam room. Johnny puts on dressing gown and comes out into waiting area.

LORENE (*Tries to be cheerful*) Hello, Johnny.

JOHNNY Hi.

NURSE (*To Nan*) Stand right up to the fluoroscope please.

LORENE Look, Johnny ... (*Touches his arm*) ya know I'm sorry about—

JOHNNY Sure.

DOCTOR Let's take a look inside now. Breathe in.

LORENE Johnny?

DOCTOR And out. And in again.

JOHNNY Let it rest, O.K.?

LORENE Sure, whatever you want. *Let go his arm.*

DOCTOR That's fine. Now the pneumo.

They move to the exam table. Nan lies on her side.

JOHNNY I mean, we're just goddam lucky to be in here, right?

LORENE We are?

JOHNNY More than a pig could eat, laze around in bed all day, no worries about a job.

DOCTOR (*To Nurse*) Anaesthetic.

Nurse applies anaesthetic.

JOHNNY Goddamn lucky. You know, I read about this doctor in England, got this goddamn bright idea.

DOCTOR (*To Nurse*) Needle.

JOHNNY Made all his patients beds in the loft of a barn. The vapours from the cowshit were supposed to be good for curing TB Jesus Christ! Lying in bed with your nose full of the stink of cowshit.

DOCTOR (*Puts in air*) There. That didn't hurt, did it?

NAN Thank you, doctor.

JOHNNY You know, I can't get the smell out of my room now ... carbolic acid. They moved me out onto the porch yesterday and doused the whole goddamn place.

LORENE (*Touching him*) Johnny ... I'd like to see you sometime soon...

NURSE (*Brings Nan to door. Nan goes to room, lies down. To Lorene*) Miss Evans.

LORENE O.K., Johnny?

NURSE Come along, the doctor's waiting.

JOHNNY Sure, kid.

Lorene goes into exam room. Johnny stands waiting.

NURSE Stand right up to the fluoroscope.

DOCTOR Take a deep breath. And out. And: again. Yes ... yes.

Elva finishes praying and comes out of Mariana's room.

ELVA (*To Johnny*) Haven't they got to you?

JOHNNY I got lots of time.

ELVA Yes, you do.

DOCTOR Now the pneumo.

They move Lorene to the table, lie her on her side.

JOHNNY (*Indicating Maria's room*) Whataya see for Mariana?

ELVA It's nearly time.

JOHNNY You're sure?

ELVA Yes.

DOCTOR Anaesthetic.

Nurse applies anaesthetic.

LORENE Ow, that stings.

DOCTOR Would you prefer not to have it?

LORENE No. I guess it's O.K.

He puts needle in and pumps in air.

JOHNNY So Mariana's not—

ELVA I'm praying for her.

JOHNNY (*Distaste*) Praying.

ELVA For her soul. (*She goes off.*)

DOCTOR There. That's it for you. We'll do an X-ray this afternoon.

LORENE Another X-ray? Is there anything—

DOCTOR Just routine.

NURSE This way. (*Leads Lorene to door*. To Johnny) Mr. Dombrowsky.

LORENE Your turn, Johnny.

JOHNNY Yeah. (*Goes in to exam room.*)

Lorene, left alone, goes into her own room where Nan is asleep and gets a package out of her table. She then sneaks along to Johnny's room, finds his chamber pot, and puts some powder in it. She then sneaks back to her own room, pulls down the blinds, turns off the light, and covers herself with a blanket.

NURSE (*To Johnny*) You know where the fluoroscope is.

JOHNNY Yes, I do. (*Walks over to it. Stands against it.*)

DOCTOR Let's take a look inside now. Ah yes. Mmmmm. Breathe in. And out again. (*To Nurse*) I think we'll want an X-ray here. Do it this afternoon.

NURSE Certainly, Doctor.

DOCTOR Now for the pneumo.

Johnny moves over to the table, lies down.

DOCTOR That lung isn't staying down. We'll try putting a little more air in this time.

JOHNNY Oh?

DOCTOR Yes, 600cc's should keep it collapsed, I think. (*To Nurse*) Anaesthetic.

JOHNNY I don't need it.

DOCTOR You've had this enough times to know.

JOHNNY I don't need it.

DOCTOR Fine. Needle. (*He puts needle in*) Bit too far ... that's in the lung. (*Adjusts needle*) There. (*Pumps air in*) Breathe out slowly. Yes, I think that's getting it. How does that feel?

JOHNNY Like there's a big chunk of ice in there.

DOCTOR Good, that's what we want. That's all for you then.

JOHNNY Till next week?

DOCTOR That's right. Next week.

Nurse starts to take Johnny back to his room.

DOCTOR Laura, I'd like a word with you.

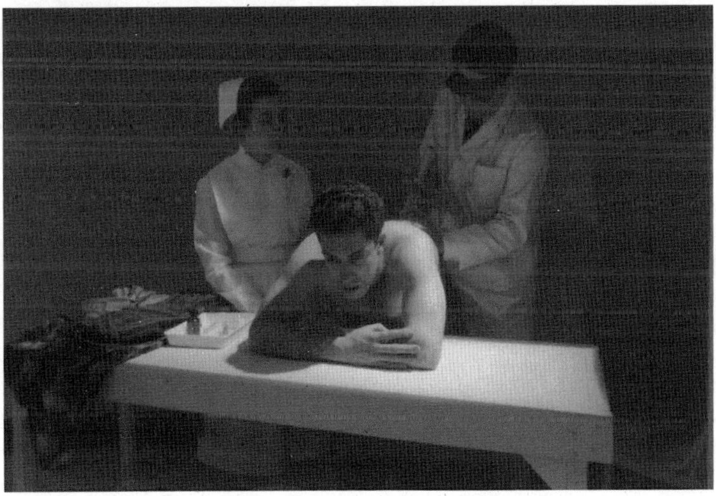

Johnny Dombrowsky (Claudio Mascuili) receives treatment for TB from the charge nurse, Laura (Linda Pollard), and Devon (Alan Tovey) in The Tenth Negative Pig, *March 1983. Photo: C.W. Hill Photography for Walterdale Theatre Associates.*

NURSE Certainly. (*To Johnny*) Go ahead, Mr. Dombrowsky.

JOHNNY Sure.

Johnny goes to his room. He picks up Hemingway and reads.

DOCTOR The first shipment of streptomycin arrived this week.

NURSE Can we start using it right away?

DOCTOR They also sent the latest clinical studies.

NURSE Yes?

DOCTOR It's effective against the bacillus, no doubt about that. But something's going wrong. They only used small doses at first, and it seemed to work. Then the disease came back, worse.

NURSE How could it do that?

DOCTOR It seems the bacilli develop a resistance to it. So they tried a larger dosage. And that did work. The disease didn't return.

NURSE Then what's the matter?

DOCTOR It does something to the inner ear. Dizzy spells ... lack of balance... in some cases even a total loss of hearing.

NURSE We won't be able to use it on everybody.

DOCTOR Not until we understand it better. Some test cases, perhaps.

NURSE Volunteers.

DOCTOR Yes. We'll review the cases. (*He starts to exit*) I better take a look at Mariana.

The Nurse stops in at Johnny's room. The Doctor looks in at Nan and Lorene and at Mariana, then goes off. Johnny is still reading.

NURSE This is supposed to be a rest period.

JOHNNY So, I'm resting.

NURSE That means sleeping, not reading.

JOHNNY Whatever you say.

NURSE It's for your own good.

JOHNNY Whatever you say.

NURSE I'll get these blinds.

Nurse pulls down blinds, flips off lights, leaves.

It grows quiet, with only mild coughing from Lorene the patients sleep.

Reprise of "In the Sanatorium."

After a moment of quiet, Johnny stirs, then sits up in bed, head bent forward resting on his hands. Then he gets up and puts on a dressing gown, peeks out into hall. Nobody. He sneaks down hall to Lorene's room and goes in. Lorene, restless, is still awake, but her back is to the door. Johnny goes quietly to other bed. He touches her shoulder, and she turns to him.

LORENE (*Quietly, but with pleased surprise*) Johnny.

JOHNNY You wanted to see me, sunshine?

LORENE Yeah, I sure did.

JOHNNY (*Indicating Nan*) She still the model patient? Goes to sleep as soon as she's told?

LORENE Just like they bashed her on the head. Out like a light.

JOHNNY O.K. then, make room.

LORENE (*Moves over*) Sure.

JOHNNY (*Stretches out on bed beside her, an arm around her shoulders*) Good.

LORENE Johnny?

JOHNNY Yeah.

LORENE I'm real glad you came along. I've missed you these past few days.

JOHNNY Yeah, well I haven't been feelin so good...

LORENE I'm sorry.

JOHNNY He was a nice guy.

LORENE What are you gonna do if you get out?

JOHNNY You mean, WHEN I get out.

LORENE Yeah, when you get out.

JOHNNY Go back to the plant, I suppose.

LORENE You know how they treat you when you get out of here? Like a walking epidemic.

JOHNNY Aw, not everybody.

LORENE You know Liz that always comes back to visit? She told me. They sorta freeze if you happen to touch them. Her sister was always sneaking off to wash her hands. Even boiled the sheets Liz used.

JOHNNY I haven't been outta here since I first walked in, so I wouldn't know.

LORENE You cough a coupla times, and that's it.

JOHNNY That's what?

LORENE They see you to the door. "Not around me, thank you. I don't want your tu-bugger-lo-sis."

Johnny laughs.

JOHNNY Hey, Lorene.

LORENE What?

JOHNNY I like you.

LORENE I like you, kiddo.

JOHNNY Then how about a kiss?

LORENE Promise not to cough on me?

JOHNNY Promise.

LORENE Well, what have I got to lose? (*They kiss*) Mmmm, that's nice.

JOHNNY You're warm and cuddly.

LORENE Don't tell me how high my temperature is ... send it higher. (*They kiss again*) Johnny?

JOHNNY Yeah, honey?

LORENE What if I had a baby?

JOHNNY A baby? You mean...

LORENE No, I'm not ... But what if I did?

JOHNNY You are a woman, right?

LORENE Right.

JOHNNY Then I guess it could happen.

LORENE Of course it could. Having TB doesn't stop that.

JOHNNY But would the kid be O.K.?

LORENE Sure. I talked to Elva about it. The baby'd be fine ... except...

JOHNNY Except what?

LORENE I'd be afraid to touch it ... afraid to kiss it ... Poor Mariana, she won't even get to hold her kid. They'll slap it right in the Preventorium.

JOHNNY Think you could stand that?

LORENE I don't know. Knowin your baby was so close, but never seeing it.

Elva walks by in hall, going to Mariana's room.

JOHNNY Shh. (*Whisper*). What was that?

LORENE Probably Elva. She's always going in to check on Mariana.

JOHNNY I better get back.

LORENE Yeah.

JOHNNY O.K., I'm off.

LORENE I'll see you again soon?

JOHNNY Real soon. Hey...

LORENE Yeah?

JOHNNY One for the road? (*She smiles and they kiss. Johnny starts to leave*)

LORENE Johnny ... (*He stops*) See ya around.

JOHNNY Sure, honey. See ya around.

Elva, in Mariana's room, has started praying. As Johnny sneaks out of Lorene's room, he overhears Elva, and moves to the door of Mariana's room. He listens, not liking what he hears.

ELVA Almighty and most merciful Father, lead this poor woman to a knowledge of Your infinite goodness. She has not taken our Lord, Jesus Christ, as her Saviour. She has erred and strayed from thy ways like a lost sheep, seeking after the devices and desires of her own heart. She has left undone those things she ought to have done, and she has done those things she ought not to have done. She has sinned in thine eyes. And there is no health in her.

Charge Nurse enters, notices Johnny about to enter Mariana's room to stop Elva. Elva continues praying during the conversation.

NURSE (*Loud whisper*) Mr. Dombrowsky. What are you doing out of bed?

JOHNNY Do you know what the hell's going on in there?

ELVA (*Continuing with prayer*) Please, O Lord, have mercy upon her sins. Let her enter thy Kingdom. In the name of the Father, the Son, and the Holy Spirit–

NURSE What are you talking about? (*Looks in door*) Stewart! What are you doing in there?

ELVA (*Comes to door*) What is it?

NURSE Is there anything the matter with Mariana?

ELVA No. She's sleeping.

NURSE Then what are you doing?

ELVA I'm trying to save her soul.

JOHNNY She doesn't need YOU to save it for her.

ELVA Yes, she does.

JOHNNY She can look after her own soul.

NURSE Stop it, both of you. The Doctor will be doing his rounds any minute. Mr. Dombrowsky, you get back to your room.

She tries to direct him back to his room. He resists.

JOHNNY Not until she leaves that poor woman alone.

NURSE Stewart, you're wanted at the admissions desk.

ELVA But I haven't finished praying.

NURSE Right now.

ELVA Of course.

Elva goes out to admissions desk. Nurse escorts Johnny to room.

NURSE Now in there.

JOHNNY (*Mumbles*) Goddamn holy roller.

Nurse waits till Johnny goes in. She goes to women's ward. Johnny turns on his light, raises the blinds. He drinks from a glass beside his bed.

NURSE (*In Women's Ward, flips on lights, raises blinds*) You can stop resting now.

LORENE Jesus!

NAN (*Groggy*). What? What is it?

NURSE You can stop resting. The doctor will be here in a moment.

NAN Oh ... the doctor ... thank you nurse.

LORENE For nothing.

NURSE You have a complaint, Miss Evans?

LORENE A complaint? Jeez, what could give you that idea? I love freezing my ass off at night, I love bright lights blazing in my eyes, I love...

NAN (*Warning her*) Lorene ... we'll be ready for the doctor.

NURSE Thank you, Miss Wilkin. I'm glad some patients are courteous.

She leaves room, and exits right.

LORENE Courteous? If I'd treated customers the way she treats us, I'd have been fired in two shakes of a lamb's tail.

NAN You must have been a good waitress, Lorene.

LORENE I had to be good ... I couldn't depend on my looks to pull in tips.

NAN You look fine.

LORENE Yeah, but not beautiful. Not like you.

NAN Oh, I'm not beautiful, especially in this getup! (*Laughs.*)

LORENE You could be sensational if you'd ditch that old maid hairdo.

NAN It's practical.

LORENE I guess school teachers aren't supposed to look as gorgeous as Veronica Lake, eh? Might take the kids' minds off their books.

The doctor comes to the door, knocks lightly, and enters.

DOCTOR And how are we feeling now?

LORENE Oh, Nan's fine. (*Looks at Nan*). Flushed cheeks really become her.

NAN (*Laughs*) Actually, it's rouge.

DOCTOR (*To Lorene*) I hear you're having trouble finishing your meals.

LORENE Yeah, I'm just not that hungry ... and when you've seen as many hot beef sandwiches and apple pie a la modes as I have—

DOCTOR It's important to eat regular meals, Lorene. What about your cough?

LORENE I got it pretty well under control.

DOCTOR And you, Nan?

NAN I've been taking short walks, like you told me, and it seems like I'm getting more energy than I used to have.

DOCTOR Good girl. You can walk a little further as you start to feel stronger.

NAN I'd like that.

DOCTOR In fact, I'm happy to say, Nan, that things look pretty good for you. We've been going over your recent X-rays, and they show that the lesions in your lungs have shrunk way back. If you keep up the good work, chances are you'll be out of here soon.

LORENE You mean you'd let her out in the dead of winter.

DOCTOR Why not? She's used to fresh air.

NAN How soon?

DOCTOR We do a test with guinea pigs, injecting them with fluid from your lungs. They're very susceptible to TB, so if they don't get it, we consider you to be negative.

NAN And then I can go?

DOCTOR If ten pigs in a row are negative.

For a moment, Nan has to fight back tears.

NAN I want to go home.

DOCTOR We'll send you away as soon as we can. (*She nods her head, and he pats her shoulder*) Why don't you go for a little stroll right now.

NAN All right.

LORENE (*To Nan*) That's great Nan. I'm real glad for you.

Nan nods her head, exits.

So, got any good news for me, Doc?

He doesn't answer at once.

I'm not gettin any better, am I?

DOCTOR You've shown some progress since you came here. At the moment, your condition's pretty stable.

LORENE I haven't noticed any improvement, not for a long time. Isn't the pneumo helping?

DOCTOR Not as much as we'd like. You see, some people develop adhesions between the two layers of the chest wall ... makes them stick together. That means we can't get enough air in there ... the lung won't go down enough to really help you.

LORENE That's what I've got—adhesions?

DOCTOR Yes, and we don't want that lung to get any worse.

LORENE (*Scared*) Isn't there anything you can do?

DOCTOR We think the best thing in your case is if we try a surgical technique—

LORENE I don't want any cutting.

DOCTOR Lorene...

LORENE I'm not letting you cut me.

They freeze as Johnny, in his room, sings "Doctor Death."

JOHNNY (*Sings*)
oh Doctor Death
takes good care
of those bodies

in despair
oh Doctor, oh Doctor Death
oh Doctor, that Doctor Death

oh Doctor Death
don't make mistakes
when he cures
your pains and aches
oh Doctor, kind Doctor Death
oh Doctor, yeah Doctor Death

oh Doctor Death
he's your friend
brings all suffering
to an end
oh Doctor, sweet Doctor Death
oh Doctor, yeah Doctor Death

oh Doctor Death
treats you well
gives you Heaven
takes away your Hell
oh Doctor, good Doctor Death
so softly, takes away your breath

Repeat last verse, with end line:

oh Doctor, yeah Doctor Death

People in Women's Room unfreeze. Doctor pats Lorene's shoulder.

LORENE I won't do it. I'd rather be DEAD.

DOCTOR You say that as though being dead was just another way of being around.

LORENE You mean–not be? Not anywhere?

DOCTOR I'll come by another day, and we'll talk about it. (*She doesn't answer*) All right? (*Leaves.*)

Nan comes back in. Lorene is crying.

NAN I'm sorry it's just me this time. (*Pause*) I'd gladly stay longer if I could help you...

LORENE Don't say that. You get out of here as fast as you can. And don't look back ... (*Nan puts her arm around Lorene*) It's just gonna take me a little longer, that's all. It'll help me, knowin you're outside.

NAN I'll write you.

LORENE No you won't.

NAN Yes, I really will.

LORENE (*Pause*) I know you will.

After singing his song, Johnny has picked up his books and reads one. The Doctor has gone to find Charge Nurse, before visiting Johnny. Johnny looks in his cupboard for his chamber pot.

JOHNNY Where's the pisspot when you need it?

He finds it under the bed. He gets up and takes it behind his bed, back to the audience, and pisses into the pot. As the liquid hits the powder (which Lorene put there), it begins to foam uncontrollably.

JOHNNY (*Screams*) Aahhh. What's happening to me? What's happening? (*Foaming continues. He puts the pot down as Doctor and Charge Nurse run for his room.*) What is this? What is it?

Lorene and Nan also hear Johnny yelling and get out of bed. Lorene starts to laugh and follows the Doctor and Nurse down the hall to Johnny's room. Nan pauses in the doorway of the Women's Room. The others enter Johnny's room.

DOCTOR What's the matter?

JOHNNY I can't stop this foam.

DOCTOR (*Laughs*) Nothing serious, I see.

JOHNNY Whataya mean, nothing serious?

NURSE (*Annoyed*) Sedlitz Powders. The acid in urine reacts with it ... like this.

JOHNNY You mean somebody...

Lorene ducks behind the doctor.

NURSE I think I know who it was.

DOCTOR Never mind, nurse. Nothing wrong with: a little fun now and again. Things have been pretty serious in this neck of the woods lately.

JOHNNY Fun. Scared me half to death. What IS this stuff?

DOCTOR (*To Charge Nurse*) Just get rid of that, would you nurse?

NURSE I'll get an orderly.

DOCTOR Oh, I'm sure you can handle it.

NURSE Of course.

She takes the chamber pot out, exits right. Lorene starts to go back to her room, but the Doctor stops her.

DOCTOR Lorene ... don't run away.

LORENE (*Trying to cover laughter*) I ... I was concerned about Johnny.

JOHNNY I bet. (*Trying not to laugh.*)

LORENE Gee. What happened?

JOHNNY Well I had to take a ... I had to...

DOCTOR Johnny had to relieve himself, as they say, but things sort of blew up in his face.

JOHNNY You know when you shake a beer bottle and then take your thumb away...

LORENE My, I wonder what would make it do that? Like the froth on a bottle of Bohemian, eh? Of course, a lady doesn't know much about such things, but are you sure you weren't standing too far away?

They laugh.

JOHNNY Lorene, you're a little devil.

They laugh, then freeze. Lights down slightly. At opposite side of stage, Elva has wheeled Michael on. From the doorway of the Women's Room, Nun watches. Michael wears a dressing gown and carries an Air Force uniform, folded on his lap, the hat on top. He looks exhausted.

ELVA Nan—what are you doing out of bed?

Nan I heard the commotion in Johnny's room. Everybody was yelling and running around.

ELVA Well they better quiet down. I got Johnny's new roommate here.

They look at Michael, who looks up at Nan.

Lieutenant Prentiss, this is Nan Wilkin.

NAN How do you do.

MICHAEL Hello.

ELVA He's still recovering from surgery, so he'll need a lot of rest.

NAN He's come to the right place, then. You were in the air force, lieutenant?

MICHAEL Yes, I was a pilot in Ceylon.

NAN That's a long way from home. Is that where you broke down?

MICHAEL Broke down?

ELVA She means, is that where you got the TB?

MICHAEL Yes, I suppose so I...

The cap slips from his hands to the floor. Nan picks it up.

ELVA Poor thing, he needs his rest. I'll take him along to his room.

Elva starts to wheel him away. He turns slightly towards Nan.

MICHAEL My hat...

NAN Here it is. (*Hands it to him.*)

MICHAEL Thanks.

They look at each other. Freeze. Lights down slightly on them, up again on

Doctor, Johnny, Lorene.

DOCTOR Well, back to your room now, Lorene. It's nearly time for lunch.

LORENE O.K., doc.

JOHNNY See you around, Lorene.

LORENE (*Leaving*) See you around, Johnny.

She walks down hall and lights come up and scene with Elva and Michael unfreezes.

DOCTOR Actually, I was coming along to tell you you've got a new roommate.

JOHNNY Somebody new for you to practice on, eh?

DOCTOR (*Dryly*) Yes, it's a bit like playing the piano–except not all the instruments are in tune ... Ah, here we are now.

Elva wheels Michael in.

Hello ... it's Flight-Lieutenant Prentiss, isn't it?

MICHAEL Yes, sir.

DOCTOR I'm Doctor Devon. Welcome to the San.

MICHAEL Thank you.

DOCTOR This is your roommate, Johnny Dombrowsky.

JOHNNY Pleased to meet you.

MICHAEL Hello.

DOCTOR They tell me the operation was a success. Incision healed nicely?

MICHAEL It doesn't feel like a success ... but yes, it's healed.

DOCTOR Good. You're tired from your journey, I'm sure, so I'll see you later. (*Michael only nods*) You too, Johnny.

JOHNNY Yeah, see ya later doc.

The Doctor leaves the room, and exits left.

ELVA Now we'll just put your things over here.

Elva puts uniform on table. Helps Michael into bed, with assistance from Johnny. This is painful for Michael, and is done slowly. As Michael is put in bed, Nan and Lorene talk.

LORENE Didja see the new guy?

NAN Yes.

LORENE He's kinda cute, eh?

NAN I've never seen anyone look so tired.

LORENE Oh, Johnny'll look after him. You'd be amazed how kind he can be, he's like an old granny.

NAN I just saw him for a moment...

LORENE He'll do everything for him.

NAN He looks so tired.

In men's room, Elva puts the wheelchair out of the way and picks up Michael's clothes.

ELVA Now don't you worry. We'll take good care of your uniform. It'll be all cleaned and pressed for when you walk out of here.

Elva starts to leave.

MICHAEL Wait. (*Urgent*) Wait.

ELVA What is it?

MICHAEL There's something in my jacket. A small box...

ELVA (*Checks pockets*) Yes, here it is.

MICHAEL (*Holds out hand*) Thanks.

ELVA (*Places it in his hand*) You're welcome.

Michael puts box in pocket of dressing gown.

ELVA You'll have your lunch in a moment, and then you can rest all afternoon.

MICHAEL I am awfully tired.

ELVA It's no wonder. (*She exits.*)

Charge Nurse brings in lunch trays for Johnny and Michael. She gives Johnny his tray.

NURSE Lunch time. (*Serves Johnny*) Mr. Dombrowsky.

JOHNNY Thanks.

NURSE (*Serves Michael*) Welcome to the San, lieutenant. Are you getting settled in all right?

MICHAEL Yes I am, thanks.

NURSE Anything I can get you? Another pillow? (*He shakes his head*) More blankets?

MICHAEL I think I have everything I need.

NURSE I want you to know, I really appreciate what you've done ... in the war.

MICHAEL (*Embarrassed*) Less than many others, I'm afraid.

NURSE Well, you just let me know if there's anything I can do. Enjoy your lunch now.

MICHAEL Thank you ... we will. (*Nurse exits*)

Elva brings lunch trays in for Nan and Lorene.

ELVA Time for lunch.

LORENE Already?

NAN Thanks, Elva.

LORENE I'm still full from breakfast.

ELVA Enjoy your lunch.

LORENE Yuk!

ELVA You know what Charge Nurse says.

LORENE Yeah. (*Mimics Charge Nurse*) "Think of our boys at the front. Our boys at the front would just love a meal like this." (*Nan and Elva laugh*) We'll have to ask the new guy if it's true.

All patients start to eat as Elva leaves. Freeze scene, dim lights. Reprise of "In the Sanatorium."

Lights slowly up. Elva and Charge Nurse come in and collect the trays. These are now the supper trays. It is evening. Elva goes to collect the men's trays, while Charge Nurse takes the women's.

NURSE Are you finished with your supper?

LORENE Yeah.

NURSE It doesn't look like it to me.

LORENE I ate all I could.

NAN It was very tasty.

NURSE I'm glad to hear that someone appreciates the food.

Nurse leaves. When the women are alone again, they talk while the scene in the Men's Room freezes. Later, the women freeze while the men talk (the two conversations are, in reality, simultaneous.

LORENE O.K., let's get on with the presents.

Lorene reaches into drawer of her bedside table, takes out assorted knitted items, Christmas wrapping paper, tape and scissors. Nan gets out similar stuff from her table. They examine the knitted items. Lorene picks up a scarf.

LORENE Here's my scarf for Johnny. Nice work, eh?

NAN And here's mine. (*Holds it up*) Think he'll appreciate getting two scarves? (*They laugh.*)

LORENE He damn well better. It took us long enough. Y'know, I guess we're lucky to be here for Christmas, otherwise what'd we do with all this goddamn knitting?

NAN There is a fair bit of it.

LORENE A *fair* bit. It'd make a great hope chest for an Eskimo. Or an old crock.

NAN We'll have to not look when we wrap each other's.

LORENE Yeah, we want it to be a complete surprise. (*They laugh*) Just give me a hint, though. Is my present made of wool?

NAN I can't tell you. It's a complete surprise. (*They laugh.*)

LORENE I hear the flyboy had that operation where they take out your ribs.

NAN Yes.

LORENE Where'd he come from?

NAN He said he was stationed in Ceylon.

LORENE Pilot?

NAN I guess so.

LORENE Well, he coulda been a gunner or a navigator. Ceylon, eh? Jeez, don't some people have all the luck?

NAN You think it's lucky to travel half way around the world to fight for your country?

LORENE I mean, to travel like that, see new places. Just once I'd like to spend winter where it's warm all the time, and palm trees, and everything green ... You know, I tried to join up myself, that's when they discovered the goddamn TB

NAN I didn't know you were going to enlist. That's really brave, Lorene.

LORENE Not that brave, I guess. They don't send women to the front lines. But I'd of been some help. And it would've been a chance to get somewhere besides Swift Current.

NAN I never considered it myself. (*Picks up a pair of mittens*) What'll we do with these?

LORENE I don't know. (*Holds up socks*) And I got these. It seems a shame to waste them, they won't fit us. Do you think it'd be O.K. to give them to the new guy?

NAN I suppose so.

LORENE I mean, he wouldn't have to know...

NAN No, he wouldn't have to know ... let's do it.

LORENE O.K., let's. It'll make him feel welcome. (*They start wrapping socks and mitts for Michael*) You ever do anything else besides teaching, Nan?

NAN I helped in my dad's store when I was in high school.

LORENE What kinda store?

NAN Drug store. And we had a little soda fountain. I used to run that.

LORENE (*Pleased*) Oh–you were a waitress too.

NAN Well, not exactly a *waitress*.

LORENE I guess it was different cause your daddy owned the store. You weren't a waitress, you were just helping daddy.

NAN Oh, I guess I was a waitress.

LORENE Didja get paid?

NAN What?

LORENE Didja get paid for working? You know, money?

NAN Well no.

LORENE I see. (*Puts down the wrapped present*). Say, did I ever tell ya about the time the boss grabbed my ass?

NAN *What?* Uh, no, you never did.

LORENE Well, see, I was workin at this crummy lunch counter in the five-and-dime, and this skinny creep with greasy side-burns was the boss, and one day he sneaks up behind me when no one's lookin, and he grabs my left tit in one hand, and slides the other hand down my hip and grabs my ass...

NAN (*A bit shocked*) Lorene!

LORENE And he says to me, "you and me could have a little fun, eh, how 'bout it, sweetheart?" and he gives my ass a little squeeze. Well, I just happen to be frying up this omelette, see, it was still pretty runny, actually. And so help me God, I couldn't stop myself, I just turned nice and slow and gave it to him right in the face. You shoulda seen him wipin those eggs outta his eyes and his hair. And I'm helpin him, wipin off his shirt and tie with the dishrag, and beggin him not to fire me. I say, "I'm so sorry, sir," nice and loud so half the people in the store can hear, "it's just that when you grabbed my ass, I kinda jumped, kinda like a reflex or something. Please don't fire me sir, and maybe we could have some of that fun you was talkin about."

Nan laughs.

NAN Lorene, you didn't.

LORENE Yeah, I did! And I wish you coulda seen his face. First he turns bright red, and then he starts to go pale, when he looks around the store and everybody's watching him. Pale as his shirt collar, which was mostly white. And he says in this vicious whisper, "Be quiet, you bitch. I'm a married man." And I just kept apologizin for all I was worth. You can bet he stayed away from me after that. Except he always suggested I have the roast beef sandwich for lunch. My, they were good.

NAN I think I get the picture.

LORENE I think you do. Course, you probably had to put up with the same kinda thing from the principal, or maybe the school inspector.

NAN No, of course not. (*Thinks*) Although, there was that one inspector. I never was quite sure if he...

LORENE Probably not. He was probably a married man. (*They laugh*) O.K., I'm gonna wrap yours now, so don't look.

NAN All right, I'll turn the other way and wrap yours. Don't you look either.

LORENE Don't worry, I won't. You get few enough nice surprises around here.

They busy themselves with the presents. Lorene has made Nan knitted pink bloomers. Nan has crocheted Lorene a tea cosy.

LORENE Nan, what would you do, if you could be anything in the world you wanted?

NAN Oh, I don't know. Probably the same thing. I like teaching.

LORENE (*Dryly*) It's a nice steady career for a girl. At least until she gets married. (*Nan smiles*) But I mean, if you could really do anything in the world you wanted.

NAN (*Thinks*) I did have an idea once ... but you'd think it was crazy.

LORENE Go on.

NAN It's just that I used to read about the arctic explorers, and how they tried to find the North Pole. I think maybe I'd have liked to be the first woman to reach the North Pole.

LORENE You were right. I think it's crazy. (*They laugh*) It's too goddamn cold at the North Pole.

NAN Of course, I'd wear big fur parkas and fur pants, just like the Eskimos.

LORENE Yeah, and every time you had to take a leak, you'd freeze your ass. (*Laughter*). Besides, some Eskimo woman probably beat you to it. (*Nan looks puzzled*) the North Pole, I mean.

NAN So what would you do, if you had the chance?

LORENE I usta think I'd like to go to Hollywood and be a movie actress, but that's a load of crap. And sometimes I think I'd like to work in a really nice restaurant, like you see in movies, only there aren't any like that in Swift Current, and besides that's a loada crap too. But what I might really like, and I never told this to anybody ... what I think I might really like, and I know it's not gonna happen in a million years ... but I might've liked to be a doctor.

NAN Why not be a nurse, then? That's easy enough.

LORENE I said a doctor. I don't wanna be a goddamn nurse. Get pushed around like Elva does ... Besides I haven't got my goddamn grade twelve.

NAN I suppose you could always go back.

LORENE That's why I thought of enlisting. Seemed like the one chance to break out ... of course, bein here is pretty different from back home too.

NAN Will you go back there when you get out?

LORENE Jeez, I don't know. My old job's gone, and my boyfriend went and married some good breeder with no diseases ... bastard said he'd wait for me.

NAN Lorene, anybody could get TB

LORENE Yeah, but it sure helps to be poor and live in a shack and think that everybody coughs. Our place was like a goddamn sieve in the winter. And now I gotta freeze here.

NAN It's really not so bad, is it?

LORENE Look, I may come from a poor family, Nan, but by Christ, we didn't have to sleep out in the winter. Any place else, they wouldn't expect somebody healthy to do it ... here they got sick people out there freezin.

They haven't noticed Charge Nurse enter. She's come to settle them for the night. She carries "pigs" to warm their feet.

NURSE Complaining again, are we? If some people would just start to realize how lucky (*Placing a pig at the foot of Nan's bed*) they are—

LORENE Lucky!

NURSE —to be where they're looked after, and well fed. If they would just realize that complaining is not the way—

NAN Nurse...

Nurse stops in mid-sentence.

Uh, thank you very much.

NURSE You're welcome, I'm sure. I only wish that everybody—(*Goes to place Lorene's pig.*)

NAN And nurse...

NURSE (*Looks up*) Yes?

NAN Merry Christmas.

Charge Nurse is caught off guard. Somewhat embarrassed. Lorene won't look at her at all.

NURSE Oh ... yes ... Merry Christmas.

They all freeze. In Men's Room we go to beginning of their conversation. Elva is removing the supper trays.

ELVA And how was the supper?

MICHAEL Fine.

JOHNNY I'll say one thing for this place, they sure do feed you. Butter on everything.

ELVA There's no rationing here.

JOHNNY I musta put on twenty pounds.

Elva exits with trays.

MICHAEL Do they always feed you so much?

JOHNNY Yeah, and you've only had lunch and supper ... wait till you see breakfast.

MICHAEL I don't usually eat breakfast.

JOHNNY (*Sitting up on edge of his bed*) There's not much choice around here. Anyway, it's surprising how you start to feel like a starving coyote five minutes before the food arrives.

MICHAEL You been in here long?

JOHNNY Long enough. One year, two months, seventeen and three-quarter days.

MICHAEL You must be nearly better.

JOHNNY My condition has, as they say, "stabilized." I'm not getting any worse... I hope.

MICHAEL I hope I'm not here that long.

JOHNNY You had that operation.

MICHAEL Yes ... thoracoplasty.

JOHNNY Keep your shoulder up.

MICHAEL What?

JOHNNY Didn't they tell you that? "Keep your shoulder up." Helps things to heal right.

MICHAEL (*Tries it*) I see. It hurts when I do that.

JOHNNY Yeah. Harold had one and he ... nah.

MICHAEL Harold?

JOHNNY (*Lying down again*) One of the patients who left.

MICHAEL Oh. (*Johnny stares at ceiling. Michael touches his scar and winces*) When's lights out?

JOHNNY Soon.

Pause.

MICHAEL What did you do?

JOHNNY Do?

MICHAEL One year, two months, seventeen and three-quarter days ago.

JOHNNY You mean outside ... I worked in a slaughterhouse ... chain gang on the hog floor.

MICHAEL What's that again?

JOHNNY Chain gang's the men who kill and cut up the pigs.

MICHAEL Oh.

JOHNNY I was the sticker.

MICHAEL You killed them?

JOHNNY Yeah. Guy'd shackle'em by one leg ... pigs'd get hoisted up, hanging head down, and they'd come along towards me on the hoist.

MICHAEL One at a time?

JOHNNY One every thirty seconds. And the noise ... you wouldn't believe the noise pigs make. On the farm, all you hear is those little grunts they make when they slop the feed. But they're coming at you and you got a knife—a long blade, sharp on both sides—and you're stickin it in their throats and they know what's comin and they scream ... that's all it is, screamin. And kickin their bodies in the air, trying to get out of the shackle ... sometimes they break their legs ... and sometimes they make you miss, so you have to stick'em twice. And if you miss'em completely, the hoist just keeps movin and they keep screamin till they hit the steam trough ... water scaldin hot and in they go ... and then they stop.

Johnny hasn't noticed Michael's distress, which increases as Johnny speaks. The description sends Michael into a memory of his surgery. Their speeches overlap.

MICHAEL It's not going to hurt, the doctor said ... but you'll be awake ... better if you don't look ... and I didn't want to, but they were cutting in my chest, and I had to look ... at first I couldn't believe ... no pain, but I could feel the cutting, I could hear ... at home I helped dad butcher steers ... and I saw it over and over as they worked on me ... I tried not to see ... my dad slipping the knife between the bones ... and the blood ... I was awake, I could feel ... the bone stripped from its case ... and I was alive, awake, I could hear...

Michael covers his face. Johnny comes over to his bed, puts a hand on his shoulder.

JOHNNY Take it easy, boy.

MICHAEL I could *feel*...

JOHNNY (*Firmly*). Just take it easy ... it's all over now. Just try to let it go ... breathe slow and easy.

Michael uncover his face, tries to do as Johnny says. Johnny pats his back lightly.

MICHAEL I'm sorry.

JOHNNY It's all right. It was stupid of me.

Johnny stays by Michael, who gradually recovers himself.

MICHAEL I guess I've been trying to wipe it out of my mind.

JOHNNY (*Sounds in hall*) Elva's gonna be here in a moment. She gets us settled for the night.

Michael is trying to be his normal self. Elva enters.

ELVA I've got your pigs. (*Positions one in Michael's bed*) That'll keep you nice and cosy.

MICHAEL Pigs?

JOHNNY They're full of hot water. I guess they're called pigs because of their round bellies. Elva brings Johnny's pig.

ELVA Looks to porch. It gets pretty cold out there.

MICHAEL On the porch?

JOHNNY I forgot to tell you. We sleep out there.

MICHAEL In the open?

ELVA It's screened in.

MICHAEL Yes, but the cold.

ELVA With your nice thick Hudson Bay blankets and this cosy little pig, you won't feel it at all.

MICHAEL Oh my God.

ELVA Here we go. (*Pushes Michael's bed out, comes back for Johnny*) You ready?

JOHNNY Ready as I'll ever be.

ELVA Here we go, then. (*Pushes his bed out.*)

At the same time Charge Nurse is pushing Women's beds out.

ELVA AND NURSE

Good night, and Merry Christmas.

Lights fade down, leaving a dim light around Mariana's bed. Patients sleep. Moments of Silence. Then Musician begins to play music for "Spirits of Night." Mariana wakes, gets up. Her long hair falls loose to her shoulders. Music continues softly as Mariana speaks.

MARIANA I couldn't live around here ... I'd always feel too exposed, too defenceless. At least here we're in a valley, but up there on the prairie there's no place to shelter ... Where I come from there's trees all around. Even in winter, when their boughs are weighed down with snow, the trees are still green, you can see they're still alive under the snow. Here, when the leaves fall away, there's only bare branches, like when the flesh falls away from your body and there's only bones, naked bones...

It's still cold back home, yes, it's cold. Deep snow everywhere, ice three feet thick on the lakes. But under that snow, under the ice, there's life. Small animals in their tunnels, fish and beaver under the water ... and over us all, in the night, white shadows of owls drifting, and the sky filled with stars, and the moon ... large and cold ... like a big piece of ice cut from the lake ... floating across the darkness...

At night, when my husband came back from the trapline, we would lie together after love, our hands on my belly, sheltering the child inside me ... and we would listen to the cold. You could hear it, easing into the trees, to their hearts ... and when the cold touched them, their hearts would go *crack! crack!*

I knew there was something wrong when the cough I got in summer wouldn't go away. It's only a summer cold, I thought, they always last longer. But I started coughing blood during the time of the autumn moon. Still, it wasn't for me that the doctor flew into the village ... there was a child with a bad fever. But my husband asked the doctor to come to our cabin. I was pretty weak, coughing a lot, coughing blood. The doctor said unless I came to this place, we might lose the child. I didn't want to leave my husband, but we didn't want to lose the child...

I don't understand anything they say around here ... I never learned their language. I'd like my husband to visit me, but I don't know where I am ... the plane brought me so far ... They never understand me when I speak, so I don't talk to them any more ... They don't even know my name my name isn't Mariana...

This land speaks to me in voices I haven't heard before ... the wind speaks too loud, it's trying to tell me something, but I don't want to hear ... the wind calls me ... it calls and calls...

I only came because we didn't want to lose the child.

Music up. Lights dim. She gets into bed. Silence, sound of cold wind. Silence. Lights out. Music stops.

End of Act One.

Act Two, Scene One

Lights up. Christmas morning. Musician plays traditional carols. Johnny, Lorene, Michael, and Nan are gathered in a lounge (beds turned sideways, pillows removed) with small artificial Christmas tree on a table in the centre. There are presents under the tree, some of which they have opened. Each has a glass, and there is an open mickey of rye on the table, from which they're drinking. Johnny, particularly, is getting quite a glow on. They are wearing pyjamas with dressing gowns over them. Johnny wears a bright woolen scarf around his neck. They all stand around the tree, as Johnny proposes a toast.

JOHNNY Here's to chasing cure!

ALL To chasing cure!

They drink. Michael returns to his wheelchair and sits down.

JOHNNY (*Pulling another scarf from wrappings*) Oh boy. Another scarf. You girls sure know how to take care of a guy. (*Kisses Lorene's cheek*) Thanks, honey.

LORENE Glad ya like it, kid. (*Opening Nan's gift*) Oh say, this is really nice. (*Puts it on her head. To Johnny*) How's it look?

JOHNNY Oh, "swave," Lorene—real "swave."

NAN (*Laughing*) It really suits you. I don't know what made me think it was a tea cosy.

Lorene takes off the tea cosy, looks at it, and they both laugh. She puts it back on.

LORENE Hell, I'm not gonna waste anything this warm on a teapot. (*Takes a sip of her drink*) Besides, they're my colours.

Nan has opened her gift from Johnny: a box of chocolates.

NAN Oh these are beautiful, Johnny. Thank you so much.

JOHNNY Glad you like 'em, Nan. I thought you could always use the box after to keep stuff in.

NAN You'll all have to help me eat them.

Lorene opens her present from Johnny. It's a flat fifty of Player's cigarettes.

LORENE Johnny. You dreamboat. A whole flat fifty. (*She breaks open the wrappings*) Anybody got a light?

Johnny produces matches from his pocket and lights her cigarette. She takes a deep drag.

Aaah (*Coughs*) that's good. (*Others laugh.*)

Johnny goes around and tops up all the drinks, although Nan tries to refuse. They all drink. Nan and Lorene go to the tree and pick up their gifts for Michael and take them to him.

MICHAEL For me? But I don't ... well, thank you.

LORENE Go ahead, open them.

MICHAEL I'm afraid I don't have anything...

LORENE Hey, don't worry about that. You didn't know.

MICHAEL You two didn't know I'd be here either.

NAN Maybe not, but we do a lot of handicrafts here.

Michael unwraps a pair of mittens.

LORENE Comes in *handy* sometimes. (*They laugh.*)

MICHAEL Thanks, they're really nice. (*Nan smiles*) You made them yourself?

NAN Yes. Try them on ... see if they fit.

He does, and they do. Then Michael opens Lorene's present. A pair of socks.

MICHAEL Thanks, Lorene, these are really well made. And I like the pattern.

LORENE You're welcome. And I expect to see them on your feet one day soon.

MICHAEL Why put off until tomorrow what you can do today? (*Starts removing his slippers with great difficulty*) I can't wait to try my new toe warmers.

Women help him change to the new socks. He looks at his feet, pleased.

There, snug as a pig in a blanket.

JOHNNY Real sharp. Just because we're old crocks, don't mean we haven't got the latest fashions—my God, Nan, what is that?

Nan has unwrapped the pink bloomers from Lorene and holds them upside down.

NAN Oh Lorene, it's beautiful. What ... is it? (*Then turns them right side up. Embarassed*) Oh, I see ... why they're ... lovely.

LORENE You gonna put your present on too?

Nan shakes her head.

Come on, you gotta.

Lorene goes over and puts them around Nan's neck, like a collar.

Nice collar, eh? Why you could wear that anywhere.

JOHNNY Oh hell, yes, opera, theatre, you name it.

Laughter. There are still three presents under the tree. One by one they turn to look at them.

MICHAEL There's three presents left. Who're they for?

JOHNNY (*Examines tags on presents*) Well, there's one for Nan, one for Lorene, and one for me.

MICHAEL Why don't you open them? (*Nobody moves*) Who're they from, anyway?

Nobody answers. Michael is confused.

LORENE They're from Harold.

Michael looks at her, trying to understand.

NAN Harold was Johnny's roommate before you came.

They let that sink in. Johnny opens his present.

JOHNNY (*Pulls out a "26" of whiskey*) Well, how about that? He really did'er up proud.

LORENE Wow, we can have some party with that.

MICHAEL What happened to Harold?

Again, no one wants to answer. Lorene takes a deep breath and speaks calmly.

LORENE Harold won't be back. (*Pause*) The bone wagon hauled him away.

MICHAEL (*Shocked*) What?

JOHNNY It's what we say ... when somebody ... dies.

MICHAEL But that's ... horrible.

NAN You have to find some way...

JOHNNY You have to able to laugh, or you'd go nuts.

LORENE The mickey's empty. Let's crack Harold's bottle.

Johnny opens the bottle and pours everyone a shot. No one tries to refuse. They drink solemnly.

LORENE Here's to Harold.

They raise glasses and drink.

ALL To Harold.

JOHNNY Let's see what he got you girls. (*Hands them presents.*)

Lorene opens hers and pulls out a pair of long woolen stockings.

LORENE Oh boy, are these NICE. So warm. Bet they'll come right up to my ... knees.

Johnny smiles, but they're getting choked up. They take another swallow. Nan opens her present, flannelette pyjamas.

LORENE Watcha got there, Nan?

NAN Pyjamas. Feel how nice and soft they are. Good ones.

Nan, Lorene, and Johnny are near tears, especially Nan. Johnny takes a drink.

JOHNNY Look, Nan, he was a good guy. But he's gone.

NAN I know.

LORENE (*Sings softly. It's a song they all know*)
He's just another one who won't be goin home.

LORENE AND JOHNNY
He's passed along to a place that we don't know
He'll never get to see another day
And the bone wagon hauls another one away

Oh, he's gone but not forgotten
Till we meet at judgement day
And we'll all chase cure tomorrow
If the bone wagon hauls another one away.

Michael watches them; Nan hasn't joined the singing.

JOHNNY Come on, Nan.

Johnny begins second verse, joined by Lorene, and then by Nan, softly at first, then with greater strength. They may cry, but don't stop singing.

JOHNNY, NAN AND LORENE

He's just another one who won't be goin home
He's found himself a home where the wind don't blow
So you better have a good time while you may
Cause the bone wagon's hauled another one away

Oh, we'll wait here in the valley
As they cover him with clay
And we'll warm ourselves with his whiskey
As the bone wagon hauls another away

More quietly.

He's just another one who won't be goin home
He's passed along to a place where we can't go
He'll never take another tumble in the hay
And the bone wagon hauls another one away

JOHNNY (*Drinks*) I didn't think Christmas was gonna turn into a wake for Harold. (*Drinks*) How about that? A Ukrainian wake. (*Smiles and drinks.*)

MICHAEL How old was he?

JOHNNY Oh, about forty-five. Nice little guy—bald head, shiny as a billiard ball.

Lorene and Nan laugh, a little ashamed.

LORENE And little stick legs like billiard cues. He was kinda cute. Always talking about his wife.

JOHNNY Until she ran off with the boarder.

LORENE Actually, the boarder just moved downstairs. She didn't have to run off.

JOHNNY Not with Harold away. (*He refills glasses. They're all getting drunk.*)

LORENE I think he was kind of sweet on Nan.

Michael looks at Nan, disturbed.

NAN He said I reminded him of his sister.

LORENE He used to play cribbage with Johnny.

NAN And he always used to win.

LORENE He never caught on that Johnny let him win. He was just so darned pleased. But a real good sport.

JOHNNY Oh yeah, Harold was a great sport.

MICHAEL But I don't quite see...

NAN You will.

LORENE I'll always remember Harold.

Johnny begins the first chorus of the song again. "Oh he's gone but not forgotten." Lorene and Nan, and even Michael, join in. Elva, on her way to Mariana's room, looks in. She is carrying a wrapped Christmas present.

JOHNNY (*Spotting Elva*) Hey, Elva ... c'mon in and have a drink to old Harold.

ELVA You know I don't drink liquor.

LORENE Sure, Elva, come and join us.

ELVA No, thank you very much ... not even for poor Harold.

JOHNNY Ah, come on ... just this once.

NAN What have you got there, Elva? Is it a present?

ELVA It's a blanket for Mariana's baby.

JOHNNY Oh, on your way to prayers again, are you?

ELVA It wouldn't hurt you to think upon the Christ child today.

LORENE We'll do that, Elva. Don't mind him...

JOHNNY Prayin all the time ... gabble, gabble, gabble.

ELVA What's wrong with my prayers?

JOHNNY They're a goddamn insult to the human race!

NAN Johnny!

JOHNNY No health—pile of crap.

MICHAEL Oh, for heaven's sake.

ELVA There's no need to say that. It's Christ's birthday. I won't listen ... no... (*She leaves, nearly in tears.*)

LORENE Didja have to jump on her like that?

JOHNNY I got no use for the kinda religion says people are nothin but shit.

NAN Elva doesn't think that.

JOHNNY Do you know those crummy prayers she mumbles in Mariana's room? Do you?

NAN No, how would I?

JOHNNY Well, I do. I heard them. And let me tell you, I don't think Mariana understands one word of English, and it's a goddamn good thing, because it's bloody well the last thing she needs to hear. How she's a lost sheep who's let God down, and how she's left undone things which she ought to've done, and done things she ought not to've done,' and—

Lorene starts to speak the works with him, softly.

—there is no health in her.

LORENE "There is no health in us."

JOHNNY (*Notices Lorene joining in*) You know it?

LORENE Sure, I've said it a million times in church. So what?

JOHNNY So *what*? Have you ever thought what it means? Why say people are no good?

Michael has been growing increasingly distressed.

MICHAEL For God's sake man, don't be so literal.

JOHNNY Whattaya mean?

MICHAEL No one literally believes that there is no good—

JOHNNY Yeah, well they're still teachin it to poor stupid fools like Elva.

NAN That's not the only thing we're taught.

JOHNNY "There is *no health*"—no good. Tell people that enough times and they won't even think of trying to change anything.

NAN Didn't you ever belong to a church?

JOHNNY No, I never did. My old man broke with the church way back in the old country.

LORENE Weren't you even baptised?

JOHNNY None of us kids ever set foot in a church.

LORENE I think I believe in the church ... sort of.

JOHNNY Why not believe in people?

LORENE People can let you down.

JOHNNY And people can help you, and work with you ... and fight with you.

LORENE Sometimes people cause their own troubles. I mean, I worked hard for everything I ever had ... but back home we got some neighbours, the Huckabees, and none of them ever did a day's work in their lives. They never seemed to care if their kids had good food or not, wouldn't even bother to grow a garden. What do you do about Huckabees?

JOHNNY Look, I don't know. We had neighbours too, the Zalinskas, lost everything they'd sweated for, and it sure as hell wasn't any fault of theirs.

NAN In the Depression?

JOHNNY Yeah. And they weren't the only ones. There wasn't much work anywhere. I saw a lot a people like the Zalinskas when I was movin around. In the Okanagan it was all the fruit you could eat ... sounded good at first, but believe me, you can't live on fruit. The more you eat, the more you... (*They all laugh*) ... the more you toot. (*Laughter*) After I'd had enough a that, I rode the rails back to Moose Jaw ... ended up in the jungle.

MICHAEL The jungle?

JOHNNY Hobo jungle ... just south of the town by the river, place called Round Hill. I heard there was this camp, so I walked over ... across a trestle ... at first I couldn't see anybody, and then, way down in the trees, I see a campfire. So I walk down towards the smoke and this guy ... Jigger Ericson...

LORENE Jigger? What kind of name's that?

JOHNNY Oh, he used ta work for the CPR on the section gang and he liked to ride the little jigger they travel around on. Anyway, Jigger jumps out at me from behind a tree and asks me what the hell I want. They'd been havin trouble with the CPR bulls ... the cops, ya know ... and I say I've just come in from the Okanagan and I need someplace to sleep. He asks me if I've eaten, and I say not for two days. So he takes me into the camp—there musta been 30 guys around the fire—and he finds me some beans. A whole can of pork and beans. Jesus, would you believe, no food's ever tasted that good, before or since, not even in Spain ... Ya see, it was Jigger who told me that the Communist Party was trying to get men to go and fight in Spain.

NAN Were you a communist?

JOHNNY Close to it. Things weren't working in Canada, and I couldn't see anybody doing much about it. Anyway, Jigger said they were looking for men ... "to help fight for democracy" was how he said it.

MICHAEL They're still saying it about this war.

JOHNNY Yeah, they are. Anyway, it seemed pretty clear to me. The fascists were trying to destroy the government people had elected. And I guess it was a way of fighting back against the whole goddamn Depression, the work camps, the union busting...

NAN But you mean you just up and went, just like that?

JOHNNY I took a coupla days to think it over. But there was never much question.

LORENE You had a lotta faith in people.

JOHNNY Still do. There's a lot of people like the Zalinskas ... and they're worth fighting for.

LORENE Too much faith, maybe.

JOHNNY Keep up that kinda thinkin and you're gonna end up like Elva.

LORENE That so?

JOHNNY (*Relaxes a little*) Well, I guess you'll never be exactly like Elva.

NAN Elva was right about one thing, Johnny. This is a Christian holiday.

JOHNNY Like hell. Mid-winter's always been a pagan celebration. Solstice ... lowest point of the sun in the sky. Shortest day, longest night. They were celebrating the death and rebirth of the sun. The Christians just took it over. Christ ... if there was a Christ ... wasn't even born on the 25th of December. Hey Lorene ... want another drink?

LORENE Sure.

JOHNNY A girl after my own pagan heart.

Lorene joins him in half-hearted laughter, but Nan looks offended. She and Michael try to turn the conversation. Johnny pours drinks all around.

NAN (*To Michael*) Did they celebrate Christmas in Ceylon?

MICHAEL Yes, some of them did. People in Ceylon ... the Christians anyway ... believe Ceylon is where Adam and Eve went after they were cast out of the Garden of Eden. They think the island is the closest thing on earth to Paradise.

JOHNNY So nowhere better to find God, eh?

MICHAEL (*Treats it as simple question*) At times it seemed so ... but not on land, beautiful as the land was...

NAN Flying.

MICHAEL Yes. Flying.

JOHNNY And coal-miners dig down to hell.

MICHAEL I don't mean in that way, not that you could get physically closer to Him by flying. I mean, it's simply a different place, the sky. Look, the plane I flew was big, a hundred-foot wingspan, a crew of seven. It was a flying boat ... we took off from the water, landed on water. We could stay up there for a whole day, even more. Just lose touch with the earth. Forget after a while what the ground felt like.

Music for "Where is God" begins, softly.

Flying ... high, high over the Indian Ocean ... away from all land ... out past the small dots of green and gold, coral islands ... then no land anywhere ... only ocean, blue-green like emeralds, like sapphires. All of us snugged into sheepskin jackets with electric coil in them to keep us warm, and oxygen masks ... and below, the tropical heat and the drift of soft air laden with spices, laden with salt from the sea. Flying. On my first missions I used to feel ... every moment in the air ... a sensation just below my ribs ... a floating bubble of fear ... that never burst, but never escaped from my body. And I'd pray ... pray we wouldn't find anything. We never did. Then one day the fear wasn't there any more. It just went away.

Sings.

> Where is God
> when you fly?
> blue-green sea
> blue, blue sky
>
> Where is God
> when you die?
> salt sea of tears
> cold sea of sky
>
> Where is God
> where does He hide?
> warm sea of death
> flows into sky

NAN (*Near tears*) Oh, Michael... (*She takes his hand.*)

JOHNNY (*Under his breath*) What a load of crap!

LORENE Let it go, Johnny, it's Christmas.

JOHNNY (*Getting up*) A load of crap is a load of crap, no matter what day it is.

LORENE Johnny...

Johnny storms out. Lorene goes after him.

JOHNNY There's something the flyboy should see—so he'll know what this war's really about.

LORENE (*Leaving*) I better talk to him.

JOHNNY (*On way out*) Tropical paradise, Jesus!

Lorene leaves.

LORENE (*Off*) Johnny! Johnny, wait!

Michael feels unjustly attacked.

MICHAEL Boy, he sure takes things seriously.

NAN Look, don't take it to heart.

MICHAEL I can understand how he feels about Harold...

NAN It's not only that.

MICHAEL What is it then?

MICHAEL I think when he sees you, he feels he should have been in the war too. And that what he did in Spain went for nothing.

MICHAEL Because he couldn't prevent the war?

NAN And because no one honours them. You've seen how Charge Nurse treats servicemen—nothing's too good for you. But Johnny she always accuses of being a Communist.

MICHAEL Why take it out on me? I'm willing to give him his due.

NAN It's not only the war. Johnny thinks he should be working.

MICHAEL Yeah ... I sure feel useless enough. Just sitting here, taking up space, using up food ... but why'd he fly off the handle at Elva.

NAN He's got a thing about religion.

MICHAEL I can see that.

NAN He thinks if people can have religion and still do bad things, what's the use of religion? So he just tries to be good all on his own.

MICHAEL But why pick on Elva?

NAN She can get on your nerves.

MICHAEL Simple faith ... what's wrong with that?

NAN If you don't happen to take the Bible literally ... and somebody acts like they were *there*, and if it's all they talk about...

MICHAEL But she seems so kind.

NAN She can be very kind.

MICHAEL How'd she get stuck away in this place?

NAN She had it too.

MICHAEL Had what?

NAN When she was young, just finished training to be a nurse, they found out she had pleurisy, and they sent her here for a few years.

MICHAEL So she was cured.

NAN She got over it. But by the time she got out her mother was sick. Her heart. Elva was the only unmarried one in her family, so she had to stay home.

MICHAEL Being a nurse and all.

NAN Exactly.

MICHAEL She tell you all this?

NAN Oh, in bits and pieces. She probably doesn't realize how much she's told me.

MICHAEL Did her mother die?

NAN Yes, and Elva stayed on to keep house for her dad. Then he got sick, and she had to look after him. She spent more than ten years nursing the two of them.

MICHAEL She never lived on her own all that time...

NAN And when her father died, there she was, thirty-five years old, no money, no furniture—her father left the house to her eldest brother...

MICHAEL Bastard.

NAN Elva told me she didn't even have decent clothes to wear to look for a job in.

MICHAEL But why come back here?

NAN She had another bout of pleurisy after her dad died. When they got her back on her feet, I guess this place seemed safer than the outside world.

MICHAEL Was she always religious?

NAN Oh, in the ordinary way, she probably was. But I think it's really blossomed since she came back here. It's all she's got, really ... her "dear little Christ child."

MICHAEL She seems pretty interested in Mariana.

NAN Whenever a women has a baby here, Elva waits on her hand and foot. You can see how she wants children, she needs to touch them...

MICHAEL Poor woman.

NAN But there's something wrong about it. She wants to hold them and hug them ... but children grow into people. You have to see them for themselves, not just as cuddly bundles...

MICHAEL (*Smiling*). You wouldn't cuddle them...

NAN Of course, I would. I just mean, there's a lot more to it. You have to *think*.

MICHAEL I wonder where Johnny's got to?

NAN Oh, Lorene's calming him down. (*Changing subject*) Have you heard from your family?

MICHAEL *Morose*. They probably don't know I'm here. I imagine they sent my presents to the veterans hospital in Winnipeg.

NAN Where do they live?

MICHAEL On a ranch near Canmore.

NAN You haven't seen them...

MICHAEL For over two years. Last time was just before I went overseas.

NAN (*Trying to divert him*) So you were a rancher.

MICHAEL My mother wanted me to go to university. Her father was a lawyer, and that's what she wanted for me. My brothers were supposed to stay home and run the ranch.

NAN What did *you* want?

MICHAEL Oh, who knows at eighteen? But I would've gone. Except the war came along.

NAN I've never been to a ranch.

MICHAEL I used to ride up into the mountains. Go fishing for rainbow trout or just walk in the summer meadows ... I wonder if I'll ever see them again.

NAN You have to believe you will. You have to work at it.

MICHAEL Is that what you do?

NAN I want out of this place.

She holds out her box of chocolates.

NAN Like a chocolate? (*Shows him diagram from box*) Here's the diagram showing you what's in them.

MICHAEL Yeah, let's see where the soft ones are. (*He chooses one and eats it.*)

NAN I like the hard centres best ... they last longer. (*Takes a candy*) Funny, that's the only thing dad ever brought home from the store ... except medicines.

MICHAEL It was a drugstore?

NAN Yes. I used to think there was a medicine for every sickness. I'd watch him mixing them, measuring the coloured powders on a shiny brass scale, and filling the capsules ... they looked so pretty, I figured they were a kind of candy.

MICHAEL (*Eating*) Ummm, this is good ... Turkish Delight.

NAN Whenever mom or I got sick, he always got the pharmacist in the next town to fill the prescription.

MICHAEL Why?

NAN He said it was like a doctor treating his own family ... Especially with mom.

MICHAEL What was wrong?

NAN There was nothing they could do. She died when I was twelve.

MICHAEL I'm sorry, Nan.

NAN Then I'd see him sifting through the bottles of medicines, staring ... as if he didn't believe in their power any more, because they hadn't helped her ... and when I got TB...

MICHAEL I guess nothing can cure it.

NAN It's a disease, like the others. They haven't found the drug yet, but they will.

MICHAEL You don't think it'll always be with us?

NAN It'll disappear like the Black Death ... but in the meantime, we have to cure ourselves.

MICHAEL You know what you want.

NAN I don't want my father to lose me too. And I want to go back to teaching children.

MICHAEL But did you ever feel ... it seems as though TB singled me out...

NAN No.

MICHAEL ... as though I have to learn something from it.

NAN You can't think that way. You have to prepare your mind to defeat it.

MICHAEL God knows that's how I got through my first missions in Ceylon. You make yourself believe you'll get back.

NAN And you got back.

MICHAEL Yes ... but changed. The war changed me ... Nan, do you have a sweetheart at home?

NAN No.

MICHAEL Did you?

NAN No, I never did.

MICHAEL The men must be blind back where you came from.

NAN (*Smiles*) Maybe it was me that was blind. I don't think I ever found anyone that interested me that much.

MICHAEL I'm trying to be as interesting as I can. Would you like to hear more about the mountains, about cold lakes that look like turquoise ... about wildflowers in the alpine meadows, where the air seems closer to the sun, where everything is so new and clean...

They look at each other a moment, then are distracted by sounds from the hall.

LORENE Johnny, forget it.

JOHNNY I'm going to show him.

Johnny returns, angry, gripping a newspaper in his hand. Lorene follows along.

JOHNNY You see this, fly-boy?

LORENE C'mon, Johnny, don't.

MICHAEL See what?

JOHNNY A story in the paper. From the Russian front. They captured some German prison camps for Russian soldiers and for civilians. And they found graves, mass graves.

LORENE Johnny...

JOHNNY You wanta know how many bodies?

NAN No, Johnny.

JOHNNY Bodies of people killed by the fascists. Seven hundred thousand. *Seven hundred thousand*. In one goddamn camp.

NAN Please.

JOHNNY If we'd stopped those bastards in Spain...

LORENE Let's have another drink. For godsake, Michael was only about 14 years old when you were in Spain.

JOHNNY You girls like to hear war stories so much, I'll tell you war stories ... only mine aren't about tropical paradises, flying high above the fighting...

LORENE *Johnny...*

MICHAEL No, let him talk.

JOHNNY I saw my friends die ... guys from work camps, slaughterhouses, lumber towns ... Finns, Ukrainians, English ... we were the MacPaps! ... And we didn't fly to the front, we bloody well walked ... through mountains, snow to our ankles ... it was misty ... we had to go slow, so we wouldn't fall off the cliffs ... *three weeks* of training and they sent us to Brunete, to try to save Madrid ... and we *held* them ... we could've finished it then, if only we'd had some help ... the fascists had help ... lots of it, but with us everybody wanted to be *neutral* ... (*In recalling the war, Johnny has partly forgotten Michael*)

Michael (Rainer Kraps) endures the pent-up anger of fellow TB patient Johnny Dombrowsky (Claudio Mascuili) in The Tenth Negative Pig, *March 1983. Photo: C.W. Hill Photography for Walterdale Theatre Associates.*

And that goddamn Charge Nurse is always at me about the boys at the front as if I'm some kind of coward or something, and I'm not supposed to talk about my war because I fought with the *communists*, and *she* doesn't think it's nice...

They were *practicing* on us ... and the goddamn British were too dumb to see it ... and now their cities are getting it ... the fascists bombed hospitals, Red Cross trains, refugees, they didn't care ... they were practising ... for the big war...

Practicing... (*Shakes paper*) Practicing even for this. When they first invaded Spain they took a couple of towns by surprise. At Badajoz they rounded up everybody they figured was against them, men and women ... herded them into a bull ring, nearly 2,000 people. They had machine guns set up in the stands. And they started shooting and shooting and shooting. That's *war*, goddamn it.

MICHAEL All right, that's war.

Johnny coughs a couple of times.

LORENE Johnny, take it easy ... you'll hurt yourself.

JOHNNY I never got hurt all through the whole damn war ... not once. My friends dropping all around me, gut-shot, shrapnelled, bayonetted ... men I knew better than brothers, and we were lucky if we could get them out and bury them ... hand to hand fighting ... sometimes we were so close we could spit into each other's faces...

(*Short coughs*) And that's what war is like. Shitting your pants from fear, men bleeding and screaming and dying all around you ... that's war. A war we could've won if those son-of-a-bitch politicians hadn't been so scared of making Hitler mad ... and they've made us all pay for it now...

LORENE Johnny, Johnny, stop!

JOHNNY (*Shouts*) That's war!

Johnny "throws" a spectacular haemorrhage, blood frothing from his mouth. Michael gets up from the wheelchair, takes a step toward him. Johnny continues haemorrhaging.

LORENE No! No!

Lights out.

Act Two, Scene Two

The New Year's Eve dance at the San. The space around the Musician(s) or the exam/op room is the dance floor. Darkness. The Muscian(s) begin(s) to play and the song begins. The first verse of the song is in darkness gradually getting brighter. All join in on the chorus. The Doctor and nurse are dancing circles around the patients—Johnny and Lorene, Nan and Michael—who simply shuffle along. The song is "Temple Gardens."

SINGER

In from the country on Saturday night
From high in the hills see the city's bright lights
Warm bodies close in the car
Summer can't be very far
A voice on the radio says
"There's a dance at Temple Gardens!
Find romance at Temple Garden!
Steal a kiss as you waltz
Through the tunnel of love!"

Up on the stand see the band members play
They're dressed in white and the couples all sway
Floating around the floor
Or laughing beside the door
Coloured lights swirl through the air
At the dance at Temple Gardens
There's romance at Temple Gardens
Steal a kiss as you waltz
Through the tunnel of love

Down at the Serpentine in Crescent Park
Swans glide and couples stroll in the half-dark
Music drifts around
Breezes lift the sound
Up to the moon and the stars
Oh the dance at Temple Gardens
The romance at Temple Gardens
Steal a kiss at Temple Gardens
Take a chance, Temple Gardens
Oh romance, Temple Gardens
Steal a kiss as you waltz
Through the tunnel of love!

Song Ends. All Applaud.

JOHNNY (*To Musician*). Hey, how about a polka!

Music starts to play.

LORENE (*Laughs*) Oh Johnny!

NURSE You're lucky we let you dance at all!

JOHNNY Oh, yeah, I almost forgot there for a minute. I was just about to show you some Ukrainian dancing.

DOCTOR (*Stopping Musician*) How about something slower for a change?

Musician begins another waltz.

MICHAEL (*To Nan*) I think I better sit this one out.

NAN All right.

He sits in wheelchair.

MICHAEL Do you think we could go somewhere a bit quieter for a few moments?

NAN Let's do that.

She wheels him out of the Dance Room and down towards his Room in the Ward. As they leave the dance, the music fades, the lights dim, and the scene freezes. In Michael's Room, Nan sits on a bed with Michael in the wheelchair beside her.

NAN There, that's better.

MICHAEL Yes.

They sit in silence for a moment.

MICHAEL Where were you last New Year's?

NAN Where? Oh, I was here ... sometimes it seems I've been in this place all my life.

MICHAEL I suppose there was a dance then too.

NAN Only I wasn't at it.

MICHAEL No?

NAN I had to stay in bed. "Typhoid" rest is what they call it ... couldn't even get up to use the bathroom.

MICHAEL You've got quite a bit better since then.

NAN Yes ... yes I have. But what about you?

MICHAEL Me?

NAN Where were you last New Year's?

MICHAEL Oh ... I was at a dance. Much bigger than this. At our base in Ceylon ... a town called Trincomalee. It's a British Naval headquarters, so their officers threw a party, invited our squadron to come. All kinds of food and drinks ... a big dance band...

NAN And lots of girls. (*Laughs.*)

MICHAEL Oh yes, lots of girls. (*Laughs*) The daughters of all the important people in town were there. Their duty, you see. Part of the "war effort." Anyway, the limeys got the biggest hall they could find, an old wooden building, with verandahs looking out over the sea. And you could go out there and gaze at the ships riding in the harbour, dark shapes on a dark sea, only with a river of gold flowing away towards the full moon.

NAN An esplanade along the shore...

MICHAEL Couples walking along in the moonlight and the warm night air...

NAN Walking with a girl...

MICHAEL ... with a dark, dark face, and the bluest eyes you've ever seen ... her father was Dutch ... strolling arm in arm, and telling her about winter in Canada, just like I'm telling you about Ceylon ... (*Laughs ... this turns nearly into tears*) ... and now this...

NAN It won't steal your life away.

MICHAEL Sometimes I think I loved the beauty of the world I found there too much ... and this illness is merely my love transformed

NAN I don't think it has anything to do with love ... it's only a disease.

MICHAEL Then why does it seem as if my whole life has been speeded up, as if I'm living months in days, years in the space of weeks? As if there's a fire burning in me, intensifying my perceptions, purifying my spirit? It's been so strange, that as I've been told I'm getting sicker and sicker, I've felt more and more alive to the marvels of this world.

NAN That must have been in you always ... you never took the time to understand it before, that's all.

MICHAEL But the disease has freed it! Don't you see. I might never have taken the time. It's almost like a privilege. To feel things so strongly, to feel my own uniqueness responding so completely to the world. (*Pause*) Look ... (*Pulls small box from pocket of dressing gown*) Look at this.

NAN What is it?

Michael takes a large black pearl from the box and places it on the palm of his hand.

MICHAEL I was on leave ... just wandering around the island. I ended up on the West Coast, at a small village called Marichukaddi ... it used to be a pearl fishing centre, even the Phoenicians knew about it. I was poking around in the market ... the only white man there ... when an old man grabbed my arm. "Per-al," he kept saying, "per-al." He had pearls wrapped up in all kinds of little packages, and he showed me hundreds—seed pearls, pearls big as the end of your thumb, flawed and misshapen, a set of matched pearls for a necklace, even some small pearls the colour of pale roses. He could see I wasn't really interested. But then he showed me this. "Per-al kalu." The black pearl. (*Pause*) I could feel something turning in my life as soon as I held it in my hand. Now I know what it was. The bacillus was working in me the same way that a piece of sand works in a pearl-oyster ... they both force something precious to grow.

NAN No, Michael, don't ... don't...

MICHAEL You're almost all better. And I know you'll stay that way. I also know what we're feeling about each other. And how fast my love for you is growing. These things burn through me like prairie fire. (*He holds her hand, placing the pearl in it*) This is for you.

Nan does not look at the pearl. She looks into Michael's eyes, while he closes her hand over the pearl.

Lights dim on the scene, as lights and music rise on the dance again.

Applause. Elva goes over to the Doctor.

ELVA Excuse me, doctor.

DOCTOR Yes.

ELVA Do you think I should check on Mariana?

DOCTOR I don't think that's really necessary, nurse. Why not enjoy yourself a little?

ELVA She's so near...

DOCTOR She'll be all right for another hour or so. I looked in on her before I came here.

ELVA Oh. Well, that's fine then.

DOCTOR You have to be here to see the New Year in.

ELVA Thank you, doctor.

DOCTOR Not at all. Would you like to dance?

ELVA Oh, really...

DOCTOR (*To Musician*). How about another waltz?

Music begins. Doctor and Elva waltz. Johnny touches Lorene's arm.

JOHNNY Let's slip out for a breath of air.

LORENE Yeah, you know how I love fresh air.

JOHNNY That's not all I've got in mind.

As Johnny and Lorene leave, Nan wheels Michael back in. They waltz as well. Johnny and Lorene walk, slowly, because they're tired from dancing, to Lorene's room. Behind them, lights dim, music fades, and the scene freezes.

JOHNNY You got the rest of Harold's rye tucked away somewhere?

LORENE Yeah, like a little snort?

JOHNNY Sure.

LORENE It's in my night-table.

Johnny gets it out from the table and pours a drink in one glass. They both drink.

JOHNNY Mmmmm, isn't it good?

They drink some more, then put the glass down. They snuggle and kiss.

JOHNNY Hey, take it easy kid. That dancing kinda wore me out. (*They laugh.*)

LORENE And you wanted a polka.

JOHNNY It's in the blood, eh? But I couldna danced one to save my soul.

LORENE (*Pressing close*) I want you so much, Johnny.

JOHNNY Me too, babe ... I like to be with you.

LORENE Johnny ... I want to have a baby with you.

JOHNNY (*Pretending alarm*) You mean, right now?!

LORENE I want a baby to love ... I want her to be happy, and to have a lot of things I never had, and...

JOHNNY Now hold on, Lorene. (*Teasing*) First my dad has to talk to your dad about how many chickens and cows and pigs he'll give us.

LORENE Hey, wait a minute! What would your folks give my folks for taking you off their hands?

They laugh.

JOHNNY Of course, I'd have my wedding clothes, and hand-tooled boots, and my mom'd give you this big cast iron pot for making cabbage rolls in.

LORENE I don't know how to make cabbage rolls.

JOHNNY Doesn't matter! You'll have to learn. And of course everybody at the wedding chips in to make one big wedding present. Mind you, the wedding won't be cheap, but we should come out maybe $500 ahead.

LORENE Five hundred! That'd sure come in handy, setting out. (*Pause*) Johnny ... will your folks mind that I'm not Ukrainian?

JOHNNY No, I don't think so. Not any more. Like my dad said once, after he had a fight with our neighbours. "Well, Johnny, I guess we got-it the sonsabeeches too, just like the other peoples."

LORENE So there's hope for me?

JOHNNY Baby, they'll love you ... just like I do. The main thing we'll have to worry about is me finding a job.

LORENE You think you could work at the slaughter-house again?

JOHNNY I'd like to, cause that's what I know how to do and with the union the money's pretty good now ... but I don't know if I'll have the strength. Doc says, it's a matter of learning to pace yourself, and I can see that. Right now, I wouldn't last half an hour. (*Pauses, depressed at his loss of health*) Jesus.

LORENE Don't they have any jobs that aren't so hard?

JOHNNY Yeah, caretaker or night watchman. I don't wanna do that. Pig sticker might not sound very glamorous but you gotta understand what it's like on the floor. A guy's proud to be able to do it.

LORENE I thought maybe I might get on there too for a while ... before I had the baby.

JOHNNY There's gutters and sausage stuffers and chicken pluckers. How'd you like to be a chicken plucker?

LORENE I can't say it's been my life's ambition. But they'll never take me back at the Uptown Cafe. The boss doesn't want me scaring off customers. (*Depressed*) Oh well, I guess it'll be quite a while before I have to worry about a job.

JOHNNY Maybe not so long.

LORENE I been wondering something, Johnny. How come a big dreamboat like you's still loose?

JOHNNY Oh, I had a sweetheart once and we came pretty close to getting married. But I couldn't get any work, and we kinda drifted apart. Hey, what happened to our drink? Let's top it up a bit, if there's any left.

They fill the glass again and drink.

LORENE Johnny ... you don't think we make it happen do you?

JOHNNY Make what happen?

LORENE I mean, we don't get TB because of anything we do that we shouldn't?

JOHNNY What?!

LORENE Well, the way they talk around here, about how you have to chase cure and make yourself well, sometimes it's like they think we do it ourselves.

JOHNNY Don't be silly. How could we do that?

LORENE I don't know. But it's almost as if they think we let up for a minute and the germs jump in when we aren't looking.

JOHNNY Aw, that's a crock of ... bananas.

LORENE It couldn't be ... like a punishment ... for anything bad we've done?

JOHNNY Lorene, what gave you a crazy idea like that?

LORENE Well, I don't think that, not really, but once Elva said, maybe the Lord is punishing us for our sins...

JOHNNY Look, you can't pay attention to what that poor stupid bitch says. If there is a God—which I doubt—I don't imagine he works that way. Besides, you never did anything to deserve TB.

LORENE I guess it does sound kinda dumb...

JOHNNY I'll say! You know what my mom thinks? That you get TB from drinking cold water. (*They laugh*) Getting it from sin makes about as much sense.

LORENE But I'm not getting any better, Johnny.

JOHNNY You will.

LORENE And Doc's gonna be at me again about that operation.

JOHNNY They wanta take out some ribs?

LORENE Yes.

JOHNNY It's not so bad.

LORENE But what's it gonna make me look like?

JOHNNY Oh ... not that different, I suppose.

LORENE What'll it do to my ... to my breasts?

JOHNNY You'll always look beautiful to me.

LORENE Johnny—what do you think happens when you die?

JOHNNY There's just what you see here—when you're gone, you're gone.

Musician(s) start(s) to play "Auld Lang Syne" quietly. The lights start to go up and the frozen dancers move again.

JOHNNY Look, we hafta get back—don't want to miss the big moment. Come on, sweetie.

LORENE Ok.

Johnny and Lorene arrive back just as the Doctor is announcing the New Year.

All sing "Auld Lang Syne." The song ends. They cheer.

Johnny Dombrowsky (Claudio Mascuili) shows his growing fondness for fellow patient Lorene Evans (Suzi Max) in The Tenth Negative Pig, *March 1983. Photo: C.W. Hill Photography for Walterdale Theatre Associates.*

DOCTOR Happy New Year everybody!

ALL Happy New Year! Happy New Year!

NURSE Remember, no kissing!

Elva goes to Mariana's room. Mariana is asleep. Elva tucks her in.

NURSE Everybody off to bed now!

JOHNNY (*Hugs Lorene*) See you around, sweetheart.

LORENE Happy New Year, Johnny.

JOHNNY And Happy New Year to you.

NURSE It's time for bed.

MICHAEL Goodnight, Nan.

NAN Goodnight, Michael.

DOCTOR All right, break it up. Let's all get some sleep.

They move to the Wards. The Doctor wheels Michael in the wheelchair, followed by Johnny. The Nurse leads the other women to their Ward. She then goes to Mariana's room, while Nan and Lorene get into bed, after removing dressing gowns.

NURSE Stewart, come and give me a hand.

ELVA Yes, Nurse.

Elva goes off and gets the "pigs" for the foot of each bed. She places them at the foot and helps Charge Nurse move Nan out.

NAN Mmmm, this is warm.

They come back for Lorene. In the Men's Ward, Johnny is putting his scarves on, Michael his mitts.

LORENE It must be 40 below out there! Where's my tea-cosy?

Elva gives it to her. She puts it on. She and Charge Nurse move the bed.

They come back to the Ward and turn the lights out.

JOHNNY Give us a break. Doc. How about a New Year's holiday from chasing cure?

DOCTOR You, my friend, need to chase cure all you can!

He pushes Johnny out, then Michael.

DOCTOR Good night.

MICHAEL AND JOHNNY
Good night, Doc. Goodnight.

ELVA (*To women*) Good night ... sleep tight.

The Doctor comes back into the Ward, shivering. He turns the lights out.

NURSE (*To Elva*) That will be all, Stewart.

ELVA Thank you, Nurse. (*She leaves. Exit left.*)

Doctor and Nurse meet in the hall. They leave.

DOCTOR Good night.

NURSE Good night, Doctor.

The wards and porches are dark. There is only a dim light in the hall. The patients are asleep.

After a few moments of quiet, the Musician(s) play(s) a verse of "Spirits of Night." The music stops. Mariana, called by the music, stirs slowly and rises from her bed. Pale, flickering light, the beginning of Northern Lights, touches her. She moves forward into the growing light.

MARIANA Who calls me? Who calls? I'm falling, drowning, looking up from the bottom of a dark lake, shadows swirling around my body like cold, cold water. Above me, upon the shores, people are calling to me, "Come back! Come back!" But their voices echo and quaver through the water that touches me everywhere, filling my lungs. No! No! There is something moving in the night. Yes, moving, above the high walls of this valley. I hear you, I know what you want. Calling my name, wishing me to come with you, to join your dance. Your shapes a burning wind in the black sky, beating and swaying, dipping to earth like tongues of fire all speaking my name. Coming so low, so low, licking at my face, my hands.

The Northern Lights have grown in power, pulsing around her.

MARIANA Oh, ancestors, spirits of our ancestors, I can't join you now! Please... not now! Not now!

Sings "Spirits of the Night"

Spirits of night move in the sky
Circling around, making no sound
Leaping in flame, calling my name
Come, dance again!
Feel no more pain!
Come dance again!
Feel no more pain!

Spirits of night, don't call me now
I have to stay, see the new day
A child will be born, free from all harm
Then I'll dance again
Moving in flame

Spirits of night move in the sky
Flowing in fire, burning desire
Lighter than breath, dancing in death
Wait, oh wait for me!
Soon I'll be free!
Wait, oh wait for me!
Soon I'll be free!

The music and the song have pulled Lorene, Johnny, Nan, and Michael from their beds. They remove scarves, mitts, and tea-cosy. Nan's hair is loose. As the song ends, they begin to speak, as if from their dreams.

MICHAEL I'm standing in the jungle ... watching the plane burn. It's evening. No one else is with me. They must have died in the crash ... or they will die when the fire reaches the fuel tanks. I can't get at them. Have to take off this jacket ... I'm covered in sweat. Where are my boots? Snakes ... there's small, green poisonous snakes. The plane burns.

LORENE ... northern lights ... northern lights sway and twist ... like the sky's on fire, but there's no warmth ... tired ... you'd swear it'd set the snow on fire ... want to fold myself in warmth and brightness ... but it touches my skin and I'm cold ... my bones are cold...

MICHAEL ... can't see, can't see any sky at all ... vines thick as my arm loop themselves down from the highest branches ... where the trees explode into branches, into hanging mosses and ferns ... shutting out the sky...

NAN Snow melting and dripping from the eaves, a drum inside my body ... and I'm outside ... moving ... no clothes ... the soft air on my skin, light as a kiss ... snow melting on the hills ... pale shoots of new grass and plants, crocuses pushing through, the feathery petals falling open ... and I lie on the earth ... press my body against them...

LORENE ... they hum and sing ... calling to me ... they say ... they say ... no, gotta keep moving, gotta keep warm ... but they're touching me ... their long cold fingers ... they wanna make me crazy, make me dance in the light ... cold shifting light...

MICHAEL ... can't see ... must be a clearing somewhere ... if I run ... darkness closing in ... can't see ... noises ... the plane burns ... shuddering glare swallowed by shadowless black ... things out there ... slither of bodies over leaves ... a strange, coughing cry that moves in a circle ... mosquitoes crawl over my face ... sting it raw ... closing my eyes...

LORENE ... it's the wind now ... little knives slash into me, cut away at the flesh ... can't let them cut ... no! Johnny? ... where's Johnny!? ... Johnny! ... where are you?

JOHNNY ... in the tank room, down in the cellar of the slaughterhouse ... it's night, the room pitch black ... the scurry of rats across the floor ... rats everywhere ... they've chewed tunnels in the cork walls of the freezers ... hide in every corner ... the smell ... not like I remember ... blood from the slaughter draining down and pouring into the huge steel tank ... stench of blood and lungs and crushed skulls ... but the smell ... no ... strange...

NAN ... dry lightning over the pale hills, touching brown matted grass, dry leaves around me the old buffalo-back hill leaps into flame ... the fire catching, flaring through brush in the ravines ... and I am in the fire ... climbing the hill ... my body moving in flame and not harmed by flame ... my legs strong as when I was a child...

LORENE ... there's a baby inside me ... yes ... a little baby ... oh, the wind is so cold ... but nothing can touch her, not cold, not sickness ... brushing her hair so soft and shiny, the clean sweet smell of it ... so warm when she's sleeping...

NAN ... a man at the top of the hill ... he waves ... I think he is calling ... the crackle of fire all around me ... earth hot beneath my feet ... see him waving, calling ... I can't hear ... it's Michael ... Michael! ... I run up the hill, and the fire leaps with me, leaps ahead ... his face now ... calling ... flames roaring in my ears...

MICHAEL ... you have to burn them ... burn them and they fall away ... slimy leeches that cling and suck ... can't lie down to rest., scorpions, spiders ... things crawling ... snakes, lizards ... the jungle crawling with poisonous, poisonous creatures...

JOHNNY ... rats scuttle for cover when I flip on the light ... up the stairs ... concrete cool beneath my bare feet ... air dank on my naked body ... up into the darkness of the ground floor, the shipping floor, the beef-killing floor ... I flip on the lights ... rats scatter as if an invisible shell, exploding, blows them away ... no one here ... the chute empty, the hoist silent ... climb another flight of stairs, to my floor, the hog-killing floor ... lights already on ... the foreman sees me, yells, "where the fuck have *you* been?" ... grabs a meathook from the hoist, swings it in a whistling arc towards my eyes ... "get out there, you son of a bitch!" ... and he shoves me towards the front of the slaughter line...

NAN ...running faster, running to Michael ... fire around his body ... Michael on the hill, burning ... his body writhes ... blackens ... when I reach the top he will already be consumed ... only a tangle of dead black things where he stood...

JOHNNY ...I don't know any of these men ... I walk down the line of them, towards my place at the front ... past the one who splits carcasses, carefully, carefully, down the backbone with his cleaver ... past the one who slices them open, spilling the guts, yanking out the heart ... past the one who scrapes the bristles off the steaming hides, bodies scalded in a long, long tank of hissing water ... past them all ... to my place ... to the one who stands in my place ... the thin blade, cold as ice, waiting to slide into the jugular, blood spurting, washing over his hands...

NAN ... the first drops of rain, on my face, my breasts ... rain streaming down my arms, my body, flooding my fiery skin and the thick tendrils of flame ... and where I walk the flames are put out, but inside I am filled with fire...

JOHNNY ... the foreman slams me between the shoulderblades with the meathook ... "out there, you stinking hunky!" ... shoves me through the doors, out into the glare of searchlights, dazzling the night, out into the freezing cold, the shivering, silent rows of naked men and women, naked children...

LORENE ... I can feel the lights ... moving around me ... looking just like fire, only cold as ice ... I'm so tired—no! ... there's a baby inside me ... the cold flakes on my skin, melting on my face, like tears ... thicker now, covering me like a blanket ... gathering, growing round my body ... just a rounded bank of snow ... the shape of a woman ... the lights...

MICHAEL ... and light! light! ... a thunderous roar ... the darkness flung far away ... fragments of hissing metal plunge through the air ... and now I can't see, can't see at all! ... and things are on me, crawling! crawling!

JOHNNY ... the squeal of the hoist and the guards prod us with bayonets and the people shuffle forward through the doors one at a time and I hear the first screams cut short and I am shouting "no! no! no!" and a rifle butt smashes the small of my back and I stagger forward and hands grab my ankle and clasp it in metal so cold it burns and I am dragged hopping on one foot until my leg is pulled into the air and I flip upside down and I try to curl myself into a ball, all my muscles straining to hold me there while I free myself from the shackle, until I can't hold myself like that any more and upside down I see the chain gang at work in the midst of an uproar of metal and screams and the sizzling steam the blade coming for my throat!

NAN ... the rain cools everything, the hillside cool against my feet ... I look down, and the grass has started to grow again through the black spikes and ashes, sending tiny shoots that lick and pull, tugging at my ankles like the current of a creek in summer ... I can't see Michael any more, only the returning grass and the shiny new leaves forming one by one on the charred branches ... the air clear now, no smoke ... everything turning green, deepening green ... and this is where he stood ... already he has grown into something else...

Musician plays verse of "Spirits of Night" and all do dream dance without touching.

MARIANA

Spirits of night move the sky
Flowing in fire, burning desire
Lighter than breath, dancing in death
Waiting for me
Waiting for me!

Musician plays more of song while they all go back to their beds. Lights fade away. They sleep. Moments of silence.

Morning. Lights in hall come up. Doctor and nurse come on.

DOCTOR (*Yawning*) Dear me.

NURSE You're tired.

DOCTOR No, I'm fine ... all those long nights as an intern were good training.

Elva enters.

DOCTOR Good morning, Elva.

ELVA Good morning, Doctor.

DOCTOR Why don't you check on Mariana ... I haven't had a chance to see her yet.

ELVA Of course, Docotor.

Elva goes into Mariana's room.

DOCTOR (*To Nurse*) Have a talk with Johnny about the drug treatment before you bring Michael in.

NURSE Certainly.

DOCTOR Fine. I'll see Nan and Lorene after I've got a cup of coffee.

He turns away and exits left. The Nurse heads for the men's ward. She goes in and moves Johnny's bed in from the porch. His scarves are draped across the bed. She flips on the light.

JOHNNY (*Hands over eyes*) No! No!

NURSE What's wrong?

JOHNNY (*Sits up*) What? (*Coughs*)

NURSE Did I startle you?

JOHNNY (*Awakening. Looks around, moment of panic*) Where's Michael?

NURSE Still on the porch.

JOHNNY Oh.

NURSE It's morning. Time to wake up.

JOHNNY Another year.

NURSE The Doctor wanted me to talk with you.

JOHNNY I'm not getting any better, am I? (*Coughs.*)

NURSE You're at a critical stage. As the Doctor says, "A good haemorrhage can be the beginning of the end, or—"

JOHNNY Like that afternoon when Harold got on his hands and knees and coughed his life away.

NURSE You know we can't do anything with a haemorrhage like that.

JOHNNY Five minutes. That's all it took.

NURSE I'm sorry.

JOHNNY Yeah, we're all sorry.

NURSE Look ... the infection has moved into your other lung.

JOHNNY I figured as much.

NURSE There are no more procedures—

JOHNNY You can't collapse both lungs, can you?

NURSE No.

JOHNNY So an operation's out.

NURSE Yes ... but there's a new drug we'd like to try.

JOHNNY (*Angry*). And you made me wait this long to get to it?

NURSE It's just been discovered. It's only been used on an experimental basis.

JOHNNY So you want me to be a guinea pig.

NURSE We won't hide the fact that you could suffer certain effects.

JOHNNY Of course.

NURSE But it works against the infection.

JOHNNY What effects?

NURSE You could have spells of dizziness ... a lack of balance ... you might even lose your hearing.

JOHNNY But I could be cured.

NURSE We won't really know until more cases have been treated.

JOHNNY For God's sake, I'm not a case. I'm me, I'm Johnny Dombrowsky! And I want to get the hell out of here.

NURSE So you'll accept the treatment?

JOHNNY Why me? Why not that poor bastard out there? (*Motions to Michael*) Hey? Why not that kid? I may be sick, but I'm in better shape than he is.

NURSE It might not ... be suitable for him.

JOHNNY He's too far gone ... is that what you mean?

NURSE No. But the drug...

JOHNNY You might have to give him so much you'd cripple him in some other way.

NURSE In such cases ... we don't know how much...

JOHNNY But you might learn something from giving it to me?

NURSE Yes.

JOHNNY Enough to be able to help him?

NURSE It's possible.

JOHNNY Well, I've had enough of lying around to last me a lifetime. When do we start?

NURSE Right now, if you like.

JOHNNY Sure. Let's go.

Johnny gets up, puts on his dressing gown. She leads him out. She stops at Mariana's room.

NURSE (*Call quietly*) Stewart.

ELVA (*Coming to door*) Yes?

NURSE How is she?

ELVA Very close.

NURSE Move Michael's bed in from the porch. Then come back here.

ELVA Thank you, nurse.

Nurse and Johnny go to op room. When they reach there nurse flips on the lights. She prepares things to give him an injection. Lights dim and they freeze. During this, Elva goes to men's ward and brings Michael in. His mitts are on the bed. He does not move very much and coughs weakly.

ELVA It's morning.

MICHAEL ... the plan...

ELVA (*Hand on brow*) You've got a bad fever.

MICHAEL ... I can't see...

ELVA (*Pats his arm*) You rest now. I'll be back soon with the Doctor.

MICHAEL ... crawling ... things crawling...

Elva exits and goes back to Mariana's room. She watches over Mariana. Michael continues to cough and stir restlessly.

The doctor comes in with a cup of coffee in one hand. He puts it down on Nan's table, moves her bed in, and flips on the lights.

NAN (*Starting awake*) Michael!

DOCTOR Good morning, Nan.

NAN Is it morning already?

DOCTOR And a new year.

NAN Yes.

DOCTOR And a good year for you ... I've seen your latest test.

NAN Yes?

DOCTOR (*Smiling*) It's what I hoped I could tell you.

NAN The last test was negative?

DOCTOR (*Nods*) You can leave.

NAN When?

DOCTOR As soon as you can arrange for someone to pick you up. We won't throw you out in the snow.

NAN What about Michael?

DOCTOR We'll have to keep him here for a while yet, I'm afraid.

NAN I see. (*Pause, thinking about Michael*) Could I phone my dad?

DOCTOR Of course.

NAN And I'd like to spend some time with Michael before I go.

DOCTOR I'm sure that can be arranged (*Pats her shoulder.*)

NAN Now you've said I can go, I'm almost afraid to.

DOCTOR When you've been an "old crock" it takes a bit of courage to go out into the world again. But you'll do well, I know you will.

NAN Thanks Doctor ... for all your help.

DOCTOR It's been a pleasure.

NAN Is it all right if I go and visit Michael now?

DOCTOR I think so ... I have to talk with Lorene.

NAN With Lorene ... oh.

DOCTOR We'll take care of her.

NAN I never had a sister.

DOCTOR (*Nods*) Why don't you go along now?

NAN (*Puts on dressing gown*) Yes. (*Leaves.*)

Nan goes to Michael's room. Doctor brings in Lorene's bed. Her tea-cosy is on the bed.

NAN Michael? Michael?

He does not answer, she goes in. Michael is restless and coughing weakly.

Oh Michael...

She sits on the bed and touches his forehead. She holds one of his hands in hers. She watches for him to awaken.

LORENE (*Shivering*). I'm cold ... cold...

DOCTOR Wake up, Lorene.

LORENE ... shouldn't have fallen asleep...

DOCTOR Lorene.

LORENE (*Wakes up fast*) I won't let you cut me!

DOCTOR Take it easy.

LORENE No!

DOCTOR We think it can give you a better chance.

LORENE You'll send me out a cripple.

DOCTOR No, we'll send you out to a nearly normal life. Of course, you'd always have to be a little more careful, to make sure you don't break down again.

LORENE (*Bitterly*) Kind of like rationing yourself, eh?

DOCTOR The war's given a lot of people a taste of that.

LORENE How many?

DOCTOR What?

LORENE How many ribs?

DOCTOR It could be as few as three ... possibly six or seven...

LORENE Oh my God.

DOCTOR ... until we get collapse.

LORENE Doc, I'm a *woman*. I don't wanna get better if I'm gonna be deformed.

DOCTOR Look, it's not so bad.

LORENE It's not fair. (*Cries*) You don't give us any goddamn decent choice.

DOCTOR It's a chance to get better.

LORENE I wouldn't mind so much, the pain and boredom and the bloody endless hours of *nothing*, if I thought it was doing any good. But it's all so meaningless.

DOCTOR We have no way of knowing, Lorene.

LORENE (*Low*) Stuff it. Doc.

DOCTOR (*Ignores this*). I have to tell you we can't use a general anaesthetic—too dangerous—

LORENE (*Horrified*) I'd be awake?! I'd hear you cutting?!

DOCTOR We only want what's best for you.

LORENE (*Crying*) Oh sure...

Elva flips the lights on in Mariana's room. Mariana is moaning softly and moving. The labour pains have begun. Elva goes quickly to the women's ward, calling.

ELVA Doctor! Doctor!

DOCTOR (*Going to door*) What is it?

ELVA It's Mariana! The baby!

DOCTOR I'll take a look.

He goes out with Elva. They go to Mariana's room. He examines Mariana briefly.

DOCTOR Let's move her. That baby's in a hurry!

They wheel the bed to the op room (or, they get the wheelchair and move her in that). The nurse has finished giving Johnny his injection. Elva takes the baby's blanket.

(*To Johnny*) On your way now.

JOHNNY Just leaving.

They all prepare for the birth, scrubbing up, etc. The Musician(s) begin(s) to play "Spirits of Night" softly. Johnny goes to his room and looks in.

JOHNNY (*To Nan*) Lorene's alone?

NAN Yes.

JOHNNY Mariana is having her baby.

NAN Oh.

JOHNNY I'm going to see Lorene.

NAN Yes.

JOHNNY There won't be anybody around here for quite a while.

NAN I suppose not.

JOHNNY Pretty bright in here.

Johnny flips out the light. Nan looks at him. He closes the door. He goes down the hall to Lorene's room. He stands at the door, listening to her crying. The birth is starting.

MICHAEL (*Waking up from a fevered sleep*). The pearl ... (*Urgent*) You haven't lost the pearl?

NAN It's right here. (*Takes box from robe. Opens it*) It's safe.

MICHAEL (*Looks at it*) Look ... look into it.

NAN (*Looking*) There we both are.

MICHAEL Look deeper ... beyond our reflection.

NAN Past the surface.

MICHAEL To the heart ... the pain in the heart...

NAN Pain that enclosed itself in beauty...

MICHAEL Until it couldn't feel that pain any more.

NAN I love you.

MICHAEL You'll have the black pearl.

NAN I want more of you than I'll ever be able to have.

MICHAEL I'll be inside you ... (*Touches her head*) ... here.

NAN Memory...

MICHAEL More than memory...

Nan lets her robe fall to the floor. She lifts up the cover and gets into bed with Michael. They caress. She moves on top of him. They lie together.

Johnny goes into Lorene's room.

JOHNNY Lorene...

LORENE It's getting so cold...

JOHNNY We're gonna get better. (*Moves to her, touches her.*)

LORENE (*Not hearing him yet*) Johnny, don't leave me ... the coldest part of winter's yet to come...

JOHNNY We're gonna get out of here.

LORENE On the porch at night you can see the stars and you know they're nothin but ice...

JOHNNY We'll have a good life together.

LORENE I can feel the snow now ... touching my face, so soft and cold...

JOHNNY And we'll help make a decent life for other people.

LORENE ... until there's just a mound of snow where I was ... and they'll come in the morning to look and I'll be gone.

JOHNNY And our kids'll have good food and a good home and they'll be able to see the doctor if they need it...

LORENE Johnny? What did you say?

JOHNNY We're getting out of here!

LORENE About our kids?

JOHNNY You're gonna get better!

LORENE And we'll get married?

JOHNNY Yes ... and have kids!

LORENE I'm still young.

JOHNNY (*Fiercely*) We have to go home!

JOHNNY AND LORENE

We're going home!!

In the op room, Mariana cries out loudly as the child is born. The music stops at once. The Doctor holds the child up, slaps it. The child cries out.

ELVA Mariana look! The child is here. The child is here!

DOCTOR Get it to the Preventorium right away.

Elva takes the child, wraps it in the blanket and carries it towards the front. As she does so the Doctor speaks to the Nurse.

NURSE Shall I tell the orderlies?

DOCTOR Yes, I'll do the autopsy this afternoon.

Lights dim and they freeze. Lights on all three scenes are dim and characters freeze. Elva walks into a pool of light at centre front.

ELVA (*Comforting the child*) There, there ... there, there ... She looked at you ... looked right at you. And you are so beautiful ... yes, you are. The poisons didn't reach you. Your mother wouldn't let them. She kept you safe. And now here you are, looking at all this with eyes so new ... and small fingers not yet uncurled to touch the world ... and your sweet body welcoming the air.

I don't know if she understood my words. There is sin, I know there is. We have left undone ... how many times ... I could always have done better, been kinder, remembered God ... for we all have sinned ... there is no health...

Yet Jesus said, "suffer the little ones to come unto me." Perhaps I am a foolish woman ... she didn't know what I was saying.

And here you are in the world. And there are more poisons all around. But child, you came through. There is health in you. Even after that journey. Yes. There is health in you.

Lights fade fast on all scenes.

End of play.

The Three Sillies (1983)

by Mary Glenfield

It may seem unusual to find a children's play, particularly an English folktale, printed in a collection that is not devoted on the whole to children's theatre. But the fact that *The Three Sillies* stage adaptation by actor and longtime Walterdale member Mary Glenfield appeared during the company's fruitful new play years in the early 1980s grants leave for such an opportunity. Glenfield's nimble activation of the story's ranging and outrageous quest narrative is aimed at very young audiences, but as with all lively children's theatre, the accompanying adults can expect the child within to find enjoyment too. The fact that a number of other published and frequently presented adaptations of the story have appeared since Glenfield's 1983 version is a testament to the tale's rich performative potential.

Anyone who has practised theatre in Edmonton during the past fifty years would find it hard to dispute that Mary Glenfield and her husband Frank may be counted as the soul of Edmonton's theatre community. Mary Ross Glenfield (née Baldock) was born in London, England, in 1921. She moved with her family three months later to Bangor-on-Dee in North Wales, where her father took up a position as rector at an Anglican church; her mother was a classical scholar. Glenfield attended boarding schools in Chester and then Denbigh in North Wales before World War II, when she moved to work in Bletchley, England, at the Government Code and Cypher School (known for cracking Germany's Enigma Code). After the war, Glenfield worked in London doing editorial work with the *Red Cross Review* and the magazine *Women's Own*, as well as acting with the Liberal Theatre Group, until 1951, when she travelled to Edmonton to visit an aunt. Within three months, Glenfield was cast in a production of *The Barretts of Wimpole Street* produced by the Alberta Legislature's Civil Service Playhouse. Two years later she married Frank Glenfield, a staff member at the University of Alberta's Drama Division, while he was acting in a Studio Theatre production of Labiche's *The Italian Straw Hat*. After she had lived in the city for thirteen years, the

Edmonton Journal noted that as an actor Mary Glenfield was "well known to Edmonton theatre audiences" ("Fool's Day"). While raising two adopted children with Frank and acting with a number of companies, including Walterdale and Bette Anderson's Theatre for Children, Glenfield intermittently took undergraduate courses at the University of Alberta until she earned a BA in drama in 1992. Several years later she re-enrolled at the Drama Department, completing an MA in 2001 with her thesis "The Growth of Edmonton Theatre: From the Early 1920s to 1965," which includes a chapter on children's theatre. At Walterdale, Glenfield served not only as an actor, but also as board secretary, wardrobe mistress, and founding librarian. Today she continues to act, having appeared in well over fifty plays, including memorable performances in Walterdale's *Hedda Gabler* (April 1964), *Arsenic and Old Lace* (February 1967), and *Hay Fever* (March–April 1972).

The Three Sillies, Glenfield's only play, fits within Canada's long tradition of producing children's theatre.[39] She records in her thesis that in Edmonton, children's theatre began in the early 1950s at city playgrounds (107) and that in 1954 Bette Anderson began the company Theatre for Children, which ran until 1969 (110).[40] In December 1973, Walterdale began to produce plays that would appropriately accommodate young actors under the name Young Walterdale. Offered outside of the regular season package, the shows were presented by young actors in the context of "on-the-job" training. These plays frequently received popular and critical praise and provided early stage time to a number of now well-recognized professional actors in Edmonton. They were presented as Young Walterdale productions until 1979, when the slot was repackaged first as the Walterdale Christmas Show and then, following the production of Glenfield's play, as the Christmas Pantomime. This format, in turn, lasted until 1995, when Warren Graves's adaptation *Beauty and the Beast* ran as the last children's show. The spot has since been given over to more general (i.e., adult) shows, though in 2007 artistic director Randy Brososky directed Reakes's *Sinbad the Sailor* as a "classic pantomime in the true tradition" (Walterdale, *Walterdale Playhouse*).[41]

Among Walterdale's two dozen children's offerings, *The Three Sillies* stands out. Glenfield wrote the play and its accompanying songs specifically for the slot because Walterdale had had recent trouble finding an appropriate children's show (the company presented the musical *The Fantasticks* in the December slot the year before). *The Three Sillies* was hailed in the *Walterdale Newsletter* as "a welcome return of the children's production."[42] Moreover, with this play we see how Glenfield's longstanding personal connection to a company whose reputation she helped to build is intertwined with her childhood exposure to English folktales. The play stages her memory of one tale; the process of creating it was Glenfield's personal journey.

Three months after *The Three Sillies* closed, Walterdale president Vivien Bosley wrote a thank-you letter to Mary and to Frank, who had directed the play. Bosley's letter highlighted the play's marketability as a children's show, with its "fairy-tale charm and cast of people and animals." (The *Walterdale Newsletter* took a humorous tack: "It sounds like the only person missing in this production is a vet!") Bosley's encouragement to Mary in her letter to "go on to other playwriting ventures [because] it's obviously something you have a talent for—not to mention the very catchy songs," unfortunately, went unheeded.

Mary Glenfield's *The Three Sillies* is a light-hearted musical children's play adapted from the English folktale of the same name with humour and imagination. The play opens in an English farm courtyard with the simple confusions of preparing the evening meal, including the trouble of catching the chicken and bringing in the water. While standing outside, young Sally cries when she sees an axe, worried that it will fall on someone. The play takes an adventurous turn when young Peter tells Sally that before he can marry her, he must go on a journey to discover if there are any "sillies" sillier than she. Meanwhile, two thieves plot to follow Peter and steal his money. In Ireland, Peter finds an old woman who pulls her sheep up onto her grass roof to graze; in Scotland, he finds a man who tries to run and jump into his breeches to put them on; and in Wales, he finds three villagers fishing for the moon in a pond because it fell in the night before. Populating the play are sheep (staged as a cow in the premiere), dogs and cats (actors in costume or puppets, some of which speak and sing), and a chicken (a puppet on a wire). Glenfield specifies geography (England, Ireland, Wales) in her play, while the original folktale does not. The two thieves were added at Bette Anderson's suggestion are two robbers to raise the stakes for Peter. The language and characterizations in the world of the play are convincingly childlike. The musical score is printed in Appendix II.

The Three Sillies ran December 16–20, 1983, at Walterdale Playhouse (firehall) with the following cast and creative team:

SANDY	Robert Harle
SALLY Saucer	Joan Robertson
MRS. SAUCER	Teresa Griffiths
MR. SAUCER	Dave Parker
COOK	Deirdre Swan
TOM	Steven Sparke
TOWNSFOLK AND CHILDREN	Josephine Stebbings, Tobrina Smith, Jane Glenfield, Jennie Wigmore, Robert Jahrig, Amanda Clarke, Alexandra Sydie, Eric Brown, Ron Otten
LITTLE BOY	Matt Booi
PETER	Ted Soutar
FIRST THIEF	Claudio Masciulli
SECOND THIEF	Godfrey Budd
IRISH WOMAN	Malka Lerner
COW (TWO HALVES)	Dennis Robinson, Dave Parker
INNKEEPER	James Kemschead
DOGS	Jane Glenfield, Ron Otten, Amanda Clarke
CATS	Jennie Wigmore, Robert Jahrig
MICE	Tobrina Smith, Josephine Stebbings, Mary Tymo, Alexandra Sydie
SCOTTISH MAN	Dennis Robinson
HARRY	Eric Brown
WELSH WOMAN	Deirdre Swan

DIRECTOR	Frank Glenfield
SET DESIGNER	Cheryl Krausher
CHOREOGRAPHER	Karen Anthony
MUSIC	Mary Glenfield
PIANO PLAYER	Rhuanedd Meilen
STAGE MANAGER	David Glenfield

The Three Sillies

by Mary Glenfield

Act One, Scene One

As a rough plan. A farm courtyard in the west of England—Devon, Cornwall, Dorset, Somerset, what-have-you. A summer's evening—the sun still warm, but slanting gently through the trees, and the peculiar quietness of this time of day in England—a quiet expectancy.

Suddenly a dog starts barking from SL, and then bounds in after an amorous butterfly. The dog skids to a stop, looks around for the butterfly, which has disappeared, and suddenly sees the audience. He comes forward, DSC.

DOG Well, hello, children—glad to see you here. (*Softly*). Can you all hear me? (*Waits*). CAN YOU HERE ME NOW? – Okay, okay, that's good. My name's Sandy and my master's name is Peter Piper. He doesn't known I can speak—he thinks I can only bark; (*Barks laughingly*); but I can talk to you, and every now and then I'll come and tell you the next bit of the story. You see, this house is where Sally Saucer lives and tonight they're having a BIG party to announce her wedding day to my master, Peter Piper. She can NEVER make up her mind about anything, but I hope she has this time. (*Sees centre door opening*) Goodness, someone's coming—see you later—(*Bounds off, USL*).

BILLY (*Entering centre door, with a pink dress and a blue dress over her arm*) I just can't decide which dress is prettier, the blue or the pink. (*Turns*). Mother! – Mother!

MRS. SAUCER
(*Looking out of window SL of entrance door*) Good heavens, child, what's the matter? I'm so busy.

SALLY Which dress shall I wear?

MRS. S. Sally, I do wish you'd make up your mind about SOMETHING. (*Calls inside*) Father! (*Calls outside*) Father! (*Window SR of entrance door opens suddenly*)

MR. S. (*Irritably*) I've lost my best tie. What's the matter?

MRS. S. Which dress should Sally wear tonight?

MR. S Oh, how should I know? It's HER party.

SALLY (*Looking at the sundial*) Oh goodness, look at the time!

MRS. S. And Cook still hasn't caught a chicken for supper. Everything's always so LATE in this house. (*Slams her window shut*)

SALLY (*Still dithering*) Now, which one WOULD be best...?

Suddenly there is a commotion and wild clucking noises, and in dash Cook and Tom, chasing a chicken. Chicken is on wire from left corner of house to DSL. Cook is large and red-faced, in voluminous skirts and apron. Tom has string round his trousers at the knee, a chopper in his hand, and is willing, but dumb. He must, however, inspire affection rather than derision.

CHICKEN Cluck, cluck, cluck *etc.*

Chicken stops. Tom and Cook creep up to it; it goes on again. Stops. Both creep up to it again. Tom raises chopper and—"cluck, cluck, cluck, cluck" — off chicken goes. Tom and Cook bump into each other and fall in a heap, Tom with chopper above his head, Cook with petticoats over hers.

COOK (*Disentangling herself*) Of all the clumsy, idiotic men! I nearly had that chicken by its tail. (*Tom hangs head*) What we SHOULD do is creep up to it BACKWARDS, so that it thinks we're walking AWAY from it—like this. (*She demonstrates*) Now you try.

Tom puts down his chopper, walks backwards and falls over the chopper, sending the chicken offstage in a fine scurry of cluckings.

COOK (*Vexed*) Oh— (*She flounces off*)

SALLY (*Who has been watching all this with amusement*) Hello, Tom.

TOM Hello, Sal.

SALLY Well, cheer up. She doesn't mean to upset you.

TOM But I'm so clumsy. I always fall over everything.

SALLY Never mind, Tom; if everyone had as big a heart as you've got, the world would be a happier place to live in.

TOM Oh, Sal, you always make me feel better. (*Suddenly, shyly*) Here—I've got something for you. Guess which hand.

SALLY (*Dithering*) I can't decide—BOTH. (*Tom holds out both hands with an enormous lollipop clutched between them*) OH! —A lollipop, how lovely, just like when we were children—I haven't had one for ages.

TOM (*Sadly*) And soon you'll be getting married to Peter Piper and going right away from us.

SALLY (*Who has been dreaming and not listening to a word*) My goodness! I've got to change my dress—I can hear people coming. (*She runs off through centre door, dropping lollipop as she goes.*)

TOM (*Picking it up*) You've dropped your— (*Resignedly*) —oh well. (*Picks up his chopper and takes it over to a large hook in the beam SR*) Might as well stay there for now. We'll never catch that chicken.

He goes off through door SR as villagers come dancing in upper SL. Music of "Little Sally Saucer" has started up quite quietly in the distance with faint humming just before Sally goes off. It grows louder as villagers come in and then fade to background again before Little Girl speaks.

LITTLE GIRL Mummy, Mummy, when's Sally going to get married?

MOTHER Well, we're not sure, dear, but they'll tell us tonight.

1ST NEIGHBOUR
We none of us know.

2ND NEIGHBOUR
I wonder if Sally knows.

3RD NEIGHBOUR
She can't make her mind up.

All these remarks must be said very quickly one after the other.

ALL (*Hands up theatrically*)
Oh WHAT ... a silly girl! }

Then the song starts. One girl sings slowly "Little Sally Saucer," then all girls join in for first verse. Boys sing second verse all together. Then everyone sings last verse.

ONE GIRL'S VOICE

(*Deliberately, setting the tune*)

Little Sally Saucer — (*Pause*)—

ALL GIRLS (*Regular speed*)

She's going to marry
Peter Piper soon in the springtime.
When a girl is certain, then she musn't tarry.
She must settle on some day soon.

ALL BOYS

She wasn't certain, pretty pretty little Sally;
Peter Piper knew he must win her.
He didn't waste time, didn't dilly-dally,
Kissed her under the yellow moon.

ALL TOGETHER

Little Sally Saucer, she's going to marry
Peter Piper soon in the springtime.
We don't know the date yet, rumours seem to vary,
All we know is it's some day soon.

The music goes on and all do a country-dance, one circle round the pump USR, the other circle round the sundial DSL.

A little boy has been standing on the steps leading to centre door, and as everyone curtsies and bows at the end of the dance, he glances towards the villagers' entrance, USL, and calls out:

LITTLE BOY (*Shouting*) He's coming—the guest of honour's coming! (*Mr. and Mrs. Saucer push each other out through the front door*)

MRS. S. Oh dear, we'll have to have cold meat, they haven't caught the chicken yet.

MR. S. Bother this collar. (*It flips open again as he does it up*)

Mrs. Saucer fans herself vehemently and puts on an overbright smile; Mr. Saucer stands with one end of his collar ludicrously in the air.

LITTLE BOY (*Dramatically*) Here he is! Peter Piper!

Peter Piper strides on with great assurance towards Mr. and Mrs. Saucer. He MUST MAKE AN ENTRANCE! Sandy is at his heels and gives a little bark towards the audience.

MR. S. Hello, my boy, hello—bother this tie!

MRS. S. (*Twittering*) Peter—I have the feeling—I don't KNOW, but I THINK that SALLY'S MADE UP HER MIND about the wedding date!

EVERYONE (*Turning to each other, and speaking almost in chorus*) She's made up her mind, she's made up her mind! Oh, how wonderful, she's made up her mind!

PETER That's marvelous! If she really does know her own mind this time.

MR. S. Yes, well—humph—everyone's invited to supper, if it's—humph—ready, that is, my love?

MRS. S. (*Giving him a look*) I'm sure it is, now. But where's Sally?

TOM Well, the last time I saw her, she was going to change.

MRS. S. (*Rudely*) Who asked you?

EVERYONE Yes, who asked you?

TOM Well, I thought—

PETER Thanks, Tom, that's very good of you to tell us.

MR. AND MRS. SAUCER AND EVERYONE
Yes, that's very good of him to tell us.

Sally comes in through centre door and rushes over to Peter.

SALLY Have I kept you waiting?

PETER Of course not.

SALLY Well, go on in, everyone. The dining table's laden with things to eat.

All the villagers troop in behind Mr. and Mrs. Saucer. Peter and Sally and Sandy stay behind.

PETER Have you really made up your mind, Sally?

SALLY Yes, Peter, I really have; and I'm so happy. But I'm going to miss all my friends—the ducks and the chickens and the village folk, and Mother and Father.

PETER (*Pulling her laughingly by one hand*) Come on, for goodness' sake, else you'll change your mind again.

Little Boy appears at top of steps, centre door, with a large water jug.

SALLY Hello, what are YOU doing?

LITTLE BOY They've forgotten the water; I've come to get it.

SALLY Give me the jug. Go on in, both of you, I'll be there in a minute.

PETER Don't be long. (*To Sandy*) Stay there, old fella, and I'll bring you some food later on. (*Sandy wags his tail*)

Peter and Little Boy go in together. Sandy stays. Sally puts water jug under pump and leans on pump dreamily.

SALLY Yes, I SHALL miss everything. Even you, dear old pump; and you, dear house; (*Crossing to overhanging beam SR*) and you, old oak beams; (*Running her hand along underneath, but not looking*) and—(*Stops suddenly*)—why I've never noticed YOU. (*Looks and gasps*) Why, you're an axe! Suppose you fall! (*Sits down on bench DSR and talks, staring straight ahead*) Suppose Peter and I get married, and we had a little boy, and he came out one day to get water, and stood under that axe and it fell on him—what a terrible, terrible thing that would be! (*Starts to cry*)

Sandy goes across to her and nuzzles his head in her lap. She strokes him abstractedly. After a moment Mrs. Saucer comes in centre door.

MRS. S. Sally, everyone's wait—. Why, what's the matter?

SALLY Mother, look at that old axe stuck in the beam there. Suppose Peter and I get married, and we had a little boy, and he came out one day to get water, and stood under that axe and it fell on him—what a terrible, terrible thing that would be!

MRS. S. Oh, my goodness! (*Sits down with suddenness beside Sally*) Wouldn't that be awful. (*Starts to cry*)

Both of them are crying. After a moment Mr. Saucer fusses in centre door.

MR. S. Come along, come along! WOW, what's the matter?

MRS. S. (*Tearfully*) Just look at that old axe stuck in the beam there. Suppose Sally and Peter got married, and they had a little boy, and he came out one day to get water, and stood under that axe and it fell on him—what a terrible, terrible thing that would be!

MR. S. (*Sitting down on the bench beside the other two and getting out his pocket handerchief*) Dear, dear, it doesn't bear thinking about. (*Sniffs and dabs his eyes*) Oh, deary dear— (*Blows his nose violently*)

All three are now crying together. After a moment Peter comes through the centre door with the villagers crowding behind him.

PETER (*Going across to Sally and taking her hands*) Well, Sally, what's the matter?

Sally gulps and shakes her head.

MR. S. (*In a choked voice*) You see that old axe up there, stuck in the beam? Suppose you and Sally get married, and you had a little boy, and he came out one day to get water, and stood under that axe and it fell on him—what a terrible, terrible thing that would be!

Mrs. Saucer and Sally have been crying softly and nodding at intervals through the speech. Sandy looks up at the axe and howls softly.

PETER (*Incredulous*) Is THAT all? (*Laughing*) You're the three silliest sillies I've ever seen! Didn't anyone think of taking the axe DOWN? (*He removes it from the hook*) There, now there's nothing to worry about.

SALLY Oh, but there is, Peter. I couldn't marry you now.

PETER What!

EVERYONE (*Gasps*) Oh!

PETER But we shan't be living here—we'll be in our own house.

SALLY How do you know the same thing won't happen where we're going to live?

EVERYONE (*Sighing*) Oh...!

PETER Sally, once and for all, will you make up your mind about the date.

SALLY (*Wailing*) I can't, Peter.

PETER (*Firmly*) Very well; I'll tell you what I'm going to do. I'm going to go on a long journey with Sandy, (*Pats dog—everyone gasps, Mr. and Mrs. Saucer sit up, Sally's mouth drops open*), and if I can find three sillier sillies than you, I'll come back and perhaps you'll have learned some sense by that time, Sally. (*He laughs and picks up the axe*) I think I'll just take this away so you won't frighten yourself again!

Peter strides off USL, with Sandy following. Sally bursts out crying, and goes indoors, being comforted by Mr. and Mrs. Saucer, while the villagers go off shaking their heads and murmuring quietly. Two men detach themselves from the rest of the villagers—one has beckoned to the other. These are the Two Thieves. They stay behind.

1ST THIEF (*After looking quickly round to see that no one is listening*) For a long journey like that, Peter Piper will need a lot of money, won't he?

2ND THIEF I'd thought of that, too; but how can we get a hold of it? We'd soon be caught at this time of day in the village with so many people about and everybody knowing us.

1ST THIEF We'll follow him a bit of the way on his travels, and when he's sleeping in some lonely spot, we'll relieve him of such a weight of gold!

Both Thieves laugh.

2ND THIEF He should be grateful to us! And WE'LL see a bit of the world at the same time! Come on—let's go after him.

Exeunt and CURTAIN.

Peter Piper (Ted Soutar) informs Sally Saucer (Joan Robertson) and her parents (Teresa Griffiths and Dave Parker) that he must find three sillies sillier than they are before he can marry her, as Sandy the dog (Robert Hale) and the townsfolk look on in Mary Glenfield's children's folktale adaptation The Three Sillies, *Dec 1983. Photo: C.W. Hill Photography for Walterdale Theatre Associates.*

Act Two, Scene One

As rough plan, a cottage in Ireland. Flowers in garden. Fence round the garden; a sheep inside fence among the flowers. Tuft of vivid green grass and several outsize shamrocks on thatched roof. Large chimney with a long rope dangling from the inside of it over the roof and down into the garden. An old woman comes out form the door of the cottage. She looks up at the chimney.

OLD WOMAN (*To herself*) There, tha' should do it. Th'only good grass for mi sheep is on the roof. (*Goes round stage left of house.*)

Peter and Sandy come on, DSR, looking tired.

PETER (*To Sandy*) Well, Sandy, old fella, we've arrived in Ireland and never seen another silly silly yet. Maybe I can get some water for us at this cottage.

Old Woman comes round the side of the house again, carrying a ladder.

PETER Here, grandam, let me help you with that. Where would you like me to put it?

OLD WOMAN Put it up by the side of this rope, agin the roof. Thank'ee, thank'ee, that'll do fine. Where are ye come from, young man?

PETER We've been traveling for many days, all the way from the south of England. Can you spare some water for me and my dog? We're both very thirsty.

OLD WOMAN Go and help yourself. The pump's in the backyard, and the pitcher's beside it.

Peter and Sandy go round SL of house. Old Woman pulls end of rope to sheep and starts trying to fasten it round sheep's neck. This meets with a surprising show of resistance. The sheep kicks up its back legs, tugs away from Old Woman, goes round and round her in a circle, and finally after many admonitions from her—"Don't be so rough, me old dear"; "Wait now, wait" etc.—the rope gets fastened around sheep's neck. At the last the Old Woman bends to pick a flower, and the sheep butts her in the behind.

OLD WOMAN (*Crossly*) Ungrateful thing! This flower was to put on your neck—Shan't have it now. (*Sticking it in her own blouse.*)

During all this the Two Thieves have crept on, DSR, and have watched the Old Woman's antics with open-mouthed amazement. They nudge each other, and draw back, but still in sight of the audience, as Peter and Sandy come round the house again.

PETER Many thanks for the water, grandam. Are you taking your sheep to market?

OLD WOMAN No, that I'm not. It's me best companion in me old age. But it eats so much I've got no good grass left in me garden, and that sheep will start on me precious flowers if I don't get it some green stuff soon.

PETER What are you going to do about it, then?

OLD WOMAN D'ye see that big patch of green grass and shamrocks up on me roof?

Peter looks and nods.

OLD WOMAN I spent most of yesterday trying to push th'old sheep up the ladder to eat it, till we were both exhausted. Stupid creature fell off all the time; but I think I've got the answer today.

Peter looks amazed.

OLD WOMAN Th'other end of this rope is hanging down the chimney into me kitchen. When I get th'old sheep on to the ladder, I'll run inside to the kitchen and pull on the end of the rope until the creature's sitting on the roof, eating.

SANDY (*Coming forward and speaking to children*) This may be the first silly silly we've been looking for! Shush... (*Paw to mouth*)

PETER (*Aside*) I must see how this funny idea works!

OLD WOMAN (*Suspiciously*) What did ye say?

PETER I said I'd help you.

OLD WOMAN Oh, thank 'ee.

PETER I'll leave my moneybag here with you, Sandy, or it'll get in the way.

The Two Thieves look at each other, and pantomime pleasure and expectation. While Peter and the Old Woman get the sheep to the ladder, Sandy comes forward again and speaks to the children.

SANDY Can YOU think of an easier way to do it? Come on, you call it out to me while they're not looking. (*If he gets the right reply:*) That's right, just bring down a handful of grass and give it to the sheep. (*If no reply*:) Well, why not just bring down a handful of grass and give it to the sheep? I'll bet SHE'S never thought of that. I think she's going to turn out to be a silly silly, don't you?

While the sheep is being pushed up the ladder, the Two Thieves have been edging closer and closer to the moneybag. One had his hand almost over the fence when Sandy half-turns and lies across the moneybag. The Two Thieves run off quickly, gesticulating at each other. Meanwhile, the sheep has slipped back and is pushed up, back again etc., but is finally several rungs up the ladder.

OLD WOMAN (*To Peter*:) Now you hold her there. I'm going in to pull on the other end of the rope in the kitchen. When I call out "Push," you help push the old girl right up the ladder. (*She runs indoors*)

PETER (*Holding on to sheep with one hand, and slapping his thigh with the other*) I think I've found the first one!

OLD WOMAN (*Shouting from inside the house*) Push...

Struggling and bleating, the sheep is at last half sitting on the roof. Peter lets go and laughs again, while Sandy barks. Suddenly there is a startled "Baa-aa" from the sheep who falls off the roof, and the Old Woman pops out of the chimney.

OLD WOMAN Here—I'm stuck! Help, help!

PETER Hold on—I'm coming.

He climbs the ladder, pulls the Old Woman out of chimney, apparently with some effort, like drawing a cork.

OLD WOMAN I'll never get the grass for that blessed sheep.

PETER (*Standing on ground by this time*) Why don't you pick a handful on your way down, and give it to her on the ground?

OLD WOMAN (*Still on roof*) Well, by Heavens, I never thought of tha'.

The old woman *sits on roof, looking after Peter in astonishment as he goes off.*

PETER And that, Sandy, is certainly a silly silly if I ever saw one.

CURTAIN.

Act Two, Scene Two

As a rough plan, the market square in a Scottish town. Evening. The hills rising up sharply behind the town. The Innkeeper is brushing off his front steps with a broom. A young couple (boy in kilt, girl in country dress) saunter slowly across the square from SL, hand in hand. A child comes in, lower SR, bowling a hoop, and the mother rushes after, grabbing the child when it is half across the square.)

MOTHER Where have you been, Willie? It's long past your bedtime, you naughty boy. (*She drags him off again, protesting, SR.*)

The Two Thieves enter, upper SL looking around furtively.

1ST THIEF This has been a wasted journey so far, but once Peter Piper crossed into Scotland so late he would have to spend the night here.

2ND THIEF And here's the inn where he'd stay. Have we got any money left from the last traveler we (*Laughs*) borrowed some money from!

1ST THIEF Not much, but enough for supper and a night's lodging. (*Suddenly, listening.*) Quiet—do you hear a whistling?

2ND THIEF It's the tune Peter Piper always whistles. Let's hide and see what happens.

They cross stage quickly and hide behind the two market stalls.

The Innkeeper comes out on his front steps and begins sweeping off the dust with a broom. The whistling gets louder, and Peter and Sandy enter, upper SL.

PETER (*To Innkeeper*) What town is this we've arrived at?

INNKEEPER Ye're in the toon of Castlebrig.

PETER And are you the owner of this inn?

INNKEEPER Aye, that I am—and the best inn for miles around in this part of Scotland.

PETER I'd like a room for the night.

INNKEEPER Och, it's a bad night ye've come. Market day tomorrow, and the toon's fu'. But if ye wouldn't mind sharing a room wi' another traveler...

PETER I'M so tired I wouldn't mind at all. But what about HIM?

INNKEEPER He isn't in at the moment, but when he comes—. Wait, here he is now—yo're in luck. I'll ask him.

Man enters upper SR.

INNKEEPER (*To Man*:) Would ya mind sharin' a room wi' this gentleman here for the night?

MAN (*To Peter*:) I'd be glad of his company. But I warn you, I have to get up very early in the morning, before anyone else is about, so as to have my breeches on in time.

PETER (*Looking perplexed*) I probably won't waken anyway. (*To Sandy*) You stay there the night, Sandy, by the front step.

Peter, Innkeeper, Man go inside. The Two Thieves creep out from behind the stalls.

1ST THIEF Now all we have to do when we get in is find out which room Peter's in and wait till everyone is asleep. (*He knocks on the inn door.*)

The Innkeeper bustles out.

1ST THIEF We'd like a room for the night, my man.

INNKEEPER Sorry, the whole town's full up, there's not a room to be had. (*He closes the door again.*)

2ND THIEF (*To 1st Thief:*) There you are again—you and your big ideas! We should have just lain in wait for him as he came into the town.

1ST THIEF And who is it who likes to act like a fine gentlemen and sleep in fine sheets every night, rather than save our money by sleeping in the hedgerows? (etc. etc. *They go off with mutual recriminations.*)

SANDY (*Coming forward to children and speaking as he comes*) I wonder what they were talking about ... I'll stay here, as Peter Piper said, but I'll keep one eye open, because sometimes, at midnight, all the other animals come to a market square like this to play. (*Slowly and dopily*) But—I—must—sleep—a—little—first. (*He lies down at the bottom of the stage.*)

The lights gradually fade and night takes over. Suddenly there is a little pit-pat of music and two furry faces look round the upstage corner of the inn. They disappear and there is a whispering. Then another pit-pat of music and two dogs come in on tiptoe, see Sandy and run out again. More whispering. Music again and in come three dogs and two cats. They stand around Sandy. The cats are very dressed up, one in big skirts, with a fan, the other with frilled wristlets, large feathered hat etc.—17th Century.

1ST DOG I've never seen HIM before.

2ND DOG He must be a stranger.

1ST CAT (*Ominously*) D'you think he's dangerous?

All the animals whisper together.

2ND CAT Let's scratch him and see.

3RD DOG Oh, cats! That's all you can think of—using your claws!

CATS (*Together*) P-ss-ss-ss!

Dogs retreat and whisk behind inn again. Then slowly they come out. The 1st Dog courageously comes further towards the cats.

1ST DOG (*Ingratiatingly*) You sing to him with your lovely voices, and see if he wakes up.

CATS (*Mollified*) All right.
Mee-ow — Mee-ow!
Mrwow-ow —Mrwow—ow!

SANDY (*Waking up suddenly*) My goodness—Cats!

2ND DOG (*Very hastily*) They're our FRIENDS. They were singing to you.

SANDY (*Still not quite sure*) Oh, I see. (*To cats*:) Thank you. (*He gets up, feeling more sure of himself and struts to CS.*) I know a song.

ALL (*Going eagerly towards him*) A new one?

SANDY Well, I think so. I'll sing it for you, and you can join in the chorus.

He begins to sing Sandy's Song.

Verse:

SANDY When it's very late at night and the people are asleep.
Then the animals come out to play.
And in every market square, or a patch of garden, there
You can have them sing a roundelay.
Though you may not know the tune, if you listen very hard
It's not difficult to learn at all—
As you hear them singing,
Just beyond your bedroom wall.

Dogs' Chorus:

SANDY And doggies may not all sing quite in tune—

DOGS Woof, woof, woof, woof!

SANDY Sometimes they jump right to the moon—

DOGS Bow-ow, bow-ow!

SANDY Follow us, I'll show you how.
Heels together, give a little bow;

Dogs all bow to cats and each other.

And you can all start dancing now.

DOGS Bow Wow, Bow Wow!

Last four phrases of music alone are repeated, from "Follow me," while cats and dogs solemnly dance together round the village pump.

Cats' Chorus:

SANDY The cats have all come dressed for a ball—

Cats preen themselves.

CATS Purr, purr, purr, purr!

SANDY Their song sounds just like a caterwaul—

CATS Meeow, meeow!

SANDY But, if you should tell them so,
Then I think you really ought to know
They'd turn on you and start to go—

CATS P-ss, p-ss, p-ss, p-ss!

Dogs all retreat again behind market stalls. Then Sandy eases out apprehensively and stands DSR.

SANDY (*To Children*) I haven't quite finished my song. But (*With a look over his shoulder towards the cats*) I'm gong to sing it RIGHT HERE!

Verse:

SANDY But you'd better stay in bed when you hear their little song,
Don't go standing by the window-sill.
When the music comes again and you know the right refrain
You can join in—if you lie quite still.
For if you should take a peep when you're s'posed to be asleep.
Then they'll vanish from around your house.
So pretend you're simply
Singing like a little mouse—

SANDY (*Very quietly to children*) And how does a mouse sing? Wee-eek! So when I go like this (*Making a drawing-in posture with hands*) you sing "wee-eek, wee-eek, wee-eek, wee-eek" four times. See?

Mousies' and Children's Chorus:

SANDY The mousies come as close as they dare—

ALL Wee-eek, wee-eek, wee-eek, wee-eek!

SANDY They're so small, you don't know if they're there—

ALL Wee-eek, wee-eek, wee-eek, wee-eek!

SANDY S'pose they join in singing too?

Doesn't really matter if they do,
The mousies sound the same as you— (*Pointing to children*)

ALL Wee-eek, wee-eek, wee-eek, wee-eek!

Again a small dance, then suddenly comes a thud.

3RD DOG Listen! — I can hear someone coming.

The mice (Tobrina Smith, Josephine Stebbings, Mary Tymo and Alexandra Sydie) show the cats (Jennie Wigmore and Robert Jahrig) and dogs (Jane Glenfield, Rob Otten and Amanda Clarke) with Sandy (Robert Hale, second from left) what they've got, December 1983. Photo: C.W. Hill Photography for Walterdale Theatre Associates.

All animals whisk away and Sandy lies down beside steps. The set is gradually lightening. The Man opens the inn door. He has on a long nightshirt and tasseled nightcap. His breeches are over his arm. He goes across to the pump and hangs his breeches on it, the top of them gaping open. Sandy stands and watches in amazement, but flops down again just in time as the Man turns and comes back to steps. The Man takes a running jump at his breeches—falls down. Comes back again. Takes another running jump at them and goes right past them. Takes breeches off pump and is going over to hang them on one of the stalls when Peter comes out of the inn door.

PETER Hello, I heard you go downstairs and thought I'd come out myself to get a breath of fresh morning air.

MAN (*Completely preoccupied, and hanging his breeches on stall*) Could you get back a moment, please, so I can get a good run at them? (*Waves Peter back with his hand.*)

PETER Just a moment—what are you trying to do?

MAN Oh, it's terrible! I always take about an hour to jump into my breeches, and this morning, as it's market-day, I've got to be earlier than ever.

A cock crows somewhere.

MAN There, you see, it's dawn already. The farmers' wives will soon be getting up their stalls. I MUST be ready by then.

He goes right back to the inn steps and runs hard across the stage again towards his breeches. He gets one leg in and falls down again.

MAN Oh dear, dear, dear—

PETER (*Who has been slapping his sides with laughter*) Here, let me show you. Now, hold your breeches in your two hands—so; lower them; put your left foot in and pull the breeches leg over it; and now your right foot in and pull the whole thing up. See how easy?

MAN (*Clasping Peter's hands*) Thank you, thank you. I shall never forget your kindness. I must tell my wife when I get home. (*Goes off through inn door repeating "Hold breeches in both hands, lower them"* etc.)

PETER (*Too exhausted to laugh anymore*) Well, that certainly was another silly silly, if ever I saw one. And after breakfast, Sandy, old fella, we'll go looking for the last one. (*They both go in to the inn.*)

Meanwhile two farmwomen with laden baskets have come in chatting quietly and are decorating the two stalls as the CURTAIN falls.

The second silly (Dennis Robinson as Scottish Man) explains his plan to put on his breeches two legs at a time as Peter Piper (Ted Soutar) and Sandy the dog (Robert Hale) look on in December 1983. Cheryl Krausher's whimsical set captured the play's spirit well. Photo: C.W. Hill Photography for Walterdale Theatre Associates.

Act Three, Scene One

As rough plan, country edge of a Welsh village. A big pond SR and off. Villagers raking in it, if it can be arranged. Great excitement among the villagers.

1ST VILLAGER
Have you got her?

2ND VILLAGER
Harry feels something heavy.

1ST VILLAGER
Well, pull them, man, for goodness' sake. We'll lend a hand.

All behind each other like tug-of-war.

HARRY One, two, three, heave.

2ND VILLAGER
Is it moving?

Peter and Sandy enter SR. Peter stands there looking amazed.

PETER What are you trying to get out of the pond?

All the villagers stop dragging the pond and speak to each other, puffing.

1ST VILLAGER
The 'owd green moon.

PETER The moon!

2ND VILLAGER
She fell in last night. My husband saw her, right after midnight, lyin' there in the pond, calm as you please.

HARRY Something bright's comin' up on the end of my fishin' rod.

1ST VILLAGER
Careful!

2ND VILLAGER
Don't lose it...

3RD VILLAGER

Have you still got it?

HARRY Here—it—comes. (*Something bright flashes across the line, there—*)

2ND VILLAGER

Oh, it's only a silly old kettle—that makes five so far, not to mention other sorts of pots and pans.

3RD VILLAGER

(*To Peter*:) It's never any wonder to me WHAT comes out. Our ponds here in Wales are often very deep.

1ST VILLAGER

Some years back, Roberts the dairyman drove his horse and cart in, and we've never come across them yet.

2ND VILLAGER

(*Impressively*) There's people heard horses' hoofs here some dark nights, and Roberts' voice, clear as you please. (*Lowering her voice, and glancing round hurriedly before she speaks.*) They say the witches got him!

PETER (*Laughing*) Well, why do you want the moon out again?

HARRY To see by at night, you silly man.

PETER Don't you worry, she'll come sailing in the sky as right as rain in just a short while.

VILLAGERS (*In rapid succession*)

Listen to such nonsense.
He's talking daft.
What about Roberts' horse and cart, then?

All go back to dragging the pond.

PETER What a lot of silly sillies!

WOMAN'S VOICE

Gwynfor, I've found me old teeth!

Suddenly Sandy, SL, starts howling quietly, and then louder, and the moon sails into view upper SL.

1ST VILLAGER

Look at the moon...!

All stop dragging and look up. They are terrified, and lean with their bodies, saying—

VILLAGERS How did she get up there?
Ooo-ooh—look at her ride!
Ooo-ooh see the witches riding on her tail!

Moon disappears upwards SR, and, at the same moment, is reflected clearly in the pond.

2ND VILLAGER

She's in the pond again!

VILLAGERS (*All converging on Peter*)
He's got her bewitched!
Chase him out...
No room for him in this village!

All chase Peter and Sandy with brooms, pitchforks, rakes etc., Sandy barking as he goes. As the villagers nearly reach the side of the stage, on whirl the Two Thieves who appear amazed to see Peter and Sandy rushing past them. The villagers stop dead in their tracks for a moment.

WOMAN'S VOICE

And here's two more strangers come to bring us bad luck!

MAN'S VOICE Out with them, too...

The Villagers fall on the surprised Thieves, belabouring them, and to the sound of their howls, the CURTAIN falls.

Act Three, Scene Two

Same as Act One. Enter Two Thieves looking around.

2ND THIEF Well, thanks to your idea we've been half round the world and come right back to where we started without getting hold of Peter Piper's money. There won't be much of it left by now.

1ST THIEF You needn't have come if you didn't want to. And, anyway, Peter's got a lot of money left. It's still worth stealing, if we can do it carefully.

2ND THIEF Quiet! Do you hear that tune again? It may be Peter. Let's hide and see.

They hide. Sandy runs in. He rushes from one familiar thing to another, and is just about to bark joyously when Peter enters and looks quickly around.

PETER Now, Sandy, don't make a noise. It's early in the morning and nobody's awake yet. We'll just lie down here and get a little rest. I'll use my moneybag for a pillow—it's still quite full.

He sits down and then stretches out under the tree. Sandy is nearly asleep already. Peter wraps himself in his cloak and is also soon asleep. The Two Thieves come out quietly from their hiding-place. One nudges the other and points to the moneybag under Peter's head. 1st Thief quietly goes over to try and pry moneybag loose. 2nd Thief goes over to Sandy. Peter stirs and Sandy wakes up. 2nd Thief throws sack over Sandy's head, but the dog is too quick for him and, barking, shakes it off and goes for the man's legs. Meanwhile, Peter has woken up and is fighting with the 1st Thief. Barking. Shouts of "After him, Sandy"; "I'll teach you to steal money from travelers." Howls from Thieves. Finally both thieves are overpowered and tied together wrists and ankles—i.e. 1st Thief's left wrist to 2nd Thief's right wrist, ditto ankles—with the string dropped by 2nd Thief, who was going to use it to tie sack over Sandy's head. Sandy stands guard over them as they sit on ground. All the village has now woken up, except the Saucer family. Villagers come crowding in from upper SL.

1ST WOMAN Why, it's Peter Piper back again! (*Looks at men on ground*) And that's my son, Jim. What's he been doing?

2ND WOMAN (*Thrusting forward*) And my son, Arthur, tied to him!

PETER They were trying to steal my money, but Sandy woke up and stopped their little game.

The two Thieves are struggling to their feet.

1ST WOMAN I THOUGHT you were up to no good, Jim Hopkins, when you went off so sudden—to seek your fortune, YOU said.

2ND WOMAN You just wait till I get you home, Arthur Green. You'll not know what's hit you!

They go off, still yelling behind the Two Thieves who are hopping along awkwardly, three-legged, to the laughter of the crowd. Tom and Cook have appeared from door lower SR. Mr. and Mrs. Saucer have come out on the steps and are looking sleepily bewildered.

MRS. S. There's a terrible noise going on.

MR. S. (*Vaguely*) I can't see anything without my glasses.

SALLY (*Bursting through between them*) It's Peter back again! (*She rushes up to him and holds his hands*) Oh, Peter, I'm so glad to see you!

PETER I'M glad to see YOU, Sally; and I'm back for good. And you know a funny thing? After looking all over for three sillier sillies than you I've found out something else.

SALLY What?

Peter Piper (Ted Soutar) ties together the Two Thieves (Claudio Masciulli and Godfrey Budd) as Sandy the dog (Robert Hale) barks encouragement, December 1983. Glenfield and Bette Anderson, founder of Edmonton's Theatre for Children, conceived of the addition of the Two Thieves to the children's folktale to heighten the story's suspense. Photo: C.W. Hill Photography for Walterdale Theatre Associates.

PETER *He begins Peter's song.*

I thought that the silliest sillies were you,
But on looking around me, I found
That in spite of the odd little things that you do,
There were sillier sillies around.
So just listen while I sing
Of a most amazing thing

(*Singing*)

We all seem silly to someone
No matter how clever we are;
If all of us
had to be brainy
We just wouldn't get very
far.
If we had to
be sensible all of the while
and never give people the chance of a smile
We all seem silly to someone
No matter how clever we are.

We all do silly things sometimes,
And nobody minds if we do
The silliest things to others
Are things that seem clever to you.
If you find someone silly in things that they do,
They're probably thinking the same about you
We all do silly things sometimes,
And nobody minds, and nobody minds,
And nobody minds if we do!

All the villagers clap.

SALLY And I've found out something, too, Peter. But first, tell me—do you still want me to marry you?

PETER Well, of course, Sally.

SALLY Then I'll tell you—(*Raising her voice and speaking loudly to everyone*) Peter Piper and I invite you all to our wedding next Saturday—and this arrangement is definite!

Everybody laughs and they begin to sing "Little Sally Saucer."

ALL Little Sally Saucer, she's going to marry
Peter Piper, now that it's springtime.
Now that she is certain, she will never tarry,
She has made up her mind for good!

All dance again as the CURTAIN falls.

But Sandy gets in front of the curtain and says to the children:

SANDY And don't you ever, ever, tell Peter and Sally that I can talk!

He runs, barking, offstage.

Sandy the dog (Robert Hale) hams it up during the production photo shoot, December 1983. Photo: C.W. Hill Photography for Walterdale Theatre Associates.

Just (1999)

by Trevor Schmidt

Following the production of a number of successful new plays in the early 1980s, Walterdale's attention to new play production waned during the latter part of the decade and into the early 1990s. In some years the April or May slot was given over to known full-length plays such as Chekhov's *The Cherry Orchard* (May 1987), in other years to productions of known one-acts (Ayckbourn's *Drinking Companion*, *Gosforth's Fete*, and *A Talk in the Park* in May 1992, for example). By the mid-1990s the company turned in earnest to new one-act productions in the late-spring slot. Since then it has produced, and in most cases offered dramaturgical development to, nearly forty new one-act plays by local writers, including CKUA radio personality and former Walterdale board member Chris Allen, playwright Heather Morrow, choreographer (and musical theatre aficionado) Barbara Mah, playwright and screenwriter Matthew Kowalchuk, actor Dale Wilson, and former Walterdale artistic director David Owen. Counted in this list is multi award-winning playwright, director, and designer Trevor Schmidt.

Schmidt was born in Saskatoon. He graduated with a BFA in drama from the University of Calgary in 1991 and has since written dozens of plays. In 1994 he moved to Edmonton and in the following year he formed the Unconscious Collective. The group had the wide but pressing mandate to produce new works for the theatre written by Albertans. Schmidt himself wrote most of the group's plays. His writing, directing, design, and acting work have garnered him Elizabeth Sterling Haynes nominations in eight categories, as well as a Syncrude Award for Innovative Artistic Direction and an Enbridge Emerging Artist Award for his playwriting.

When *Just* made its theatre company debut at Walterdale in 1999, having had recent success at the Alberta Provincial One-Act Festival, Schmidt's playwriting star was on the rise. To offer a sense of his output, consider that in the 2000/01 Edmonton theatre season alone, he earned three of the four Elizabeth Sterling Haynes nominations for Outstanding New Play for *Only Girls* (Sound & Fury Theatre/The Unconscious

Collective), *Treatment* (Theatre Yes/The Unconscious Collective), and *The Watermelon Girls* (The Unconscious Collective), which won the award. He was also nominated that year for his costume design for *The Oedipus Project* (Northern Light Theatre). In the summer of 2002 he contributed six of his own plays to the Edmonton Fringe Festival; notably, Schmidt himself produced none of them. For the 2003/04 season, along with ten other writers who included Mark Stubbings and former Walterdale artistic director David Owen, Schmidt won the award for Outstanding Fringe New Work for his contribution to *Change Room*. Since then he has barely slowed down despite becoming artistic director of Northern Light Theatre, where he continues to write, direct, design, and act. His second play produced at Walterdale, *Mockingbird Close*, received enthusiastic responses at the 2008 one-acts.

Just, one of the few one-person shows that Walterdale has produced, is a tense yet delicate story told by a woman who comes to a home for young, pregnant girls to adopt a baby. By way of sensitive dramatic monologue we gradually learn why she has been troubled for so long as she waits for her husband to meet her.

Just ran May 31–June 5, 1999, at Walterdale Playhouse (firehall) with the following cast and creative team:

WOMAN	Michele Vance Hehir
DIRECTOR	Trevor Schmidt
STAGE MANAGER	Brad Smith

Just was presented at the 1999 Edmonton Regional One-Act Festival, where Michele Vance Hehir won the Best Actress Award as The Woman, before going on to the Provincial One-Act Festival. *Just* became, as Schmidt describes it, the "cornerstone" monologue for his award-winning play *The Watermelon Girls*, performed at Edmonton's Arts Barns the following year.

Just

by Trevor Schmidt

The Woman (Michele Vance Hehir) considers her options in Trevor Schmidt's Just, *May-June 1999. Photo: C.W. Hill Photography for Walterdale Theatre Associates.*

A woman sits alone.

WOMAN My husband should be here. Any minute.
I don't have any idea what's keeping him.
We made an appointment, he always does this, we make
an appointment and he ... sorry.
Something must have come up, some sort of emergency.

Just wait, I suppose.

This is a lovely home. I thought that as I was pulling up.
It's a lovely colour. And so big. Why, there must be ... seven
rooms? Maybe eight! It's so nice that it can be used for such
a ... good cause. I think it's wonderful, the work that's being done here.

I saw some of them. The girls. Outside. When I drove up. They were
having some kind of picnic or something, on the bench just off the porch.
They were laughing and happy, each one looking like she'd swallowed a
medicine ball.

They all looked very happy.

I don't suppose I could ... smoke a cigarette? Or is that not done here?
I'll ... wait, I'll just wait. It's a filthy habit. I'll just wait.
I don't know where he is.

I was ashamed. Earlier. In the car, out front. They all saw me, the girls, they saw me drive up, they were all laughing. I pulled up the drive, stopped in front of the house, and just ... sat there. I didn't want to get out and walk to the door. Not with all of them watching.

That was silly, wasn't it? I mean ... they must have known, they must have all known, I mean, no one comes out here unless ... it was silly of me. Stupid. To sit there in my car while they stood not twenty yards away, just sat there waiting for ... I don't know what I was waiting for.

I don't have any idea how long I would have sat there if one of the girls hadn't detached herself from the group and started coming toward me, her huge belly ... well, that was enough to practically shoot me out of that automobile, tell you. Direct contact! I couldn't face that.

She called something out to me, friendly? Concerned. I waved her away and practically ran up the walk, trying to keep my face away from them, hoping my hat would cover. Trying to keep my face away! Can you see any point in that? With my car sitting right out front, with license plates clear as day. What was I thinking!

I was ashamed. Does that make any sense? I mean ... what do I have to be ashamed of? It's not as though I'm one of those ... I haven't done anything wrong.

I suppose I shouldn't have told you that story. It didn't represent me in the most positive light. I just ... I guess it was on my mind. My conscience. And it slipped out. I thought it would be better to acknowledge the whole incident than just ... ignore it.

I should probably just sit here until my husband arrives, and not say another word. Just sit and wait quietly.

Yes, it's a very lovely colour, this house. A lovely shade. And those trees out front. Well they're quite...

They weren't laughing at me. When I drove up. I know that. They were just happy, and that's all. Though how one could be happy in that condition, knowing that in a few weeks, or months, you were going to...

Well, everyone's different. And what the good Lord takes from one, He gives to ... though in this case, He doesn't really take, as much as they give it away, all of them...

I suppose there's always someone willing—happy—to get what one of those girls has cast off.

He should be along any minute. He surely hasn't forgotten. He might be late, but he won't have forgotten. He knows how important this is to me.

I didn't mean anything about those girls. Nothing bad. I don't judge. Sometimes you just find yourself in situations ... that you're not sure how to get out of. And if you're young, and have no one to help you ... I can understand.

My sister-in-law, Betty, says that I'm chasing a dream. She's always catching me looking out the window, or staring at the wall. She doesn't understand. She says she'd love to have the time to stand around, day-dreaming, but she's got four kids to run around after. She says that's just the way it is. Some get, some don't.

Betty says we're lucky.

She came across me the other day, just crying my eyes out. Sitting in the door to the backyard, the screen door between me and her kids. She asked me why I was crying.

What could I say? That her kids made me weepy? I was bawling because her kids were happy?

Now Betty just thinks I'm crazy.

I told her I wasn't feeling well. I had an ache in my stomach, that's what I said.

Look at me. I'm smoking. Now, how did that happen? I could put it out. Should I put it out? I could. If it's against the rules— I don't want to break any rules here. I want...

I really wanted this to go well, but everything seems to be conspiring against me. First my husband...

He knew how important this was to me.

I have tried and tried ... and tried.

I understand those girls. The ones outside, having a picnic. I think ... if I'm afraid of them, ashamed, it's because I understand them.

Bert wasn't my first. No, that distinction goes to a young man who lived down from us, a boy with curly hair. His name was Cameron.

I didn't know the first thing about ... the first thing. If I'd known then ... if my mother had told me ... well, I can't help but think things would have been so different.

It didn't take long
it hurt
and the earth didn't move
he didn't talk to me the next day
I thought I'd left with only some grass down my dress
down there
but I found I had
something else
left there, too.

I don't even remember what I felt

My mother was horrified
My father could never know
She took some money from a jar
and more from a secret drawer
and drove me to a little house
smaller than this one
an ugly little house
and an ugly little man
did something
down there.

Then she took me home
and told my father
I was ill
a fever
and she brought me food in bed
and changed my dressings
and sang to me
like she hadn't done since I was
a baby

Bert says Betty means well. But I think she's purposely mean. She doesn't realize. With just the slightest amount of tact, she might notice that I'm ... pained. She might think twice about bringing her brood over.

We have a nice home. Not as nice a colour as this one but ... We have a large home, with lots of room. But there is an empty space. I have died a hundred deaths waiting for something to fill that space. That room.

You have no idea what that's like
When you wait
and each month
a drop of blood
kills you.
A tiny drop of blood
like a teardrop
my body cries

I want to meet the girl
the girl in question
I'd like to meet her
I'd like for her to see me
to see that I'm the right sort
I want to tell her
show her
how badly
I want this.

And my husband
my husband as well
he'll tell you himself
it's very important
it's what we need
what we've needed for some time now
just what we need to
remind us
why we ended
together in the first place
It seems a hundred years ago now.

Bert and I
tried very hard
we used to try
every night
but
I guess he got tired of trying
and gave up.

I can't really blame him
it's not as though
I was ever very good at it
if it had been my choice
I wouldn't do it at all
except that
The Ends Justify The Means.

I try not to think about it too much
but I think it's my fault
you know
my fault that all our trying was for
nothing
I did something wrong
at the wrong time
and now I can't do it again
even though
now
it's the right time
the perfect time
even though it may soon be
too late.

I don't know how much longer I should wait. He should have been here long before now. I don't know what kind of excuse he'll have for me. What kind of excuse I can give you for him.

He works very hard. He's tired.

The other night, when I told him about coming here today, that I'd made an appointment, he shook his head and said "I'm tired.

I'm tired..."

I made him promise to come, and that tired man went to bed.

He lay beside me and we pretended to sleep, neither one of us touching. Too tired to try.

Bert and Betty don't know, of course, I never told them. I can't imagine why I've even told you about it today.

I suppose I just wanted you to know that ... if there had been a house like this, if I had known about it, if I knew then what I know now, well ...

I would have gone to "visit an aunt." That's the proper phrase, isn't it? They still say that, don't they? "Gone to visit an aunt."

Everything would be so different.

I dread the rest of the lonely evenings of my life stretching out before me. I don't want to spend my time with the company of a man who is tired. I want to have love, even if it is the love that someone else has given away, the love they have cast out. It only seems fair. The love has done nothing wrong. It should be held close, cherished. I can do that. We can do that.

I don't mean Bert and I, although he will make a fine father. He'll leave the real work of it to me.

No, when I say "we," I mean yourself and I. We can do it. You and I can do it together. This deal, this contract, it can be between us. It can be our secret.

Not that it is anything to be ashamed of. No. I didn't mean that, by any means. It's not a secret. But I don't want to call it a deal, I mean, that sounds so...

I'd best wait for my husband. I'll just wait.

My mother kept my secret. Our secret. She'll go to her grave with it, I have no doubt. That's mothers and daughters.

> I want that.
> I want that, does that make any sense to you at all?
> I'm going to wait.
> I'm very patient.
> I'll wait to get what I want
> I'll wait forever if I have to.
> I'll sit here and wait.
> Don't rush to any decisions.
> Take your time.
> I'll wait.

The Woman smokes and sits and waits as the lights fade.

The Beaver Effect (2002)

by Mark Stubbings

More than once, Walterdale has produced plays that problematize the criteria on which Canada's cultural nationalism has been built. Including George Ryga's *Nothing But a Man* and a number of other plays presented in this collection (*The Canadian Fact*, *[ice land]*, and *Chief Shaking Spear Rides Again*), they represent one half of a dialectic current that flows through the identity of many longstanding amateur theatres. As official federal policy turned in earnest toward painting a national character for Canada in the two decades leading up to the country's Centennial, many amateur theatres sought to redefine a portion of their fare in order to support not only the federal agenda (which had often shared with these theatres Eurocentric tendencies) but also growing public and artist interest in Canadian content. The foreign, often colonial, fare that had won these theatres an audience base was, as the Centennial approached, sharing the stage with homegrown works at nonprofessionalized theatres. Notably, a selection of these homegrown plays dealt outright with questions of Canada's national character. Mark Stubbings's *The Beaver Effect* follows this tradition.

Many of these works, like Stubbings's play, are not blindly nationalist. Many express a general skepticism toward selling a unified nationalist Canadian identity to Canadians, often citing geographic and cultural differences. During the 1950s and 1960s federal policy routinely met with wry responses from the very artists, including playwrights, who wanted a bigger piece of the state funding pie. The whole mechanism, of course, is absurd: artists required to beg for state funding so that politicians could congratulate themselves for supporting the country's culture by offering their handouts; the more public begging, the more congratulating while some funds changed hands.

When plying their trade at amateur theatres, playwrights found production environments in which their messages were received and encouraged. After all, unlike their professional counterparts, most longstanding amateur theatres had never relied on government funding at any level and thus had benefitted from a unique sort of artistic freedom when new play production became a priority. As long as the box office was in good standing, and as long as the paying membership supported the programming, new play production need not be equated with experimental risk.

Like Canadian theatre, Canadian film—in particular the curiously definitive National Film Board of Canada—could be the target of quasi-nationalist satire. Historically dwarfed in comparison with Hollywood, the Canadian film industry has been seen by many writers to play out that recurrent and constitutive part of Canada's forever maturing national character: a perceived inferiority to its neighbour to the south. This is coupled with a "Hollywood bombardment," according to the first director of *The Beaver Effect*, that erodes opportunities for Canadian identity-making (DeGagné). Facing the stereotype of low-budget Canadian film productions and narrowly defined "Canadian" subject matter, along with state-sponsored, top-down cultural policy, early-career artists may perceive both the film industry and the state as narrowly focused, aesthetically exclusive, and systematically frustrating. To the struggling screenwriter both industry and state appear unsupportive of Canadian talent working outside of certain socio-economic and conceptual boundaries. In this sense, Stubbings's play *The Beaver Effect* may be as much a comment on the discipline of Canadian theatre as it is on the discipline of Canadian film. But it is also, Stubbings asserts, "an attempt to understand what it means to be an artist in Canada and to recognize the roadblocks involved in doing so" (Stubbings). He does so in *The Beaver Effect* with the characteristic "muscular, funny, profane" dialogue (Nicholls) that has increasingly earned him the respect of Edmonton theatre audiences and critics alike.

Born in Kitchener, Ontario, in 1975 and raised in the Edmonton suburb of Sherwood Park, actor and playwright Mark Stubbings made his Walterdale debut in May 1991 in Tony Cain's one-act *This Wooden O*, which presented brief excerpts from Shakespeare's plays. Stubbings graduated with a BA in drama from the University of Alberta in 2004, forming with other graduates David DeGagné, Nathan Durec, and Elizabeth Ludwig the theatre and film company Last Night Productions. Stubbings has garnered a number of playwriting awards, including a 2003 Alberta Playwriting Competition award in the Discovery category (for playwrights whose work is not yet professionally produced) for *Dust* (later produced in 2004 and 2007 by Last Night Productions) and a 2004 Sterling Award for Outstanding Fringe New Work (with ten other writers) for *Redemption Thong*. His other critically lauded plays include *In the Doghouse* (Nextfest and the University of Alberta's New Works Festival 2002), *Fran Chews* (Alberta One-Acts Competition 2004, Walterdale 2005), *Our Kind of Love Is an Ugly Love* (Edmonton Fringe 2007) and *Stars and Sons* (Edmonton Fringe 2008).

Stubbings is one of a handful of playwrights who have come to define the playwriting scene in Edmonton during the past decade. He is also one of a number of Edmonton theatre artists who supplemented their undergraduate education with non-university exposure to theatre practice. (Conversely, as if to define one contemporary "town-and-gown" approach to playmaking, Walterdale has benefitted from the participation of undergraduate and graduate students, particularly since the mid-1990s, by offering directing, stage management, and production experience and substantial roles, often in large casts, to students who gain experience from working beside non-university theatre artists. A number of university professors also have participated at Walterdale over the years, including English professors Wilfred Watson and Diane Bessai, French professor Vivien Bosley, and drama professors Piet Defraeye and Alex Hawkins.) Along with playwrights such as Scott Sharplin and Trevor Schmidt, Stubbings stands out as much for the critical acclaim his plays have received as for his dedication to an art form that has lost much popular cachet, particularly at the outset of the digital age.

The Beaver Effect, which Stubbings has characterized as "a Kevin Smith-type comedy about two (hapless) Ed Wood filmmakers trying to get a grant" (quoted in Nicholls) follows the dilemma of two twenty-something men trying to obtain Canadian funding to produce their science-fiction film. The challenge: to convince Denise at the Canadian Film Society to fund the movie, even though it does not fall under her Canadian content guidelines: "Prairie, Prairie, Prairie or a small fishing community of some kind"; "The more wheat, farmers and girls in frilly dresses the better." The play takes aim at some of the ridiculous stereotypes related to "being Canadian," while it encourages us to laugh at the parts of the stereotypes we find ridiculous, as well as at the parts we believe in. It updates the satire on empty nationalisms found in Watson's *The Canadian Fact* for those who grew up watching Degrassi High, while dealing bluntly with those who claim to speak to "What Canadians want": "Even the CBC airs American shows." It is particularly representative of Walterdale's ongoing interest in attracting young artists and audiences to the theatre.

The Beaver Effect ran June 10–15, 2002, at Walterdale Playhouse (firehall) with the following cast and creative team:

LAWRENCE SCHMIT	Jimmy Shewchuk
DENISE CURRAN	Shauna Johannesen
CLIVE ANDREWS	Mark Stubbings
DIRECTEOR	David DeGagné
STAGE MANAGER	Joelle Lemmen
DRAMATURGE	Sam Varteniuk

The Beaver Effect was produced in a previous incarnation at the Lloydminster Fringe Festival August 11–13, 2000.

The Beaver Effect

A Play in One Act

by Mark Stubbings

Scene One

Lawrence sits center stage in a pair of pajamas. He is barely visible under the cold blue lighting. Faint lighting washes over him, a gobo, the shadows of jail cell bars. As the sharp lines of the bars fall across him he begins to mutter and sing softly. He is cradling a golden statuette.

LAWRENCE (*Sung*) Wake up in the morning, alarm gives off a warning, gee, I gotta go to school. (*Spoken*) This is our independence day! (*Sung*) C'mon, give us a try, at Degrassi Junior High! (*Spoken*) sometimes you gotta take one for the team... Canadian Film Society, can you hold please? (*Sung*) There's a voice that keeps on calling me, on the road, that's where I wanna be. (*Spoken*) You killed him... Clickety click, Barba trick! Do we still have a deal? (*Sung*) You can do it, yes you can, put your muscles to it, in a jam, you can do it, yes you can, and you can too!

The lighting dramatically shifts and the stage is washed over by extremely bright lights. A projection screen behind Lawrence displays various images from Canadian film and television. Lawrence, now completely visible, jumps to his feet and excitedly addresses the audience. Awards music swells.

LAWRENCE Wooooo Hooo! Yeah! Thank you so very much. I ... I ... really don't know what to say. I am shocked. I want to thank god ... my mother that taught me the beauty of language ... my father that taught me to take care of my responsibility. My very supportive girlfriend Crystal ... we did it baby! Hooray, hooray for movies. Oh yeah, this guy in the front row knows what I'm talking about, you betcha! I have to say that you wonderful people of the academy are what make dreams come true. This film, which I shot on a handy cam for three hundred dollars, was a labor of love. It was blood, sweat and tears from the word go ... or should I say the word MAYBE, I'm talking to you there Paramount!

The projections continue but slowly the gobo of jail bars washes over Lawrence. The lights begin to dim. His tone changes from ecstatic to somber all at once. He falters through the next section of his speech.

LAWRENCE No, seriously, for a Canadian film to win best picture is ... well ... unthinkable. It's so hard, y'know, to find an artistic voice or something ... It all comes down to what you want to say. You can't compromise. You can't let people hold you back.

An alarm sounds and off stage we hear the voice of the warden.

WARDEN LAST BELL!

LAWRENCE Oh, they're telling me to wrap it up. I should thank my collaborator ... (*a second bell*) Oh, my time's up ... I guess all that's left to say is ... (*raising the statuette over his head*) It's mine! It's mine! It's all mine!

Black out.

Scene Two

A basement apartment. Lawrence lies on the couch stage right. He is dressed in his bathrobe and pajamas. He speaks in his sleep muttering things like "I'm the king of the world" until he suddenly springs up looking around in bewilderment. He rubs his eyes and crosses to a mini fridge stage left. He opens it and pulls out a can of V-8 juice. He produces a can opener from his bathrobe pocket, cracks open the can and guzzles the juice until it is empty. His Mother's voice from offstage startles him.

LAWRENCE'S MOTHER
Lawrence! Your fucking girlfriend is here! Put your goddamn pants on!

LAWRENCE Mom! Do you have to use that language? You sound like a trucker! And this would seem a lot more like my own apartment if you didn't yell at me through the vent!

LAWRENCE'S MOTHER
Don't yell at me like that! If I wanted abuse I'd go find your father! Put some fucking pants on, I'm sending her down!

LAWRENCE Mom! She's already seen me without pants! And you want to know what that means? It means we've had sex! Yeah, you heard me! I'm not the twenty three year old virgin you think I am. I have made sweet love to her! I am a love machine! I am extremely well hung!

An extended pause.

LAWRENCE'S MOTHER
Well, she just left Lawrence. I hope you're happy, you little prick!

LAWRENCE Shit!

Lawrence meanders over to his dresser upstage left. He roots through a collection of video tapes, finds the tape he is looking for and stares at it intently. Clive comes bursting in stage right.

CLIVE What the fuck is wrong with your Mother!

LAWRENCE Holy! Man, you scared the hell outta me!

CLIVE Sorry. You okay?

LAWRENCE Yeah. What are you doing here? It's like eight in the morning.

CLIVE Larry, it's two thirty in the afternoon. On a Monday.

LAWRENCE What? I ... who came up with the concept of time anyway?

CLIVE I don't know ... Christopher Lloyd? Look, I'm sick of sitting around waiting for her to call back. Let's just go see her.

LAWRENCE She just left. And I don't think she is in the mood to deal with you.

CLIVE She just left? She was here?

LAWRENCE Yes, Crystal was just here and I said the wrong thing again and she left.

CLIVE I'm not talking about Crystal. Jesus, does anything in your life ever change? I am talking about Denise.

LAWRENCE That woman at the Canadian Film Society?

CLIVE Yeah. I've called her about the arts grant meeting ten times and she still won't set up a meeting. So, I say we go down there right now and give a pitch.

LAWRENCE Right now?

CLIVE Yes. Right now. We go down there and we make her listen. She can't turn us down. Not with the revolutionary film scripts we have.

LAWRENCE Look, Clive. I'm really not in the mood right now. Crystal and I are fighting again and I have to work a drive thru shift tonight.

CLIVE She'll forgive you, she always does. And if not, you ankle her.

LAWRENCE I really screwed up Clive. I'm telling you. After last night, I'm surprised I can still count two testicles. And she was just here and I messed that up too. We weren't even in the same room and I messed it up.

CLIVE Yeah, I hear ya. Ever since the days of the fucking caveman, men have been pissing off women. Some Neanderthal didn't help clean the cave and we're fucked for the rest of eternity.

LAWRENCE I told her she was fat and smelled like fish.

CLIVE Holy shit! Why would you ... what? Out of all the things you should not say to a woman you said two out of five.

LAWRENCE It was taken out of context. We were at the carnival at the house of mirrors when I said she looked fat. And when I said she smelled like fish we were at Red Lobster.

CLIVE Even still you can never say those things to a woman if you want to keep your groinal area.

LAWRENCE Wait a second, what are the other three things you can't say to a woman?

CLIVE Where's my dinner. Your sister is hotter than you. And, "Hey, did you give me this infection"?

LAWRENCE Crystal doesn't have a sister.

CLIVE Crystal's not going to dump you. You don't sleep around, you make decent money at the burger baron. You're pretty stable and that's about all any woman really wants.

LAWRENCE I'm twenty three and I live in my mother's basement.

CLIVE Well, there is that.

LAWRENCE I go out with Crystal and the stupidest things come out of my mouth. Like some synapse in my brain is firing telling me to say the most insensitive thing I can possibly say.

CLIVE Women are trouble. Hey, did you get your DVD player fixed yet?

LAWRENCE Clive, I'm asking for help here! Could you just listen for a second?

CLIVE Alright, go on.

LAWRENCE It's just I feel like I'm being swallowed up by this thing with Crystal. She really puts me through the paces man. Flowers, back rubs, long walks through the park. I hate walking. That's why I have a car. Do you see what I'm saying? I have to walk to make her want to stay with me. I didn't know it was going to be so much like work when I asked her out. So, I'm left here, surrounded, totally besieged by this swarm of questions about us and her...

CLIVE Questions? About us? (*Indicating himself*)

LAWRENCE No you idiot! About me and her. There's like this voice in my head posing all these questions about our relationship. And it says stuff like "What? You think you're gonna marry her?" or "You think you love her you prick!"

CLIVE The voice swears at you?

LAWRENCE Yeah. And you want to know what else? When it asks these questions. I don't know how to answer. I don't know if I love her. And I should know that. I should be sure it's real and worth it. I should because that's important. It's probably the most important thing. Clive, no offense, but you wouldn't understand.

CLIVE What's that supposed to mean?

LAWRENCE You haven't dated anyone for more than a day. You just don't understand what it's like to be in love or even try to be in love.

CLIVE Look, what's all this rhetoric about love anyway? I swear to god I'm sick of it. My whole life ... both our lives we have been told that love conquers all. All you need is love. Love is a many splendored thing! Love, love, love! Well, you wanna know what I say. I say phooey! I say phooey to love!

LAWRENCE No one says phooey.

CLIVE Well, they should. They should say phooey and cockamamie and when they really like something they should say "Say, that's swell." And they should bring back that invisible cola. That stuff was awesome! The point is we have spent all our lives being told that we should be so lucky to fall in love. Can you imagine how much we could get done if we weren't always preoccupied with the notion. Think about this: Two people meet, fall in love, get married, house, car, blah, blah, blah! And then when all the sex and passion and butterflies in their tummies disappear? Then what?

LAWRENCE Divorce?

CLIVE — Work! You give up on the relationship and go through the motions of being someone's husband or wife or whatever and you focus on your career. And you try to become the best shoe salesman, garbage man or cola company executive that you can possibly be. So, why'd you waste all that time finding someone to love when you are just going to neglect them and focus on your career anyway?

LAWRENCE — That's a little too cynical for my blood.

CLIVE — Is it? Well then. Answer me this optimist boy. How many films have we finished since you started dating Crystal?

LAWRENCE — That's completely unrelated!

CLIVE — No. Answer the question.

LAWRENCE — One.

CLIVE — Correct. Now, how many films had we finished before you started dating her?

LAWRENCE — Clive, c'mon...

CLIVE — Nine. Nine films. So why don't we get on with our real life long passion and forget about love because it's irrelevant in the end.

LAWRENCE — I haven't been that bad. Have I?

CLIVE — Yes. You have. So shut up with your shit about "My girlfriend's mad." "I'm in the doghouse," "Why won't anyone love me." It's defeatist and it's not what you want. It's love or movies. You choose movies. So go and do that. Be a filmmaker. If you can do that. If you have the balls enough to do that and you still aren't satisfied. Then you can walk down that aisle and throw away your talent. Don't waste your time on your girlfriend if you don't know if you love her. You know you love making movies. So, let's go! Denise is in her office until four so we gotta hurry.

LAWRENCE — We can't go in there empty handed. She'll throw us out.

CLIVE — Alright then, it's pitch time, Larry!

LAWRENCE — What are we going to bring her?

CLIVE — Well, we should probably come prepared with a bunch of ideas but I say we bring her the last one we made. While the iron's hot.

LAWRENCE You think?

CLIVE Yeah, but like I said we'll have to have some back-ups. That's how the professionals do it and if we want to get that grant we have to be professional. Alright? So, it's your turn to go first.

LAWRENCE Alright, I'll humour you but she probably won't...

CLIVE Just do it! Movie idea number one ... take it away!

LAWRENCE Okay ... uh ... *Mortician's Academy*. A group of wacky students at the mortician's academy play pranks on their tight assed dean, madcap hilarity ensues!

CLIVE Not bad ... okay ... How about ... The *Adventures of Banana Bob*. He's an archaeologist who goes in search of petrified fruit. And in order to get that fruit, he has to battle the evil gorilla king. And I know where we can get a gorilla suit!

LAWRENCE Well ... okay ... but how about this. *The Man with Mechanical Pants!*

CLIVE Or ... how about *The Seventh Sense*. It's about this kid who sees dead people but in the end it turns out that ... THEY ARE JUST REGULAR PEOPLE!

LAWRENCE That's a little too close to the original.

CLIVE You're right. Let's just stick to the one we just shot. But we'll keep *Banana Bob* in mind just in case.

LAWRENCE What's the point? You know what she's going to say.

CLIVE Yeah, I do. She'll say yes.

LAWRENCE She never says yes. I don't think the word is in her vocabulary. She won't even say yes to a meeting. Last time I called her she said our film ideas weren't Canadian enough. What the hell does that mean?

CLIVE That's just the way these things work. You have to keep banging away at this shit. Pay your dues. And we have paid them. We've made ten films in two years. Nobody does it better or faster. These executive types just want to see that you're not just a flash in the pan. That you've got staying power. We DO. And Denise will see that.

LAWRENCE So I forget about Crystal and we pitch the film to Denise. You realize I'm going from begging to one woman to begging another.

CLIVE It ain't something for nothing. Look, we get the grant and we start running the film festival circuit and we don't stop until we're on the cover of *Maclean's* being hailed as the Canadian equivalent of Steven Spielberg! So, stand up and accept the fact that you are destined for film greatness. You, yes you, Lawrence Schmidt, are about to hit the big time!

LAWRENCE The last film was pretty great!

CLIVE Fuckin' A right!

LAWRENCE We have a good chance at getting the grant or at least some sort of funding.

CLIVE It's almost a guarantee!

LAWRENCE Crystal's a pain in the ass anyway.

CLIVE Like a Drano enema!

LAWRENCE Okay! Let's do it! Let's make some movies!

CLIVE Atta boy! I'll be waiting in the car. (*He moves to exit snatching some loose DVDs as he goes and hiding them in his pants*) And Larry. Bring some pants okay?

Clive exits as Lawrence notices his lack of pants.

Scene Three

The office of the Canadian Film Society. A desk with three chairs is stage right. There is a projection screen down centre. Clive and Lawrence enter and conspire.

LAWRENCE Alright, keep your mouth shut and let me do the pitch. I know how to handle women.

CLIVE Really? Because between Crystal and your mother I never would have guessed it.

LAWRENCE Look, do you want to be in my Oscar speech or what?

CLIVE I really inspired you didn't I? I got you talkin' the Oscar talk.

LAWRENCE Yeah, you did alright. Just let me do this.

Denise enters and crosses to greet them.

LAWRENCE Alright, here she comes. You just stand here, smile and try not to have an aneurysm or go off on a rant. (*Loudly to Denise*) Ms. Curran, I'm Lawrence Schmidt and this is my collaborator Clive Andrews.

DENISE Gentlemen, how magnificent to finally meet you. Lawrence, how have you been? Good, fantastic! Clive, you look every bit as handsome as I thought you would. You must work out. I bet you do. Wonderful. Spectacular. Great. Now, down to business. I see you have brought me a little piece of cinema, have you?

LAWRENCE Yes, we have. Let me have a second to pitch this to you. (*He clears his throat and speaks with great importance. Clive acts out the story silently as Lawrence delivers the pitch*) The year is 2049. The place: Earth. Not the earth you and I know, however, but an earth that has been over run by a race of three-legged aliens!

DENISE (*Interrupting*) Three legs, yes, good.

LAWRENCE Now, these aliens feed on the human soul. Something Clive and I call The Kinesphere. Now the most powerful kinesphere on earth belongs to our hero Blade Simco...

DENISE Lawrence, darling, I'm seeing a lack of ... oh, how shall I say it ... content. Of the Canadian variety.

CLIVE Aw, c'mon. Not this shit again.

LAWRENCE Listen, Ms. Curran ... Denise, I've been thinking about what you said about making my films more Canadian and...

DENISE Shall we go to the chart, Gentlemen? Yes, let's take a look at my little chart.

Denise produces a remote from her pocket. As she makes her points during the following exchange she clicks the remote to display various images, graphs and figures to support her case.

DENISE Let us consult the Canadian Film Society's guidelines for cinema. These rules, designed and enforced by yours truly, are what decide whether we issue a grant to wonderful filmmakers such as yourself.

LAWRENCE Wait a second, they're your rules not the Canadian Film Society's?

DENISE Lawrence, let's be honest with each other. We both know they're the same thing. So, alright, back to the guidelines. Rule number one: Location, and I can't stress this enough. Prairie, Prairie, Prairie or a small fishing community of some kind. Because let's face it, wherever you are in this great country of ours you are either near the ocean or on the prairie.

LAWRENCE What about the Northwest Territories? And there are other places...

DENISE Lawrence, really, as if they count. Rule number two, let's talk time period. Think pioneers, covered wagons or at least the depression era. Trust me gentlemen. People don't want to see the road to Avonlea paved. The more wheat, farmers and girls in frilly dresses the better.

LAWRENCE Hold it. What about *Degrassi Junior High*?

DENISE I know, I know. A contemporary television program with a cast made up of completely hideous children. I warned them but they had a moral in every episode and that seemed to keep the soccer moms happy so we kept airing it.

CLIVE You consider Joey Jeremiah hideous?

DENISE Yes. Then and now. Hideous. It's what we were all thinking, I just have the courage to say it. Moving on there is the issue of the representation of all cultural groups. Native Canadians, African Canadians, Asian Canadians, French Canadian and of course let's not forget the Newfies!

CLIVE Newfies! That is so prejudiced! The proper term is Newfoundlander.

DENISE Clive, all linguistics aside, be realistic. Have you ever heard those people speak? They call themselves Newfies. Whatever the case, everyone must be represented and heard from. No matter how unintelligible.

LAWRENCE You know, we do have an African Canadian in the film.

DENISE Really! Where in god's name did you find him? This is Alberta.

CLIVE Now that is definitely prejudiced! And racist!

DENISE Now, now, boys, this is counterproductive. You obviously don't meet the criteria so why are we beating a dead horse here?

CLIVE She's prejudiced against horses too!

LAWRENCE Look, Ms. Curran, all of these guidelines are based on the success of shows like *Anne of Green Gables* and *The Beachcombers*. And it is my contention that these shows suck! Do you know why Canadians watch more American shows than Canadian ones?

DENISE Because they have breasts and violence?

LAWRENCE No, because people don't have friends like Relic. They have friends like Chandler or Phoebe. And they don't live in log cabins anymore or walk thirty miles through the snow to school! Let's get modern alright! And what could be more modern than the year 2049 when the earth has been over run by a race of three-legged space aliens!

DENISE Look Lawrence, I would like to help you. I really would. But we here at the Canadian Film Society have made a commitment to the people of Canada. A commitment to provide quality, non-threatening entertainment. Canadian people don't want to turn on their TV and see violence or wise cracking thirty somethings. They want pioneers, beavers and Mounties! They want the farm report or at least a nature program about bison.

CLIVE So much for freedom of expression then! The fact that we are Canadian and we make films isn't enough. No, we have to represent a minority or tell a certain kind of story to be heard! A great movie about three-legged aliens isn't as important as a show about some neon rider guy who helps out wayward teens, is that it?

DENISE That's about the long and short of it, yes.

LAWRENCE Hey, could you just watch it? How are we supposed to get ahead in the business if we can't even get you to watch our films?

DENISE I'm very busy and your time has elapsed. I wish you luck and happy filming. You know, I have a good feeling about you two. In twenty years or so when you've paid your dues I'm sure we'll work together. Good afternoon.

She moves to leave.

DENISE And Gentlemen, nobody likes science fiction, at least nobody who matters.

Denise exits.

CLIVE Excuse me! Have you ever heard of Trekkies! There's about a million of 'em!

LAWRENCE Calm down! It's over.

CLIVE Just watch the damn tape! This will not stand! We will overcome! We will be heard! I got my eyes on the prize you fuckin'...

LAWRENCE Clive! Clive! She's gone.

CLIVE This is not over.

LAWRENCE Clive, this was a total dog fuck! She won't even watch the tape. What's the point any way. Even if she saw it she wouldn't give us a grant. She thinks we're too young.

CLIVE Just hold on.

LAWRENCE You hold on. It took us two months to finish *The Tripods Have Landed* and three months when we made *Indiscreet Merger*. And how long did it take for us to finish *Being John Tesh*? And Tesh wouldn't even sign on for that film.

CLIVE Hey, I thought you made a very convincing John Tesh. Look, don't you give up now. You want to go back to your girlfriend a failure? A man who can't make a living without a paper hat?

LAWRENCE No.

CLIVE We just have to try a different approach.

LAWRENCE How long are we going to do this? You tell me that I'm wasting my time with Crystal. How do I know I'm not wasting my time with movies?

CLIVE Because you can't love something this much and fail at it.

LAWRENCE Clive, I think you can.

Lawrence exits. Clive remains for a beat or two then follows.

Scene Four

Lawrence's room. Lawrence is on the phone trying to reason with Crystal.

LAWRENCE Don't you see what I mean, baby? It was just a misunderstanding about Red Lobster ... Why? Because the whole place smells like fish! It's not a comment on your personal hygiene.

Lawrence's Mother yells from off-stage.

LAWRENCE'S MOTHER
Lawrence! Put some fucking pants on! Your mongoloid friend Clive just pulled up!

LAWRENCE I'm wearing pants!

LAWRENCE'S MOTHER
Go fuck yourself, you little prick!

LAWRENCE Mom, what is wrong with you! (*To Crystal*) Look, Crystal, Clive is here, I should go ... No ... he's not weird...

Clive enters in a beaver costume. He begins rummaging through a knapsack he has brought with him. Lawrence doesn't notice him or his attire.

LAWRENCE He's not weird ... he did that to you as a joke ... hasn't anyone ever frozen your bra at a slumber party? ... I know it wasn't a slumber party but ... What do you mean I should stay away ... from him or from you? Crystal?

Lawrence hangs up the phone after realizing Crystal is no longer on the line.

CLIVE She's not taking you back, eh?

LAWRENCE What do you care?

CLIVE You're right, I don't. Listen up, we have to get ready for our next meeting with Denise.

Lawrence rises and suddenly notices Clive's costume.

LAWRENCE What the hell are you doing Clive?

CLIVE Getting into character.

LAWRENCE Did you join the ice capades?

CLIVE No, I'm going to go back to Denise's office and I'm going to make a statement. I believe it is called a protest.

LAWRENCE Or an episode in your case.

CLIVE Say what you will but the way I have it figured, she'll have no choice but to watch our film. And when she does, we are definitely going to get a grant. Or at least some media exposure.

LAWRENCE You're not serious? You're actually going to do this?

CLIVE WE are going to do this. I got you a costume too.

Clive reaches into his knapsack and produces a Mountie uniform.

LAWRENCE What?

CLIVE You'll be a Mountie and I'll be a beaver. Get it? They're representational. She wants Canadian content, that's what we'll give her.

LAWRENCE She'll call the police. Do you hear me Clive? If a giant filmmaker beaver walks into her office, she will call the police.

CLIVE So we get some attention. It's a peaceful protest. When people see that we are so dedicated to creating Canadian art that we are driven to protest in costumes like these, they'll see how unfair Denise is being. Then, we'll meet other film reps who will be dying to give us a grant. Or Denise will respect our efforts and give us a grant herself.

LAWRENCE We might as well pitch that patriotic porno you wanted to shoot. Y'know, *Canuck Fuck*? Get it through your head Clive. She's not going to watch our movie and we're not going to get a grant. Think Clive. We grew up on American television and movies. We know more about Bill Clinton's wang and O.J.'s golf swing than we do about Louis Riel or how parliament works. Even the CBC airs American shows. So how the hell are we supposed to know what is Canadian much less make distinctly Canadian films. We are just American byproducts. And we'll never get past these Canadian content regulations if we make the kind of films we want to.

CLIVE I don't have a problem with ALL of the regulations. So the radio stations have to play a Canadian song once an hour, fine, good, so be it! But does it have to be that sell out Bryan Adams or Celine Dion. I mean, if I hear that fucking boat song one more time I'm gonna shoot myself! We get it Celine! The boat sunk, Leo drown, your friggin' heart will go on. What the fuck does the Titanic have to do with Canada anyway?

LAWRENCE James Cameron is Canadian.

CLIVE Yeah, but he moved to the states to make it big.

LAWRENCE So did William Shatner and he's a good actor.

CLIVE Shatner! Are you kidding me? You could drive a Mack truck through those dramatic pauses!

LAWRENCE Lorne Greene was Canadian.

CLIVE Who's Lorne Greene?

LAWRENCE Y'know, Lorne Greene's new wilderness?

CLIVE Never saw it.

LAWRENCE He was the starship captain on *Battlestar Galactica*.

CLIVE Oh yeah. (*Pause*) But that show was just American space propaganda.

LAWRENCE We are arguing the same point! They defected and they made it. Don't you get it? If they can't make a great film here then we don't have a chance. And if we follow Denise's guidelines and make a shitty one, well, we might as well give up and get day jobs.

CLIVE Not in this lifetime. C'mon Larry, let's do this. It's the only way.

LAWRENCE They'll arrest us.

CLIVE So what? I can read the headlines now, "Artists suffer for their work," "Canada needs to wake up and smell the movies." Sometimes you gotta take one for the team ... THE MOVIE TEAM!

LAWRENCE What are you talking about?

CLIVE I'm talking about the little guy. All the other brilliant filmmakers out there that can't get their film shown because of some spoiled executive. I'm talking about giving the Canadian moviegoer what he wants! Explosions and Aliens! I'm talking about the beaver, the Mountie and the good ol' hockey game! I'm talking about winter in Alberta, summer in Saskatchewan and the almighty toonie! Because you want to know what? I AM CANADIAN!

LAWRENCE YOU ARE AN IDIOT!

CLIVE You lost your girlfriend over this. Do you want that to be for nothing?

LAWRENCE I miss her.

CLIVE If you become a success, you can get her back.

LAWRENCE I don't know.

CLIVE You are such a pussy, you know that? Every fucking time I had a vision, some brilliant moment of completely Zen thinking, you back down. Remember when we were twelve and I said "Hey, let's get on our bikes and go to the D.Q. and get some ice cream"? And you were like "No, that's too far. My Mom will get mad if I go all that way on my bike." And then I said "Let's get some fucking ice cream, you asshole!" Then you were like "okay." And what happened?

LAWRENCE I don't even remember this.

CLIVE We got some ice cream and it was awesome! And you wouldn't have done it if I didn't call you an asshole. Don't you want to have some ice cream Larry? Because I am offering you some ice cream.

LAWRENCE I have no idea what you are talking about.

CLIVE I do. So just listen to me and you'll be happy. We do this, the film gets shown. And if we do a couple of nights in the joint, so be it. We gotta represent.

LAWRENCE Represent, huh?

CLIVE Nothing ventured, nothing gained. Find your balls and use 'em.

LAWRENCE Give me that uniform.

CLIVE I've got the car running outside. Now let's get that coat on you.

LAWRENCE Thanks buddy.

Scene Five

Denise's office. Denise sits at her desk arranging and rearranging papers. Clive enters from behind her. He is dressed in the beaver suit as before. He carries a knapsack and a sign that reads "Make Movies, Not Love." He startles Denise as he begins to sing "O Canada" off key, getting all the lyrics wrong. Denise springs to her feet.

DENISE What is this?

Clive stops singing and stares at her silently.

DENISE What do you want?

CLIVE (*In a ghostly voice*) You, Denise Curran, you have made a grave error! You have used your position to corrupt Canadian art! I have come to teach you the error of your ways!

DENISE (*Immediately recognizing Clive's voice*) You are a beaver, yes?

CLIVE (*Ghostly voice*) I have taken this form so I may represent all that you have turned your back on. You will listen to the beaver or you will be punished!

DENISE Is this supposed to be like an Ebenezer Scrooge thing? Like you are the beaver of Christmas past and you've come to teach me the evils of eating beaver meat or something to that effect?

CLIVE (*Dropping the voice*) You've eaten beaver before?

DENISE Yes, once, in college.

CLIVE (*Again with the voice*) Listen to me! Since the dawn of time the beaver has represented Canada. Therefore, the meaning behind...

Lawrence bursts in wearing the Mountie uniform. He carries a sign that reads, "Film 3:16."

LAWRENCE Clive, where have you been? It's a fucking madhouse out there. People kept throwing cans at me as they drove by and a preschooler punched me in the nuts!

CLIVE Silence! The beaver is speaking to the corrupt woman!

LAWRENCE Why are you talking like that? You were supposed to wait for me!

CLIVE (*Pulling off his mask*) Great Larry, way to ruin the whole mystique of the thing.

DENISE Gentlemen, shall we explain ourselves? You know, as to why you two are having your little costume parade in my office.

CLIVE We're here to give you one last chance.

DENISE Boys, don't waste your time. You have no appointment. So, tragically, I cannot help you. It's called professional courtesy. And, sadly, you don't seem to be extending any to me.

CLIVE Courtesy? Fuckin' courtesy? If you had just had the courtesy to watch our film in the first place then I wouldn't be here now dressed as a beaver trying to scare you!

DENISE Yes, and why are you dressed as a beaver?

CLIVE It's representational!

LAWRENCE Alright, calm down. Denise, this is a protest. All we want is for you to watch our film with an unbiased eye. If you just let go of your preconceptions as to what Canadian film has to be, you will like it.

DENISE The guidelines I've set out are in place for a reason...

LAWRENCE Forget about the guidelines for a second. Forget about who the film may offend or who it does or does not represent. Forget about geography and educational value and just watch a movie. It's supposed to be fun.

DENISE Well, what are the themes involved?

LAWRENCE Forget about themes. Let me ask you something, did you like *Star Wars*?

DENISE The original or *The Phantom Menace*?

LAWRENCE The original.

DENISE Of course I did.

LAWRENCE It didn't provoke thought. It didn't have covered wagons or fishermen. And you liked it. Would you have used your guidelines to stop that film from being made?

DENISE Alright then Lawrence. You made your point. If Canadian content doesn't really matter perhaps we could consider negotiating. Perhaps agree on a few alterations to your work, yes?

CLIVE Artists! We are artists and we don't alter or negotiate! We create, we emote, we rock your emotional world or at least mildly sway it.

LAWRENCE Wait a second Clive. She has a point. My dad used to say that a deal only works if both parties benefit.

CLIVE Who benefited when he left your mother to become a rig pig?

LAWRENCE He did. Work not love. Remember?

DENISE Excuse me but I was in the process of offering you a grant.

Clive and Lawrence freeze.

DENISE What if I were to promise you a film grant if you take my suggestions about your film, and, you know, alter it accordingly. I won't even expect a credit.

LAWRENCE You would do that? Why would you do that? You haven't even seen the film.

DENISE Because I am sick of it. I am sick of the four phone calls a day. Because I want you out of my office and I realize that to get you out of my face for five seconds I have to give you a grant. So I just want to change the film enough to justify it to my bosses. Alright, okay, good, let's do this.

LAWRENCE We get this down on paper then?

DENISE Darling, I wouldn't have it any other way. Yes, good, let's begin.

Denise moves to her desk to get the contracts.

CLIVE Larry, don't do this.

DENISE Clive, you're wearing a beaver suit. You don't exactly exude credibility. Lawrence can do this without your input.

LAWRENCE Clive, it ain't something for nothing. We do this, we get a grant.

CLIVE Fine. Continue. But Denise I am warning you, don't fuck up our movie.

DENISE Such vulgarity. Do you kiss your beaver mother with that mouth?

LAWRENCE Let's just get this done.

DENISE Yes, let's. Now, I will ask you some questions about your film, yes, and then for each question I will offer a possible solution. The grant relies on how accepting you can be in regards to said solutions. I'm only proposing minor changes to the look and feel of the film, agreed?

LAWRENCE Yes, go on.

DENISE First, where is the film set? I mean location.

LAWRENCE As I said before, it's earth in the year 2049.

DENISE Can we localize that? Because the Earth is a pretty large place. It's a location scout's nightmare.

LAWRENCE How about Toronto?

DENISE Little more specific, please?

LAWRENCE Downtown Toronto?

DENISE Alright, let me provide you with a similar solution. Let's say ... Lloydminster!

LAWRENCE How is that like Toronto?

DENISE Well, Lawrence, it's not. But it is cross provincial.

LAWRENCE Fine. Lloydminster.

DENISE Good, yes, we're making progress here. You say earth, I say Lloydminster. They're the same thing really.

CLIVE You're on thin ice over here!

DENISE Fine, good, whatever, Clive. Alright. Let's talk protagonist here. Is he swarthy?

LAWRENCE Swarthy? I guess.

DENISE Because he must be swarthy. Women love swarthy. What about abs, does he have great abs? Like cheese grater abs?

LAWRENCE Not exactly cheese grater but he's a really talented actor.

DENISE So was John Candy but no one wants to see him in a shower scene with Neve Campbell.

CLIVE There is no shower scene.

DENISE I see. I'm getting ahead of myself. Lawrence, people don't want to see fat people fight aliens or take showers. They want hotties. So you'll have to cast a ridiculously handsome leading man.

LAWRENCE We could recast. Stewart's not going to like it though.

DENISE He'll live. We'll find him a nice supporting role as a pretzel vendor or a Kiwanis member.

CLIVE Alright, I draw the line at Kiwanis!

LAWRENCE Shut up, Clive!

DENISE We are almost finished if you don't mind. Finally, let's talk climax, the ending. How does your little epic come to an end?

LAWRENCE This is the best part. They swap planets!

DENISE I don't follow...

LAWRENCE Well, the aliens have taken over Earth, right? So all the humans leave Earth, blow it up, and go live on the aliens' home planet which is in much better shape environmentally.

DENISE The humans blow up Earth? I mean Lloydminster?

LAWRENCE Yeah. Which kills all the aliens! Pretty cool, huh?

DENISE Yes, yes, cool. However, Lawrence, and hear me out. And keep in mind that this is the last thing I propose to change before I bestow upon you this film grant. Let's say the humans don't blow up the Earth.

LAWRENCE They don't?

CLIVE That's how it ends!

DENISE I propose that instead of blowing up the earth, let's say that the United States army rescues the people of Lloydminster and sends the aliens back to their planet. And the humans blow up their planet!

CLIVE The US army? Are you shitting me? How does that represent Canada in any way?

DENISE Lawrence, you told me to forget about Canadian content. This way I think people will enjoy the film more. Because, well, it's more American.

LAWRENCE We came to you so we wouldn't have to make American films. So we could do what we love here in Canada.

DENISE You can't have it both ways. You throw out the guidelines and what are you left with? An American film ... made by Canadians. Only this way you don't have to defect. As I said before, it's all about location.

LAWRENCE (*Shyly*) But I am Canadian.

DENISE The film you've made isn't any different than the kinds of films that come out of America. They make these kinds of films all the time, so no offense boys, but they do a much better job than you. So, in the end, doesn't it make sense to give grants to people who make unique films?

CLIVE You call *Anne of Green Gables* unique?

DENISE Compared to *Independence Day*? Yes, I do. So Lawrence, do you accept the changes?

LAWRENCE I...

DENISE Because the grant is here if you want it.

LAWRENCE I'll take it.

CLIVE No, no! This is horseshit! It's the same thing as defecting. She's just feeding you a different set of rules.

LAWRENCE It will be a success Clive.

CLIVE Oh, I see, I get it. You're just doing this to get Crystal back. Crystal doesn't know what you need. I do. You're whoring yourself for her. You're a corporate whore!

LAWRENCE It was your fault that I lost her in the first place. Wasting my time with you and our movies! Well here it is Clive! This is what we want.

CLIVE This isn't what we want. It's what you want. You can't do a fucking thing without being led by the hand. Told what to do. And when you do decide on something you make the wrong fucking choice!

Clive removes a pellet gun from his knapsack.

CLIVE Well, I won't let you, you are not doing this!

LAWRENCE Holy shit! What the hell are you doing!

CLIVE I'm leading you by the hand, as usual.

LAWRENCE Where did you get that?

CLIVE Shut up. Denise, you are not going to change a single frame of our film. You will shut the fuck up and give us a grant for the film as is.

DENISE Don't shoot. I have something to tell you. Please, put the gun down.

CLIVE No, you don't get to tell us what to do any more. Canadians can't make films as well as Americans, fuck that! It's people like you that fuck it all up. Well, sister, you will not drive me across the border!

LAWRENCE Are you fucking nuts, put the gun away!

CLIVE I will not sell out. I will not let you sell out! Did you hear what she said? The U.S. army saves the day! (*To Denise*) You ... you get out that contract or so help me...

DENISE I'm not who you think...

CLIVE Get out that fucking contract.

LAWRENCE Don't shoot Clive. If you don't shoot we can get out of this.

CLIVE I love you Larry.

Clive abruptly grabs Lawrence and kisses him full on the mouth. Lawrence and Denise are dumbstruck. There is a short pause.

CLIVE This is for us. We have been together our whole lives. If we do this we can share ourselves with the world our way. I love you, I really do but you won't help yourself. So I have to do it for you.

DENISE You're insane. I can't give you a grant I'm just...

Clive pushes her to her knees. Lawrence goes towards her but Clive turns the gun on him.

CLIVE Stay right there.

LAWRENCE You call this help?

DENISE All right, I'll do whatever you want, just put the gun away. I'll give you the grant. Just don't shoot anyone.

CLIVE (*Throwing his arm around Lawrence*) Look Larry, she's going along with it. Shit, I should have pulled the gun earlier.

LAWRENCE Give me that!

Lawrence tackles Clive. They struggle for the gun.

DENISE Listen to me! I'm not ... stop it ... I...

Denise runs to the phone and dials 911.

DENISE I need some help. I'm being held hostage...

Lawrence, having overcome Clive and snatched the gun, pauses and looks closer at it.

LAWRENCE Hey, this is just a pellet gun?

Clive lunges at Lawrence and Lawrence instinctively fires. Clive is hit and falls to the ground.

LAWRENCE (*After a long silence*) Clive ... c'mon Clive, it's a pellet gun. Clive?

Denise drops the phone and rushes over to Clive.

DENISE You ... you shot him in the eye.

LAWRENCE What?

DENISE He's dead. Oh God. You killed him.

LAWRENCE What? No ... you saw it ... it was self defense ... oh, shit, I'm sorry. He was going to hurt you, I protected you.

DENISE You killed him.

LAWRENCE I didn't mean it.

The faint sound of police sirens is heard.

DENISE Get out. Get out of here!

Lawrence moves to exit.

LAWRENCE I ... Do we still have a deal?

DENISE What?

LAWRENCE A deal. I change the film and you give me a grant.

DENISE I can't do that Lawrence.

LAWRENCE Why not?

DENISE Because I'm just the secretary.

LAWRENCE What? You promised...

DENISE I'm just the secretary, Lawrence. They tell me to pretend I'm an executive so they don't have to deal with people like you, so you don't waste their time. There never was a grant for you. You have to apply. You can't just show up with some hand held piece of garbage and expect them to pay for it. Just because you want it. Just because you are Canadian.

LAWRENCE Then why did you do all this?

DENISE Because I put up with people like you all day, every day. And I'm sick of it. Space aliens and action flicks. You people are a waste of my time. I was teaching you a lesson. (*Pause*) I'm sorry.

Lawrence crosses over to Clive's body.

LAWRENCE Shit.

Lights fade as the sirens grow louder.

Scene Six

The scene is as it was in the beginning. There is a gobo of jail bars lighting Lawrence. The screen behind him projects images of American films, Independence Day, *etc. Lawrence is standing centre stage and is still dressed as a Mountie. He is holding a golden statuette.*

LAWRENCE I would like to thank the Academy and the Royal Canadian Mounted Police for this award. I would also like to thank Denise Curran for allowing me to be here tonight and for the next few years...

OFFICER (*Offstage*) Lights out Schmidt!

LAWRENCE (*Quietly*) They are telling me to wrap it up. I would most like to thank the great country of Canada for being a country that supports unique talent. A country that uses brains to make movies instead of special effects and explosions. That's why it's such a shock for me to win this. Because my films tend to use violence and special effects. There is one more person I would like to thank...

Clive enters still in the beaver suit. He has an American flag wrapped around him.

CLIVE I'm sorry, Lawrence. There's been a recount.

LAWRENCE What?

CLIVE (*Approaching him*) You didn't win. There's been a recount.

LAWRENCE What do you know about it, you're dead.

CLIVE I just do what they tell me. The recount says you lost.

LAWRENCE Who won then?

CLIVE *Anne of Green Gables: The Next Generation*. Sorry, pal, nice effort though.

Clive snatches the award away and struts off holding it over his head. The projection now shows Anne of Green Gables.

LAWRENCE No, no, that's not right. It's mine. I won. It's mine, it's mine...

Lawrence continues raving.

Officer (*Offstage*) LIGHTS OUT!

The lights fade and Lawrence is left being lit only by static.

[ice land] (2003)

by Jonathan Seinen

One strength of the corpus of contemporary Canadian plays may also be a weakness: its tendency to label its constitutive elements. Thus, we might turn to our bookshelves to find plays clearly "about" teen, feminist, queer, prairie, nationalist, and even "official" experiences and histories. We might then turn to an assortment of critical collections of plays and essays that further clarify, explore, and indeed reify these fields of knowledge around which Canadian theatre has been arranged. Proceeding further we might discover that those works that fit into these now-recognizable genres have proven (and provable) attendance records and therefore have been successfully produced at state-funded professional theatres; in certain cases they have garnered issue-specific professional artist grants to enable their creation in the first place. Indeed, entire theatre companies have emerged fully mandated to tackle one or more of these issues by developing and producing representative new plays. But in parallel with this discussion of genre reification, consider the place of Walterdale. It has not limited its mandate in order to back one or more ideological fields. It operates outside of the "popular issue" dramaturgy within which so many of Canada's play producers are often trapped. An important example is Jonathan Seinen's vivid and violent *[ice land]*, which ignores none of these popular issues, yet wears none on its sleeve.

Seinen was born in Terrace, British Columbia, in 1980 to Dutch-Canadian parents. In 1985 he moved with his family to Slave Lake, Alberta, and, following a year in Ancaster, Ontario, he moved to Edmonton in 1995. He studied theatre at Royal Holloway (2002, London, England) and the University of Alberta, where he graduated in 2004 with an honours BA in drama before attending the National Theatre School's acting program in Montreal, from which he graduated in 2007. His other plays include *Regeneration* (2004, University of Alberta's Working Titles Festival and Theatre Network Nextfest) and *this.it*, a short piece presented at the Edmonton International Fringe

Festival in 2004 as part of the multi-author production *OuterSpaces*. His play *Unknown Pleasures* premiered in Calgary in June 2008 at Sage Theatre's Ignite! Festival. Seinen currently lives in Toronto, where he continues to write.

[ice land] was initially developed in a University of Alberta playwriting course led by Alberta playwright Conni Massing. As Seinen explains, the play began as a personal writing exercise, "an experiment to find out how I really saw the world and what I could dare myself to write. After living in England and falling in love with Sarah Kane's astounding talent, confrontational ideas and bleak imagery, I wanted to see how her sensibility could translate into Canadian English" (Seinen). Indeed, *[ice land]*'s high tension and graphic violence are more reminiscent of plays by British playwrights such as Kane and Howard Brenton than they are of many Canadian plays. As a personal "experiment," *[ice land]* uses powerful language and situation to stunning effect. And notably, it finds ways to discuss Canada in both regionalist and internationalist perspectives with a dreadfully straight face.

[ice land] is a brutal and disturbing incursion into the extreme depths of torture and human suffering. Coming upon a bunker in the basement of a house in prairie Saskatchewan some time after a nuclear holocaust, Iris finds herself held hostage by three "desperate, dangerous" men bent on survival and growing "mad" by the day: the blind and controlling Frederick, the aggressive Luther, and the simple Pluto. As Luther contemplates shooting and eating campers in a nearby settlement, Frederick is consumed by his own sexual appetite (primarily for Pluto), and Pluto, keeping house, admits that he loves Frederick. Iris tells Luther about the terrors she has seen in this post-apocalyptic world but admits, somewhat sardonically, that she would rather be on the prairies than in the farming co-ops on the West Coast: "The prairies have always been about individual initiative, right? I proudly carry on that tradition." But when Luther returns covered in blood, having roasted one of the nearby campers, and Frederick orders Pluto to poison Iris's food, tradition, it is clear, has been annihilated by the drive for in/human survival. Though it is a work of intense imagination, *[ice land]*'s violent prophecies are difficult to ignore as world tensions, we are reminded daily by the news media, rise in perpetuity.

[ice land] ran June 9–14, 2003, at Walterdale Playhouse (firehall) with the following cast and creative team:

FREDERICK	Mark Henderson
PLUTO	Kevin Gojmerac
IRIS	Sarah Hoyles
LUTHER	Brian Bergam
DIRECTOR	Michael Cowie
DRAMATURGE	Heather Inglis
STAGE MANAGER (REHEARSAL)	Mary Anne Trann
STAGE MANAGER (PERFORMANCE)	Evan Pang

[ice land]

by Jonathan Seinen

I exist on the best terms I can
The past is now part of my future
The present is well out of hand
"HEART AND SOUL"—JOY DIVISION

Characters IRIS
FREDERICK
LUTHER
PLUTO

Setting A basement bunker. To the back of the stage is a stairwell, coming down from the upstairs. Stage left is a kitchen area with a hotplate and cupboards. Upstage from this is a door in the wall, into the sleeping area. There are some chairs in the main area. A large Canadian flag hangs at the back of the room. A bare light bulb hangs from the ceiling.

The Time *This play is set a short time into the future (+/– 10 years).*

Note When a "/" appears, it indicates an overlapping of dialogue. It acts as a cue for the next line to start. "(...)" indicates the intended completion of an interrupted sentence.

Scene One

The room is dark. Frederick is sitting with a bowl of beans, his cane beside him. Pluto stands in front of him. Frederick eats a spoonful.

FREDERICK Take your shirt off.

Pluto does so. Frederick takes a bite.

FREDERICK Take off your pants.

Pluto does so. Frederick takes another bite.

FREDERICK Come here.

Pluto walks towards Frederick. Frederick offers him a spoonful of beans.

FREDERICK Eat.

Pluto eats.

Frederick puts the bowl down on the ground. Stands in front of Pluto.

FREDERICK Take off my shirt.

Pluto starts unbuttoning Frederick's shirt. Frederick touches Pluto's head, hair, shoulders. Pulls him forward. They kiss. Noises from upstairs. Then, Luther struggling with Iris to get her down the stairs. Luther pushes Iris down the stairs and eventually she's on the ground, standing up to defend herself as Luther circles her, pointing a gun. She is soaking wet and carrying a jerry can.

IRIS What the / hell is this?

LUTHER Look what I found sneaking around outside.

IRIS (*Watching Luther circling her.*) What are you going to do? Huh?

LUTHER Sneaking around on our property.

Luther pulls chain on light bulb and the room fills with its incandescent light. Iris realises there are others in the room. Pluto grabs clothes and moves to the side, Frederick standing still, his shirt undone. He has a scar running across his chest.

IRIS What's going on?

LUTHER This is our home, girl, and you're trespassing and we don't like trespassing persons.

FREDERICK Who is this, Luther?

LUTHER She was trying to bust in, sir.

IRIS I was just looking for a place in from the rain. Why'd you have to / drag me ... (down here like this)?

FREDERICK (*To Iris*) What is your name?

Iris spits in Frederick's face. She realises he's blind.

LUTHER (*Approaching Iris. She is staring at Frederick, sizing him up*) Tell him your name!

Iris doesn't respond. Luther is ready to strike.

FREDERICK (*Slowly wiping the spit off his face. Smells it*) This is going to be an unpleasant evening, friend, if we don't know each other's names, don't you think?

Pause.

IRIS Iris.

FREDERICK Thank you. My name is Frederick. This is Pluto. I believe you've already met Luther.

IRIS Charmed.

LUTHER The pleasure's all mine.

FREDERICK Now that we all know each other, why are you here?

IRIS This fucker came out of nowhere and dragged me down the stairs.

FREDERICK Why might he do a thing like that?

IRIS It was raining outside and the house looked abandoned. I was looking in the windows to see if anyone was home.

LUTHER But the house isn't abandoned.

IRIS I realise that now.

LUTHER And now you're trespassing.

What's with the jerry can?

IRIS I'm looking for gas.

LUTHER You're not American, are you?

IRIS What?

LUTHER If you're American, I'll fucking slit your throat. Americans always stick their noses in other people's business, showing up where they're not expected...

Iris doesn't dignify with a response.

LUTHER (*To Frederick*) She was looking around the house, Frederick. Peering in the windows. She was going for the front door. She was going to come in here and find us.

IRIS So?

FREDERICK So we don't want anyone to know we're here. We want to keep this bunker to ourselves.

LUTHER But perhaps we can make an exception. In your case.

FREDERICK What were you doing out in the rain?

Pause.

IRIS Taking a stroll.

Pause.

FREDERICK Was it a pleasant stroll? Was the rain crisp, clean, the kind of rain on a warm spring evening on the coast, or more of a biting acid rain, the kind of rain that burns your eyes, burns holes through your skin, down to the bone? What was the rain like, Iris?

IRIS I was looking for a place, that's all. I saw this house...

FREDERICK What did you think of the house when you first saw it? Did you think "well, there's my safe haven, there's my protection, there's my future"? When you walked along the road and saw this little house on the prairie, surrounded by absolute nothingness, and the rain falling – how did it make you feel?

IRIS I'm freezing.

FREDERICK Ah. Pluto, get her a blanket.

Silence as Pluto goes into sleeping room and gets blanket. Crosses to Iris and wraps her in it.

FREDERICK How do you feel now, Iris?

IRIS Better.

FREDERICK Good.
Where were you walking?

IRIS North.

FREDERICK Why?

IRIS My car broke down.

FREDERICK Where?

IRIS About 2 hours south.

FREDERICK Where were you driving?

IRIS North.

FREDERICK Why?

IRIS Looking for gas. Food. Whatever I can find.

LUTHER Well, you found us.

IRIS Yes, I found you.

FREDERICK Where are you coming from?

IRIS Last night I was in Regina.

FREDERICK Regina?

IRIS Yes, Regina.

FREDERICK What did you find there?

IRIS Some food.

FREDERICK Anything else?

IRIS There is nothing else.

Pause.

FREDERICK Are you going to Saskatoon?

IRIS I might.

FREDERICK Why?

IRIS I haven't been there yet.

LUTHER Ha! There's nothing there. Nothing but deserted shopping malls and burnt out homes. We burnt out the homes.

IRIS I'll see for myself.

Pause.

FREDERICK Is there anything you'd like to tell us?

IRIS What?

FREDERICK Anything you'd like to share? About the world beyond these four walls? About the remnants of a once great country? Anything at all?

IRIS No.

FREDERICK No?

IRIS What's there to say?

FREDERICK Indeed. (*Pause*) Empty your pockets.

IRIS What?

Iris looks at Frederick.

LUTHER Do what he says. Empty your pockets.

Iris empties her pocket. Car keys. Luther is watching her carefully with the gun. She tosses them on the floor. Luther forces her to pick them up and give them to him.

LUTHER Car keys.

Iris reaches into another pocket. A pack of Marlboro cigarettes and a box of matches. She hands them to Luther.

LUTHER Where the fuck did you get those?

IRIS I found a case in Regina. I was going to use them to barter for food.

LUTHER (*Grabbing them*) But these are Marlboros.

IRIS So you're observant too!

FREDERICK What else?

Luther has put his gun away and is readying to light the cigarette. The lights flicker and go out.

LUTHER Oh, great.

IRIS What the hell?

LUTHER Frederick, the lights / have gone out.

The lights return, but at a reduced level. Luther is about to strike a match. Iris has dropped the jerry can and pulled out a small handgun, aiming it at Luther.

LUTHER Shit. She's got a gun, Frederick.

Pluto pulls out a gun, aims at Iris.

PLUTO PUT THE GUN DOWN.

IRIS Give me my keys and let me leave. I will let you get on with whatever it is you guys do down here. Just let me leave.

Luther very still. Frederick moves over to where Luther is, grabs cigarette packet and matches from his hand, and lights cigarette. Smokes.

FREDERICK As appealing as that sounds, I'm afraid we may need your car. We're running out of food. And we don't want to leave our home just yet, you see, so a car will make gathering food much easier.

What you ask is simply out of the question.

PLUTO Give me the gun. Or I'll blow your brains out.

Iris gives up. Pluto takes her gun. Luther quickly moves to kitchen and grabs handcuffs. Meanwhile, Pluto, gun still trained on Iris, moves to Frederick and gives him Iris's gun.

FREDERICK Nice work, lover. (*Frederick kisses Pluto.*)

Luther goes to Iris and binds her hands behind her.

LUTHER Fuckin' bitch. No more misbehaving, yeah?

FREDERICK Now why do you want to carry one of these around with you?

IRIS Because I plan to stay alive.

FREDERICK Luther, take a closer look. Make sure she hasn't any other surprises up her sleeve.

Luther searches her pockets.

LUTHER Nothing.

FREDERICK Good.

Are you hungry, Iris?

IRIS If I'm staying here, I might as well eat something.

FREDERICK Well then, Iris, have a seat. Pluto, serve up some beans for our new friend.

Luther forces Iris to a chair. Pluto serves up beans for Iris. Luther's gun still trained on her.

IRIS Do you need to wave that thing in my face? I'm not going anywhere, you shit.

Lights flicker again.

FREDERICK Luther, go see what's up with the generator.

LUTHER Good idea.

FREDERICK And make sure Iris doesn't have any friends waiting outside for her.

LUTHER Right.

Luther takes the gun upstairs to look outside. Frederick moves to his original position and sits down. Pluto crouches downstage of Iris in order to feed her.

FREDERICK So, tell me, where were you when ... when nonsense took over?

Pause.

FREDERICK Tell me. I haven't had a decent conversation in months. What have you been doing the last few years?

Pause. Iris looks at the spoonful.

FREDERICK Eat the beans.

Iris eats the spoonful. Pause.

FREDERICK We used to live in Edmonton. We were members of a certain organisation. Now, as in any organisation, order is key. Strict discipline was essential. If you had guys getting out of line, making demands, stepping beyond their reach, you'd have chaos. Disorganisation. Completely unacceptable.

We had this guy who thought he was a big shot. Thought he was "cock of the walk." One night, on a raid, he went crazy, lighting houses on fire, spraying innocents with gasoline, bashing in car windows. Now, none of this was particularly uncommon. The only problem was, he was doing it on another organisation's property. And this kind of insubordination was unthinkable, after the hard-fought peace we had established between ourselves and this other organisation.

And so this organisation demanded that this particular member be made an example. So, in the public square – Churchill Square it was called – they extracted their payment. They stripped him, poured acid in his eyes, cut off his dick, and branded him across the back with the word "TRAITOR." Then they sent him on his merry way. The example had been made, the peace had been spared.

I think he drowned in the river.

Examples must be made, Iris. So that order does not fall into disorder.

I'm sure you understand.

Where have you been?

IRIS On the road.

FREDERICK Before that.

IRIS I was south of Regina, near the border. I was living with my brother and his wife on their farm. They went out for food and never came back.

One night, this soldier drove up. I guess he had gone AWOL or something. He tried to rape me. I killed him with my brother's hunting rifle, took his jeep and started driving. I've been on the road for five months.

FREDERICK What are you doing here? It seems most people have gone far, far away from here.

IRIS Yes.

PLUTO Why did you stay?

IRIS ... I'm a solitary creature.

FREDERICK That's too bad. (*Pause*) We've not had the pleasure of a woman's company in a long while.

Pause. Frederick is "staring" at her. The lights return to normal. Iris eats another spoonful.

IRIS So you used to live in Edmonton?

FREDERICK Yes.

IRIS I remember watching the riots on TV.

FREDERICK This was the real thing. We owned that town ... for a while, at least. Others would loot and bring us the merchandise as a sign of good faith. The street wars I orchestrated were glorious to watch. We'd torch an entire neighbourhood and kill them as they came running out. Just for kicks. Nothing stood in our way. (*Luther comes down the stairs.*)

But, soon enough, we were invaded. For our resources. Calgary was first, and Edmonton was next on the list. We decided to jump in a car and head east. But it got out of hand in Saskatoon. It went too far. So we came out to this little bunker on the prairie to settle down.

Did you find anything out there?

LUTHER Nothing. As usual.

FREDERICK How's the generator?

LUTHER It needed some gas. But it's getting old, Frederick. I'll take a look in the morning. See if I can fix it.

IRIS You have gas?

LUTHER Maybe.

Where's your car?

Iris sits still. Luther threatens her.

PLUTO (*Quietly to Iris, getting another spoonful ready*) You might as well tell him.

IRIS (*Looks Luther straight in the eyes*) It's two hours walk south from here along the highway. Highway 11. It's a US Army jeep. It's got California plates, license number FUCK U.

I left it sitting in the middle of the road.

Iris takes another spoonful. Pluto readies another.

LUTHER It's from the army?

IRIS Yes.

LUTHER Cool. How 'bout I go find it, bring it back here. What about that, Frederick?

FREDERICK Good idea.

LUTHER Then we can get outta here, huh? Find someplace else to live. Maybe drive south, show those Yanks who's boss, whaddya say?

FREDERICK We'll worry about that later.

Pause. Iris eats another spoonful.

FREDERICK (*To Iris.*) Is there anything you would like to ask us?

Pause. Iris is eating her beans. She's hungry—she hasn't eaten in quite a while. She turns to Pluto, directs all questions to him.

IRIS Well, first of all, How long have you been here?

LUTHER 'Bout two months.

IRIS Where did you get the beans from?

FREDERICK They were here when we arrived.

LUTHER Six dozen cans. One a day.

IRIS You must be running low.

FREDERICK Yes, we are.

LUTHER Hope you're enjoying them.

Iris looks at Luther. Eats another spoonful.

IRIS So, what do you guys do?

LUTHER What do we do?

IRIS Yeah, what do you do around here? For fun? For shits and giggles? It must get pretty dull sitting in the dark.

LUTHER I used to go out with the rifle and shoot gophers, mice, birds. They've all disappeared. Guess I killed 'em all.

FREDERICK We used to play chess. I just kept beating them.

IRIS Maybe we can have a game sometime.

FREDERICK (*Surprised*) I'd like that.

Pluto invents new ways of cooking beans.

IRIS (*To Pluto*) You do?

PLUTO Yes.

IRIS What's your favourite way?

Pause. She eats another spoonful.

PLUTO I once cooked a mouse to see what it would taste like. Put it in the beans.

IRIS (*With beans in her mouth*) And...? What was it like?

PLUTO Chicken.

IRIS Really?

Pause.

IRIS What about sex? You guys have a lot of sex?

LUTHER What?

IRIS How do you feel when your roomies are fucking, hey, Luther? Do you like it when they screw?

LUTHER You little shit.

Luther starts to roll up his sleeves as a threat of violence to Iris.

IRIS I know it's the 21st century, but you're from Alberta, so, I thought maybe you MIGHT have a problem living with gays. Maybe not a PROBLEM as such, but a difficulty nonetheless...

Maybe you like to watch.

FREDERICK (*Frederick distracting Luther*) Luther, while you were outside, Iris and I were chatting.

LUTHER (*Luther playing along*) Oh, yeah? Learn anything interesting?

FREDERICK It seems Iris killed a man when he tried to rape her.

LUTHER Really?

FREDERICK With a hunting rifle.

LUTHER (*Approaching Iris. Pluto is moving away*) A hunting rifle?

FREDERICK A hunting rifle.

LUTHER Well, we've got a hunting rifle, don't we, Frederick?

FREDERICK Yes, I believe we do. But where is it? I don't think we've used it since you killed all the gophers.

LUTHER No, that's true. I haven't used it in months. It's in the cupboard.

FREDERICK In the cupboard, way on the other side of the room.

LUTHER Be difficult to get to. Especially if you're tied up.

FREDERICK Did you know, Luther, that Iris has been driving around for five months?

LUTHER Five months? That's a long time. Must get awful lonely. (*Luther is touching Iris's hair. She glares at Frederick.*)

IRIS (*Under her breath. To Frederick*) You fuck.

Lights down as Luther continues to play with her hair.

Scene Two

Lights come up on the basement. Iris is lying battered on the stage. She is now on the floor, her left hand handcuffed to a post. Her clothes are torn. Pluto has draped the blanket over her. He sits watching her. He has a gun by his side. Nothing happens for a moment. Then Iris stirs. She slowly regains consciousness and looks around. Sees Pluto. Pluto sees her. She crumples back to the ground.

PLUTO Are you okay?

IRIS (*Indecipherable mumble.*)

Pause.

PLUTO Are you okay?

Iris vomits.

IRIS (*Raising her head*) I feel like shit. (*Drops her head*) Have you been sitting there watching me?

PLUTO I wanted to make sure you were alright.

IRIS Where's Luther?

PLUTO He's gone to get your jeep.

IRIS Did I fall asleep?

PLUTO Yeah.

IRIS How long?

PLUTO Couple hours.

Pause.

PLUTO Need some water?

Iris spits.

IRIS I need a cigarette.

PLUTO Luther has them. Sorry.

IRIS Figures. (*Iris sits up.*) So, let's get to know each other, shall we? How are you?

PLUTO How am I?

IRIS Yeah, how are you? It seems your roomies don't care too much for either of us. I've only been here a matter of hours and I already want to leave. You live here. Why's that?

Iris doubles over in abdominal pain.

IRIS Ah, shit.

Iris lies back down.

PLUTO Would you like a chocolate?

Iris groans.

PLUTO I've got some hidden away. Thought you might like one.

Pluto scavenges in the kitchen, finds his box and takes it out.

PLUTO I've had these since we left Edmonton. I save them for special occasions. (*Pluto takes out a half bag of Hershey's Kisses*) Would you like a Kiss?

IRIS Sure.

Pluto moves to Iris with the box, takes out two Kisses, and slowly unwraps one in his hand, and watches it as he slips it in her mouth. She chews as he gets one out for himself. Iris grimaces.

IRIS It's rotten.

PLUTO Is it? (*Pops the Kiss in his mouth*) I can't tell.

They sit chewing, Iris grimacing, Pluto delighted.

IRIS What else have you got in the box?

PLUTO A few little personal things. A stuffed animal. Some cash – not really worth anything now ... My diary. More candy. Pictures.

Pluto is rifling through, flipping through photographs.

IRIS What are they?

PLUTO They're from before all this happened. My family. Friends. My parents. My dog, ... Gabriel.

IRIS Gabriel?

PLUTO Yeah. My boyfriend. Well ... / ex-boyfriend.

IRIS Oh really? Let me see.

PLUTO I haven't shown anyone. These are the only pictures I have of us ... of him. One night we found one of those photo booths that take your picture and it still worked...

IRIS He's cute.

PLUTO Yeah.

IRIS What happened to him?

Pluto takes pictures and puts everything back in the box. He crosses back to the cupboard.

PLUTO One night we went out to try and find some food – Gabriel was getting ill. Malnutrition, I think. We raided this abandoned Safeway and found some cans of peaches and some cans of beans. Green beans. On the way back to our apartment, we ran into these enormous guys. Shaved heads. Big boots. Y'know, militia types. They demanded the food, but Gabriel said no. They pulled a knife out and stabbed him. Beat me up. Took me back to their place...

Pause.

PLUTO Frederick was their leader. He had people believing he could see the future.

IRIS Fucking hell. And can he?

PLUTO Well, no. Not since ... Luther used to think he could. I don't know.

IRIS Isn't that a tad problematic? He's your master...

PLUTO He's my partner ... We're partners.

IRIS Right. Shouldn't you believe him, then?

PLUTO Yes, well ... He believes he's going to die in my arms ... I guess I like the sound of that.

Pause.

PLUTO At least I'm safe. Nothing else matters, really.

Pause.

IRIS I was married once. When I was 21. He was in the army. He was one of the first to go. I knew I'd never see him again.

He only wrote me one letter. "Some nights my arms ache because I'm not holding you," he said. "These guns are cold companions." He died in his sleep.

What was Gabriel like?

PLUTO I can barely remember ... not even his smell, the way his skin felt to touch. Sometimes I imagine he's here.

But Frederick's here.

Pause.

PLUTO Do you still have the letter?

IRIS Letter?

PLUTO From your / husband.

IRIS No. I burnt it.

PLUTO Why wouldn't you keep it?

IRIS I burnt it, alright?

PLUTO I would have kept it.

I keep things.

IRIS Well, I don't.

Pause.

IRIS So, Does your partner let you fuck him?

PLUTO What?

IRIS Does Frederick let you fuck him? Huh? Does he?

Pluto is silent.

PLUTO I can't.

IRIS Oh.

Pause.

IRIS How'd you find this bunker?

PLUTO It was my uncle's house.

IRIS Your uncle built a bunker?

PLUTO The house was built back in the '50s or something. It's a Diefenbunker.

IRIS A what?

PLUTO Nevermind. My uncle believed the world was going to fall apart at the year 2000. You know, Y2K? He stocked it up back then. Cans of food. Water. Emergency supplies. Even guns. But the food's running out.

IRIS No more mice to hunt either.

What are you gonna do?

PLUTO I count on Frederick.

IRIS You love him?

Pause. Pluto smiles to himself.

PLUTO Tell me what you've been doing.

IRIS I drive around the prairies, searching.

Now and then I find settlements. But these people ... they're not people anymore. They'd eat you on the spot. I think there's some poison in the air ... if you stay in the same place too long...

I keep driving and I stick to myself.

Around here, except for you guys, I've seen nothing. For miles in all directions. Nothing.

PLUTO What are you doing here then?

IRIS I haven't much choice right now, do I, kid?

PLUTO No, I mean ... We haven't seen anyone in months. And here you are, appearing out of nothing ... Are you an angel?

IRIS What? ... You're not serious...

PLUTO Angels don't have to have wings, you know. That's what I believe. They can look like humans ... like you. Reminding us that ... that we're human. And that we need each other ... that we need hope and love ... that, that...

IRIS I'm tied up in a bunker. What are you talking about, an angel?

PLUTO Maybe you're a devil, then.

IRIS I'm just a person trying to survive in a fucked up world. That's it.

Pause.

PLUTO I used to dream about angels.

IRIS I don't dream at all anymore.

Pause.

PLUTO I do love Frederick. I know he doesn't feel the same, but I don't care. I'm alive. Sometimes I'm cold, sometimes I'm hungry. But I'm alive.

We hear Luther returning upstairs.

LUTHER (*From upstairs*) Honey, I'm home!

Pluto goes to sleeping room and looks in the door. He keeps the gun trained on Iris, never looking away from her.

PLUTO Frederick, Luther's back.

Pluto moves back to where he was and sits down, still looking at Iris.

IRIS Would you even know what to do with that thing?

Pluto looks at gun. Holds it to his head. Laughs to himself. Luther comes down the stairs, stands at the back of the room. He's carrying a bag with cans and powdered milk in it, a carton of Marlboro's under his arm. He's eating from a package of cookies. Iris and Pluto look at him.

LUTHER Where's Frederick?

Pluto indicates the sleeping room. Luther notices Iris has vomited.

LUTHER Clean that up.

Pluto moves to clean up the mess. Luther crosses to Iris and demonstrates his affection. She rejects him.

LUTHER Would you like a cookie? They're raisin oatmeal.

Iris just stares at him.

LUTHER It's snowing out there now. Fucking climate change.

And thanks for the jeep. Pretty cool.

IRIS I'm happy for you.

LUTHER Yeah. We can drive around and find things to kill.

IRIS Great.

LUTHER I looked through the jeep to see if there was anything useful. Not much, but I found this. (*Pulls out a small vial*) I'm curious, Iris. What is this? Is it poison? Is it, like, strychnine or something?

IRIS Why don't you drink it and find out?

Luther crosses to Iris.

LUTHER Why don't YOU drink it?

Luther tries to force it on Iris.

IRIS It's rat poison. Meant to kill big rats. I got it off this guy. I cut his throat with a screwdriver. A whiff and you're fucked; a drink and you're dead.

LUTHER (*Tossing vial up and down*) Interesting. Here, Pluto, catch. If you ever get lonely.

Throws vial to Pluto. He sits back down and looks at it. Frederick comes in.

FREDERICK So, Luther, did you get the jeep?

LUTHER Yes, sir.

FREDERICK It will make gathering food and supplies easier.

LUTHER Right. I've got a solution to the food problem. So I'm driving back here and I drive past this little settlement about 15 kilometres south. It's like this little camp. A couple kids on this old homestead. They had a fire going and this guy on guard ... I took him out – target practice, you know. And I threw him in the back of the jeep. We're set for at least a week. He's a bit skinny, but...

I figure we could go out late at night with the jeep and a gun ... knock a few of them off, cook 'em up good and tasty ... mix 'em in with the last of the beans.

PLUTO You're sick.

LUTHER I'm being practical. Frederick, they'd never expect it. A gun shot under cover of night ... Really, I mean, how else are we going to survive?

PLUTO Frederick, please, this is unacceptable. We aren't animals...

IRIS Yes you are.

Pause.

FREDERICK Some animals eat their children.

Pause.

FREDERICK Before we descend into madness, we will use the jeep to visit towns within driving distance, looking for food and supplies. Iris has managed to survive this way, so we should be able to find something. Pluto has been studying the map, and there are enough towns within an hour or two to hit a few and grab what they've got for us. You and Pluto will head out in the morning and I'll stay here and look after our guest.

LUTHER C'mon ... You can't even SEE her.

Frederick pulls out Iris's gun from his pocket, moves towards Luther, and points it directly at his groin. Frederick keeps gun trained on Luther as Luther tries to avoid it during his speech.

LUTHER Fine. But, Frederick, you haven't been outside in three months. You know what's out there? Dick-all. I saw these three kids. That's it. I passed through a couple towns on my way back here. Bodies lying on the streets. There are no windows in the shops. The grocery stores are ransacked completely. This is all that was left. I'm tired of beans, I'm tired of the same thing every day. I need some meat.

Frederick puts the gun away.

FREDERICK Then eat Iris.

Luther moves to Iris, crouches, touches her hair, her face.

LUTHER I could never do that.

Iris maliciously smiles.

IRIS How big of you. Give me a cigarette.

Luther takes out cigarette packet from his pocket. Takes one slowly, puts it in her mouth, takes out lighter, lights it. She smokes.

IRIS Thanks, lover.

Pause.

FREDERICK Are you two finished?

Pause. Luther sits down next to Iris. Eats cookies. Frederick puts the gun away.

FREDERICK Okay, then. You can watch Iris. Pluto and I will head out in the morning and find some supplies. I'm going to get some rest before the sunrise.

Frederick exits into sleeping room.

PLUTO So you killed this kid and now you're going to ... eat him?

LUTHER Desperate times...

PLUTO You don't have any respect for life. You just kill people like, like...

LUTHER Pluto, I've never felt more alive. When I'm this close to death, I feel like I hold my life, I hold it in my hands. This is what it was like back in Edmonton. And I miss this feeling.

PLUTO You treat death like some toy, some game, some TV show...

LUTHER There's a fucking war on! I'm not the only one / killing people.

PLUTO It doesn't matter how many million die. Or where. Or how. It still means something. Life still counts for something. (*Almost to himself*) So does love...

LUTHER What? You're kidding, right?

Look, if you can't handle the way things are, if you can't survive according to the new rules...

PLUTO Then what?

LUTHER Then maybe that poison will come in handy.

PLUTO Maybe we're dead already and nobody bothered to tell us.

LUTHER Yeah, maybe. And maybe we're still alive and the world is a shit hole.

FREDERICK (*From sleeping room*) Pluto. Come here.

Pluto looks at Iris. Stands. Gives gun to Luther. And goes into the sleeping room. Luther is mindful that Frederick may hear him.

LUTHER (*Whispers to Iris*) These faggots are fucking crazy.

Pause.

LUTHER That kid must be about 15, 16. The thing is, he hasn't known anything but this. The world was fucked up from the moment he was born. There must be someplace where they're trying again, someplace where they're trying to make some kind of civilisation.

You've been out there. What's going on?

IRIS The world is a rapist.

Pause.

IRIS I'll tell you a story.

LUTHER Okay.

IRIS I stopped into a deserted gas station. I wandered inside hoping to find some food – Twinkies or Oreo cookies or some other non-perishable food item meant to last past the end of the world. The shelves were bare, candy wrappers on the floor. I walked through to the diner. There, under a table,

I found three children huddled together. A girl of about 8, and two boys a little younger. I asked them "What are your names?", but they didn't answer. They were ... their eyes were full of ... rage. I reached out my hand and said, "My name is Sarah. I want to be your friend." And this girl leapt out and bit my hand. Hard; it started bleeding. She was clawing at me, flashing her teeth. The boys followed, grabbing at my legs, digging in with their fingers, their teeth. They were screaming, making noises like wild animals. I tripped over backwards ... tripped over a dead body, but it had been picked clean ... I saw dried blood on the girl's clothes, blood around their mouths ... I fought them off, desperate ... I ran back to the car and drove off. They chased me down the highway...

Those are the only children I've seen.

LUTHER They were going to eat you.

Pause.

LUTHER Your name isn't Sarah.

IRIS And what's Pluto real name?

Pause.

LUTHER There was a time when I thought I would never kill anybody. I once killed for a jug of sour milk, some eggs, and some stale bread. I once killed for a bicycle. I once killed for spite. Someday I may even kill myself.

I didn't plan on this.

But I'm making the best of it.

IRIS You're a fucking animal.

LUTHER And what are you, huh? Guns, rat poison. I saw the blood inside the jeep. You try to come across as some kind of victim when you / yourself...

IRIS I'm adapting.

LUTHER And so am I.

But this basement is driving me mad.

Pause.

IRIS I've been to the west coast.

LUTHER Yeah?

IRIS Yeah. After the bomb fell, I started driving west. See what was happening on Vancouver Island. And there were all these little communities set up, all these little towns. People growing their own food. They were completely unaware of the madness on the rest of the continent.

LUTHER Why'd you come back?

IRIS I'm not ready for that kind of cooperative shit.

LUTHER You'd rather live in this wasteland than somewhere warm?

IRIS The prairies have always been about individual initiative, right? I proudly carry on that tradition.

Luther is looking at Iris.

LUTHER I need to go somewhere warm, where fruit grows on trees, where the ocean laps on the beach. Someplace safe and warm. Down south, far away from here. Maybe I'll take you with me. We'll go south, find someplace to settle, somewhere to raise a family. We'll leave them behind, we'll leave them here because this is where they want to stay.

IRIS How you gonna get across the border?

LUTHER What?

IRIS The border's been closed for years, you know that.

LUTHER Do people actually give a damn about the 49th parallel anymore? I figured they'd have something better to do than try to keep them out.

IRIS IT'S TO KEEP US IN, you idiot.

Pause. Luther takes cigarettes and matches out of front pocket. Takes one himself. Lights it.

LUTHER (*Singing quietly.*)
O Canada
Our home and native land
True patriot love
In all our son's command...

LUTHER Name your favourite Canadian of all time.

IRIS What?

LUTHER Favourite Canadian. All time.

IRIS Ummm...

LUTHER Okay. I'll go first. William Shatner.

IRIS William Shatner? You mean...

LUTHER Yeah, yeah, James T. Kirk of the Starship Enterprise. From way back in the 1970's or something.

IRIS I used to watch that. I was convinced we'd be living on the moon before I was 20.

LUTHER Me too. Oh well.

Your turn.

IRIS Okay. Ummm ... Oh. Those guys who made that cartoon about that small town ... y'know, with the songs ... (*Sings*) "Blame Canada..."

LUTHER What? That wasn't Canadian. That was ... uhh ... *South Park*. Definitely American.

IRIS Oh, fuck, I don't know. Stupid question.

LUTHER JUST PICK ONE.

Luther is getting upset.

IRIS Fine. Céline Dion.

LUTHER CÉLINE DION?! ... You don't have a clue. I thought you'd pick someone cooler than that. Like Neil Young or Ron Peterson or even Mr. Dressup. Geez...

IRIS SORRY.

Pause. Smoking.

IRIS Is that your flag then?

LUTHER Yeah.

IRIS Looks pretty beat up.

LUTHER (*Laughs*) How symbolic.

Pause.

IRIS You're going to take my car whether I go with you or not, is that right?

LUTHER Yes, well, that's the way it is, I suppose.

IRIS Well, fuck you then.

LUTHER No, fuck you. I'm offering you a way out here.

I want you along, Iris, because ... well, you're intelligent, you're like me.

IRIS Yeah?

LUTHER Yeah, sure.

IRIS Really?

LUTHER Listen. The two of us could make it, y'know. Start over. Like the Garden of Eden.

IRIS The Garden of Eden?

LUTHER Yeah, where our children can grow healthy and strong.

IRIS Our children?

LUTHER Just imagine how perfect they'd be. Your looks, my strength, our survival instinct. It'd be perfect. Exactly what this world needs now.

IRIS (*Indicates her belly*) Maybe you're right.

LUTHER They'd be fucking gorgeous.

Pause.

LUTHER Y'know, I had a twin when I was born – when we were born. But she died when we were six.

When I first saw you, I imagined you were her.

Iris is silent.

LUTHER From a distance, you really look like what I would imagine her to be. Tall. Beautiful. Determined. My sister would have walked through the front door too.

Did you have any siblings?

IRIS No.

Iris lies down as if to sleep.

LUTHER (*Singing softly again.*)
God keep our land
Glorious and free
O Canada we stand on guard for thee
O Canada we / stand...

Lights flicker again to a lower level.

LUTHER Fucking generator.

Lights fade to black.

Scene Three

Morning. Iris is sleeping on the floor where she was the night before. Pluto, "on watch," has fallen asleep too with the gun fallen out of his hand, beside him. He is quietly snoring. Frederick emerges from the sleeping area, himself just woken up. A moment. He smiles. Moves to Pluto and crouches. Gently nudges Pluto. Pluto doesn't wake. Nudges again. Doesn't wake. Frederick leans in and kisses him on the cheek. Whisper in his ear.

FREDERICK (*Whisper*) Wake up.

Pluto opens his eyes. Turns to look at Frederick.

FREDERICK You fell asleep.

Pluto, realising what's happening, grabs gun and jumps up. Looks around. Sees Iris sleeping. Relaxes.

PLUTO Luther woke me up and told me to look after her. He went outside. Guess I fell asleep. Sorry.

Pluto sees vial on the ground – it's fallen out of his pocket. He bends down and grabs it.

FREDERICK What is that?

PLUTO Luther found a vial in the jeep.

Pluto hands it to Frederick. Frederick lifts stopper, goes to sniff it. Pluto stops him.

PLUTO Iris says it's rat poison, but like really strong rat poison.

FREDERICK Why do you have it?

PLUTO Luther gave it to me. Said I might get lonely.

Pause. Frederick replaces stopper.

FREDERICK Cook up some breakfast.

Pluto gets up, goes to kitchen area. Grabs can of beans. Opens it, puts it on the stove. Frederick stands, thinking, playing with vial in his hand.

PLUTO Beans, beans, the musical fruit ... the more / you eat the more...

FREDERICK What's he doing out there?

PLUTO Fixing the generator. I think we're running low on gas, too. Might be stumbling around in the dark soon.

FREDERICK Nothing new.

Pause.

PLUTO Frederick, it sounds like he's heading off south and taking Iris with him.

FREDERICK I know.

PLUTO I think he's losing it. He thinks Iris and him are going to start a family. If he's going to eat that boy ... Frederick, he's going to eat me.

FREDERICK I won't let him.

He'll come 'round. He'd be lost without me. That jeep is our means to find some food and bring it back here, where we're comfortable. If we need to, later, maybe we'll take off. But not right now.

PLUTO Have you talked to Iris? She said to Luther that on Vancouver Island there are settlements, there are people...

FREDERICK Iris will tell you whatever she wants.

Pause.

FREDERICK (*Tossing vial up and down*) Pluto. We have to make an example. For Luther's sake. (*Moves in Pluto's direction*) Here. (*Holds out vial to Pluto*) Make her some beans.

PLUTO (*Moving to Frederick*) You want me to poison Iris?

FREDERICK Yes.

Pluto slowly takes vial. He slowly turns back to beans, hesitates, then pours the whole vial into the pot. Quickly stirs it.

FREDERICK Good. That solves that. Now go see what he's doing.

Pluto goes upstairs. Iris stirs, sees Frederick, sits up. Watches him.

FREDERICK Have a good sleep?

IRIS Great.

FREDERICK Good. Glad to hear you're getting on well.

IRIS Can I have some water, something to drink?

FREDERICK No.

Pause.

IRIS Please?

Pause.

IRIS Your boyfriend is really quite lovely. Seems to care about you a great deal.

FREDERICK Yes, he does.

Pause.

IRIS Luther's a bit of a dick.

FREDERICK Seems to care about you.

Pause.

IRIS You know, Frederick, you're really fucking ugly.

FREDERICK I know. You see my dead eyes, you see all the dents and cuts and bruises and burns on my skin, and you turn away. You can't help it. Ugliness is repulsive. To you, I am repulsive. I can feel the ugliness creep under my skin, into my blood, into my bones. There is no fighting it.

It happens to all of us, sweetheart. These days, we haven't a choice.

Let me get you that water.

Frederick crosses to the kitchen to get cup of water.

IRIS What's it like being blind? Stumbling around in your own darkness, never being quite sure what's going on around you. Having to rely on others. And you're not getting any younger, Frederick. Why, by the look of things, you're already a senior citizen.

FREDERICK You're about 6 feet tall, you've got dark hair, you've got lovely teeth, and you're in fantastic shape. I dreamt about you, Iris. I haven't had a dream in months. And last night I saw you ... and you were on the ground, surrounded by this smoky haze ... green grass on a foggy morning ... and you were coughing / ... coughing up blood.

IRIS ... coughing up blood. And the air smelled like aluminum and I'm coughing my lungs out of my chest ... I used to have that dream when I was a child. All the time. And I'd wake up and I'd be holding a pillow over my face with my own hands.

FREDERICK I used to dream all my teeth had fallen out.

Pause.

IRIS Let me ask you something. Does Luther have any tattoos, markings, scars, that sort of thing?

FREDERICK We all have scars.

Pluto comes back down the stairs.

PLUTO Frederick, Luther has gone crazy. He's built this huge fire outside and he's ... he's ... roasting that boy. He's covered in blood ... It's gross.

FREDERICK I'll go talk to him. Here, give this to Iris. (*Frederick hands him the cup.*) And give her some beans.

Frederick heads up the stairs. Pluto goes to kitchen and stirs the beans. He turns to Iris.

PLUTO You alright?

IRIS Yeah, sure. You got that water?

Pluto goes over with the glass of water.

PLUTO Here.

IRIS (*Looks at Pluto*) You first.

PLUTO What?

IRIS (*Indicates glass*) You first.

PLUTO You don't trust me? Iris, I gave you a chocolate Kiss.

Iris takes a long drink.

IRIS Do you believe dreams can tell the future?

PLUTO I don't believe in anything.

Iris hands back the glass. Pluto takes it back to the kitchen area.

IRIS Pluto, I think you should take the jeep and get the hell outta here.

PLUTO No.

IRIS You can't seriously want to stay here.

PLUTO I want to be with Frederick.

IRIS Look, Pluto, this is a fucking wasteland. Get out of here while you can.

Pause.

PLUTO Why are you telling me this?

IRIS Because I'm your friend.

I'm American. Well, I guess we're ALL Americans now, but...

I was in California. Another bomb came last Tuesday. And everyone decided to leave. So, there they were, in their cars, stuck in a traffic jam on the edge of the world at the end of time.

I stole the jeep and started off down a secondary highway, going north, stealing gas and food from abandoned stations along the way. People starving on the streets, families huddled around fires. Desperate, dangerous people. And coming up behind me – I could feel it – the great exodus.

I crossed the border two days ago.

PLUTO How'd you get across the border?

IRIS There's nothing a woman, some ingenuity and a gun can't do.

I won't be the first coming this way, Pluto. The south is worse than it is here; expect a lot of visitors.

PLUTO Why are you telling me this?

IRIS Because, Pluto, you can leave this shit hole before you die here.

Pause.

PLUTO You just want me to give you your jeep back.

IRIS Sure, of course I do.

PLUTO (*Irritated*) So why should I trust you? Why should I believe anything you say? Last night you / told me...

IRIS I know what I told you last night. This is what I'm telling you now. You don't have to believe me, Pluto, but if you want to survive, if / that's at all important to you...

PLUTO You think you can come in here and fuck with us? We're not going anywhere. We're staying here, Frederick and Luther and I. It's safe, it's warm. It's our home.

IRIS What are you talking about? Luther's gone mad. He's going to eat you sooner or later. It's no longer much of a safe haven, is it?

PLUTO Thanks to you. Everything was fine before you showed up.

IRIS No, it wasn't. Look, I thought you might like to know what's really going on. But you've convinced yourself you love Frederick, that that means something...

PLUTO I heard you talking to Luther last night. Telling him ... giving him some hope and ... and now you're telling me there's nothing out there...

IRIS THERE'S NOTHING HERE EITHER.

Pause.

IRIS Can I ask you something? What happened in Saskatoon?

Pluto doesn't respond. He crosses to kitchen. Pluto scoops up some beans into a bowl and moves towards Iris.

PLUTO (*As a "peace offering"*) Here. Eat some food. You need your strength.

IRIS I couldn't eat a thing.

PLUTO (*Kneeling beside her*) It'll make you feel better.

IRIS Pluto, your beans make me sick. How you could eat those for two months / I'll never know.

PLUTO (*Insistent*) You have to eat / sometime.

IRIS (*Equally insistent*) FUCK OFF WITH YOUR BEANS.

Pause. Pluto gets up and goes back to stove. Luther comes down the stairs. He is wearing an apron that says "Kiss The Cook" which is covered in blood. There is blood on his face, hands.

LUTHER Breakfast is just about ready, folks. It tastes mighty fine. Rather like chicken, imagine that. I've got a cut especially for you, love.

Luther kisses Iris.

LUTHER Yes, a piece of meat especially for you ... You and the baby better get some strength for the long journey ahead. Now, we should have enough supplies to make it to the border. There should be more gas over there, I'm guessing.

PLUTO Luther, listen to me.

LUTHER (*To Pluto*) We're taking off. My woman, my baby and me have had enough of you cocksuckers. (*Walking towards him. Grabs him, grabs his ass*) Unless you want to come with me, prettyboy. Let a real man take care of you.

Pluto struggles free. Luther laughs.

PLUTO Frederick won't let you leave.

LUTHER You think I care about him anymore? Look around, Pluto. Look where we ended up. Some hole in the ground. In the middle of nowhere. Not REALLY what I'd call the promised land.

I should have let the fucker drown.

PLUTO And you're going to find this "promised land" out there somewhere, is that it?

LUTHER Yeah, I am.

C'mon, Pluto, I'm giving you a chance here. Take it. I'm giving you a chance to be part of SOMETHING, something real. The start of a new civilisation, a new world. Frederick can't see it, but maybe you can.

PLUTO And who are you? The beginning of this new world?

LUTHER Yes. Yes, Iris and I are the lifegivers, the new Adam and Eve. Right honey?

IRIS (*Quietly*) Right.

LUTHER RIGHT HONEY?

IRIS RIGHT.

PLUTO You've lost it. Look at you, you think Iris loves you or something, you think she's pregnant, you think ... God, Luther, what happened to you?

LUTHER You and Frederick are happy to just stay here and live your own little married life. She found this place, and she won't be the last.

I don't know what you think you've found here, Pluto.

PLUTO No, no, this is our home, this is where we live. You know there's nothing out there. This is our only safety.

I know you and Iris talked last night. I know you believe her. But you can't. Just now she / told me that...

Frederick stumbles in from upstairs. Luther has beat him with his own cane. Pluto crosses to support him.

PLUTO Frederick! (*To Luther*) What have you done?

LUTHER He's old. He's getting in the way.

FREDERICK So, I guess you're heading out there to find your future. Pluto and I are staying here on our own then.

LUTHER That's right.

FREDERICK You're not taking the jeep. It belongs to all three of us. And two of us want it to stay here.

LUTHER Who stole it? Who went out there and got it?

FREDERICK Luther, we have been together for a long time. We've survived. Trust me, Luther, this is the safest place for us to be. I know it.

Listen to me, Luther. This is no way to deal with this. I've seen what it's like out there, Luther. I know you'll find nothing...

Frederick falters. Pluto supports him.

LUTHER Answer this, Freddy. Will you answer a question for me, huh?

FREDERICK Ask.

LUTHER Right. Let's think back a couple years. Back to the time we first met up, and you had all these stories about the future. Remember that?

FREDERICK Yes.

LUTHER Great. Well, so do I. And here's my question, Freddy, here's my question: When you dreamt about the future, is this what it looked like? Huh?

Pause.

FREDERICK What if I said yes?

Luther. We've looked out for each other. We've fed each other. We've survived. I saved your life. You've saved mine.

Now let me ask you a question. Since Iris is such a good friend of yours, tell me this: What is her brother's name?

LUTHER What?

FREDERICK Her brother's name. Well, she told me she had a brother. She lived with him just a few short months ago. Is that what she told you?

Luther is silent.

FREDERICK Where is Iris from?

LUTHER She's from ... I don't know. Who cares?

FREDERICK Why does she have American cigarettes? And why does she have a U.S. Army jeep?

LUTHER I guess she stole it off some American soldier.

FREDERICK Right. The border's been closed for years. How'd it get across?

Luther is silent.

FREDERICK Alright, Iris – What's the capital of Quebec?

IRIS What?

LUTHER What are you trying to prove?

FREDERICK ANSWER THE QUESTION.

IRIS Fuck off.

FREDERICK Who was Canada's first Prime Minister?

Who was Wayne Gretzky?

When did Canada build its first nuclear bomb?

Iris?

IRIS Go to hell. This doesn't mean anything.

FREDERICK It proves we don't know who you are, where you come from, or what you're doing here.

(*To Luther*) Why don't you ask her the name of her brother?

LUTHER Iris, you told me you didn't have any siblings.

Pause.

PLUTO Luther, we've been together for a long time. Frederick's right. We've survived. Now, Iris isn't the person you...

Luther walks over to Pluto. Stares. Pluto turns away. Luther grabs the bowl of beans and starts eating them. Pluto turns back. Luther spits some of the beans on Pluto's face. Pluto madly wipes the beans off his face.

LUTHER Yum, these beans are so good...

FREDERICK Luther.

LUTHER ... I want to eat these beans for the rest of my life...

FREDERICK Luther.

LUTHER ... I want to be stuck in a hole in the ground eating these beans...

FREDERICK LUTHER.

LUTHER WHAT?

Pause.

LUTHER Freddy, this is over. I've lived here for three months because I had nowhere else to go. Now, there's a jeep and you still want to stay in this shit hole? C'mon, we used to take chances, things used to be exciting. Now we just sit here and rot. Come with me, let me show you...

FREDERICK (*To Iris*) You've been around, Iris. You know there's nothing out there.

Why do you insist on pulling us apart like this?

IRIS I haven't done anything. You're all so paranoid that all you needed was a push. Now it's all coming crashing down. And I've had the pleasure of sitting here and watching.

FREDERICK (*Stumbling towards her*) I think you've said enough, Iris.

LUTHER (*Gun to Frederick*) Frederick, leave her be. She's my partner, and I don't appreciate you threatening my partner.

FREDERICK Fine.

Pause. Frederick goes for Iris with his cane, starts hitting her. Iris crumpled on the floor. Luther follows Frederick with the gun. Luther is starting to feel the effects of the poisoned beans.

LUTHER Frederick.

Frederick pauses. Turns to Luther.

LUTHER Frederick ... I'll shoot you.

Frederick starts kicking Iris.

LUTHER FREDERICK. I swear to God...

Frederick freezes in mid-kick, looks to Luther. Eye contact. Frederick goes to kick again.

LUTHER STOP!

The lights flicker as Frederick goes to kick her and go out. A gunshot. A groan is heard as Frederick falls on Iris. She screams. Lights flicker and come up. Iris pushes Frederick off of her, looks at him.

IRIS (*To Luther*) Give me the key for this.

Luther shocked, grabs key to handcuff from pocket and throws it to her. Iris frees herself and slowly stands. Looks down at Frederick, who is writhing in pain. Kicks him. Looks at Luther.

IRIS Thanks.

Luther, shocked, can only nod.

IRIS Okay. Let's get going. You ready?

Luther nods.

IRIS Okay. Well, I don't see the point sticking around here. (*Turns to Pluto*) You sure you're not coming?

Pluto doesn't move.

IRIS Well, sorry to leave you like this Pluto, but, hey ... C'mon, there's nothing here worth sticking around here for.

Pluto doesn't move.

IRIS But I guess its up to you. Not much out there anyways.

Luther falls to his knees, grabs his stomach. Fights for breath. He's dying.

IRIS (*Goes to him and kneels beside him*) Luther? What the fuck? Luther?

Luther spits up blood. He falls to the floor and shakes.

IRIS Well, well...

Iris looks over Luther's body and as he's still shaking, she reaches into his pocket and grabs the car keys. Grabs a gun from another pocket. Pluto takes out his gun and aims it at Iris. He pulls the trigger. The gun clicks.

He pulls the trigger. The gun clicks.

He pulls the trigger. The gun clicks.

He pulls the trigger. The gun clicks.

He pulls the trigger. The gun clicks.

He pulls the trigger. The gun clicks.

He pulls the trigger. The gun clicks.

He pulls the trigger. The gun clicks.

Pluto drops the gun. He falls to his knees, crying.)

PLUTO Rat poison in the beans. Frederick wanted to poison you. You ruined everything.

IRIS (*Standing. She jangles the keys in her hand*) Thanks for the help.

Iris grabs everything she can – the blanket, cans of beans, Luther's bag of food, the carton of Marlboros – and moves to the stairs. Pluto isn't following her. She stops and faces Pluto.

IRIS It doesn't really make a difference if you stay here or take off. It's all over anyways. This is a war that no one wins. Some just bleed less than others.

I hear nuclear winters are a treat. Enjoy yourself.

Iris exits. Pause. Hears Frederick's laboured breathing. Pluto moves to Frederick's body. Kneels. Takes his body in his arms. Holds him close.

FREDERICK Pluto...

PLUTO Yes, we'll be fine. Don't worry.

Frederick tries to sit up, tries to feel for the wound. Too painful.

PLUTO Frederick, just relax...

FREDERICK Let me feel the wound.

Pause.

FREDERICK TAKE MY SHIRT OFF. (*Lovingly reaches to Pluto's face, brushes his cheek*) Please?

Pluto takes off his shirt. The bullet hit his abdomen; his stomach is covered in blood.

FREDERICK Doesn't look too bad.

PLUTO Just a scratch.

FREDERICK (*Suddenly shivering*) I'm so cold...

Pluto grabs the Canadian flag from the wall and wraps it around Frederick, holds him close. Pause. Frederick pulls Pluto close and they kiss.

FREDERICK What are you going to do?

PLUTO What? I'm staying with you, here...

FREDERICK No, you can't...

Frederick reaches with not a little bit of pain, and grabs his gun. Holds gun out to Pluto.

FREDERICK Shoot me.

PLUTO What?

FREDERICK I want you to shoot me.

PLUTO No, I can't...

FREDERICK PLUTO. Please.

Pluto pauses for a moment. Then takes the gun. Stands.

FREDERICK You've taken such good care of me.

Pluto raises gun, aims at Frederick. He starts crying, shaking. The lights flicker and out. A gunshot is heard in the blackout.

The End.

The Trial of Salomé (2007)

by Scott Sharplin

Theatre companies in Edmonton spring up every year dedicated to developing new plays, while many companies that have appeared since the early 1970s have retained new play development as a priority. The city thus entered the millennium as a hub of support for new writers—at least for workshops. Playwright David Belke has noted the "clear lack of systemic assistance for production-based writing. Nearly every playwright support system in Canada, including the Alberta Playwrights' Network, is designed to serve development, not production" (3). Full productions of long-form new plays by emerging writers are rarities at established theatre companies in the city. The repeated argument from the local media and the theatre community is that a large number of very good new plays exist; if only there were sufficient opportunities to produce them. As critic Paul Matwychuk pointed out in the fall of 2005, the production of new plays in the city ebbs and flows.

> Edmonton is supposedly a theatre-mad town—and yet, whenever I sit down to talk with a group of playwrights, talk inevitably turns to how difficult it's become for a local writer to get a script produced by a professional theatre company.
>
> This isn't just the usual bellyaching. It seems as though substantial mainstage productions of new scripts by Edmonton playwrights have become the exception and not the rule.
>
> But good scripts are out there.

Walterdale could potentially take the lead in the production of full-length new plays, while continuing to thrive on a useful and unique mixture of period fare and contemporary hits.

Within this context, it had been nearly twenty-five years since Walterdale produced a full-length new play when artistic director Scott Sharplin programmed his play *The Trial of Salomé* into the end of Walterdale's 2006/07 season. This slot had been reserved for the summer musical in the previous seven years, and the melodrama for thirty-five years before that.

When Sharplin was appointed Walterdale's artistic director in 2005, the Edmonton theatre set was already familiar with his work. An award-winning playwright, director, and administrator, Sharplin was born in Edmonton in 1974. He began writing plays at Victoria Composite High School and at The Citadel's Teen Festival of the Arts. At the age of nineteen he gained city-wide notice when he co-founded the Carnival of Shrieking Youth theatre festival in 1993, which has since become the city's longest-running youth-driven festival. In 1995 he founded Sound & Fury Theatre, primarily dedicated to modernizing and adapting classical works (particularly Shakespeare), but also to producing new works by Sharplin and a host of young playwrights. The company, which began producing full theatre seasons in 2000, made fostering new talent in the city its priority. Sharplin's savvy in finding government grant money to pay his company a guaranteed minimum, whenever possible, gained notice from other independent companies. He stepped down as Sound & Fury's artistic director in 2004 before the company integrated with Edmonton's Image Theatre in 2006. He has also served on the board of Alberta Playwrights' Network and as artistic director at Walterdale from 2005 to 2007. While directing *King Lear* (2006) and the Edmonton debut of *Antony and Cleopatra* (2007) at Walterdale, Sharplin maintained Internet blogs called "Lear Year" and "Stage Whispers," respectively, on which he recorded his ongoing experiences and musings while preparing and directing the productions. His original plays include *Purity Test* (2006, Chill Room Co-op/Fringe, winner of the 2002 Alberta Playwriting Competition), *Truth Factory* (2003, Lunchbox Theatre), *Burnt Remains* (2002, Sound & Fury/Fringe), *Troll Girl* (2002, Sound & Fury), and *Touch* (2000, Sound & Fury).

The Trial of Salomé is a historical comedy set during World War I when Canadian dancer Maud Allen played her ingénue role as Oscar Wilde's Salomé in London. When Roger Pemberton-Billing, MP, interrupts a performance of the Independent Theatre's production of *Salomé* in order to save the audience from certain lecherous intrigue, Allen announces that they will instead perform the trial, "Exactly as it was performed before the King's Bench." She casts Billing as himself in order to ensure authenticity (and Billing's consent). The play rolls through the World War I trenches and London's back stages and back alleys to chronicle British distaste for licentious discourse while also invoking the celebrity gossip columns of today. By including lines from Wilde's *Salomé*, trial transcripts, debates on ethics in the media of the day, and a deft dose of theatricality in the context of a nation at war, the play reaches its climax as Allen agrees to dance Salomé's Dance of the Seven Veils if the judge agrees to present plaintiff Pemberton-Billing's head on a platter. She dances...

The Trial of Salomé ran July 4–14, 2007, at Walterdale Playhouse (firehall) with the following cast and creative team:

MAUD ALLEN	Leslie Caffaro
ROGER PEMBERTON-BILLING	Denny Demeria
JACK GREIN	Nathan Coppens
ACTOR ONE	Bill Roberts
ACTOR TWO	Tania Gigliotti
ACTOR THREE	Amir Shah
ACTOR FOUR	Bradley Bishop
ACTOR FIVE	Lee Conrad
ACTOR SIX	Kelsie Acton
ACTOR SEVEN	Carolyn Barker

DIRECTOR	Amy Neufeld
STAGE MANAGER	Erin Voaklander
SET DESIGNER	Jim Herchak
COSTUME DESIGNER	Tara-Lee LaRose
LIGHTING DESIGNER	Joanne Soetaert Lantz
SOUND DESIGNER	Mark Senior
PROPERTIES	Jessica Haak
CHOREOGRAPHY	Heather Taschuk

The Trial of Salomé

by Scott Sharplin

Characters MAUD ALLEN, *the Salomé Dancer*
ROGER PEMBERTON-BILLING, *Member of Parliament, "The Prophet" (also plays The Marquess of Queensbury)*
JACK GREIN, *the Manager of the Independent Theatre (also plays Oscar Wilde)*

Actors in the Independent Theatre production of Salomé:

Actor one, who plays:
- HEROD, *Tetrarch of Judea*
- GENERAL SIR WILLIAM "WOOLY" ROBERTSON
- BOWLER-HATTED BLOKE 1
- QUEENSBUDDY 1
- JUSTICE DARLING

Actor two, who plays:
- THE YOUNG SYRIAN
- TOMMY 1
- SPY

Actor three, who plays:
- THE PAGE OF HERODIAS
- TOMMY 2
- BOWLER-HATTED BLOKE 2
- BOSIE (ALFRED LORD DOUGLAS)

Actor four, who plays:
- RICHARD VON BEMTINCK, *German Foreign Minister*
- DOCTOR SERRELL COOKE
- BOWLER-HATTED BLOKE 3
- QUEENSBUDDY 2
- THE SEVERED HEAD

Actor five, who plays:
- LORD BEAVERBROOK, *Minister of Information*
- CAPTAIN HAROLD SPENCER
- PROPSMASTER
- BOWLER-HATTED BLOKE 4
- YOUNG OSCAR

Actor six, who plays:
HERODIAS, *the Tetrarch's Wife*
EILEEN VILLIERS-STUART, *an agent provocateur*

Actor seven, who plays:
JANE SMUTS, *sister of the unsubstantiated assumption*
TOMMY 3

Setting London, April 1918. The final year of World War I.

Note A successful production will be fast-paced, with a crisp, slightly exaggerated delivery. Very little about the production should be naturalistic; settings can be suggested through very simple, overtly theatrical set pieces, props, lighting and sound.

Act One

Scene: The opening tableau of Oscar Wilde's Salomé. *The Young Syrian and the Page of Herodias are reclining on the terrace outside Herod's palace.*

SYRIAN How beautiful is the princess Salomé tonight!

PAGE Look at the moon!

SYRIAN She has a strange look.

PAGE She is like a woman rising from a tomb. An ageless face.

SYRIAN She is like a dancer who has silver doves for feet.

PAGE She is mad and sorrowful, reckless and repentant.

SYRIAN She is like the shadow of a white rose in a mirror of silver.

PAGE She sees everything and says nothing.

SYRIAN Perhaps she will dance. Do you think she will dance?

PAGE You must not look at her. You look too much.

SYRIAN Oh, she is rising! She is leaving the table!

PAGE It is dangerous to look at someone in that fashion.

SYRIAN She looks troubled.

PAGE Something terrible will happen.

SYRIAN She is coming this way!

PAGE How pale she is. She is a silver flower in a swift flood.

SYRIAN Do not look at her!

PAGE Yes, she is coming towards us.

SYRIAN Put out the torches! Hide the moon! Hide the stars!

PAGE She is like...

SYRIAN She comes! The princess Salomé!

PAGE She is—

Enter Billing, carrying a legal document. He is dressed as a British gentleman circa 1918, and his entrance totally destroys the mood.

BILLING Cease and forbear! Desist and discontinue! Cancel, terminate, and halt!

SYRIAN Who's this damp dishrag, then?

PAGE Admirer of yours?

BILLING No more of this obscene and rancid verbiage!

SYRIAN Now there, he must mean you.

BILLING I mean this filthy play! The play is over! *(to the audience)* Out!

PAGE Hang on a jif, there, mate.

SYRIAN The play's just gettin' started. Salomé's not even danced yet.

BILLING Nor shall she, now nor never. (*gives Syrian the paper. To the audience again*) Gentlemen and ladies—and I use the terms equivocally—

SYRIAN "By order of the Grand High Court of London—"

BILLING You are here under false pretenses.

SYRIAN "This twenty-third of April, 1918—"

BILLING You came to witness this insipid drama.

PAGE "*Salomé* by Oscar Wilde—"

BILLING I've come to liberate you from that fate.

SYRIAN "All performances repealed!"

PAGE "Re-pealed."

BILLING Yes.

PAGE Does that mean we've been pealed once already?

SYRIAN Naw, I told ya, Salomé's not danced.

PAGE Now THAT is what I call a pealing.

BILLING (*Grabbing the paper back*) It means bugger off back to your fleapits and stop spreading plague—

PAGE She's coming! Look!

SYRIAN Do not lay eyes on her!

BILLING Excuse me. What did I just say?

PAGE She is a spire of ivory that rises from the sea.

SYRIAN She is—

BILLING Now stop that! We've heard quite enough!

Enter Grein (instead of Salomé).

PAGE She's really not herself today.

GREIN Roger Pemberton-Billing, Member of Parliament.

BILLING Jack Grein, Theatrical Nancy-Boy.

GREIN This is a private perfomance, Mr. Billing.

BILLING That doesn't matter, Mr. Grein. The ruling is inclusive. ALL performances—

GREIN These gentle folk have paid their coin already. They await their art.

BILLING Oh, art? (*To audience*) It's art you seek?

GREIN A densely splendid tapestry of verse and drama—

BILLING If art is your intent, you'll find the British Gallery next door.

GREIN Please! Keep your seats!

BILLING They have a splendid painting of Sir Henry Irving playing Hamlet.

GREIN Irving is deceased, sir. These are theatre aficionados. They crave—

BILLING Crave? Live flesh?

PAGE The moon is rising.

BILLING Crude poetical conceits and pornographic choreography?

SYRIAN She is a perfumed breeze that carries secrets.

PAGE She is coming.

GREIN True art is neither moral nor immoral. It just IS.

BILLING Not anymore, it's not.

SYRIAN Hide the moon in sackcloth!

PAGE She is coming!

BILLING You were there. The Judge was firm.

SYRIAN I beg you not to look at her.

PAGE The princess!

BILLING *Salomé* is over. End of story.

PAGE She is here!

Maud Allan enters, dressed as Salomé. By now, the rest of the cast has assembled on stage also.

MAUD And now, the play begins.

GREIN You are a jot late on your entrance, Miss Allan.

MAUD Mr. Grein, the Lord our Saviour took three days to rise up from the grave. Thus tardiness is next to godliness.

BILLING A charming opener, Miss Allan. Blasphemy and hubris, very nice. Where shall you go from here?

MAUD I'm taking offers.

BILLING Take them somewhere else. (*To audience*) You've had your opportunity to gawk, it's what you came for. Now, by order of the Grand High Court of London, pry your filthy eyes off this slut's flesh and scuttle home.

GREIN Now see here!

SYRIAN No one speaks such words of this celestial—

PAGE Fear not, Miss Allan, I'll defend your honour.

SYRIAN I was doing so. You interrupted.

BILLING (*To Maud*) Did you truly think I'd let this pass?

MAUD Perhaps I merely hoped to see you one last time.

PAGE You think YOU can defend her honour?

SYRIAN If you'd let me—

GREIN Mr. Billing—

MAUD That is why you came, is it not?

GREIN Miss Allan—

MAUD To see me.

BILLING I have seen quite enough of you, of late.

MAUD Then look away.

PAGE Get in there. Start defending.

SYRIAN After you.

GREIN Please, everyone, please calm yourselves. We have an audience, a very cultured, dignified, impatient—

BILLING Squirming deviants. A press of orgiasts. That's right, you two, I see you pressing back there. Pervert proletariat.

GREIN Perhaps. But they did pay.

BILLING Then reimburse them. This play—

GREIN Sainted stars! That IS perverse!

BILLING This play is censored. One more word will land you all in prison.

The Syrian and the Page boo and hiss. Billing glares at them.

SYRIAN That wasn't from the play.

MAUD I believe I have a resolution. (*To audience*) Mr. Billing is correct, of course, the Bailey has declared the play of *Salomé* unfit for your discerning ears and eyes.

GREIN No refunds, no exchanges.

MAUD But your patronage is dear to us. And we would not have a gathering disperse unsatisfied. We therefore hope to offer you a drama, slightly modified, but of comparable excitement, stimulation, and release.

BILLING I shudder to imagine what you mean.

MAUD And I shall overlook your fear, Mr. Billing, so long as you can keep your shuddering from escalating. (*She claps her hands*) Ladies and Gentlemen, in lieu of *Salomé* by Oscar Wilde, the Independent Theatre presents a true account of recent scandals, intrigues, and litigious pandemonium in war-torn London.

BILLING You don't mean...?

MAUD All who seek accounts for this grand act of censorship shall be appeased, as we enact the accusations and the trial itself, its every word.

BILLING Oh, for the love of Ben.

MAUD The trial of *Salomé*. Exactly as it was performed before the King's Bench.

GREIN She's astounding!

PAGE What a brain within that head!

SYRIAN And what a pedestal beneath it!

BILLING No.

MAUD You do not wish to see your victory reflected on the stage?

BILLING You'd never show it truthfully.

MAUD Indeed; in fact, I promise to make you look good.

GREIN Ah, Mr. Billing is, of course, most welcome to remain, to verify the facts of the affair.

MAUD And to ensure that he himself is played with dignity.

BILLING And which of these iniquitous grease-painted poofs would play me?

The Page and the Syrian mimics Billing overtop of his line.

PAGE AND SYRIAN

And which of these iniquitous grease-painted...

MAUD You're correct, of course. No mere artiste could recreate your idiosyncratic self. And our account cannot proceed without a Mr. Billing in the wings. He is the prime attraction, after all. Wait! A thought occurs.

SYRIAN Stand back!

PAGE That brain again!

MAUD It's hazy, but I'm quite sure I recall ... yes, you were once yourself an actor, Mr. Billing. Were you not?

BILLING Well—

MAUD Back before you were a demagogue, I mean.

BILLING I s'pose I did—a few times—back at Oxford—

MAUD In your salad days ... when you were green in judgment, and morality?

BILLING I do suspect, Miss Allan, you are preying on my vanity.

MAUD And I suspect that there is much meat there to feed upon.

GREIN (*Claps his hands*) So it's settled! Jolly good!

SYRIAN A rousing re-creation of the trial that shook the nation!

PAGE Starring both the personalities who featured in reality!

BILLING But under MY direction—this must all be—

The actors bustle into new positions.

PAGE As the bullets rain on bodies off in Belgium and in France—

SYRIAN We present the great Maud Allan, the Sultana of the Dance—

PAGE Who had traveled here to act in our salacious interlude—

SYRIAN Until her Salomé was stifled by the scheming of a prude.

BILLING You see? That is precisely the malarkey up with which I will not put—

GREIN (*Running over Billing's line*) Now, where to start? Eh? That's the question.

MAUD Perhaps the moment of conception?

GREIN Yes! Oh, yes!

MAUD Eighteen hundred ninety-two. The fertile mind of Oscar Wilde lights upon a subject for a new play.

PAGE *Salomé!*

GREIN May I play Wilde? I do a splendid Wilde.

BILLING We do not need—

GREIN "Life imitates art, and art returns the favour."

BILLING Drivel. That's enough.

GREIN "It is the spectator, and not life, that art truly mirrors."

BILLING No one needs to see a loathsome pervert writing horrid poetry.

MAUD He's right, Mr. Grein. The scene would scarcely be dramatic.

GREIN But if we added Lord Douglas? Or a strapping young secretary—?

BILLING No. The beast Wilde's play may have begun its wretched life in ninety-two, but this account starts now. Nineteen eighteen. England's darkest hour. (*Claps his hands*) The Great War.

Another scramble, as the next scene is set up.

GREIN That IS dramatic.

MAUD Mr. Billing is a natural.

BILLING (*To the audience*) For four years, England's star has sputtered balefully upon the Vosges and the Ardennes. Attrition and retreat. The Hun's advance, relentless. Their barbaric rage seems poised to overcome the genteel sportsmanship and derring-do of British Tommies.

The Scene: In the trenches, two Tommies approach their commander, General Robertson. Both the soldiers are wounded. Incessant bombing above. Robertson sips tea and listens to a phonograph. Throughout, Billing whispers cues in their ears.

TOMMY 1 General, Sir! Private Biggs reporting from the Front, sir!

TOMMY 2 Private Mills reporting from the Back Front, sir.

ROBERTSON The Back Front?

TOMMY 2 Yessir. Seems the Huns have us surrounded, sir.

ROBERTSON Oh, jolly good.

TOMMY 2 Not ... really, sir.

ROBERTSON I'll be the judge of that. Reports?

TOMMY 1 Our Italian allies have been quashed at Caporetto, sir.

ROBERTSON Well, at least we have the French.

TOMMY 2 The French keep trying to surrender.

ROBERTSON To the Germans?

TOMMY 2 Yessir. Well ... to anyone.

ROBERTSON But, the Russians! Eh? Don't forget old Ivan, Private.

TOMMY 1 Sir. The Russians had their revolution last October. They've been quarreling with one another ever since.

TOMMY 2 I'm losing ... noteworthy amounts of blood, sir.

ROBERTSON Are you implying that we're out of allies?

TOMMY 1 No sir, not quite. The boys from Canada—

ROBERTSON Oh dearie dog. They're just as vulgar as the Huns.

TOMMY 2 A veil of red, across my eyes.

TOMMY 1 If only Britain could be made to see in what grave danger she has placed her children.

TOMMY 2 It is like a scarlet curtain plunged from Heaven.

TOMMY 1 Why does she ignore our cries for aid?

TOMMY 2 It is a purple shroud.

TOMMY 1 Is she both blind and deaf?

TOMMY 2 It is a silken winding sheet.

TOMMY 1 Or is some sinister and traitorous alliance holding back her hand?

ROBERTSON Hold up, hold up. I've got the ticket. What you need's a damn fine cheering up.

TOMMY 2 I hear the angels' wings. Like thunder!

ROBERTSON Patriotic culture. Good old British razzmatazz. Pip pip, eh wot? Make you right as rain. Let's see now...

TOMMY 1 Er ... sir ... it's Mills, he's...

ROBERTSON (*Begins tapping out a telegraph message*) Urgent, Lord Beaverbrook, stop.

TOMMY 1 I think it's more than just morale at stake, sir.

TOMMY 2 Look, there she is! The moon!

ROBERTSON Front line requests immediate assistance, stop. Send British acting troupes and pantomimes, stop.

TOMMY 2 She dances! How she dances!

TOMMY 1 Look away, mate. Look away.

Tommy 2 dies.

ROBERTSON One or two celebrities a bonus, stop. Always been partial to Sarah Bernhardt.

TOMMY 1 Cor, she's lovely.

ROBERTSON Full Stop.

Billing addresses the audience. Upstage, Grein prepares the next scene.

BILLING So our boys are still found, in dark tunnels of the earth. The poison seed of Germany is planted there, and swims across to British shores. The Hunnish spawn flows upward, through the corridors of law and power, and inseminates the inner chambers of our government—

MAUD Mr. Billing. We are not at Speaker's Corner. You lack a soapbox, which would make you tall. And your harangue, I fear to say, is far too illustrative for the theatre.

BILLING Miss Allan, I could never paint a more disclosing picture than the one you shame us with.

MAUD "Disclosing" is ambiguous. There is a chasm of distinction between you "disclosing" and I "dis-clothing." The one is moralizing, and the other, art.

Maud exits. The scene begins, startling Billing.

BEAVERBROOK
That's it! It's art! That's what they need out there! Inspiration! Beauty!

GREIN I am utterly in your accordance!

BILLING Who said we were starting?

BEAVERBROOK
Mister Grein, my dear, dear, Jack.

GREIN Lord Beaverbrook!

BEAVERBROOK
Your nation needs you. Britain craves your art.

GREIN I'm yours entirely!

BILLING (*To audience*) I never witnessed this exchange. It may be fictional. A cock and bull—

SYRIAN I'll fix your cock an' bulls.

BEAVERBROOK
As Minister of Information, I am hereby naming you Ambassador of British Culture. You have thirty days to choose a repertoire of hearty British theatre, and I mean ripping thick and meaty plays, man, really pounding patriotic spectacles. Can you do it?

GREIN I shall rise to the occasion.

BEAVERBROOK
There's a chap.

Across the stage, Billing has coordinated a separate scene, which interrupts the first.

ROBERTSON You've come at last, Herr Bentinck.

BENTINCK *Ja*, I have. General Robertson. *Mein freund.*

ROBERTSON I have the book.

GREIN What is this cloak and dagger tommyrot? This isn't relevant.

BILLING Just wait.

Robertson passes Bentinck a Black Book. He inspects it.

BENTINCK *Ja*, this is bloody *wunderbar.*

ROBERTSON We still need more. The list is not complete.

GREIN But I was, just now, I was in the middle—

BILLING Shush!

GREIN And I was interrupted—

BENTINCK It will be a book of fifty thousand names, *das* men *und* women, English all, but in our power. Servants of the big, blond German Kaiser.

GREIN Somebody! Miss Allan! Make him stop.

ROBERTSON Herr Bentinck, we require more names. But time is short.

BENTINCK We need a way to gather them together. English traitors.

Grein crosses back and his scene resumes. They alternate.

ROBERTSON I believe I have a plan.

GREIN Lord Beaverbrook, my repertoire is done.

BEAVERBROOK
Oh? Jolly good.

BENTINCK *Vas is, das* plan *sie got?*

ROBERTSON Er, yes, the plan...

GREIN I entreat you, ask me what I have selected.

BEAVERBROOK
Yes. Which plays?

ROBERTSON A spectacle. A lecherous display of fleshly ailments.

GREIN One play only, but a priceless pearl it is.

ROBERTSON
Perversion. That's what traitors of this ilk seek out.

GREIN A genius feast of art, and British through and through.

ROBERTSON They'll be there.

GREIN Beauty.

ROBERTSON Every sick, demented, and susceptible-to-blackmail one of them.

GREIN Poetry.

ROBERTSON The book will be complete.

GREIN Sublimity in word and motion.

BENTINCK What monstrous performance are you thinking of?

GREIN The masterpiece of Oscar Wilde—

ROBERTSON AND GREIN
(*In unison*) *Salomé!*

Maud Allan treats this as her cue to re-enter. She has changed into 1918 streetclothes, but she still looks fabulous.

MAUD That was a much more rousing introduction. A vast improvement over "do not look at her."

GREIN The inimitable Miss Maud Allan.

PAGE The Prima Donna of the Canadas.

SYRIAN Dancer to the crowns of Europe. Known from India to Edmonton for her intoxicating–

PAGE Magical–

SYRIAN And potent piece of choreography:

GREIN The Vision of Salomé.

MAUD Another life. When I was young, and scandal was in vogue.

Grein is now addressing his acting troupe. Upstage, Billing prepares the next scene with Spencer and Jane.

GREIN I've courted her from Canada. She was retired.

MAUD Wooed across the ocean with the words of Wilde.

GREIN Her famous dance will happen at the climax of our play. Thus, Oscar's Salomé and Miss Maud Allan's Salomé shall merge, to form–

SYRIAN Quintessent Salomé!

PAGE And that'll liven up the troops?

GREIN I think it will.

MAUD A Salomé so great she shall be spoken of by every mouth, in every ear.

SYRIAN I hear she danced for Persian princes once.

MAUD And la, the thing's they'll say!

PAGE I heard her dancing cured a blind man.

SPENCER Rot!

SYRIAN I heard–

SPENCER Blank poppycock!

SYRIAN I heard she was seen recreating after hours with the Lord Prime Minister.

GREIN It wasn't the Prime Minister.

SYRIAN Oh no?

GREIN It was his wife.

SYRIAN Oh, so!

PAGE Oh my.

MAUD My fellow thespians. I am ecstatic to embark with you upon this great artistic voyage. Our time is short, and we must use it well. I shall, therefore, be in my dressing room, practicing my climax.

She exits. Everyone but Billing stares after her.

SPENCER Pumpernickel! Canterbury! Spatchcock!

BILLING The scene now turns to Fleet Street, where the editors of one small patriotic ... (*Everyone is still staring the other way*) The scene now TURNS ... thank you ... to Fleet Street, where the editors of one small, patriotic newspaper are toiling to deliver truth and root out German insurrection.

SPENCER Ruddy insurrectionists!

BILLING *The Vigilante.* As in vigilant. Chief editor, yours truly, Roger Pemberton-Billing. Facts checker, Captain Harold Spencer, Special Forces.

SPENCER Doctor!

BILLING And on special discharge.

SPENCER Doctor Spencer! Who told ye Captain, eh? Who told ye that?

BILLING March twenty-fifth, 1918.

SPENCER Can't trust 'em, what they say. The ruddy sausage-eaters.

BILLING Captain Spencer—

SPENCER Doctor!

BILLING Very well, then, Doctor. We must keep our focus on the tasks at hand. The afternoon edition is about to print. I have to get to parliament in time for questions. And we lack a leading headline.

SPENCER How 'bout this, then? "Jerry Bosche-Buggerer in Every Bedroom in the British Isles."

BILLING Apart from the alliteration? No.

SPENCER I seen 'em, eh. Teutonic deviants ... in West End flats, erotomanically furnished...

BILLING This is not productive.

SPENCER Bars in Portsmouth ... then they hook 'em in, see, German gigolos, seduce an' sap the stamina of British sailors.

BILLING Actually, that isn't bad. (*Takes a few notes*)

SPENCER Then, in the throes of buggery, they spill their guts. Our plans, our numbers, the positions of our fleets ... and t'ain't just sailors on a bum-lark, neither. Generals, chiefs of staff, ay, members of parliament—

BILLING I am an MP, you know.

SPENCER The WIVES of members of parliament—

BILLING How fortunate that I'm a bachelor.

SPENCER In orgiastic ecstasy the secrets of our State have been betrayed!

BILLING Yes, ripping stuff, old boy, but we need proof.

SPENCER It's in the book, I tell ya. All their names in one perverted book.

BILLING You've seen the legendary Black Book?

SPENCER Who told ya? Who's been on about the book?

BILLING You have, Doctor.

SPENCER Captain!

BILLING Fine, whatever. Look, I have to run. We need a headline. Make yourself lucid and write something down. Can you accomplish that?

SPENCER Pish nappy pederast!

BILLING Yes, truly, this is England's darkest hour.

Jane Smuts enters, passing Billing as he strides offstage.

SPENCER (*Muttering to himself*) Ruddy blight, uranians, prick-pounding blaspheming puberty.

JANE I beg your pardon.

SPENCER Eh?

JANE Was that ... was that HIM?

SPENCER Who wants to know?

JANE Roger Pemberton-Billing? The Prophet?

SPENCER Hey, who's a bonny lass, then?

JANE Why do they call him "The Prophet"? Is it—

SPENCER Captain Harold Spencer, at yer service!

JANE Oh. I, cheers. I need to speak with him most urgently. I have some information—

SPENCER Succotash! Fudge ripple!

JANE Captain Spencer? Are you—

SPENCER Doctor.

JANE Sorry?

SPENCER Doctor Spencer.

JANE I thought you said Captain.

SPENCER Who's been tellin' ye what I been sayin'?

JANE You—well, you did—Doctor—

SPENCER Captain!

JANE Doctor Captain –

SPENCER Harold Spencer, Special Forces, Special Discharge, SIR!

JANE I think I'll leave now.

SPENCER Don't buy all ye hear about me, lass. Or anythin' ye read.

JANE Read—yes, yes, read, I read it in the *Times* this morning!

She hands him a news clipping.

SPENCER "Two private performances of *Salomé*, starring the Canadian Maud Allan, will occur on April ninth and tenth."

JANE I thought he, maybe—I don't know, he seems to print things about scandals. And Miss Allan, with her dance, and all—well, mercy—

SPENCER "Applicants should contact Mister Jack Grein, nineteen Duke Street."

JANE Do you think he likes to print such things? Or is it that he feels compelled? A higher force that urges him to root out vice?

SPENCER Ay, ruddy viceroys.

JANE So perhaps he'll print it?

SPENCER "Maud Allan," "Canadian Maud Allan" ... there's a chime-tingler...

JANE And perhaps then I could meet him?

SPENCER Here's the neat and narrow. This will be our leading article. Miss Marbles, take this down at once!

JANE Sir ... my name is—

SPENCER "To be a witness to Maud Allan's filthy exhibitionism, one must first become a private member."

JANE (*Struggling to write it down*) "To be ... witness..."

SPENCER "If the belly-shakin' scugs at Scotlard Yard had the bullocks to confiscate this list of members, they'd be lookin' at a hefty chunk o' names from out the Huns' Black Book itself!"

JANE I fear I cannot write the word "bullocks," sir.

SPENCER Ay, the Black Book ... Sadists. Maso-kites. Necrophiles. Uranians.

JANE And—sorry, which one is Maud Allan?

SPENCER Sodomites!

JANE My hollyhocks!

SPENCER "Maud Allan" ... damn, but that's a fine thought-knocker of a name.

JANE But can she—that is, I, I did not realize that ladies ... could be ... that.

SPENCER That? What?

JANE That word you said.

SPENCER Thought-knocker?

JANE Sod—som—somdom—

SPENCER Sodomite? Ay, bleedin' willowy, the tonne of 'em. Ye can't right sneeze these days without a pansy passin' ye his silken la-dee-das.

JANE But LADIES. Surely ladies lack the ... apparati to be s—s—

SPENCER Naw, see, the female sodomite is every drop as dirty as the male. They do it differently, is all, they—see, there's one that gets up on 'er—first, and then the lady number two, she's sorta—well, that is—it simply isn't for a lady's ears to know what ladies do.

JANE Amen to that.

SPENCER But in the cause of journalistic accuracy, we must travel that dank path. (*He goes to the telephone*) Doctor Serrel Cooke, please, Ipswich four-nine-one. On a matter of utmost national importance. (*To Jane*) We shall consult a medical professional.

JANE But I thought you were—never mind.

Across the stage, Dr. Cooke answers the phone.

COOKE Doctor Cooke speaking.

BILLING Serrel! This is Harold.

COOKE Harold! How's your down-abouts? Has all the swelling settled down?

BILLING Er, something much more urgent, Doctor. We're in need of expertise upon a circumstance of national security. For the safety and survival of Dear Mother Britain, tell me quickly, Doctor: what do ye call it when two lasses stoke the stove together?

JANE (*Covering her ears*) Grandmother's begonias!

COOKE A question for the ages, Harold. Hippocrates believed it was impossible. But thanks to rational physicians of the day, we have an answer.

BILLING Swimming!

COOKE No, it's rather dry, in fact. It all revolves around a naughty little organ called the cli—

Grein interrupts the scene (*with impeccable timing*).

GREIN Now that will certainly be all we need to hear of that.

Billing comes back on stage. Maud will re-enter also.

BILLING Mr. Grein, my oily friend, do you recall the point of this recital?

GREIN Yes, yes, to tell, of course, what happened, but—

BILLING The truth. In all its grim veracity.

GREIN Our audience is scarcely set to hear such vulgar phrases.

BILLING Vulgar! What about Miss Allan's former costume?

MAUD I am glad you found it so provoking.

BILLING Truth. The social and immoral truths that weaken our defences from within. And yes, disgraceful anatomical truths also. Does anyone believe, beneath your harlot's garb, you harbour only silk and pearls?

MAUD Your comments show your lack of research, Mr. Billing.

GREIN I will simply not have that—that WORD ... with ladies present!

MAUD Oh, permit it, Mr. Grein. It's my belief that ladies who have not yet heard the word—nor probed its implications—are well overdue.

BILLING You still think this is,all just titillation?

MAUD Once again, your anatomical expressions lack precision, sir. (*To Cooke*) I pray, continue with the scene, that everyone—including Mr. Billing—may depart endowed with knowledge.

COOKE Quite. Where was I?

SPENCER "Cli—"

COOKE Right. Cheers, sport.

SPENCER Not at all, mate.

COOKE "—toris."

SPENCER Bonny Prince Charly! What the fadge is a cli-toris?

COOKE No one's really sure. But in the hands of certain female deviants, it's deadly.

JANE (*Still covering her ears*) Fellas and fillies like lilacs and lilies...

COOKE Rumours flourish of a monstrous sub-species of the female whose dexterous manipulations of the cli-toris have made all males redundant.

SPENCER Scotch and succubi!

COOKE My thoughts precisely.

SPENCER Just as ruthless Germans want to make all Brits extraneous. Ay, it fits together perfectly.

JANE It does?

SPENCER (*Hangs up the phone*) Miss Mackerel, here's a headline you can wager ought to make the Huns and perverts soil their lederhosen: are ye ready?

JANE I fear not.

SPENCER Too late! "The Cult of the Clitorites!"

Jane swoons. Billing serves as chorus while the scene hops about quickly.

BILLING And so *The Vigilante's* headline ran, March twenty-sixth.

BOWLER-HATTED BLOKE 1
The Cult of the who?

BILLING Harold Spencer's daring revelation left all London stupefied.

BOWLER-HATTED BLOKE 2
Clitorite? Now isn't that a kind of monk from Devonshire?

BOWLER-HATTED BLOKE 1
A breed of racing horse, I rather think.

BILLING So potent were its words, the article sent shockwaves through the nation—even to our British boys abroad.

In the trenches, a Tommy reads the article to his chums. They all collapse into uproarious laughter.

TOMMY 1 "To be a witness to Maud Allan's filthy exhibitionism, one must first become a private member."

TOMMY 3 Do the Clitorites need members?

TOMMY 1 Sign me up!

BILLING But other, more important parties were not laughing.

General Robertson and Herr Bentinck peruse the article, fighting to restrain their laughter.

ROBERTSON "If the belly-shakin' scugs at Scotlard Yard had the bullocks to confiscate this list of members, they'd be lookin' at a hefty chunk o' names from out the Huns' Black Book itself!"

BILLING Yes, these traitorous fifth columnists found Spencer's words completely serious.

BENTINCK (*Still stifling giggles*) Is serious, *ja*.

ROBERTSON Bloody serious. I'm very sobered by this, Bentinck.

BENTINCK I do not think I've been more humourless in all my life. And I am German!

ROBERTSON Who owns this newspaper, this *Vigilante?*

BENTINCK A man named Roger Pemberton-Billing.

ROBERTSON Ah yes, the Prophet. Is he on the list?

Bentinck consults the Black Book.

BENTINCK *Nein,* he's clean like kindergarten.

ROBERTSON Then he is a threat. This Clitorite claptrap is too close to the truth. He must be silenced. (*Bentinck hauls a German pistol out of his trenchcoat.*) Not like that, Bentinck. This is the twentieth century, man! Assassination is *outré*. The modern skullduggery is blackmail.

BENTINCK *Ja, ja, das blachenmail.* So tell me. Billing, what are his Achilles' heelses?

ROBERTSON Well, he's rather young. Impetuous. And he's a bachelor.

BENTINCK You mean a *jiggen-mit-den-fraülein-herr?* Why did you not say so? (*Claps his hands. Eileen saunters into the spotlight.*) I have just the man for the job.

Scene change: Maud Allan enters, surrounded by a gaggle of production assistants. Grein tries to get her attention, a copy of the Vigilante *in his hand.*

MAUD Vexatious. Reprehensible. Intolerable. Ah, Mr. Grein, I hope your day is passing more agreeably than mine.

GREIN Er, not exactly, Miss Allan—

MAUD These costumes are caricatures. They invite lampooning. What are these supposed to be, exactly? Tails? Shall I be playing Salomé, or some Darwinian reject? Send it back.

GREIN Miss Allan—

MAUD And those sandals! Tell me now, however did you get two ploughman's lunches on such tiny little plates? Appearances are everything, my dears. It is only shallow people who do not judge by appearances.

GREIN Well put.

PAGE She has the most intoxicating taste.

SYRIAN For a colonial, no less.

MAUD If our performance is to be the quintessential *Salomé,* then each detail, each pearl and stream and sequin must contribute to the myth. Our aim is to be whispered of in admiration in one hundred years.

GREIN Indeed, a hundred. Two!

SYRIAN I would have thought, as a Canadian, she would be most content in beaver furs, or bear skins.

MAUD Truly, all transcendent garments have an element of bare skin.

GREIN Ha ha! Very clever. But Miss Allan—

MAUD Now THIS outfit is TOO good. The hundred years of whispering must fixate on my face.

PAGE She has the most intoxicating face.

SYRIAN The face that launched a thousand lawsuits.

PAGE Now, don't get ahead of things.

GREIN Miss Allan, there is something in this tabloid that concerns us both.

MAUD Does it refer to me by name?

GREIN I fear it does.

MAUD Delightful. Let me know when every other rag in London does the same.

GREIN But you must read—or rather, I could summarize—oh dear—

PROPSMASTER
Your head, Miss Allan.

The Propsmaster lifts the lid from a silver charger, revealing the head of John the Baptist. Maud takes it.

MAUD Ah, Iokanaan. John the Baptist. How thy hair entwines about thy head. Thy hair is like clusters of grapes, like the clusters of black grapes that hang from the vine-trees of Edom. The long, black nights, when the moon hides her face, when the stars are afraid, are not so black as thy hair. And thy mouth! Thy mouth is like a pomegranate cut in twain with a knife of ivory. Redder than vermillion, redder than the feet of those who tread the wine-press, redder than the feet of him who cometh from a forest where he hath slain a mighty lion. There is nothing in the world so red as thy mouth. Ah, Iokanaan, Iokanaan, thou wert the man that I loved alone among men! All other men were hateful to me. But thou wert beautiful!

Applause.

GREIN Sheer poetry!

SYRIAN She is a diamond among dirt!

PAGE A narcissus trembling in the wind!

MAUD (*Handing the head back to the Propsmaster*) Be sure to moisten his lips with jelly—just a dab—for when I kiss him.

GREIN That was marvelous, Miss Allan. Surely yours will be the finest Salomé to ever tread the boards. That is, if we are not undone by scandal first.

He finally gets her to read the Vigilante *article.*

MAUD "The Cult of the—" My word. I have a sudden urge to swoon.

She passes the article to Page, who reads (*while she threatens to swoon*).

PAGE "To be a witness to Maud Allan's filthy exhibitionism..."

SYRIAN Slanders! Sullies! Slurs!

GREIN That part might actually boost ticket sales.

SYRIAN "Belly-shaking scugs ... the bullocks ..."

GREIN Yes, you see. It gets worse.

SYRIAN " ... hefty chunk of names from out the Huns' Black Book itself!"

GREIN And more cryptic.

PAGE Defamations! Calumny!

SYRIAN Unbearable vituperations!

GREIN Less than two weeks till we open.

PAGE Who dares write such lies about our tender moonbeam?

SYRIAN I shall call them to accounts immediately!

PAGE I was going to say that.

MAUD I must go.

GREIN What? Where?

MAUD To Canada. Or anywhere. Away.

GREIN You mustn't go! The play—

PAGE Fear not, Miss Allan. I shall find the scoundrel—

SYRIAN What he means is, *I* shall find—

PAGE You had your chance!

SYRIAN —And knock him into paste!

MAUD I cannot stay. The scent of scandal is perfume in moderation, but an excess can be cloying.

GREIN But the play—Lord Beaverbrook, Ambassador of British Culture—my entire future—

MAUD Find another Salomé.

GREIN Impossible! There IS no other Salomé.

PAGE I have the right to defend Miss Allan's honour.

SYRIAN I think not.

PAGE Let's have it then.

Page and Syrian politely engage in fisticuffs. Maud tries to escape the stage, but Grein keeps blocking her exits.

GREIN It's really not so bad, I mean, scandal is just gossip made tedious by morality, and tedium is simply nature's way of making truly brilliant moments stand apart, and if you leave, the tour shall be revoked, and what the devil do they mean by this, I mean it's rubbish, anyone can see, "The Cult of the—"

MAUD Mr. Grein. I opted not to swoon the last time. Do not force the issue.

GREIN Please. I'm begging you. There must be something I can do to make this right.

Maud goes over to Page and Syrian and gently stops them.

MAUD These fellows have an inkling, sir. But in an age of bellicose solutions, we of the aesthetic bent must find less violent means of compensation.

GREIN You don't mean...?

MAUD Fisticuffs are *outré*. The modern form of chivalry is...

Quick cut to a new scene: Billing and Spencer, reading a notice.

BILLING " ... Immediate legal action." Bloody hell. They're going to sue us.

SPENCER Ruddy suzerains!

BILLING This is all your fault, you know. I'd *rather* you'd called her a tart and left it at that—

SPENCER Bilgewater! Trollop!

BILLING Now she's got the home field. The onus is upon us—

SPENCER Ruddy onanists!

BILLING Will you cease your maniac ejaculations for five minutes? We must think!

SPENCER Mouldy fig.

BILLING If we could prove your daft-wit allegations, we'd be fine. But Miss Maud Allan does not belong to any cult. You made it up.

SPENCER She's one of 'em! I know. There's something in her past, I just can't place it.

BILLING Well, until you place it, we are facing infamy, derision, and high legal costs. If we're not careful, they can shut us down.

SPENCER Ruddy shuttlecocks.

BILLING But till that happens, god forbid, we've still got something that she doesn't.

SPENCER Bullocks!

BILLING No, the printing press.

SPENCER Ahhh. In fer a penny...

BILLING We shall rake her systematically through every shade of muck. Before the courts can settle in her favour, we shall make the public come to loathe Maud Allan and the Independent Theatre.

SPENCER And that means...

Another quick cut, back to Grein and Maud Allan. Grein reads off a telegraph.

GREIN "Mr. Grein, your services as the Ambassador of British Culture are no longer needed, stop. There shall be no theatrical tour to the continent, stop. In fact, we never even spoke of such a project, stop. You may therefore, with all due respect, and at your earliest convenience ... stop."

MAUD Never. Do not heed them, Mr. Grein. The show, she must go on.

GREIN I thought you wanted to return to Canada.

MAUD That was a ploy to goad you into action.

GREIN Oh.

MAUD You don't know women very well, do you, Mr. Grein?

GREIN Does anyone?

MAUD Women defend themselves by attacking, just as they attack by sudden, strange surrenders.

GREIN We cannot afford to mount the play, not now. Without the sponsorship—

MAUD We have another benefactor. Mr. Billing will supply us with the backing.

GREIN Mr. Billing would rather sing on our graves, I think.

MAUD His tune will change. For once we win the lawsuit—

GREIN You seem very sure of victory. If you knew Mr. Billing—

MAUD Well, perhaps it's time I did.

Scene change: Page and Syrian serve as chorus.

PAGE Their first meeting!

MAUD Roger Pemberton-Billing.

SYRIAN On the front steps of the Parliament.

MAUD The Prophet, I believe they call you?

BILLING Guilty as charged.

MAUD Because you utter dire portents in the House of Commons?

BILLING Actually, I got the sobriquet at Oxford. I had a talent for predicting the flight patterns of young ladies.

MAUD You are a bird enthusiast!

BILLING When given time.

MAUD And what can you deduce of my activities?

BILLING You have migrated here from far away. Your plumage still carries the lustre of youth, but your wings have the guidance of age. And you may, perhaps, be seeking for a spot to make your nest?

MAUD You are astute, sir. But a songbird seldom settles quietly.

BILLING You are a singer?

MAUD Not exactly.

BILLING Then, an actress?

MAUD Only recently. My passion is the dance.

Beat.

BILLING Miss Allan.

MAUD I could not wait to meet the man whose moralistic sideshows threaten to upstage my comeback.

BILLING Your career is more important than morality? You have a sick view of the world.

MAUD Unlike your view of merely moments past?

BILLING Forgive my eyes, if they mistook you for an honest woman.

MAUD But a woman's virtue is forever being written by the eyes of men. In that regard, you are all prophets, of the self-fulfilling sort.

BILLING I don't have time for this.

MAUD Your readers have the time.

BILLING I have another job.

MAUD If you keep me from doing mine, I'll do the same to you.

BILLING There is a war on, if you hadn't noticed! British boys are dying while you gyrate on the stage.

MAUD And it offends you more that I can dance, than that they die?

BILLING Not so. They are the same offense.

MAUD Are you accusing me of—

BILLING When we meet tomorrow, at the arraignment, you will hear my accusations in full fusillade.

MAUD Perhaps your hormones have confused you. I am not the one on trial.

BILLING No? We shall see.

MAUD Until tomorrow, then, when one of us shall meet his match.

BILLING Until tomorrow.

Maud exits. Opposite, Eileen enters, unseen by Billing.

And before which time, it seems I must invent some accusations.

EILEEN Roger Pemberton-Billing.

BILLING Hello, yes?

EILEEN You are the man they call the Prophet?

BILLING Guilty as—I mean, well, yes.

EILEEN You must come with me at once.

BILLING Who are you? Have I printed anything unsavoury about you?

EILEEN My name is Eileen Villiers-Stuart. I am a loyalist, like you. And I have information.

BILLING Of what sort?

EILEEN Pertaining to the Black Book.

BILLING Moses on toast!

EILEEN Hush! Come this way!

They criss-cross the stage as they talk.

BILLING D'you mean the Huns' Black Book? The list of British backsliders? I thought it was just one of Spencer's loony tunes.

EILEEN I assure you, it is real.

BILLING But then, perhaps the rest is true as well. Perhaps there is a cult.

EILEEN (*Stopping them, turning to Billing, close*) A cult of Clitorites? You're closer than you know.

BILLING Um ... close to where, exactly?

Behind them, Bowler-hatted Blokes circulate, surreptitiously goosing and fondling each other.

EILEEN This is where they congregate.

BILLING Where who...?

EILEEN Degenerates. Uranians. Nymphomaniacs. They're all the same. No moral fibre whatsoever, they would sell their country to the Germans for a ding-dong in the park.

BILLING It truly buggers—I mean beggars—the imagination.

EILEEN Get closer. Don't be shy.

As Billing inches towards the Blokes, a Spy pops up from another bush with a camera at the ready. Eileen sees him, and approves.

BILLING I must confess, I've always been a little curious—but no. I must resist.

EILEEN Oh no, you mustn't.

BILLING It is not for Christian eyes to see.

EILEEN Then get up close and listen.

BILLING Mrs. Villiers-Stuart—

EILEEN Miss.

BILLING I thank you for your patriotic zeal. But I must go.

EILEEN So soon? But surely—

BILLING Something in this place has got me rather buggered—BOTHERED.

Since the Spy hasn't got his photo, Eileen tries something different.

EILEEN But Mr. Billing, you are such a hero to me. Being here, this close to you, I scarcely can restrain myself.

BILLING Steady on, then.

EILEEN I believe that decent people like ourselves should be permitted peccadilloes now and then.

BILLING Oh, peccadilloes, yes? With marmalade?

EILEEN For saving Britain from the Germans is a long, hard task. And getting harder. Wouldn't you agree?

BILLING Miss—Miss Allan—I mean, Mrs. Villiers-Stuart—I mean, Miss, I mean—what, exactly, do you want from me?

EILEEN I want to roger, Roger.

They are nearly intertwined—and the Spy is about to snap a photo—but Billing hurls himself away.

BILLING I must resist. You are a most agreeable companion, but I have a task. There is a war. It must be won. And wars are won with tanks and things, and tanks wear armour, and they never take it off. Not even for a quickie.

EILEEN Mr. Billing, I was wrong about you.

BILLING Not at all. I'm still a man, inside my tank, you know.

EILEEN But other men are easily entrapped. You have the strength of your convictions.

BILLING Yes. God damn them.

EILEEN Mr. Billing, I believe I am in love with you. Hear me out. I came upon assignment, the fifth columnists decided you were dangerous. But now I am convinced that you alone can save this country from destruction.

BILLING This so rarely happens to me.

EILEEN How may I assist you, Roger? Besides—yes, besides that.

BILLING Right now, the welfare of the man you see before you—and, by extension, as you say, this country's ongoing existence, and all that—depends upon the outcome of a single, perilous event.

SYRIAN The trial of SALOMÉ!

PAGE Day One: The arraignment!

MAUD Wait one moment, if you please. Before proceeding, there is one more salient event—

BILLING More *prima donna* antics?

MAUD No, it does not feature you, sir.

GREIN But that was such a lovely segue into the arraignment. Maybe we should—

MAUD Mr. Grein, the second act will have a surplus of judiciary scenes. Ere we retire to the courtroom, I should like to linger briefly in the bedroom.

GREIN Oh my.

BILLING Typical.

MAUD The night before the arraignment, Maud Allan received a visitation from the ghost of Oscar Wilde.

BILLING Oh, for crinoline.

GREIN Oh! Oh! Oh! May I be Wilde? I do a splendid—

MAUD (*Nodding assent to Grein, who quickly changes*) It befell as follows. The encounter with my nemesis had left me nervous and distracted. Sleep was not forthcoming, so I indulged that fickle mistress with a laudanum nightcap. Shortly afterward, the room began to rotate like a dervish, and the floral decoration on the walls began to leer with demon faces. I was once more greeted with the impetus to swoon. "Either this wallpaper goes, or I do!"

She falls, but Oscar Wilde catches her. They begin to dance.

OSCAR It takes a thoroughly good woman to do a thoroughly foolish thing.

MAUD Am I good, Oscar? Mr. Billing says I am a threat to purity.

OSCAR Men who are trying to do something for the world are always insufferable.

MAUD But I'm so sick of men who love me. The ones who hate me are—

OSCAR AND MAUD

So much more charming.

OSCAR My warning to you, Maud. I was destroyed by a most charming man.

MAUD Alfred Lord Douglas.

They step back and watch, as the romance of Young Oscar and Bosie is re-enacted downstage. Across the stage, Queensbury and his buddies look on disapprovingly.

OSCAR Bosie. How they talked of us. It is so monstrous, how people go about, these days, saying things behind one's back that are absolutely and entirely true.

MAUD I share your pain.

OSCAR My pain had but begun. For Bosie had a father—the Marquess of Queensbury.

QUEENSBURY Disgraceful.

OSCAR He could not abide to see his son seduced by such a handsome devil. I mean me.

QUEENSBURY There are no words to describe that—that—that—

QUEENSBUDDY 1
Beast.

QUEENSBUDDY 2
That buggerer.

QUEENSBUDDY 1
That sodomite.

QUEENSBURY Oh, that's a good one. (*Writing on a calling card*) "To Oscar Wilde, posing as a sod—som—somdom—"

QUEENSBUDDY 1
Sodomite, you ruddy twit.

QUEENSBURY Close enough.

He sends the calling card to Oscar. The players reconfigure into a trial.

OSCAR The Marquess had slipped up, or so I thought. With the pejorative in his own hand, I struck back confidently in the courts of law. I sued the father of my love for libel, and I thought, with Bosie by my side, we could not fail.

MAUD What happened, then?

OSCAR Betrayal. Tables turned. My libel charge was twisted round in court, until it was apparent that I was the one on trial. My darkest secrets, flushed out into light. My private life, grist for the public mill. I was found guilty of indecency. I was imprisoned. Bosie never spoke to me again. I was alone.

MAUD But I have always been alone. Well, nearly always ... certainly, since...

OSCAR Maud. My ill-considered legal action led me down the path of misery and shame. I died a broken man, my foes triumphant.

MAUD But your astounding works of genius shall outlast your suffering a hundred years. Nay, two! Does that not make it all worthwhile?

OSCAR Actually ... it does, now that you mention it. I thank you, Maud, from one aesthete to another. You have set me straight.

MAUD Well—

OSCAR Well, not literally straight.

They laugh. Oscar retreats into the ether.

BILLING Well that was useless.

GREIN But ART is useless. That is what we're trying to tell you. "All art is quite useless."

BILLING And you've proved your point a thousand different ways. And I applaud you.

MAUD More than just applaud. You're one of us now. You are a part of the art.

BILLING And therefore useless, I suppose?

MAUD Yes. But, at the least, you are no longer vulgar. Shall we move along?

SYRIAN The trial of SALOMÉ!

PAGE Day One: The arraignment!

Maud, Grein, Page and Syrian at one side of the stage; Billing, Spencer, Eileen, and Jane at the other.

BILLING Quickly, now. Miss Villiers-Stuart, you must summon the attention of the Press. I doubt it will be difficult.

JANE Mr. Billing—

BILLING Spencer, you forgot the law books at the office. Run and fetch them.

SPENCER You've no time to read them.

BILLING Doesn't matter. At this point, I shall content myself with the appearance of knowledge. Now go.

JANE Mr. Billing, my name is—

BILLING Ah, the Jezebel herself.

MAUD That is a separate Bible story, Mr. Billing.

BILLING Both are fallen women in need of repentance.

MAUD Repentance is quite out of date.

JANE Mr. Billing, if you please—

MAUD Besides, if a sincerely penitent young lady is to be believed, she must go to a bad dressmaker. Would you wish such horrors on me, sir?

BILLING What I would wish on you, my dear Delilah— (*Eileen has re-entered with a Newsman*) is a life of calm reflection and serenity.

An offstage voice calls out (*as Spencer returns with a stack of books*)*:*

VOICE Oyez, oyez. Civil court of London, the Honourable Mr. Justice Darling presiding.

BILLING Oh, blooming socks, not Darling.

DARLING This is a preliminary hearing in the case of Miss Maud Allan and the Independent Theatre versus *The Vigilante* newspaper.

SPENCER Jabbernowl! Where have I heard Maud Allan's name before?

DARLING Where are the accusers?

GREIN Here, my lord.

DARLING And the defendant?

EILEEN Here he is! The brightest star of Britain's long, dark night!

SPENCER Maud Allan ... Canada ... Maud Allan...

BILLING My lord, as you no doubt are cognizant, I have, on past occasions, made disparaging remarks about your conduct and, indeed, your competence, as judge. And since the news of my complaints has already reached your ears, you cannot but be prejudiced against me in this case ... unless, of course, the news had NOT reached you ... until this moment, which I see from your expression is the case. How regrettable.

DARLING You penned this article about Miss Allan, sir?

BILLING Not I. My facts checker, Captain Spencer.

DARLING But you own the newspaper.

BILLING Correct. But I was out to lunch.

DARLING And you entrust the content of your paper to this Spencer fellow?

BILLING Yes, of course. I mean, he is a thumping patriot. He fought for Britain in the Boer War.

SPENCER Allan! Yes! Beefeating bastardy! Of course!

He throws the stack of books onto the floor and starts combing through them, muttering to himself.

BILLING Took a bit of shrapnel to the head, mind you...

Billing urges Eileen to try to calm Spencer down while Darling talks.

DARLING Mr. Billing, I sincerely hope you understand the gravity of your predicament. You are answerable within this court to up to three counts of libel. I mean defamatory libel, for impugning Miss Maud Allan's reputation and affiliates.

BILLING (*Distracted*) Yes.

DARLING Then provocatory libel, which is print that may incite a public outrage or disturbance of the peace.

BILLING (*Distracted*) Yes, yes.

DARLING And finally, licentious libel, for when one publishes material which may corrupt the pure and innocent at heart.

BILLING "Corrupt the pure"—I'm not the one corrupting, here.

MAUD They are your words, Mr. Billing.

DARLING Of course, licentious libel is a criminal offense.

BILLING Is it indeed? Oh my. And what would be the average sentence ... if one were to be convicted ... of that ... thing?

DARLING Imprisonment for up to nine years.

BILLING Nine...

DARLING How do you plead, Mr. Billing?

JANE Nine years! Merciful lady's slipper!

She faints. Billing catches her.

MAUD Some ladies lack the art of swooning.

EILEEN Who the hell is this, who's so upset about you getting your two-timing arse locked up, and may they throw away the key, to boot!

MAUD My lord, it seems that Mr. Billing's grip on the proceedings is unstable. May we skip his brutish cross-examinations and receive the sentencing instead?

DARLING My dear, you are a spring of reason in a desert of—

SPENCER I've got it! Allan! William Henry Allan! I'm a ruddy crackerjack, I am!

Billing takes the book that Spencer was looking at, while Spencer does a ridiculous victory dance.

DARLING Sir, you are out of order.

MAUD (*To Grein*) Jack, I want to go.

SPENCER Who's a ruddy genius? Spencer is! Spencer!

DARLING That will do, sir! Someone please eject this lunatic from—

BILLING Miss Maud Allan. Well, well, well.

MAUD My lord, I'd like to drop the charges, please. This instant.

DARLING But you just said—

MAUD I cannot abide a scandal in my life, my lord.

BILLING She means ANOTHER scandal. Captain Spencer has directed my attention to a chapter in *Amazing Criminal Cases of Canada*. You are Canadian, Miss Allan?

MAUD Yes. But—

BILLING And your brother, William Henry Allan, he was a Canadian as well?

DARLING I fail to see how that is relevant.

BILLING (*Hands the book to the judge*) William Henry Allan, convicted, executed, 1898, upon the charge of murdering two girls.

SPENCER Ay, bonny schoolgirls. Studying to take the veil.

DARLING (*Reading*) And outraging their bodies after death!

MAUD Bravo. You have succeeded in exposing to the world the single scar I bear which will not heal.

BILLING Oh yes, a terrible ordeal, no doubt, to learn one's brother was a sadist and a necrophile. But your distress does not concern us here, today.

DARLING Then what, exactly, does?

GREIN Yes, what has this to do with anything? The libel, or the article?

DARLING "The Cult of the..."

BILLING Permit me, and I'll tell you. Yes I will. I'll tell you that Maud Allan and her brother are two perverted peas in one pernicious pod. That, like her brother, she is drawn to deeds of an impious tenor—not only the lewd dance that made her famous, but the deeds of a true Salomé. Sadism. Exhibitionism. Homosexualism.

GREIN Do you mind, sir?

BILLING I do, indeed, because whereas in private, Miss Maud Allan may commit whatever sins she fancies—

GREIN Yes, and, private—these are PRIVATE PERFORMANCES—

BILLING But in truth, her odious activities affect us all. Justice Darling, you were fishing for a plea? I'll give you one: justification. I will demonstrate, within a court of law, that Maud Allan is the apex and epitome of all that is profane and treacherous in England's frightened heart. And, yes, "The Cult of the ... Clitorites." That too.

A spot on Maud Allan. She addresses the audience.

MAUD It was just as Oscar had predicted. He had turned the trial around, and trapped me here, in court. Surrounded by men in a man's world. Why am I even here? This war is not my war, this play is scarcely even mine. I am a dancer. What can a dancer do to defend herself within a court of law? There is but one thing only: that which she has done a thousand times, in every corner of the world. That which she's born to do: entice the ears and eyes of men. And yes, when necessary, other vulnerable parts of their anatomies.

These men are desperate, furious, afraid. Their blood is hot. And sitting there, and smelling it—the blood of Englishmen—I saw the truth of things. I am not trapped in here with these men. Not a whit. I am Maud Allan, the Salomé Dancer. THEY are trapped in here with ME.

End of Act One

Act Two

The act begins with a tight, sultry spot on Maud Allan.

MAUD The Vision of Salomé. It begins with the smallest of gestures: a flutter of lashes, like two midnight moths; or else a slight curl at the corner of the mouth, like the tail of a cat preparing to pounce. Or just a breath, but one that makes the bosom swell, and summons up a rustling of pearls as they arrange themselves beneath the seven veils.

The music begins. Persian strings, a clap of small brass cymbals, and then an oboe, waving like a wounded snake. The drums are heavy, distant thunder drawing nearer. You can see the electricity that pulses underneath the skin. It makes the fingers hum like strings upon a harp. The mouth, still poised to pounce.

And then a step. A firm and unexpected thrusting of the hips, and everything is energy at last. And how the movement of the hips is amplified and echoed by the veils! And how the limelight seems to penetrate their gauzy shield. How the belly sways and beckons—you can see the diamond cluster in the navel, winking, casting glittering come-hither glances through the room.

And then the veils begin to fall. The first: lush verdigris, a delicate and patient hand directs it from its bed of pearls and lets it sigh onto the floor. The second: marvelous vermillion, this, the veil that hides that sculpted neck, you watch as it appears and starts to sway, acquiring a secret rhythm that the hips had not detected. And it is this, this secret rhythm, that controls you, guides your eyes from veil to veil and you are helpless in the dance's thrall.

Then veil the third: the shoulders rise like twin moons. Veil the fourth: that wide, bronze valley of the flesh, where pearls and gazes nestle down to sleep in opiated trances—but the rhythm will not let you sleep. It pounds, it thrusts and bucks and surges, and the hand that plucks the fifth veil seems to tremble slightly, as if frightened of the coming culmination. Veil the sixth: a sullen turquoise, sad to be drawn from the glistening skin.

A dervish, now. The sandals spin around the veil-stained stage. The body turns so quickly now, that all you see are colours, pearls and flesh, and all you hear are drums and breath, and all rhythm, tugging, forward from your seats, you yearn to see the final veil erupt, you NEED that ending. You need something—you need

The spot has widened enough to reveal Billing, standing close, taking notes.

Do you mind, Mr. Billing?

BILLING On the contrary. I have recorded every sinful, sordid moment of your monologue, enumerating the profanities, the symptoms of degeneracy, and so forth. In combination with your contributions from the first act, you now have ... three hundred fifty-six blasphemies to your name. Congratulations, Miss Allan. You now comprise your very own black book.

MAUD Splendid! When I pass away, I pray you, publish it.

She breezes away, as the lights come up to full and the stage fills.

Maud Allen, the Salomé dancer (Leslie Caffaro), dances the Dance of the Seven Veils for the courtroom in Scott Sharplin's The Trial of Salomé, *July 2007. Photo: C.W. Hill Photography for Walterdale Theatre Associates.*

SYRIAN The trial of SALOMÉ!

PAGE Day Two. The trial begins!

SYRIAN *The London Times* declares:

BOWLER-HATTED BLOKE 3
"Passchendaele Lines Lost! Fighting Retreat of Allies. News From France Never Grimmer."

DARLING No mention of the trial, what what?

BOWLER-HATTED BLOKE 3
Don't see it, mate.

DARLING Hm. Pity.

BILLING Ladies and gentlemen, the foreigner Maud Allan has accused me and my publication of attacking her with words of slanderous libel. She says that I implied she was a lewd, unchaste, immoral woman; one who gives private performances of prohibited plays, designed to foster and encourage obscene, unnatural practices in men and women. And she is right—correct in all details but one. My accusations are not of a slanderous nature—because, my lord, they are completely true.

DARLING You shall have to prove that.

BILLING I intend to. For my first witness, I call Mister Jack Grein, producer of the Independent Theatre.

GREIN My stars and garters!

MAUD Courage, Jack. For me.

GREIN For you, my flower.

DARLING Mister Grein, if you will take the stage—er, stand.

BILLING Jack Thomas Grein. Are you an Englishman?

GREIN I am.

BILLING Of British origin?

GREIN Of Dutch.

BILLING You founded several theatres in London, did you not? Including, I believe, the German Theatre.

GREIN Before the war.

BILLING Of course. And now you are producing *Salomé* by Oscar Wilde.

GREIN I am indeed.

BILLING By Wilde, the pervert.

PAGE I object.

BILLING But Wilde was a convicted sodomite. His perversion is a matter of law.

GREIN I never had the privilege of meeting Mister Wilde, or seeing him in action, as it were.

BILLING But now you are familiar with his writing, are you not? Describe his play.

GREIN It is a masterpiece.

BILLING Of perversion?

SYRIAN I object!

GREIN I have never found it perverse, myself.

BILLING Are you aware that *Salomé* has been forbidden by the British Censor?

GREIN Not for perversion. It contains Biblical scenes, which are forbidden on the public stage.

SYRIAN Hence Mister Grein's decision to hold PRIVATE spectacles.

GREIN Indeed.

BILLING On page twenty-seven, Salomé says, "I desire thy mouth, Iokanaan. It is redder than a pomegranate cut with an ivory knife."

GREIN Ah, beautiful.

BILLING How old is Salomé?

GREIN She is a child, awakening to womanhood.

BILLING And this desire for John the Baptist's mouth, does not read like an awakening of lust?

SYRIAN Oh, I object.

PAGE No, no, it's my turn.

GREIN It is but the spring song of the soul. It is a spiritual lust.

BILLING And when she dances for the head of John the Baptist? When she dances to appease the lust of Herod? Is that spiritual?

GREIN That's more an act of spite.

BILLING I thought you said her soul was waking up.

MAUD In women, the awakening of spirit goes often hand in hand with spite.

DARLING I see where this is headed, Mister Billing. You wish to demonstrate that this play, *Salomé,* is unacceptable. Well, I have read the play, and I confess I found it much to my distaste, for there is no representment of a calm domestic life. Nobody slaps anybody else on the back all through the play. And there is not a single reference to roast beef from one end of the dialogue to the other.

GREIN Roast ... beef?

DARLING And though there are some passing references to Christianity, there are no muscular Christians, as it were. The fact is, if the court will permit a judge his own opinion, I found it tedious beyond all reason.

MAUD Oh, but my Lord, there is a vast divide between the reading of a thing, and its enactment.

BILLING There she has my point exactly. We must all of us engage with our imaginings to bring this scandal out into the light.

GREIN But it is poetry.

BILLING Page seventy-eight. "A huge black arm comes forth, bearing on a silver shield the head of Iokanaan." Salomé speaks. "Ah! Thou wouldst not suffer me to—"

DARLING Let her read.

BILLING I beg your pardon?

DARLING Let Miss Allan read. That we may better picture it.

BILLING Ah. Quite. Miss Allan, if you please?

MAUD "Ah! Thou wouldst not suffer me to kiss thy mouth, Iokanaan. Well, I will kiss it now. I will bite it with my teeth as one bites a ripe fruit."

BILLING That's fine. Now, Mister Grein, do you know what a sadist is?

GREIN I do not believe so.

BILLING It refers, sir, to the vice as revealed here, in the text of *Salomé*, the lust of a child for the part of a dead body.

PAGE I object to such outrageous—

BILLING It refers—

SYRIAN And in the presence of a lady!

BILLING It refers to one who would derive arousal from the biting of a dead man's lip.

PAGE My Lord, please stop him! He will make Miss Allan swoon!

BILLING Can you deny, Jack Grein, that this play panders to the vicious lusts of moral perverts? That Salomé is not an innocent, but a sadistic necrophile?

GREIN It's poetry, I tell you. It can do no harm.

BILLING Oh, then it is to England's benefit that we receive such spectacles in wartime?

GREIN War and art have no relation whatsoever.

BILLING Does this play assist us to resolve the tribulations which all Britons face today?

GREIN It helps us to find solace in beautiful language.

BILLING Solace? To the families of the three million men in France?

GREIN (*Dissolving into tears*) "True art is neither moral nor immoral" ... and, and "all art is quite useless" ... and "vice and virtue ... materials ... in equal measure..."

MAUD My lord? Perhaps a recess?

DARLING Hmm? Oh yes. Adjourned. And very fine, Miss Allan. Your delivery, I mean.

The trial breaks apart. Maud and Billing breeze past each other.

BILLING Your delivery will not sustain you long, in court.

MAUD All the world's my stage, Mr. Billing, for as long as men have eyes and ears.

She exits. Billing is left alone onstage.

BILLING Damn and blast her eyes and ears. And Shakespeare! The audacity—a Canadian quotes Shakespeare. But she's right, by Isaac. I played every card exactly right back there, and still the judge's eyes were stuck to her like glue. There must be something. (*As he rants, Jane Smuts enters behind him. She tries to speak.*) Make her say the wrong thing, that's the job! And then he'll see the demon underneath the damsel. But I tried already—threw her dead, demented brother in her face, and did she even blanch? Well, yes, a bit of blanch, but not enough. It's bloody odd. Most women turn to jelly when I'm in the room. Can barely form a sentence. But now I'm faced with this, this wretched WHORE— (*He turns and sees Jane, mouth open.*) Oh! Uh ... I ABHOR Maud Allan. Was my meaning.

JANE It's all right, sir. One can say "whore." It's in the Bible.

BILLING Is it?

JANE Yes. The Whore of Babylon. (*She happens to step forward with her hand out at that moment.*) Oh! Not me, of course. She's the Whore. I'm merely—

BILLING Quite.

JANE Jane Smuts. A most devoted fan of yours.

BILLING You are the swooner from the other day.

JANE And also, she who brought the article about Miss Allan to your office.

BILLING So I've you to thank for all this ... business.

JANE Yes. She truly is the Whore of Babylon, you know. It's no exaggeration.

BILLING Quite. Well, thanks for popping by, and all.

JANE I think her coming is a sign, don't you?

BILLING (*Pacing again. To himself*) If I could call somebody to the stand. Someone to really shake her up.

JANE It's like this war.

BILLING The war, yes. Good idea.

JANE Everything's been written. And foreseen.

BILLING A more political approach would catch her napping. Find the moral ground.

JANE You've seen them, haven't you? The Signs of the Apocalypse? My church says that you've seen them.

BILLING No, the best approach is still the medical. It makes her seem unclean.

JANE The Second Christ is nigh. But if He is to rise again, He first requires a vessel, Mr. Billing.

BILLING Sorry, who requires what again?

JANE The Christ. He urgently desires to be born.

BILLING Which church did you say...?

JANE We are called the Sisters of the Unsubstantiated Assumption. We believe the Christ will come to us in flesh, born unto a Prophet and a Virgin.

BILLING Heh. A Prophet, eh?

JANE OH YES.

BILLING And ... a virgin?

JANE Yes, Mr. Billing.

Pause.

BILLING All right, fun is fun. Where are they?

JANE Where are what?

BILLING The photo men. Jig's up, laddies. Come on out, now.

JANE This is not a joke.

BILLING A frame-up, then. In moments, you'll be crawling all over me—

JANE Heavens to bluebells! Well, I didn't mean to rush things, but—

BILLING And then it's flashbulbs and blackmail all the way to Germany.

JANE No, Mr. Billing. This is not a trick. The Sisters have selected you. You are to be the sire of the new Christ.

BILLING This is simply too absurd to be a ruse.

JANE The congress must be soon. And if your trial goes poorly, you may face imprisonment, a long and solitary term.

BILLING In the service of morality, one must endure great hardships.

JANE If we were to conjugate, your child could raise the holy torch up in your absence.

BILLING Conjugate ... now that is not found in the Bible, Miss Smuts.

JANE Beget. Have knowledge. Lie together, as the lion and the lamb.

BILLING Miss Allan ... er, Miss Smuts, I mean ... I can't. I must stand firm. I need my stamina. This trial. I feel the war now hinges on its outcome. Ludicrous, I know, but ... then there's you.

JANE You do not wish to be the father of the Christ?

BILLING Perhaps another time.

JANE The sisters will be so dismayed.

BILLING Please pass on my condolences.

JANE We'll have to choose another Prophet. You really were the best of all the candidates.

BILLING Go on.

JANE Clearly, fitted with the best physique. I mean, Queen Anne's lace, but for a lady to resist all THAT, she'd have to be—

BILLING (*Mutters*) Maud Allan.

JANE —Blind.

BILLING Or blind to men. That's it! (*Kisses Jane on the lips.*) You've found her weakness! I'd forgotten, that's what got this business started in the first place.

JANE Do you mean ... the cult?

BILLING Exactly. Blind to men. Because they lack the proper apparati. Whereas a woman...

Eileen Villiers-Stuart has returned to the stage. Billing turns to her.

EILEEN Absolutely not.

Scene change: The stage fills up again.

PAGE Day Three!

SYRIAN *The Daily Chronicle.*

BOWLER-HATTED BLOKE 4
"Germans Reach the River Marne. The Bosche is Dug in Deep."

DARLING And is there—?

BOWLER-HATTED BLOKE 4
Page Two. "Scandalous Trial Afoot in London Court! MP Billing Levels Shocking Accusations at the Independent Theatre."

BILLING No photo, though.

DARLING Oh! Oh! Miss Allan! In light of what you said, I have endeavoured to re-read the play.

MAUD How studious.

DARLING And yet I still cannot exactly picture it, as such. The stage directions leave so much to be desired.

MAUD I am sensing something of desire.

DARLING I thought, perhaps, if I were able to, well, see you. In performance.

MAUD I'm sure that Mr. Grein will offer you a ticket to the play, when it resumes.

DARLING I—yes, well. Generous. And yet. I thought—a private sort of—thing?

MAUD My lord. When I was in my prime, I performed in all the grandest halls of Europe, and before the courts of Kings and Queens. And yet, each time I danced the famous Dance of Salomé, I danced in private.

She goes to sit down.

DARLING Remarkable lady.

BILLING My lord, I call unto the stand one Doctor Serrell Cooke.

SYRIAN I object!

PAGE We haven't even started yet.

BILLING My lord, he is an expert witness, and a specialist in sexual disorders.

DARLING More of that unpleasantness, what what?

BILLING 'Fraid so, my lord.

DARLING Be very careful, Mr. Billing. There are ladies present, and I would not have their winsome sensibilities dismayed.

BILLING (*Scans the courtroom*) Oh, if you mean Miss Allan? Not to worry. (*To Cooke*) Doctor Cooke, please describe your qualifications for the court.

COOKE Well, my speciality is nose-and-throat, in fact. I do enjoy an article on sexual perversion now and then. Who doesn't?

BILLING And who pens these articles?

COOKE Uh, Reinhold Bloch. Sacher Masoch. Krafft and Ebing.

BILLING Germans, mostly?

COOKE Now you come to mention it...

BILLING But sexual perversion does exist in England too?

COOKE Oh yes. In greater numbers every day. Or so I've read. Uranians, fetishists, satyriasists.

BILLING And what distinguishes all these sub-categories?

COOKE Well, various ... that is, in many cases ... I can't precisely say.

BILLING So, in your medical opinion, then, all perverts are the same.

COOKE Well—

BILLING One who is a sadist, for example—that is, one who would derive arousal from the biting of a dead man's lip—that one might ALSO be a homosexual?

COOKE It's possible, of course. Well, yes. Yes, certainly.

BILLING Or if it is a WOMAN who is biting?

COOKE Ah, we doctors call those lesbians.

DARLING From Lesbos? As in, Greece?

BILLING No, no. From Germany. Yes, Doctor?

COOKE I ... don't...

BILLING You said these vices all originate in Germany.

COOKE I did?

BILLING I think you did.

COOKE Well. German. Yes. Of course.

BILLING Or possibly Canadian?

MAUD (*To Page and Syrian*) Gentlemen?

PAGE AND SYRIAN
Objection!

MAUD Thank you.

BILLING Doctor Cooke is fully qualified to offer his opinions.

MAUD Biting the lip of the severed head is a directive in the play. You are confusing art with life.

DARLING Well put, Miss Allan. Jolly good.

BILLING Very well, then. Doctor? What breed of actress do you think might be disposed to take the role of Salomé in this, this PLAY by Oscar Wilde?

COOKE I rather think that is beyond my purview, sir.

BILLING But speculate. What does it tell us of her character?

COOKE That she is ... drawn to perverts.

BILLING And to acts of a perverted sort?

COOKE I ... yes...

BILLING And therefore?

COOKE Possibly a pervert. Probably.

DARLING Hold a moment there. You've gone too far. I can see this amiable lady with my own two eyes. She clearly is no pervert.

BILLING Ah, but these are hidden things, correct?

COOKE Well, yes, primarily—

BILLING The unseen enemy among us.

COOKE In many cases, so I've read, it's generally what's underneath that counts.

DARLING What? Underneath? What do you mean?

COOKE Well, in considering a, a female, um, that is ... one would examine, first and foremost, her ... (*He makes an "under the skirts" gesture.*)

DARLING D'you mean her knickers?

COOKE No. Beneath those.

DARLING Her ... her frillies?

COOKE Further still, my lord.

DARLING Further still than frillies? What could possibly be ... blimey!

COOKE Yes. The medical key to assessing the sexual degeneracy of females is the cli-toris.

DARLING The ... the cl—

COOKE Cli-toris. A superficial part of the female organ. The sensations which arise from this improper region are allurements which do not in any way assist the race.

BILLING And the indications of degeneracy in this unpleasant area?

COOKE I've never, actually, myself, seen—

BILLING Speculate.

COOKE Well, then, enlarged. Engorged with blood. Erect.

GREIN My lord, I beg your intervention.

DARLING Yes, this really is, um, rather—

BILLING Ladies in the thrall of this...

COOKE Cli-toris.

BILLING How do they behave, exactly? Speculate.

COOKE Insatiable. Nympho-maniacal. Why, an exaggerated cli-toris might even drive a woman to an elephant.

A great hubbub in court.

MAUD I believe you are exaggerating rather more than the cli-toris.

DARLING This—I'm finding all this talk a little—surely, um, Miss Allan, you must be—

MAUD Apart from having to restrain my mirth, my lord, I am in no distress.

BILLING You find this funny, then?

MAUD Unlike you gentlemen, who seem alarmed by your discovery, I learned about this superficial organ quite some time ago.

BILLING How interesting! For, as Doctor Cooke here will inform you, those who know about the cli-toris are either medical experts or manifest perverts. Which are you, Miss Allan?

MAUD An enlightened female, sir.

BILLING I rest my case.

DARLING Then may we please close the book upon the cli-toris?

BILLING Another question, Doctor. Do you think the reading of perverted literature provokes perverted acts?

COOKE I s'pose it might be very common, yes.

BILLING And what about the viewing of perverted plays? Would watching one provoke excitement?

COOKE Well yes, that's interesting. Might be how those cli-torises get engorged to start with.

BILLING So, normal gentlemen and ladies, watching plays replete with sadism and dancing, and it makes them, what? Aroused?

COOKE Yes.

BILLING Perverts? Members of the cult?

COOKE Yes, dancing I should think, would be especially infectious.

BILLING Dancing. Like the Dance of Salomé.

COOKE Yes, yes. A very interesting theory, Mister Billing. If vibrations travel through the air—

DARLING Let's see it.

BILLING What?

MAUD My lord?

DARLING The dance. The one that Salomé performs, the Seven Veils.

BILLING You ... want Miss Allan to perform her dance, in court?

DARLING Exactly. Well, as evidence, you see. The doctor, here—I mean, if watching perverts dance makes one a pervert, then—

MAUD My lord.

DARLING Let's cut the chatter, do the dance, and then we'll see what's what, what what?

MAUD My lord, although your invitation is appealing, I must respectfully decline.

BILLING And what, exactly, do you fear, Miss Allan?

MAUD This is not a fitting venue.

BILLING That you'll turn us all to deviants?

MAUD The light is wrong. And I am not warmed up.

DARLING If you are pure, as you maintain yourself to be, what is the fear?

GREIN (*Whispering to Maud*) This may be our way out of this.

DARLING A harmless dance. A dalliance.

GREIN Just do it. And when nothing happens—nothing untoward—

DARLING Miss Allan, dance for me. I order you.

MAUD My lord. To ask a lady once to dance, that is the privilege of all gentlemen. To ask repeatedly, and once she has declined? Some may perceive that as a great dishonour.

SYRIAN A dishonour? Here I come!

PAGE Now hang a jif, I heard it first!

Everyone's lines begin to overlap, as the trial dissolves into bedlam.

DARLING Now, order! I, I will have order!

SYRIAN You have ruffled the feathers of this rare bird.

PAGE You have spat in the eye of Miss Manners, and she's cross as hell!

COOKE May I step down?

BILLING Your honour—

DARLING Order! Order is in order!

SYRIAN That was a ghastly declaration.

PAGE Oh, and yours was better?

SYRIAN Here we go, then!

DARLING Order!

Page and Syrian start in with the fisticuffs again.

BILLING My lord, it seems that we shall have to take a recess.

DARLING Yes, well ... bloody hell, then. Court adjourned!

Darling hurries off. The rest of the court also breaks apart. Maud pauses to separate Page and Syrian, to pat them both on the cheeks and send them off.

GREIN Now the judge will be against us.

MAUD Yes.

GREIN If you had simply gone along with it, the truth—

MAUD The truth, Jack ... is rarely pure, and never simple.

They exit. New scene: Billing, Eileen, Spencer, and Jane. Spencer talks to Billing, who mostly talks to Eileen.

SPENCER The time is right, I'm telling ye.

BILLING You must.

EILEEN Don't even ask.

BILLING You know I'd never ask you to do something—

EILEEN Yes you would.

SPENCER I'm ready as a rock. Just put me up there, and ye'll see.

BILLING But it may be the only way to get to her.

EILEEN Forget it, Roger.

SPENCER Judges love me. Always have.

BILLING It's like Miss Smuts here said.

JANE (*Reading from news clippings*) "Miss Allan, often rumoured to prefer the company of ladies—"

BILLING There. You see?

EILEEN Then send her. She's a lady.

JANE Oleander!

SPENCER AND I'm photogenic.

BILLING She's not up to it. She frightens easily.

EILEEN That's not what I heard.

BILLING And anyway, if you were Maud, which one would you pick? Her, or you?

SPENCER It's time somebody stumped up on the state of things. The ruddy scheme.

BILLING She's weak. She's vulnerable. The time is right.

EILEEN I do not do such things.

BILLING You do. You did. To me.

JANE She did?

BILLING She tried to. I resisted.

EILEEN But it's different with a lady.

JANE I think she should do it.

SPENCER (*Practicing*) "Ay, my lord. The intestinal parasites of Europe are among us."

BILLING Spencer, shut your gob. I am not putting you upon the stand.

SPENCER Pumpship! Skivvy-bin! Why not, then, eh?

JANE (*Reading*) "When not in court, Miss Allan is reclusive. A pariah in this country."

BILLING Go to her. Befriend her. That is all I ask.

EILEEN "Befriend her." Has the age of euphemisms not yet passed?

BILLING Perhaps, in her anxiety, she'll slip you some incriminating facts.

EILEEN When I vowed love to you, I did not figure it would lead to some colonial dance-trollop trying to slip me things—

JANE "Often, after sessions, she is seen to promenade alone along the Serpentine."

BILLING For me. For all we've fought for. And for England.

SPENCER God, His Majesty, and Country, SIR!

EILEEN I'll do it, then. But only if you put him on the stand.

BILLING What? Why—

EILEEN Because. If you are going to make me squirm, I will ensure you do the same.

Scene change: Billing preps Spencer for the stand.

PAGE Day Four!

SYRIAN All papers! Take your pick! You'll see the same words!

BOWLER-HATTED BLOKE 3
"Scandal!"

PAGE "Allegations! Accusations!"

SYRIAN "Extraordinary Scenes and Outrageous Euphemisms!"

BILLING Try to keep your head, and tongue, about you.

PAGE "Perverse Anatomical Secrets Revealed!"

BILLING Say only what we have rehearsed. About the Black Book—

SPENCER Who told you about the Black Book?

BILLING My career is flashing before my eyes.

DARLING Mr. Billing, call your next witness.

BILLING Captain Harold Spencer, Special Forces, Special Discharge.

SPENCER Your eminence, it is a great, great honour—

BILLING Captain Spencer. Will you kindly and directly tell the court what post you held before your discharge?

SPENCER Secret Service. Ultra-Secret Section, Number two-six-seven-S. The S, for Secret.

BILLING And your mission, as of last November, 1917?

SPENCER I was assigned to infiltrate the German conspiracy that ravages our shores.

Hubbub and hullabaloo.

DARLING Order! Order!

PAGE My lord, I fail to see what bearing this might have upon the case.

BILLING Then you are blinkered, sir. Thus far, we have been altogether focused on the offending headline, "The Cult of the Clitorites." But let us now recall the full text of the article beneath. "If the belly-shaking scugs at Scotland Yard had the ... presence of mind ... to confiscate this list of members, they'd be looking at a hefty chunk of names from out the Huns' Black Book itself!"

SPENCER The Black Book! I have seen it with my own two ears!

BILLING Will you explain its purpose, Captain?

SPENCER Doctor.

BILLING CAPTAIN.

SPENCER Right. The Black Book. That's where Jerry keeps the names of all the ruddy Britishers that he's got wrapped around his filthy digit.

BILLING British men and women that the Bosche can blackmail. Why?

SPENCER Because they're deviates that should be locked away!

BILLING And what does Germany intend, with all these deviates?

SPENCER Subversion. Treason. Insurrection. Every man and woman on the Isle eating ruddy sauerkraut by Christmas.

SYRIAN I object!

DARLING To what?

SYRIAN I ... do not like sauerkraut.

PAGE And, plus, this witness is a braying loony.

DARLING You shall have to prove that, counsel.

SPENCER (*Under his breath*) Pebbledash! Poopnoddy!

PAGE Would the Captain please inform us where he learned of this Black Book?

SPENCER 'Twas in the words of Kaiser Wilhelm himself.

SYRIAN In Germany, then?

BILLING No, no. The Captain has not been to Germany.

PAGE The Kaiser came to him, then? To his house?

SPENCER Who told ye that? Ya ruddy—

BILLING I believe, in his capacity as Ultra-Secret Secret Servicer, the Captain has been able to construct a history of this most volatile tome.

SPENCER I have?

BILLING (*Under his breath*) You've always been a fan of rampant speculation, Spencer. Why stop now?

SPENCER I have. The Black Book has a convoluted past—

BILLING But highly relevant.

During Spencer's next speech, the other actors scramble to enact vignettes which illustrate the various stages of the Book's history. Only Maud does not participate in this.

SPENCER —Which started in the shameful year of eighteen hundred forty-seven, when Ludwig of Bavaria was King. Disgusting and debaucherous, the bastard took a mistress, in the form of Lola Montez, the Irish-Spanish "Spider Dancer." Jezebel with dahlias. She taught him how arachnids fornicate; he made her Countess of Landsfeld. The Bavarians revolted! Lola fled the country, and the King was made to sign a dastardly confession, listing all the aberrant aristocrats they'd dallied with. And then he was defenestrated!

But the book survived, and, smuggled through the hands of simple peasants, settled in St. Petersburg. It fell into the hands of sexually obsessive siren Antonina Milikova, who employed the dreadful testimony as imaginative fodder for her lustful thoughts. She shared it with her music teacher, Peter Ilyich Tchaikovsky, then attempted to seduce him. But the man was an horrendous homosexual, despite involvement with no fewer than three women. Scorned and horny, Milikova entered all the names of the composer's lovers, man and woman both. Tchaikovsky was disgraced! Attempted suicide by standing in a freezing river, praying for pneumonia.

And then! The Russian Revolution! All the traitors and conspirators set down by servants of the Tsar. This web of lechery converged upon the name of one whose sexual charisma gathered all of Russia in its grasp: the Mad Monk of the Muskovites, Grigory Rasputin. Impervious to blackmail, Rasputin was assaulted by assassins: poisoned, stabbed, and shot. As he collapsed, he reached for what he took to be a Bible—but which was, in fact, none other than the same Black Book which brought his evil down!

From thence, the Book passed through the hands of infamous and vile personalities. Isadora Duncan used it as an address book. And Mata

Hari—yes, another dancer, and a spy—she used its pages to enlarge her bosom. Robert Falcon Scott bore that Black Book with him to the Antarctics. Charlie Chaplin accidentally autographed it at the opening of *Dough and Dynamite*. The Archduke Ferdinand was said to thumb its pages just before the shot heard 'round the world. And now, most recently, where has the Book been sighted? In whose terrible and treacherous possession?

BILLING (*Gesturing to Maud*) Tell us! Tell us!

SPENCER There's the culprit! Miss Maud Allan! Prob'ly got it with her at this very moment.

MAUD Nonsense.

DARLING Then, Miss Allan, you'll have no objection to distributing the contents of your carryall?

MAUD A lady's purse, my lord, is sacred ground.

SPENCER Ay, so is England, hussy!

DARLING If you please, Miss Allan?

Maud begins to remove items from her purse. The tension mounts, as she removes a series of increasingly suggestive items. After four or five items, out comes a large black book.

SPENCER Ah ha!

BILLING I don't believe it.

DARLING We must see that book, Miss Allan.

MAUD I would rather not.

SPENCER The safety of our nation and the outcome of this war—

DARLING Miss Allan? (*Maud hands the book to Syrian, who hands it to Page, who hands it to Darling. He reads*) "London has never seen such graceful and artistic dancing. It is of a magical beauty; but the magic is black and the beauty is baleful and insidious." (*He flips through the book. News clippings and photos tumble out.*)

MAUD You have revealed my greatest failing, gentlemen. The sin of pride. Though if you truly think the contents of my scrapbook will affect the outcome of the war ... perhaps my pride is justified? Would you say so, Mister Billing?

BILLING This proves nothing.

MAUD I heartily agree.

DARLING I shall have to, uh, retain this. For, for evidence. Especially these photos.

MAUD Naturally.

DARLING Adjourned! I shall be in chambers, not to be disturbed!

The court breaks apart.

GREIN Well, that was abject nonsense.

MAUD Not fortuitous for us, I fear.

GREIN But surely no one could believe all that conspiratory claptrap.

MAUD It is wartime, Mr. Grein. Anxiety is palpable. And a conspiracy is rather like a dance: it is not concerned with facts, but only feelings.

Scene change: Maud walks through Hyde Park, carrying a parasol. Eileen approaches her cautiously.

MAUD (*Singing to herself*)
Blow, blow, thou winter wind,
Thou art not so unkind
As man's ingratitude.
Thy tooth is not so keen
Because thou art not seen,
Although thy breath be rude.
Heigh ho, sing heigh ho, unto the green holly!
Most friendship is feigning, most loving mere folly;
Then heigh ho, the holly,
This life is most jolly.

EILEEN Is there no end to your talents, Miss Allan?

MAUD You have found it, I'm afraid. If I had known I had an audience, I should not have sung.

EILEEN I'd rather you continued, and will therefore leave you.

MAUD No. As someone cleverer than I once said, if one hears bad music, it becomes one's duty to drown it in conversation.

EILEEN I shall stay, then.

MAUD Splendid. Miss Maud Allan.

EILEEN Yes, I know. Miss Villiers-Stuart. You may call me Eileen.

MAUD I believe I saw you striking Mr. Billing recently.

EILEEN Ah. Well ... that was regrettable.

MAUD Oh? I'd thought to thank you for it.

EILEEN No, I mean associating with him to begin with. The striking part was rather fun.

MAUD I'll have to try it out sometime.

EILEEN Shall we sit?

MAUD After you.

They sit on a park bench.

EILEEN You must grow weary of celebrity. Besieged in public by your fans and your detractors.

MAUD Which are you, Eileen?

EILEEN A fan, of course.

MAUD And are you planning to besiege me?

EILEEN I—I—

MAUD For my defences are quite spent, I fear.

EILEEN Miss Allan, I would never dream of—

MAUD Goodness, no, whatever you do, don't dream. I'm sure you know what someone said of dreamers. Society may pardon criminals, but forgive a dreamer? Never.

EILEEN Yet I do suspect that you are one, yourself.

MAUD One what, Eileen?

EILEEN A dreamer.

MAUD Yes. Perhaps I am.

EILEEN What do you dream about?

Pause. When Maud describes her dream, it is recreated on the stage.

MAUD My brother. In the dream he finds me, firstly like a lover, but then sternly, like a judge. His head is covered by the execution hood; he has no face. Then music. We begin to dance. And then he steps away. I dance alone. He shows me something, on a silver charger. It's the head of John the Baptist—the old prop head from my Vision days. But now the face is his, and now it speaks.

THE SEVERED HEAD
Keep dancing, Maud. You must keep dancing.

MAUD And the music grows more fervent and I start to lose my breath, but still his voice is echoing, like drums, inside my head.

THE SEVERED HEAD
Keep dancing.

MAUD And I realize with horror that he means to make me dance forever. Trapped. A whirling, churning, dizzy world for all eternity. And then I wake.

EILEEN Doctor Freud believes that dreams are symbols for our deep desires. Perhaps you want to dance forever.

MAUD Yes, perhaps. And what do you dream of, Eileen?

EILEEN Your face.

MAUD I see. Any feature in particular?

EILEEN Your lips. Like grapes. That one might bite.

They are, of course, very close to kissing. Behind them, Billing and Jane rise up from the bushes with a camera. Eileen sees this and shifts away on the bench.

Maud Allen, the Salomé dancer (Leslie Caffaro), engages in a lurid kiss with Eileen Villiers-Stuart (Kelsie Acton) as Roger Pemberton-Billing (Denny Demeria) and Jane Smuts (Carolyn Barker) get their "evidence", July 2007. Photo: C.W. Hill Photography for Walterdale Theatre Associates.

MAUD Not hungry, then?

EILEEN Someone might see us. Take advantage—

MAUD I do not fear being taken advantage of. Do you?

EILEEN It's just that—now, and with the trial at such a stage—

MAUD You speak to someone who has danced to scandal's rhythm many times. Come here, Eileen. I'll tell you something secret. I don't bite. (*Eileen shifts closer again*) When I returned to England for this play, my aim was immortality. By appropriating some small measure of the fame of Mr. Wilde, I thought I could achieve it. But then the trial, its endless intermingling of Maud and Salomé, Salomé and Maud ... and what's the point of immortality if you are not allowed to be yourself?

EILEEN I see.

MAUD We must therefore be ourselves, Miss Villiers-Stuart. No matter what the cost. Can you endure that fate?

EILEEN I—I— (*Once again, they are almost kissing. But Eileen pulls back, rising this time*) I must resist. My secret, Maud, is this. I am *agent provocateur.* World-class. Adept at seeming anything but what I truly am. In fact, for so long now, I have not been ... myself ... I fear to do so would destroy me utterly. Forgive me.

She flees. Maud rises. Her gaze follows Eileen—away from Billing —yet she speaks to him, as if she'd known about his presence all along.

MAUD Do you care to give the little one a try, as well? Or shall we call it a day?

Billing looks at Jane (the "little one") and seriously considers it. Jane sees what he's thinking and runs off the other way. Then Maud and Billing gaze across at one another for a beat.

You are out of pawns, Mr. Billing.

BILLING I don't need to catch you *in flagrante* anyhow. (*He snaps her photograph*) Your face alone bespeaks how hideous you are.

Scene change.

SYRIAN Day Five!

TOMMY 2 Dispatch from Paris. Writing now, before breakfast, I find it difficult to realize there is a possibility, perhaps a likelihood, of France falling utterly unto the Hun. Does anyone in England hear our tragic calls for help? Will no one answer?

SYRIAN *The London Times.*

BOWLER-HATTED BLOKE 3
"TRIAL OF THE CENTURY!"

BOWLER-HATTED BLOKE 4
"Pemberton-Billing Grills Secret Servicer About Germanic Book of Perverts!"

BOWLER-HATTED BLOKE 3
"Never has England seen such Scandals!"

BOTH BLOKES "What Will Billing Drag Out Next?"

SYRIAN My lord, by now, a child could see what this man is playing at. The article was calculated to incur a libel, and to breach the peace. And naturally, he couldn't merely plead "Not Guilty," no—for that would not have given him the soapbox he required. Now if he honestly believes in some weird German scheme, then let him undertake his campaign howsoever he sees fit. But do not let him march to victory upon the knickers of this lady's reputation!

DARLING Did you say "knickers"?

SYRIAN I ... my lord, I think I need a recess.

DARLING But we've barely started.

BILLING Fear not, my lord. I shall put counsel's fears to rest with my last witness.

GREIN More dancing ponies, Mr. Billing?

BILLING A dancing Canadian. Ladies and gentlemen, I call Maud Allan to the stand.

MAUD Perhaps, to save the court some time, I should declare right out that I know nothing of a secret German plot, nor of a Black Book containing fifty thousand names.

BILLING The court appreciates your candour, but we cannot ... Did you say "fifty thousand names"? I never—that is—where did you—? That wasn't in the article.

DARLING You must ask the witness proper questions, Mr. Billing.

BILLING Very nice. You mean to ruffle me. Well, two can play. Miss Allan, can you tell us where you trained to be a dancer?

MAUD In America.

BILLING And elsewhere?

MAUD Yes. In Germany.

BILLING And so, Miss Allan, this performance that has made you famous—what's it called?

MAUD The Vision of Salomé.

BILLING It is a German art, then?

MAUD No. It is an art which any man with eyes may comprehend.

BILLING And what is it, Miss Salomé, which motivates this dance?

MAUD Miss Allan, if you please.

BILLING I'm sorry?

MAUD You just called me Salomé. My name—

BILLING Forgive me, yes, of course. Your CHARACTER is Salomé. But why does Salomé—I mean your character—perform her dance?

MAUD She dances for the head of John the Baptist.

BILLING Dances, so she may, what, kiss it? Bite it?

DARLING We've been over this before.

MAUD She simply needs it.

BILLING John the Baptist scorned her. Called her harlot. Child of Sodom. Whore. He was the one man she could not possess with looks alone.

MAUD Perhaps.

BILLING So she possesses him through death. Is that not so, Miss Salomé?

MAUD I am not Salomé.

BILLING Then why does Miss Maud Allan dance?

MAUD She—why—?

BILLING If you and Salomé are not the same, then surely you must have a separate motivation.

MAUD I dance because the muse invites me.

BILLING No. You dance because of men who hate you. Men—and women, yes—that you cannot control.

PAGE My lord, I must object.

BILLING And when you dance, what happens to them, Salomé?

MAUD I couldn't say.

BILLING But why did you decline to dance for us in court the other day? What was your fear?

DARLING She did seem frightened.

BILLING If you dance for art, then all is well. But if you dance for lust, or out of anger, or revenge for all the power you do not possess—

MAUD You really think I'm powerless?

BILLING (*Quietly*) Miss Allan, you're a single woman. It is 1918. What d'you think will happen if you prove that you have power? (*Aloud*) Let's review. The play is Salomé by Oscar Wilde, the sodomite. The character is a sadistic girl with anatomical embellishments. The plot to overthrow Great Britain, masterminded by the Germans, hinges on the deviants, degenerates, and perverts who pollute our streets. And where, in all of this, is Miss Maud Allan? Is she a helpless dove among the kites? Or is she Salomé?

MAUD I never met a sadist in my life, sir, till the day I met you.

BILLING What about your brother, William?

MAUD Mr. Billing. Let us not return there.

BILLING There are many forms of sadism which are, in fact, hereditary. And are you not your brother's sister?

MAUD I must ask you, in all decency, to stop.

BILLING Are not the violent lusts which led to his transgressions also circulate within your blood?

MAUD I am not Salomé.

BILLING But it's the role you chose, my dear. Your whole career—

MAUD I urge you, sir—

BILLING By dancing for the death of John the Baptist, and by biting, after death—

MAUD I, I implore you.

BILLING The same sin your brother once committed! He, at least, was punished.

MAUD I am warning you.

BILLING Oh. Warning? Well.

DARLING Miss Allan, I will tolerate no threats within my courtroom.

What do you intend to do? What power do you have?

Maud stands.

MAUD My lord, I would approach the bench. (*She does so. Speaking very low*) You wish me to dance?

DARLING I, do I—? Well, I thought, when I suggested—

MAUD Yes or no, Judge. Now or never.

DARLING Yes. God, yes. You must.

MAUD What will you do for me?

DARLING Whatever. Anything you ask.

MAUD I want the case.

DARLING What?

MAUD In my favour. I want him to be found guilty.

DARLING But—

MAUD I want the head of Roger Billing on a bloody platter.

DARLING Yes, but—

MAUD Anything, you said.

DARLING Yes. Anything. All right, then.

MAUD Do you swear it, Judge?

DARLING I swear it, Salomé.

MAUD Bring me my perfumes, and the seven veils.

SYRIAN She is going to dance!

Maud steps behind a screen to change back into her Salomé costume. Commotion downstage as people place themselves.

PAGE Look at the moon!

SYRIAN She is a gale that sweeps all branches clean!

PAGE The moon is turning red!

SYRIAN She is a gilded tiger in the wild!

PAGE The stars are falling from the trees like unripe figs!

SYRIAN She is a force of nature!

PAGE All the world beyond this room has tumbled into darkness!

SYRIAN She's a maelstrom!

PAGE And all that's left is—

SYRIAN She's a vortex!

PAGE That which is reflected in—

SYRIAN She's everything!

PAGE Her eyes!

BILLING (*To the audience*) And so, Miss Allan danced. And we shall spare you that irreverent event, and move directly to the verdict of the trial.

Page and Syrian grab Billing's arms.

Do you mind?

They haul him upstage.

DARLING Why dost thou tarry, Salomé?

MAUD I am prepared.

BILLING Wait! Stop! You cannot dance. The order of the court forbids it.

GREIN It forbids the play of *Salomé*. But we present the trial.

DARLING I can wait no longer!

GREIN As it happened. Every factual event.

BILLING But not the dance! Not after what befell in court.

GREIN The truth, you said. In all its grim veracity.

BILLING The truth. The words, the facts. But not this!

DARLING Dance, my Salomé! Dance for me!

Maud moves downstage, preparing to dance. Music begins.

BILLING (*To the audience*) You must not look at her. Avert your eyes, I beg of you. Her power—do not look at her!

Page and Syrian cover Billing's mouth. Maud Allan dances the Dance of the Seven Veils. When she is done, everyone onstage (including Billing) is transfixed in silent ecstasy.

MAUD (*To the audience*) So much bother over such a tiny thing. When men sense something they cannot control, they panic. And like Adam, they adore the game of names. Pervert. Sadist. Lesbian. "Clitorite." How fortunate that even in this day and age, there still are things which have no name, nor never shall.

DARLING (*Snapping out of his trance*) The court will hear the verdict.

MAUD And the rest, I fear, you know already.

DARLING This judge finds in favour of the defendant, Roger Pemberton-Billing.

MAUD Broken promises.

DARLING And does hereby order all performances of *Salomé* repealed. Court adjourned!

MAUD At least the original Salomé got to cradle her prize.

GREIN But once she had the head of John the Baptist, Herod ordered all his guards to kill her.

MAUD And she died with her enemy's head in her hands. It is as close as any woman gets to triumph.

BILLING Violence and death. Is that all you think of?

MAUD You have proved as much, sir, in a court of law. I am officially degenerate.

BILLING Thank God we menfolk are not so malevolent.

MAUD Oh, that reminds me, Mr. Billing. How's your war these days?

BILLING The tide has turned at last. They are predicting victory by winter.

MAUD Really! And with all those pervert traitors on the loose?

BILLING One less, at least.

MAUD Oh yes. You've done great service to your countrymen. And I must thank you, too.

BILLING The trial is done, Miss Allan, and you lost. No need for your polite façade.

MAUD I promise you, my thanks are genuine.

BILLING And why the devil would you thank me? I destroyed your life. Your play, your final chance at immortality. I tore the false face of Maud Allan off, and found the Salomé beneath.

MAUD And still, I thank you. It is rare and good to see one's true self shine so clearly, sir. And as for immortality...

A long line of Bowler-hatted Blokes hold up copies of The Vigilante. *The covers sport huge photos of Maud, with the word "SCANDAL!" underneath.*

You have ensured my story, and my face, shall last a hundred years.

BILLING A hundred...

MAUD Even two.

She pats him on the cheek, then moves her hand to cradle his chin—a gesture which resembles holding the head of John the Baptist.

And everything, I owe to you.

The lights fade out.

The End.

"It begins with the smallest of gestures: a flutter of lashes, like two midnight moths..." Maud Allen (Leslie Caffaro) describes the Vision of Salomé dance, July 2007. Photo: C.W. Hill Photography for Walterdale Theatre Associates.

APPENDIX I: NEW PLAYS PREMIERED BY WALTERDALE THEATRE ASSOCIATES

New Plays Premiered by Walterdale Theatre Associates

Below is a list of new plays premiered by Walterdale during its first fifty years. Every effort has been made to ensure accuracy and completeness. In some cases records may not have been available.

DATE OF PREMIERE	PLAY	PLAYWRIGHT	DIRECTOR
Dec 14–16, 1961	*Is This a Friendly Visit?* (one-act)	Mary Baldridge	Barry Vogal
Nov 2–10, 1962	*Barranca*	Jack McCreath	Jack McCreath
Mar 8–18, 1967	*Nothing But a Man*	George Ryga	Marjorie Knowler
May 26–28, 1967	*The Canadian Fact* (one-act)	Wilfred Watson	Peter Montgomery
Nov 13–18, 1967	*Jackpot* (musical)	Chet Lambertson and Jimmy Richardson	Dr. Norman Ibsen Music: Frank Glenfield
Mar 15–17, 1968	*Yes, Dear* (one-act)	Warren Graves	Warren Graves
Mar 15–17, 1968	*Two Teardrops Frozen on a Rearview Mirror* (one-act)	Wilfred Watson	Joan Krisch
Nov 7–16, 1968	*Love in a Greenhouse*	Warren Graves	Warren Graves
July 19–31, 1971	*The Mumberly Inheritance or His Substance Frittered* (melodrama)	Warren Graves	Warren Graves
July 15–27, 1974	*Chief Shaking Spear Rides Again or the Taming of the Sioux* (melodrama)	Warren Graves; songs by William Thorsell	Warren Graves
Feb 20–22, 1975	*Pause* (one-act)	Frank Moher	Jack Wilson
Mar 1–5, 1977	*The Girl I Left Behind Me* (one-act)	Erika Ritter	Warren Graves
April 17–21, 1979	*The Coal Branch: A Documentary* (one-act)	Duane Mills	Duane Mills
Jan 29–Feb 9, 1980	*Shikata Ga Nai*	Kevin Burns	Kevin Burns
Jan 27–Feb 7, 1981	*Mutants*	Brad Fraser	Brad Fraser
May 19–30, 1981	*The Apprentice of Swipe*	Gordon Pengilly	Larry Farley
Mar 17–26, 1983	*The Tenth Negative Pig*	Barbara Sapergia and Geoffrey Ursell	Frank Glenfield
Dec 16–20, 1983	*The Three Sillies* (children's play)	Mary Glenfield	Frank Glenfield

DATE OF PREMIERE	PLAY	PLAYWRIGHT	DIRECTOR
May 9–12, 1984	*The Immortelle* (one-act)	Raymond Storey	Art van Loo
May 9–12, 1984	*Would You Like a Cup of Tea?* (one-act)	Warren Graves	Gaye LePage
May 9–12, 1984	*Sister Virtue* (one-act)	Gerald St. Maur	Gerald St. Maur
July 17–28, 1984	*Pamela Frankenstein or Adam and Eve Meet Apple 2* (melodrama)	Warren Graves	Warren Graves
May 9–14, 1988	*The Poet's Pig* (one-act)	Eric Rice	Eric Rice
May 15–19, 1989	*Funny* (one-act)	Tom McGovern	Eric Rice
May 15–19, 1989	*Love at First Sight* (one-act)	Peter Adamski and Michael Sturko	Robert Corness
May 16–20, 1989	*Spiders in My Bed* (one-act)	Andrea L. Toma	Marilyn Mercx
May 16–20, 1989	*Scrap Paper* (one-act)	Gerald Osborn	Gerald Osborn
May 20–25, 1991	*Mother Tongue* (one-act)	Gerald Osborn	Gerald Osborn
May 29–June 3, 1995	*Chameleon's Romance* (one-act)	Mary Ann Trann	Andrea Martinuk
May 29–June 3, 1995	*More Past than Future* (one-act)	Charles Lendzion	Matthew Kowalchuk
May 29–June 3, 1995	*Lady in a Barrel* (one-act)	Chris Allen	Dmitri Baranov
June 3–8, 1996	*The Pegasus Bridge* (one-act)	Andrew Schuster	Michele Vance Hehir
June 3–8, 1996	Alien Among Us (one-act)	Darin Saretzky	David Newton
June 3–8, 1996	*Raven Morningstar* (one-act)	Kari Klassen	Lisa Newman
June 2–7, 1997	*Crushed* (one-act)	Heather Morrow	Darin Saretzky
June 2–7, 1997	*Fragments* (one-act)	Anthony King	Petros Efstathiou
June 2–7, 1997	*Waiting for the Fish to Die* (one-act)	Barbara Mah	Eric Brown

DATE OF PREMIERE	PLAY	PLAYWRIGHT	DIRECTOR
June 1–6, 1998	*Save a Prayer* (one-act)	Matthew Kowalchuk	Heather Taylor; Dramaturge: Ken Brown
June 1–6, 1998	*Tunnel Vision* (one-act)	Paul Sveen	Dramaturge: Dave Clarke and Eileen Sproule
June 1–6, 1998	*The Retreat* (one-act)	Marily Hussey	Dramaturge: Janet Hinton
May 31–June 5, 1999	*The Burner* (one-act)	Stephanie Benger	Donna Detka
May 31–June 5, 1999	*Just* (one-act)	Trevor Schmidt	Trevor Schmidt
May 31–June 5, 1999	*Gimcrackery* (one-act)	Chris Rice	Bob Klackowich
May 29–June 3, 2000	*A Special Latitude* (one-act)	Sandy Knowler	Dimitry Baranov
May 29–June 3, 2000	*Enter the Giants* (one-act)	Peter Chriss	Elizabeth Day
May 28–June 2, 2001	*On the Subject of...*	Dale Wilson	Donna Detka
May 28–June 2, 2001	*Bang!* (one-act)	William R. Cramer	Darin Saretzky
June 10–15, 2002	*The Beaver Effect* (one-act)	Mark Stubbings	David DeGagné; Dramaturge: Sam Varteniuk
June 10–15, 2002	*Infidelity* (one-act)	David Owen	Matt Kloster; Dramaturge: Sam Varteniuk
June 9–14, 2003	*[ice land]* (one-act)	Jonathan Seinen	Michael Cowie; Dramaturge: Heather Inglis
May 4–8, 2004	*Fran Chews* (one-act)	Mark Stubbings	Brian Bergum
May 4–8, 2004	*Double Occupancy* (one-act)	Blaine Newton	Stewart Burdett
May 9–14, 2005	*The Open Mouth* (one-act)	Cat Francis	Jaclyn Thomey; Dramaturge: Caroline Livingstone
May 9–14, 2005	*Chance Moments* (one-act)	Charles Netto	Sarah Van Tassel; Dramaturge: Scott Sharplin

DATE OF PREMIERE	PLAY	PLAYWRIGHT	DIRECTOR
May 9–14, 2005	*Kissing the Armadillo* (one-act)	Leland Stelck	Heather Ross; Dramaturge: Kevin Sutley
May 8–13, 2006	*Lunatic* (one-act)	Jacqueline Lamb	Dramaturge: Amy DeFelice
May 8–13, 2006	*Crossword Puzzles* (one-act)	Tracy Alsenstat	Dramaturge: Annette Loiselle
May 8–13, 2006	*Swimming with Goldfish* (one-act)	A.G. Boss	Dramaturge: Alison Wells
May 21–26, 2007	*Pieces* (one-act)	Kristen M. Finlay	Marsha Amanova; Dramaturge: David Belke
May 21–26, 2007	*Perdu* (one-act)	Katherine Koller	Taylor Chadwick; Dramaturge: David Belke
May 21–26, 2007	*The Traveling Nude* (one-act)	Phil Kriesel	Sam Varteniuk; Dramaturge: David Belke
July 4–14, 2007	*The Trial of Salomé*	Scott Sharplin	Amy Neufeld
June 18–27, 2008	*Up Shit Creek* (one-act)	Taylor Chadwick	Steve Weller, Mentor: David Belke
June 19–28, 2008	*Cellar Doors, Secret Gardens* (one-act)	Nathan Coppens	Marsha Amanova, Mentor: Trevor Schmidt
June 18–27, 2008	*Bless You Billy Wilder* (one-act)	David Belke	Stacey Lawrence
June 19–28, 2008	*Mockingbird Close* (one-act)	Trevor Schmidt	Justen Bennett

APPENDIX II: MUSIC

The Tenth Negative Pig

Words and Music by Barbara Sapergia and Geoffrey Ursell

"In the Sanatorium" score

"Doctor Death" score

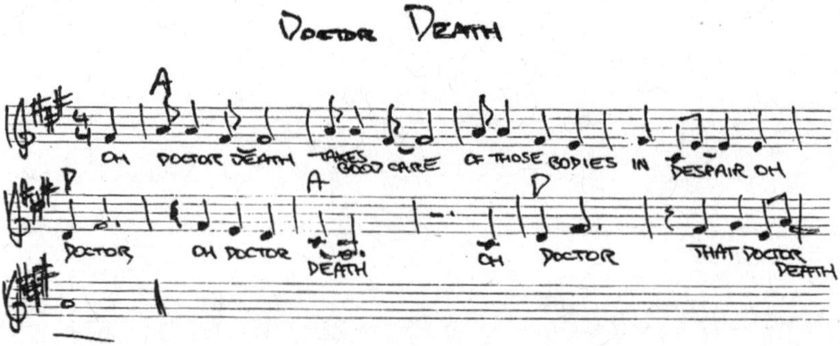

"Bone Wagon" score

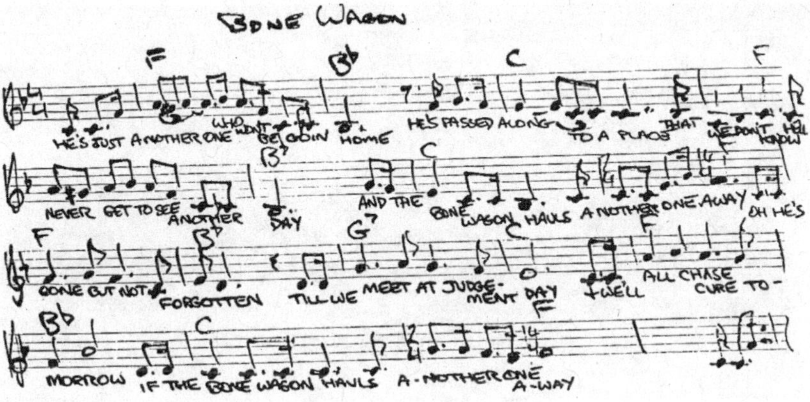

"Where Is God" score

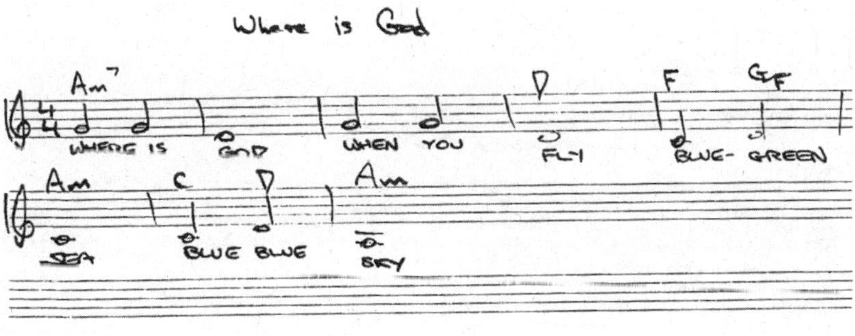

"Temple Gardens" score

"Spirits of Night" score

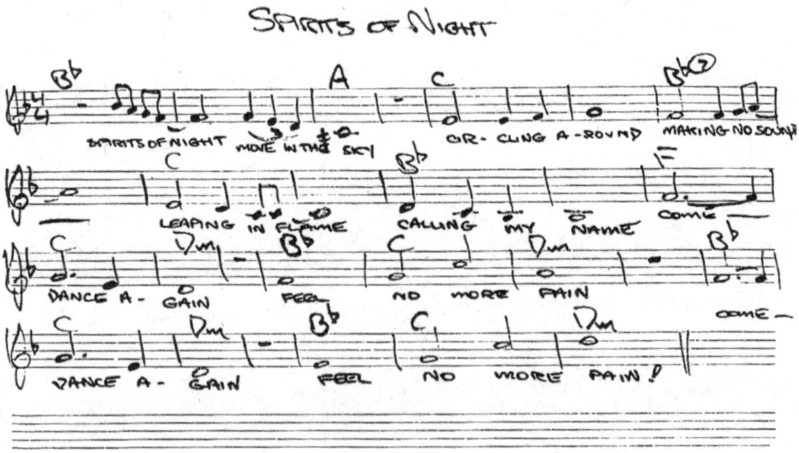

The Three Sillies

Words and Music by Mary Glenfield, Arrangements by Rhuanedd Meilen

---

"Little Sally Saucer" score

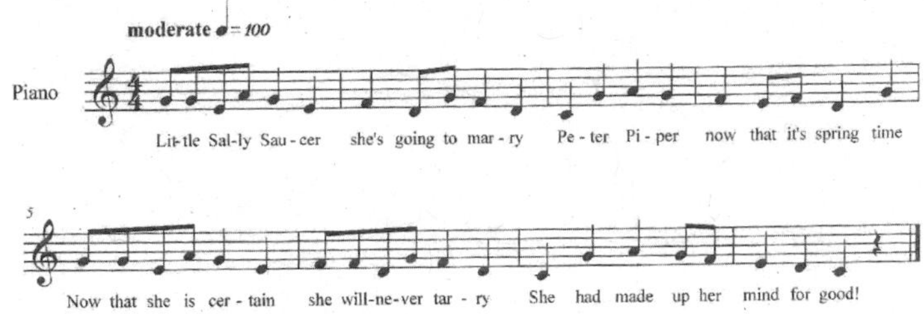

"Sandy's Song" score

cats have all come dressed for a ball. Purr! - purr! Purr! - purr! Their song sounds just like a
cat - er - waul! Me - oww! Me - oww! But if you should tell them so
Then I think you rea - lly ought to know They'd turn on you and start to go Psss - psss
psss psss. But you'd Bet - ter stay in bed when you
hear their lit-tle song Don't go stan ding by the win-dow sill, When the mu-sic comes a-gain and you
know the right re-frain you can join in if you lie quite still. For if you should take a peep when you're
s'posed to be a - sleep then they'll from a-round your house So pre - tend you're
sim - ply like a - tle mouse - The mou - sies come as close
as they dare Week! Week! Week! Week! They're so small you don't know if they're there
Week! - Week! Week! - Week! S'pose they join in sing-ing too does - n't - real - ly
mat - ter if they do Mou - sies sound the same as you Week! Week! Week! Week!

"Peter's Song" score

NOTES

1 Ottawa Little Theatre was founded May 9, 1913, as the Society for the Study and Production of Dramatic Art. The group changed its name six months later to the Ottawa Drama League. Its first dedicated venue, the Ottawa Little Theatre, was acquired in 1928. The League formally changed its name to Ottawa Little Theatre in 1951 (Winston).

Alumnae Theatre Company was founded October 19, 1919, as an all-female group of graduates from the University of Toronto's University College. In the spring of 1920 it became the Dramatic Club of the University College Alumnae Association. In 1922 members allowed men to be involved as "guests" when they decided that operating as a women-only group was "frustrating as well as boring" (Halpenny 1). The company dropped "University College" from its name in 1942 to indicate that female graduates from any university were welcome as members, calling itself the University Alumnae Dramatic Club or UADC (Halpenny 1; University 1). It subsequently updated the name to Alumnae Theatre Company as official ties to the university were shed in a series of off-campus relocations. Now located in an old firehall on Berkley Street, Alumnae Theatre allows only women to be full members of the company to this day, though everyone is welcome to participate.

Regina Little Theatre was founded in June 1926 with productions at the Regina College auditorium and the Grand Theatre. It moved into Darke Hall after 1931 but rehearsed and performed in a variety of venues (Stuart 95–98). It is now located in its own theatre, the Regina Little Theatre, on Angus Street.

The Victoria Theatre Guild at Langham Court Theatre was founded in 1929 as The Mimes' and Masquers' Guild. It changed its name to the Victoria Little Theatre Association in 1931 and again in 1938, when it moved into the new "fully functional theatre" known as the Victoria Little Theatre and Dramatic School. In 1950 the building was renamed Langham Court Theatre (Langham).

2 A 2001 survey commissioned by the Edmonton Arts Council found that when Edmontonians "were asked unaided which theatre companies they are aware of in Edmonton," Walterdale (the only amateur company mentioned) tied for fourth with Fringe Theatre Adventures (7%), after The Citadel Theatre (44%), Mayfield Dinner Theatre (26%), and Celebrations Dinner Theatre (9%). If 7% seems low, consider that more than twenty companies were mentioned less frequently than Walterdale and that 31% of those surveyed, unaided, were "not aware of any theatre companies" (Criterion).

3 In her master's degree thesis, long-time Walterdale participant Mary Glenfield lists Jack McCreath, Roman Charnetski, Larry Hertzog, Vera Rourke, Margaret Tewnion, and Bud D'Amur as signatories (with witness Connie Hertzog) to the company's incorporation (Glenfield 48). In a letter to the editor printed in the *Edmonton Journal* in 1974, long-time Edmonton thespian Mickey Macdonald lists the founders as McCreath, Charnetski, Herzog, and Jack Downey. She also lists Tewnion and

D'Amur as replacing Charnetski and Downey on the executive during the first year and Barry Vogel as joining the executive two years later (Macdonald).

4 During these early years a Theatre Associates "membership" simply entailed the purchase of a $1.00 admission ticket to the current show. This system allowed the company to operate as a "club theatre," as the exits in the school house were too small for it to be acknowledged by the city fire marshal as a "public hall" (Rivet 6).

5 From 1913 to 1976, Canadians seeking membership in a professional actors union joined American Actors' Equity.

6 Theatre 3 (1970–81) folded in 1981 and was replaced by Phoenix Theatre (1981–97). Following its last season in 1996–97, Phoenix Theatre publicly handed to Theatre Network (1975–) its "artistic vision" in order to add "contemporary, edgy" non-Canadian work to the latter's extant new Canadian play mandate (Nicholls). I am indebted to one of my anonymous readers for alerting me to the nuances of Phoenix Theatre's brief aesthetic (but not administrative) amalgamation with Theatre Network. The University of Alberta Special Collections Library holds the records of a number of professional theatres in Edmonton. The online finding aid for Theatre 3 notes that Mark Schoenberg and Anne Green founded the company as "an alternative to The Citadel Theatre and the Walterdale Theatre [*sic*]"—the other "two" theatres, as it were—with "a mandate of developing new plays, local talent, and less commercial work" (Frogner).

In contrast, Catalyst Theatre (1977–), though today an aesthetic-based professional company, was founded by David Barnet out of his interests in social action theatre and in "acting done by the nonprofessional" (quoted in Bessai 153). Referring to non-conservatory actor training such as that which he teaches as a professor in the Department of Drama at the University of Alberta, Barnet defines this type of "nonprofessional" acting as "acting which is real and meaningful and has impact without being compared negatively to the professional acting which comes out of the centre of somebody" (153). Barnet's distinction between professional and nonprofessional here refers primarily to the focus of the actor's training, whether that training prepares one for the theatre profession or for social action. Rather than offering a comparison of quality between practices, it offers an important statement on the purpose and place of the type of social action theatre that the early Catalyst Theatre practised. Thus, like Walterdale's nonprofessionalized work, Catalyst's early work operated outside of professionalized strictures, though the two differed significantly in purpose. Still, the two companies did cross paths when Catalyst's collective play *Family Portrait*, "on intergenerational stress," ran at Walterdale in 1982 (Bessai 155), and Walterdale documents reveal that Catalyst used Walterdale's building for rehearsals from time to time during the early 1980s.

7 American playwright Mart Crowley's play *The Boys in the Band* also created a stir at Walterdale in April 1977. The *Edmonton Journal* concluded its mention of *The Boys in the Band* by noting the success of the controversial production: "What bigger tribute could you get, after all, than a standing ovation from artistic director John Neville and the other Citadel Theatre members who went along with him one night?" ("Footlights").

8 Walterdale's six Sterling Awards for Outstanding Amateur Production were awarded for productions of Hare's *A Map of the World* (February–March 1988), Levin's *Deathtrap* (November 1988), Knott's *Wait Until Dark* (January–February 1990), Shaffer's *The Royal Hunt of the Sun* (April 1991), French's *Jitters* (April–May 1992), and Anderson's *Elizabeth the Queen* (April–May 1993).

9 For example, frequent Edmonton Fringe playwright Chris Craddock notes one discursive inconsistency in that "Despite being produced on Equity contracts, the Playwrights Guild of Canada refuses to allow Fringe productions to be considered as professional productions" (quoted in Belke).

10 I use the term "paraprofessional" in the sense of "a person to whom a particular aspect of a professional task is delegated, but who is not licensed to practise as a fully qualified professional" (*OED*). The designation of a theatre practitioner in these terms draws from the prefix "para": "Forming miscellaneous terms in the sense 'analogous or parallel to, but separate from or going beyond, what is denoted by the root word'" (*OED*). As practitioners operating outside of a designated "profession," but using skills parallel to professional practice, theatre practitioners who engage in both amateur and professional theatre at the same point in their career are thus "paraprofessionals." I would like to thank one of my anonymous readers for urging me to promote the comparability of the playwriting craft's demands across all three categories of paraprofessional, preprofessional, and amateur.

11 Theatre professionals, even those who were, during the mid-twentieth century, dedicated to staging Canadian voices when they could, occasionally used the success of amateur companies as leverage against amateur practice in order to recontextualize professional work. For example, Manitoba Theatre Centre, Toronto Free Theatre, and Playwrights Guild (then Playwrights Co-op) co-founder Tom Hendry remarked, "The very strength of the amateur movement is, to some extent, inhibiting the spread of professional theatre" (258). Such views, not uncommon, frequently led to exaggerated statements such as those made by Canadian actor and educator Emrys Jones: "I don't think there is any connection between amateur and professional at all. I can't conceive of any bridge" (quoted in Lee 301).

12 In 2003 Playwrights Canada Press published *Seven Short Plays from Theatre Ontario* (Doucette and Shand, eds.). Importantly, three of the seven plays premiered at a "community theatre."

13 Though it is not included here, Ryga's *Nothing But a Man* (March 1967) also contains lines from "O Canada."

14 Watson: "[I] like working underground, unless of course I could buy my own productions but not even Marshall [McLuhan] has got that sort of power" (Draft of letter to Shadbolt). Edmonton's regional theatre, The Citadel, never touched Watson's work. In fact, it was six years before The Citadel attempted a new Canadian work when it commissioned three plays for young audiences from local writer and actor Isobelle Foord and a new full-length mainstage play by Calgarian Stewart Boston, *Counsellor Extraordinary* (Peacock, "Edmonton Theatre" 62).

15 Wilfred Watson said of McLuhan, "I [...] readily fell in with his way of thinking, drawn to him because I felt that he had something vital to teach me about the writing of plays" (from the unpublished Introduction to *From Cliché to Archetype*, quoted in Tiessen 114).

16 In his general introduction to a collection of Watson's plays, Gordon Peacock explains: "During his stay in the Paris of the 1950s Watson realized that the actors rehearsing in the plays of the Absurdists could successfully quit the prevalent school of realistic character acting. He saw that rational justification of character response could be substituted for one in which all disbelief was suspended" ("Wilfred Watson" 9–10). And Watson, writing in the late 1960s, discussed one of McLuhan's notions that "banality itself, because it saves energy, is a great reservoir of psychic power. It was not hard to test the truth of this hypothesis, especially since I was under the spell of writers like Ionesco, Beckett, Genet, and Sartre" (from unpublished Introduction to *From Cliché to Archetype*, quoted in Tiessen 114).

17 A year before acquiring the schoolhouse, Theatre Associates presented at the Yardbird Suite readings of Shaw's *Man of Destiny* (October 1960) and Fry's *Venus Observed* (November 1960), as well as a production of Knott's *Dial M For Murder* (November 1960). The eclectic venue had been a jazz club on Whyte Avenue (near 104 Street) since March 1957, including the time during which Bud D'Amur was on the Walterdale executive. When D'Amur became the Yardbird's manager in the fall of 1964, he ran it more broadly as an intimate performing arts venue for poetry, music, and theatre, notably to showcase Watson's work. In March 1965 D'Amur moved the Yardbird to 81 Avenue and 102 Street. He closed it down in August 1966. It was revived as a jazz club in 1973, independent of D'Amur. Today it is a dedicated jazz club, rehearsal space, and summer Fringe theatre venue located at 11 Tommy Banks Way. I acknowledge one of my anonymous readers for emphasizing some of the details of the Yardbird's history, particularly D'Amur's central place within this history, during the 1960s. The venue's website provides further context.

18 Barry Westgate begins his review by noting that the play had introduced to Edmonton theatre a "very distinctive four-letter obscenity." He returns to the point later by stating that "[director Bernard] Engel has placed a gaggle of weird characters on stage and made them curse and swear right royally" (Westgate, "Wilfred Watson's" 59). This was not the first time Watson's complex performances had received such a scolding. As historian E. Ross Stuart notes of the 1961 University of Alberta Studio Theatre premiere of *Cockcrow and the Gulls*, "In the middle of a performance a spectator rose to proclaim the play obscene" (235).

19 Further biographical detail can be found in Diane Bessai's "Wilfred Watson" and Paul Tiessen's "'Shall I Say, It Is Necessary to Restore the Dialogue?'"

20 Certainly, the thought of an amateur theatre in Canada producing a theatre of the absurd play during the 1960s was hardly novel. By the spring of 1967, when *The Canadian Fact* opened, Theatre Associates had already introduced Harold Pinter's work to Edmonton audiences (*The Caretaker*, October 1963) and earlier, Toronto's Alumnae Theatre had staged the Canadian premiere of *Waiting for Godot* (March 1957).

21 For apt examples of mid-twentieth-century views on Canadian theatre with a nod toward British and French theatre in the context of cultural policy, see Robertson Davies's "The Theatre" and Robert Fulford's "The Yearning for Professionalism." Both pieces offer important discussions and warnings, regarding the virtues and vices of professionalization in Canadian theatre at the time.

22 Walterdale produced *Lady Audley's Secret or The Wages of Sin* precisely ten years later (again directed by Walterdale's lead founder Jack McCreath) and thirty years later (directed by Sheila Dodd).

23 Edmonton's Klondike Days Festival adopted its gold rush theme in 1962, but the festival itself is the progeny of the 1879 Edmonton Agricultural Society's local exhibition. In 2006 the Klondike Days name was changed to Edmonton's Capital City Exhibition (Capital EX) (Northlands 2007).

24 On the whole, the 1977/78 season was an unsuccessful one for Walterdale, with productions affected by poor reviews, a series of actor and director illnesses, and a car accident. However, by that season the Walterdale Melodrama had gained such a reputation for drawing audiences that income was generated not only from sold-out houses (as was the norm), but also from a series of one-time "substantial donations" from public and private sources, including the Alberta Government, the EFFORT Society, Imperial Oil, Ford, and Northwest Utilities. The Melodrama, Walterdale's president reported at season's end, "was responsible for about 60 percent of the income from shows and 47 percent of the total income that year" (Crowther).

25 Booth enumerates the main stock character types of traditional melodrama: "the hero, heroine, villain, comic man, comic woman, old man, old woman, and character actor (usually comic)" (10).

26 An *Edmonton Journal* review of Walterdale's 1970 production of Naughton's *All in Good Time* called Graves "an incredible star" and "a Walterdale stalwart who here is clearly in another league. [Y]ou, the audience, can't help loving him" (Ashwell, "Laughs"). A year later a different *Journal* reviewer lavished further praise on Graves's work in Walterdale's production of Brown's *The Girl in the Freudian Slip*: "Warren Graves, the Walterdale artistic director, gives a truly masterful performance as the unfortunate psychiatrist. His acting, timing and splendid delivery form not only the highlight of the play but also an object lesson for newcomers to the group. For the audience he is a sheer delight" (Woolner).

27 In Edmonton alone, Graves wrote twenty-two episodes for CITV's *Country Joy* as well as the plays *Goodbye, Cruel World* (1978), which he produced himself at The Citadel's Rice Theatre in collaboration with ITV; *Mors Draculae* (1979) for Stage West; the children's adaptations *Scrooge* (1978), *Beauty and the Beast* (1979), and *Alice* (1981) for Theatre 3; and *Alberta Song* (1981) for the province's 75th anniversary. His one-act *Would You Like a Cup of Tea?* (1984) ran at Walterdale. As well, Graves's *The Prisoner of Zenda* (1983) played at Toronto's Young People's Theatre, directed by Robin Philips, and was remounted by Philips at the Grand

Theatre (formerly Theatre London) in London, Ontario, and staged variously at The Citadel Theatre, the National Arts Centre, and the UK's Theatre Brambly and Chichester Festival. *The Last Real Summer* (1981), initially commissioned by Theatre 3, has proven popular at Canadian high school drama festivals. Halifax's Theatre Neptune commissioned Graves to write what was to be his last play, *Sleeping Beauty* (2002).

28 Walterdale presented *The Mumberly Inheritance* (July 1981, July 1987, July 1998), *Chief Shaking Spear Rides Again* (July 1989), *The Hand that Cradles the Rock* (October 1989), and *Beauty and the Beast* (December 1995). The *Edmonton Sun* reported of *Pamela Frankenstein or Adam and Eve Meet Apple II*, "The Walterdale executive unanimously approved the script. And the Apple computer company likes it a lot, and has provided real Apple machines for the show, plus free training for the cast" (Charles). As Graves explained, his melodrama deals with the serious matter of nuclear war. Eve is tempted by the Apple computer, "which is a great system for providing information [b]ut there's the old question of what *use* you put the information to—inventing bombs again?" (quoted in Charles, italics in original). One is reminded here of the ominous Orwellian television commercial that Apple aired to launch its new computer, Macintosh, during Superbowl XVIII (January, 22 1984), six months before *Pamela Frankenstein* opened.

29 A second melodrama was also produced during the Klondike Days Festival that week. Edmonton's Prestige Productions, a professional group headed by early Walterdale personalities Wally McSween and Ron Wigmore, remounted Walterdale's inaugural 1965 Klondike Days Melodrama *Dirty Work at the Crossroads or Tempted, Tried and True* "with six members of the original company re-creating their roles" (Adams). The reason Wigmore gave to the *Edmonton Journal* at the time was that because the Walterdale Melodrama had been selling out so fast every year, a second offering would be welcomed by the festival-goers, adding "We aren't here to compete with Walterdale" (Adams).

30 For more on the pioneer and gold rush types of nineteenth-century melodrama, see Booth (33–35). For further discussion of *Chief Shaking Spear Rides Again*, particularly its controversial treatment of racial stereotypes, see Fischlin (*Chief*) and Graves's subsequent response ("Interview") on the *Canadian Adaptations of Shakespeare Project* website.

31 George F. Walker's *Zastrozzi*, Fraser's *Mutants*, Gordon Pengilly's *Swipe*, and Warren Graves's summer melodrama *The Mumberly Inheritance* shared the stage that season with Ibsen's *The Lady from the Sea*, an adaptation of the Brothers Grimm folktale *The Valiant Tailor*, Labiche's *The Italian Straw Hat*, and Bigelow's *The Peacock Season*.

32 This point was not only mentioned at a Walterdale board meeting, but was also noted in a subsequent issue of *Canadian Forum* (Bessai 36), and for good reason. Thompson and Theatre Passe Muraille, particularly since the success of their 1972 collective creation *The Farm Show*, had been sharing their process across Canada, making them "probably the most influential company in Canada" at the time (Johnston 109). Fraser had, as they say, caught a break.

33 Vivien Bosley, artistic director at the time, noted in the play's program that the idea for the competition came from long-time Walterdale member Jack Wilson. Initially, the board intended the contest to be limited to entries from the province of Alberta, but by June 1980, having secured grant money from the city for the project, the board decided that the competition should be open to "all Canadian playwrights, due to the difficulty in defining an 'Alberta writer.'"

34 When *Swipe* was chosen as the winning entry, Wigmore stepped down as director in favour of Larry Farley because the play had already received Farley's attention in previous drafts.

35 In 1974 Pengilly's play *Sea Shanty* won first prize in the Alberta Cultural Television competition and *Peck the Woodstick* won second prize in the Alberta Culture competition. His prize-winning play *Brawler Takes the Count* was produced at the University of Alberta in 1976. *Seeds* won four awards in 1977 and was produced on CBC Radio (1978) and Global Television (1979).

36 Pengilly's plays include *Seeds* (1977, University of Alberta Studio Theatre), *Hard Hats and Stolen Hearts: A Tar Sands Myth* (1977, co-written with Theatre Network; 1978, The Performance Garage, New York), *Alice on Stage* (1985, Theatre Calgary), *God's Dice* (1989, Banff Centre), *Yours 'Till the Moon Falls Down* (1992, Lunch Box Theatre, Calgary), *Metastasis* (1995, Northern Light Theatre; 1998, Montreal Fringe Festival), *Drumheller or Dangerous Times* (2001, Prime Stock Theatre Company, Red Deer), *The Work Play* (2001, Actor's Loft, New York), and *Contraption* (2003, Jagged Edge Theatre, Edmonton). Pengilly's recently commissioned works include *Harm's Way* (2005, Alberta Playwrights' Network), *Tom Form and the Speed of Love* (2006, New Works Theatre, Toronto), and *Steffi's Garden* (2007, Lunchbox Theatre, Calgary).

37 In an *Edmonton Journal* interview with Pengilly following *Swipe*'s first-place selection, Keith Ashwell reported that Pengilly planned to spend his winnings on "records for 'an old rockie'. The rest goes against a daunting collection of T4 slips and buys the time to continue writing" ("Winner").

38 The workshop participants, limited to twenty, received a copy of the script beforehand and were obliged to attend all of the two-day event.

39 In labelling Glenfield's *The Three Sillies* "children's theatre," I maintain Dennis Foon's distinction between that form and theatre for young audiences (TYA): the former emphasizes entertainment and spectacle, while the latter emphasizes social coping mechanisms for children (Foon 253). Undoubtedly, Glenfield's play hedges toward entertainment and spectacle. See Foon's "Theatre for Young Audiences in English Canada" as well as Joyce Doolittle and Zina Barnieh's *A Mirror of Our Dreams* and M. Bronwyn Weaver's dissertation "Empowering the Children: Theatre for Young Audiences in Anglophone Canada."

40 Joyce Doolittle and Zina Barnieh record that professional theatre for young audiences began in Canada one year earlier, in 1953, when Holiday Theatre in Vancouver opened. Their important study, however, ignores on principle children's theatre work "by the young or amateurs" (11).

41 From 1973 to 1995 (except for 1982, when *The Fantasticks* occupied the slot), Walterdale presented shows that either gave young actors the chance to act in appropriate plays or provided young audiences the chance to experience children's theatre. These were normally offered in December or January. As Young Walterdale, the company presented Reach's *David and Lisa* (December 1973, dir. David Nattress), Ferber and Kaufman's *Stage Door* (January 1975, dir. Judy Unwin), Sills's *Story Theatre* (May 1976, dir. Larry Farley, the production remounted for the Canadian Child and Youth Drama Association), Raspant's *I Never Saw Another Butterfly* (January 1977, dir. Valerie Mills), Herlihn and Noble's *Blue Denim* (February 1978, dir. Rose Bene), and Swan's *Out of the Frying Pan* (February 1979, dir. George Bertwell). During this time Walterdale also presented two "Children's Theatre" productions, Cullin's *The Beeple* (December 1976, dir. Stephanie Coldwell) and Wingate and Friedman's *The Lion Who Wouldn't* (December 1977, dir. Troy Sprenke).

As the Christmas Show, Walterdale presented Bolt's *The Thwarting of Baron Bolligrew* (December 1979, dir. Troy Sprenke), *The Valiant Tailor* (December 1980, dir. Carla Nolan), Krauss's *The Ice Wolf* (December 1981, dir. Troy Sprenke), and Mary Glenfield's *The Three Sillies* (December 1983, dir. Frank Glenfield). Three one-act plays were presented in the slot in 1984 and 1985, followed by *Jack and the Beanstalk* (December 1986, dir. Sheila Dodd), *Cinderella* (December 1987, dir. Gaye LePage), Greg Palmer's *Puss in Boots* (December 1988, dir. Petra Hammond), Reakes's *Sinbad the Sailor* (December 1989, dir. Robin Bovey), Robbin's *Humpty Dumpty* (December 1990, dir. Jack Almond), Hayes's *Jardy* (December 1991, dir. Jane Barclay), Reakes's *Little Jack Horner* (December 1992, dir. Petra Duncan), Robbins's *Hickory Dickory Dock* (December 1993), Lloyd's *The Christmas Cavalier* (December 1994, dir. Robin Bovey), and Graves's *Beauty and the Beast* (December 1995, dir. Andrew Freund).

42 As reported in the December 1983 *Walterdale Newsletter*, "Mary made the auditions extra enjoyable by singing the songs she has composed as well as narrating."

BIBLIOGRAPHY

Preface

Foucault, Michel. *Discipline and Punish: The Birth of the Prison.* Translated by Alan Sheridan. New York: Vintage Books, 1995. Originally published London: Allen Lane, 1977.

Leger Marketing. *Edmonton Cultural Capital: Analysis of Findings: Benchmark Study.* July 2007. http://www.edmontonculturalcapital.com (accessed July 3, 2008).

Old Strathcona Business Association. *Entertainment and Theatre.* 2007. http://www.oldstrathcona.ca/EntertainmentTheatre/tabid/57/Default.aspx (accessed May 10, 2008).

Introduction

Belke, David. "The Hyper-Producing Playwrights of Edmonton: Or Why Alberta's Capital Breeds New Plays Like Tribbles." Alberta Playwrights' Network. *Dialogue,* March 2004, 1–4, 10. http://www.albertaplaywrights.com/html/apn_newsletters.htm (accessed December 10, 2007).

Bessai, Diane. "Canada's Citadel Theatre and the Alternatives." In *Theatre in Alberta,* edited by Anne Nothof, 144–68. Toronto: Playwrights Canada Press, 2008.

Bill, Desmond. "On The Arts" (column). *Edmonton Journal,* June 9, 1962, 26.

Bourdieu, Pierre. *Distinction: A Critique of the Judgment of Taste.* Translated by Richard Nice. Cambridge, MA: Harvard University Press, 1984.

Canada. Royal Commission on National Development in the Arts, Letters and Sciences. *Report, 1949–1951.* Ottawa: The Commission, 1951.

Citadel Theatre. "The Citadel" (history). 2007. http://www.citadeltheatre.com/citadel_history.php (accessed November 15, 2007).

Cochrane, Claire. "The Pervasiveness of the Commonplace: The Historian and Amateur Theatre." *Theatre Research International* 26, no. 3 (2001): 233–42.

Criterion Research Group. *Live Theatre Attendance in Edmonton: A Research Report.* Edmonton: Edmonton Arts Council (EAC), August 2001.

Day, Moira, ed. *The West of All Possible Worlds: Six Contemporary Canadian Plays.* Toronto: Playwrights Canada Press, 2004.

Demers, Patricia, and Rosalind Kerr, eds. *Staging Alternative Albertas: Experimental Drama in Edmonton.* Toronto: Playwrights Canada Press, 2002.

Doucette, Marian, and Skip Shand, eds. *Seven Short Plays from Theatre Ontario.* Toronto: Playwrights Canada Press, 2003.

Edmonton Theatre Associates. Notice to the Members of the Edmonton Theatre Associates. ca. November 1969.

"Footlights" (column). *Edmonton Journal,* April 16, 1977.

Fritch, J.E. (James). Untitled (historical notes on Walterdale). 1967. "Archivist" folder, Walterdale Playhouse Archives, Edmonton (accessed June 2006).

Frogner, Raymond. "Theatre 3 Fonds Finding Aid." June 21, 2004. University of Alberta Special Collections Library. http://archive1.lse.ualberta.ca/FindingAids/Theatre3/Theatre3.html (accessed November 16, 2007).

Glaser, Darlene E. Treasurer's Report. Minutes of the Annual General Meeting. Walterdale Theatre Associates. August 29, 2002. Personal files.

Glenfield, Mary. "The Growth of Theatre in Edmonton: From the Early 1920s to 1965." Master's thesis, University of Alberta, 2001.

Grace, Sherrill, Eve D'Aeth, and Lisa Chalykoff, eds. *Staging the North: Twelve Canadian Plays.* Toronto: Playwrights Canada Press, 1999.

Halpenny, Francess. "Shall we join the ladies?" *Bulletin* (University of Toronto staff newsletter), ca. 1970.

Hendry, Thomas B. "Trends in Canadian Theatre" (1965). In *Canadian Theatre History: Selected Readings,* edited by Don Rubin, 251–58. Toronto: Copp Clark, 1996.

Hutchison, Robert, and Andrew Feist. *Amateur Arts in the UK.* No. 726. London: Policy Studies Institute, 1991.

Keeping, John. "Local Play Lauded." *Edmonton Journal,* November 3, 1962, 3.

Kerr, Rosalind, ed. *Lesbian Plays: Coming of Age in Canada.* Toronto: Playwrights Canada Press, 2006.

Langham Court Theatre. *A Brief History of Langham Court Theatre and the Victoria Theatre Guild and Dramatic School.* 2007. http://langhamcourttheatre.bc.ca/history.html (accessed December 21, 2007).

Lee, Betty. *Love and Whisky: The Story of the Dominion Drama Festival.* Toronto: McClelland and Stewart, 1973.

Macdonald, Mickey. "Record Straight." *Edmonton Journal,* November 1974.

Massey, Vincent, ed. *Canadian Plays from Hart House Theatre.* 2 vols. Toronto: Macmillan, 1926–27.

Melvill, Harald. *A Complete Guide to Amateur Dramatics.* London: Rockliff, 1962. First published 1957.

Mojica, Monique, ed. *Staging Coyote's Dream: An Anthology of First Nations Drama in English.* Toronto: Playwrights Canada Press, 2003.

Music Theatre International. "Community Rentals." 2007. http://www.mtishows.com/resource_community.asp (accessed November 4, 2007).

"New Walterdale Playhouse." *Town Talk,* September 1966, 1–2.

Nicholls, Liz. "Spirit of Phoenix Finds Safe Haven: Theatre Network Expands '97–'98 Lineup." *Edmonton Journal,* May 29, 1997, D3.

Nothof, Anne, ed. *The Alberta Advantage: An Anthology of Plays.* Toronto: Playwrights Canada Press, 2008.

Oxford English Dictionary Online. 2nd ed. Oxford University Press, 2006.

Perry, Bliss. *The Amateur Spirit.* Freeport, NY: Books for Learning Press, 1969. Reprint of the 1904 edition.

Pirot, Steve, ed., with Diane Bessai. *Nextfest Anthology II: Plays from the Syncrude Next Generation Arts Festival, 2001–2005.* Edmonton: NeWest, 2006.

"Playhouse with a Future." *Edmonton Journal*, September 9, 1966.

Rivet, John G. "Walterdale Theatre Associates" (essay for J. DeFelice's Drama 616, Research in Canadian Drama course, University of Alberta, c. 1978–79). "Archivist" folder, Walterdale Playhouse Archives, Edmonton (accessed June 2007).

Ryga, George. *Nothing But a Man*. In *George Ryga: The Other Plays*, edited by James Hoffman, 35-57. Vancouver: Talonbooks, 2004.

Salter, Denis, ed. *New Canadian Drama 3: Albertan Dramatists*. Ottawa: Borealis Press, 1984.

Sears, Djanet, ed. *Testifyin': Contemporary African Canadian Plays*. Vols. 1 and 2. Toronto: Playwrights Canada Press, 2001, 2003.

"Shavian Work at Playhouse." *Edmonton Journal*, January 11, 1962, 20.

Sprenke, Troy. Artistic Director's Report. Minutes of the Annual General Meeting. Walterdale Theatre Associates. May 29, 1978. "1978–79" binder, Walterdale Playhouse Archives, Edmonton (accessed June 2007).

Stirling, Glenda, ed. *NeXtfest Anthology: Plays from the Syncrude NeXt Generation Arts Festival*. Edmonton: NeWest Press, 2000.

Stuart, E. Ross. *The History of Prairie Theatre: The Development of Theatre in Alberta, Manitoba and Saskatchewan, 1833–1982*. Canadian Theatre History. No. 2. Toronto: Simon and Pierre, 1984.

University Alumnae Dramatic Club, The (internal document). ca. 1956. Berkley Street Theatre Archives, Toronto (accessed December 2004).

Varteniuk, Sam. "Introduction." *Walterdale Playhouse Presents Hot Thespian Action!* (season brochure, 2004/05). Edmonton: Walterdale Theatre Associates, 2004.

Walterdale Theatre Associates. Certificate [of incorporation]. June 16, 1978.

________. Constitution. May 28, 1975.

________. "Walterdale Playhouse." 2007. http://www.walterdaleplayhouse.com (accessed November 16, 2007).

Warr, Jas. Letter to Edmonton Theatre Associates. September 25, 1968. "Walterdale Theatre Associates," box 2, item 69, Provincial Archives of Alberta, Edmonton (accessed June 2007).

Westgate, Barry. "26th K-Days Melodrama's On: I Can Still Remember the First." *Edmonton Journal*, July 18, 1989, B1.

Whittaker, Robin [C]. "Artistic Director's Message." *Playhouse: A Newsletter for Walterdale Members and Friends*. Edmonton: Walterdale Theatre Associates, May 2003.

Winston, Iris. *Staging a Legend: A History of Ottawa Little Theatre*. Carp, ON: Creative Bound, 1997.

The Canadian Fact

Bessai, Diane. "Wilfred Watson." In *Canadian Writers Since 1960*, 2nd series, edited by William H. New, 382–86. Detroit: Gale Research, 1987.

Bessai, Diane, ed. *Prairie Performance*. Edmonton: NeWest Press, 1980.

Davies, Robertson. "The Theatre: A Dialogue on the State of Canadian Theatre in Canada."

In *Royal Commission Studies: A Selection of Essays Prepared for the Royal Commission on National Development in the Arts, Letters and Sciences*, 369–92. Ottawa: Edmond Cloutier, 1951. Also printed in Don Rubin, ed., *Canadian Theatre History: Selected Readings*, 155–74. Toronto: Copp Clark, 1996.

Fulford, Robert. "The Yearning for Professionalism." *Tamarack Review*, 13 (Autumn 1959): 80-85.

McLuhan, Marshall, and Wilfred Watson. *From Cliché to Archetype*. New York: Viking, 1970.

Nicholls, Liz. "Watson's Trilogy Stunning Theatrical Experience." *Edmonton Journal*, March 30, 1986, B12.

Peacock, Gordon. "Edmonton Theatre News Letter: A Plethora of Playwrights?" *White Pelican*, 1, no. 1 (1971): 62.

________. "Wilfred Watson and the Modern Canadian Theatre." In *Plays at the Iron Bridge or The Autobiography of Tom Horror*, edited by Shirley Neuman, 9–11. Prairie Play Series. No. 9. Edmonton: Longspoon Press/NeWest Press, 1989.

Peacocke, Thomas. "Introduction." In *Poems: Collected / Unpublished / New*, by Wilfred Watson, xi–xix. Edmonton: Longspoon Press/NeWest Press, 1986.

Stuart, E. Ross. *The History of Prairie Theatre: The Development of Theatre in Alberta, Manitoba and Saskatchewan, 1833–1982*. Canadian Theatre History. No. 2. Toronto: Simon and Pierre, 1984.

Tiessen, Paul. "'Shall I Say, It Is Necessary to Restore the Dialogue?': Wilfred Watson's Encounter with Marshall McLuhan, 1957–1988." In *At the Speed of Light There is Only Illumination: A Reappraisal of Marshall McLuhan*, edited by John Moss and Linda M. Morra, 95–145. Ottawa: University of Ottawa Press, 2004.

Watson, Wilfred. Draft of letter to artist Jack Shadbolt, August 14, 1969. In Tiessen, 106.

________. Draft of letter to Diane Bessai, May 25, 1981. In Tiessen, 102–03.

________. "Poem and Preface." *Canadian Literature*, Autumn 1966: 33–46.

________. "Towards a Canadian Theatre." *White Pelican*, 1, no. 1 (1971): 55–59.

Westgate, Barry. "Another World." *Edmonton Journal*, November 24, 1967, 39.

________. "Nightside." *Edmonton Journal*, October 18, 1965, 22.

________. "Scant Opportunity, Less Incentive for Local Dramatists." *Edmonton Journal*, March 16, 1969, 9.

________. "Wilfred Watson's Bizarre Play Disappoints at Studio Theatre." *Edmonton Journal*, November 22, 1969, 59.

________. "Yardbird Suite Opens Another Watson Play." *Edmonton Journal*, March 10, 1967, 60.

Yardbird Suite (website). www.yardbirdsuite.com/home.htm (accessed May 14, 2008).

Chief Shaking Spear Rides Again or The Taming of the Sioux

Adams, Sharon. "GASP! HELP! Someone Save Little Nell!" *Edmonton Journal*, July 13, 1974, 73.

Ashwell, Keith. "Graves' Play Opens in Belfast." *Edmonton Journal*, May 15, 1980, A23.

________. "Laughs at Expense of Crazy Truths." *Edmonton Journal*, October 7, 1970, 84.

________. "Prolific Playwright Writes About Women." *Edmonton Journal,* April 10, 1981.

Booth, Michael. "Introduction." In *Hiss the Villain: Six English and American Melodramas with Texts in Full,* edited by Micheal Booth, 9–40. London: Eyre and Spottiswoode, 1964.

Callaghan, W.N., Jr. "Warren Graves—The Playwrite" *[sic]. The Gateway* (University of Alberta student newspaper), October 5, 1971, 9.

Charles, John. "'Disaster' looms." *Edmonton Sun,* July 1984.

Crowther, Len. President's Report. Walterdale Theatre Associates. Annual General Meeting Minutes. May 29, 1978. "1978–79" binder, Walterdale Playhouse Archives, Edmonton (accessed June 2007).

Fischlin, Daniel. *"Chief Shaking Spear, or the Taming of the Sioux."* Canadian Adaptations of Shakespeare Project. Guelph: University of Guelph, n.d. http://www.canadianshakespeares.ca/a_shaking.cfm (accessed August 24, 2007).

Fritch, J.E. (James). Untitled (historical notes on Walterdale). 1967. "Archivist" folder, Walterdale Playhouse Archives, Edmonton (accessed June 2006).

Graves, Warren. *Walterdale Newsletter.* February 1974. "1973–74" binder, Walterdale Playhouse Archives, Edmonton (accessed June 2007).

________. *Walterdale Newsletter.* May 1974. "1973–74" binder, Walterdale Playhouse Archives, Edmonton (accessed June 2007).

________. *Walterdale Newsletter.* August 1974. "1973–74" binder, Walterdale Playhouse Archives, Edmonton (accessed June 2007).

________. *Walterdale Newsletter.* December 1974. "1974–75" binder, Walterdale Playhouse Archives, Edmonton (accessed June 2007).

"Interview with Warren Graves." Canadian Adaptations of Shakespeare Project. University of Guelph, January 2004. http://www.canadianshakespeares.ca/i_wgraves.cfm (accessed August 24, 2007).

Nicholls, Liz. "Loud Popular Outcry Saves 'Meller-drama.'" *Edmonton Journal,* July 18, 1989, C7

Northlands. *Edmonton's Capital EX.* 2007. http://www.capitalex.ca/history.html (accessed August 24, 2007).

Peacock, Gordon. "Edmonton Theatre News Letter: A Plethora of Playwrights?" *White Pelican* 1, no. 1 (1971): 62.

"Today's Paper: Globe Columnists: William Thorsell." *Globe and Mail.* http://www.theglobeandmail.com/servlet/HTMLTemplate?tf=columnists/biographies.html&cf=tgamv3/columnists/TopwilliamThorsell.cfg&hub=williamThorsell (accessed May 12, 2008).

Walterdale Theatre Associates. Executive and Department Heads 1976–77. "Walterdale Theatre Associates," box 2, item 69, Provincial Archives of Alberta, Edmonton (accessed June 2007).

________. Executive Meeting Minutes. February 9, 1970. "1978–79" binder, Walterdale Playhouse Archives, Edmonton (accessed June 2007).

________. Treasurer's Report. Annual General Meeting. May 31, 1981. "1980–81" binder, Walterdale Playhouse Archives, Edmonton (accessed June 2007).

________. *Walterdale Newsletter.* May 1975. "Walterdale Theatre Associates," box 2, item 83, Provincial Archives of Alberta, Edmonton (accessed June 2007).

Whittaker, Robin C. "Graves, Warren." *Canadian Theatre Encyclopedia*. Edmonton: Athabasca University, October 5, 2006. http://www.canadiantheatre.com/dict.pl?term=Graves%2C%20Warren (accessed July 9, 2008).

"William Thorsell." Royal Ontario Museum. www.rom.on.ca/about/newsroom/pdf/thorsell.pdf (accessed May 12, 2008).

Woolner, Dave. "2 Hours of Rich Comedy." *Edmonton Journal*, November 17, 1971.

Mutants

Ashwell, Keith. "All the Writer Needed Was a Clean-Cut Cause." *Edmonton Journal*, January 28, 1981, D1.

________. "Les Belles Soeurs Strong and Touching." *Edmonton Journal*, May 21, 1980, A22.

________. "Milestone Occasion for Local Theatre." *Edmonton Journal*, May 17, 1980, I2.

________. "Mutants Set to Premiere: Novice Debuts as Playwright and Director." *Edmonton Journal*.

________. "Rewrite! Rework! Play Can Be Helped." *Edmonton Journal*, January 30, 1980, D19.

Bessai, Diane. "The Prairie Season." *Canadian Forum*, May 1981, 36.

Bosley, Vivien. Letter to Judy Tilley. June 26, 1980. "1980–81" binder, Walterdale Playhouse Archives, Edmonton (accessed June 2007).

Fraser, Brad. "Biography." 2005. http://bradfraser.net/bio/index.htm (accessed September 26, 2007).

________. Interview with author. October 2, 2007.

Glenfield, Frank, and Mary Glenfield. Interview with author. June 30, 2006.

Goldman, Emma. "*Mutants* Try to Change World: Characters Are Well-Developed." *The Gateway* (University of Alberta student newspaper), January 29, 1981, 10.

Johnston, Denis W. *Up the Mainstream: The Rise of Toronto's Alternative Theatres*. Toronto: University of Toronto Press, 1991.

Kirman, Paula E. "Brad Fraser Feels the Heat." *Suite101.com*, March 3, 2000. http://www.suite101.com/article.cfm/canadian_literature/34602/2 (accessed October 6, 2007).

Walterdale Theatre Associates. Annual General Meeting Minutes. June 22, 1981. "1980–81" binder, Walterdale Playhouse Archives, Edmonton (accessed June 2006).

________. Annual General Meeting Minutes. May 31, 1982. "1982–83" binder, Walterdale Playhouse Archives, Edmonton (accessed June 2006).

________. Executive Meeting Minutes. August 20, 1980. "1980–81" binder, Walterdale Playhouse Archives, Edmonton (accessed June 2006).

________. Executive Meeting Minutes. October 22, 1980. "1980–81" binder, Walterdale Playhouse Archives, Edmonton (accessed June 2006).

________. Executive Meeting Minutes. November 26, 1980. "1980–81" binder, Walterdale Playhouse Archives, Edmonton (accessed June 2006).

________. Executive Meeting Minutes. February 11, 1981. "1980–81" binder, Walterdale Playhouse Archives, Edmonton (accessed June 2006).

________. Executive Meeting Minutes. April 29, 1981. "1980–81" binder, Walterdale Playhouse Archives, Edmonton (accessed June 2006).

________. Executive Meeting Minutes. August 4, 1982. "1983–84" binder, Walterdale Playhouse Archives, Edmonton (accessed June 2006).

________. *Walterdale Newsletter.* December 1979. "1979–80" binder, Walterdale Playhouse Archives, Edmonton (accessed June 2006).

________. *Walterdale Newsletter.* May 1980. "1979–80" binder, Walterdale Playhouse Archives, Edmonton (accessed June 2006).

Youth Representative Report. Walterdale Theatre Associates. Annual General Meeting Minutes. June 22, 1981. "1981–82" binder, Walterdale Playhouse Archives, Edmonton (accessed June 2007).

Swipe

Ashwell, Keith. "And the Winner is ... from Edmonton? Huh?" *Edmonton Journal*, February 25, 1981, C18.

________. "A Lusty Flight of Fancy That's Made to Enthrall." *Edmonton Journal*, May 20, 1981, F10.

Filewod, Alan. "Erect Sons and Dutiful Daughters: Imperialism, Empires and Canadian Theatre." In *Imperialism and Theatre: Essays on World Theatre, Drama and Performance*, edited by J. Ellen Gainor, 56–70. New York: Routledge, 1995.

Hunt, Stephen. "Calgary Playwright Wins Illustrious BBC Award." *Calgary Herald*, August 28, 2007. http://www.pugetsoundradio.com/forum/b-GN/m-1188350815/ (accessed October 28, 2007).

Pengilly, Gordon. "Artist Biography: Gordon Pengilly" (audio download). *Alberta's Art Heritage.* Heritage Community Foundation, 2003. http://www.abheritage.ca/abarts/database/artist_bio.php?artist_id=65&section_id=0 (accessed October 30, 2007).

Purves, C.J. Letter to Ms. [Vivien] Bosley. April 21, 1980. "1980–81" binder, Walterdale Playhouse Archives, Edmonton (accessed June 2007).

Stuart, E. Ross. *The History of Prairie Theatre: The Development of Theatre in Alberta, Manitoba and Saskatchewan, 1833–1982*. Canadian Theatre History. No. 2. Toronto: Simon and Pierre, 1984.

Walterdale Theatre Associates. *The Apprentice of Swipe* (Production program). Edmonton: Author, 1981.

________. "Celebration of the 75th Birthday" (Press release). Edmonton: Author, n.d.

________. Executive Meeting Minutes. June 4, 1980. "1979–80" binder, Walterdale Playhouse Archives, Edmonton (accessed June 2007).

________. Executive Meeting Minutes. June 24, 1980. "1979–80" binder, Walterdale Playhouse Archives, Edmonton (accessed June 2007).

________. Executive Meeting Minutes. January 11, 1981. "1980–81" binder, Walterdale Playhouse Archives, Edmonton (accessed June 2007).

________. Executive Meeting Minutes. March 25, 1981. "1980–81" binder, Walterdale Playhouse Archives, Edmonton (accessed June 2007).

The Tenth Negative Pig

Coady, Vince. "Winning Play Pokes Fun at Death." *Edmonton Journal,* March 18, 1983, D6.

Glenfield, Frank, and Mary Glenfield. Personal interview with author. June 30, 2006.

Walterdale Theatre Associates. Executive Meeting Minutes. June 22, 1981. "1980–81" binder, Walterdale Playhouse Archives, Edmonton (accessed June 2007).

________. Executive Meeting Minutes. September 2, 1981. "1981–82" binder, Walterdale Playhouse Archives, Edmonton (accessed June 2006).

________. *Walterdale Newsletter.* December 1981. "1981–82" binder, Walterdale Playhouse Archives, Edmonton (accessed June 2007).

The Three Sillies

Bosley, Vivien. Letter to Mary and Frank Glenfield. March 13, 1984. "1983–84" binder, Walterdale Playhouse Archives, Edmonton (accessed June 2007).

Doolittle, Joyce, and Zina Barnieh. *A Mirror of Our Dreams: Children and the Theatre in Canada.* Vancouver: Talonbooks, 1979.

"Fool's Day Opening for Ibsen's Hedda." *Edmonton Journal,* March 13, 1964, 47.

Foon, Dennis. "Theatre for Young Audiences in English Canada." In *Contemporary Canadian Theatre: New World Visions,* edited by Anton Wagner, 253–61. Toronto: Simon and Pierre, 1985.

Glenfield, Mary. "The Growth of Theatre in Edmonton: From the Early 1920s to 1965." Master's thesis, University of Alberta, 2001.

Nicholls, Liz. "Surprises the Norm with Glenfield." *Edmonton Journal,* April 2, 1987.

Smith, Ryan. "Edmonton Theatre Queen Tells History in Thesis." *Express News.* Edmonton: University of Alberta, June 8, 2001. http://www.expressnews.ualberta.ca/archives.cfm (accessed July 7, 2007).

Walterdale Theatre Associates. Executive Meeting Minutes. February 1, 1984. "1983–84" binder, Walterdale Playhouse Archives, Edmonton (accessed June 2007).

________. *Walterdale Newsletter.* December 1983. "1983–84" binder, Walterdale Playhouse Archives, Edmonton (accessed June 2007).

________. *Walterdale Newsletter.* January 1984. "1983–84" binder, Walterdale Playhouse Archives, Edmonton (accessed June 2007).

________. *Walterdale Playhouse: 2007–2008 Season.* http://www.walterdaleplayhouse.com/current_season.htm (accessed December 2, 2007).

Weaver, M. Bronwyn. "Empowering the Children: Theatre for Young Audiences in Anglophone Canada." PhD diss., University of Toronto, 1992.

Just

Belke, David. "The Hyper-Producing Playwrights of Edmonton: Or Why Alberta's Capital Breeds New Plays Like Tribbles." Alberta Playwrights' Network. *Dialogue*, March 2004, 1–4, 10. http://www.albertaplaywrights.com/html/apn_newsletters.htm (accessed December 10, 2007).

Schmidt, Trevor. Correspondence with author (e-mail). June 16, 2007.

The Beaver Effect

Berry, David. "These Guys Are Working Nine to Six Feet Under." *Vue Weekly* [Edmonton], November 7, 2007. http://www.vueweekly.com/article.php?id=7298 (accessed May 5, 2008).

DeGagné, David. "Director's Notes." In *The Raw, the Rare and the Cooked* production program. Edmonton: Walterdale Theatre Associates, 2002.

Nicholls, Liz. "Morbid Comedy About Working Stiffs Defies Expectations." *Edmonton Journal*, November 8, 2007.

Stubbings, Mark. "Playwright's Notes." In *The Raw, the Rare and the Cooked* production program. Edmonton: Walterdale Theatre Associates, 2002.

[ice land]

Seinen, Jonathan. "Playwright's Notes." In *An Evening of Canadian One-Acts* production program. Edmonton: Walterdale Theatre Associates, 2003.

The Trial of Salomé

Belke, David. "The Hyper-Producing Playwrights of Edmonton: Or Why Alberta's Capital Breeds New Plays Like Tribbles." Alberta Playwrights' Network. *Dialogue*, March 2004, 1–4, 10. http://www.albertaplaywrights.com/html/apn_newsletters.htm (accessed December 10, 2007).

Matwychuk, Paul. "The Unproducers." *Vue Weekly* [Edmonton], December 22, 2005. http://www.vueweekly.com/articles/default.aspx?i=3073 (accessed November 17, 2007).

Sasano, Mari. "Notorious P.L.A.Y." *Edmonton Journal*, July 6, 2007, H11.

Sharplin, Scott. "Lear Year" (Internet blog). February 2005–February 2006. http://learyear.blogspot.com (accessed November 17, 2007).

________. "Stage Whispers" (Internet blog). February 2006–April 2007. http://sharplin.blogspot.com (accessed November 17, 2007).

MARQUIS
Marquis Book Printing Inc.
Québec, Canada
2008